Tennessee's Radical Army

Tennessee's Radical Army

The State Guard and Its Role in Reconstruction, 1867–1869

BEN H. SEVERANCE

THE UNIVERSITY OF TENNESSEE PRESS • KNOXVILLE

Copyright © 2005 by The University of Tennessee Press / Knoxville.
All Rights Reserved. Manufactured in the United States of America.
First Edition.

Published in cooperation with the Tennessee Civil War National Heritage Area, which
is a partnership unit of the National Park Service.

This book is printed on acid-free paper.

Library of Congress Cataloging-in-Publication Data

Severance, Ben H., 1966–
Tennessee's Radical army : the state guard and its role in
Reconstruction, 1867-1869 / Ben H. Severance.— 1st ed.
    p. cm.
Includes bibliographical references (p.   ) and index.

ISBN 1–57233-362-6 (acid-free paper)

1. Reconstruction (U.S. history, 1865–1877)—Tennessee.
2. Tennessee—Militia—History—19th century.
I. Title.

F436.S48 2005
976.8'051—dc22   2004014889

To Tara, Bea, and Josie—the Ladies of My Life

Contents

Illustrations

FIGURES

MAPS

Acknowledgments

AN ENDEAVOR AS LONG AND INVOLVED AS A BOOK CAN NEVER BE completed alone. While God predestined the ultimate success of this project, and all glory rightly goes to Him, I am nevertheless indebted to a great many people. Specifically, I want to thank Stephen V. Ash. His outstanding direction during the dissertation phase made this project a joy to work on and helped me produce a piece of scholarship of which I am very proud. I also thank Paul H. Bergeron for his excellent advice throughout my graduate school days and for taking the time to talk with me at length about a host of interesting topics. And I thank John D. Fowler, Thomas C. Hood, Karin Kaufman, G. Kurt Piehler, James Sefton, and Mark Williams for carefully reading all or portions of the manuscript and then offering many helpful suggestions as well as much encouragement.

I would also like to express my appreciation to some special colleagues—particularly Bill Drumright, John Fowler, John Pinheiro, Lewie Reece, and Mark Williams—who enlivened my years of research and writing by providing friendship and comic relief. I enjoyed our many discussions, as well as the golf, the beer, the movies, the parties, and the road trips.

A number of archivists deserve a round of applause for assisting me with much of my research: Nick Wyman and William B. Eigelsbach (Special Collections, University of Tennessee, Knoxville), Sally Polhemus (McClung Historical Collection, Knoxville), and Susan Gordon (Tennessee State Library and Archives, Nashville). For helping me create first-rate maps, I want to thank Will Fontenez of the University of Tennessee's Cartography Department. For helping me assemble and professionally develop the book's pictures, I want to thank, among others, Holly Adams, Trevor Smith, and Mikel Uriguen.

Sincere thanks must go to Carroll Van West and the personnel at Tennessee Civil War National Heritage Area for their generous financial contribution to this work. Similarly, I want to recognize the entire staff at the Univerity of Tennessee Press for their courteous professionalism from start to finish.

Finally, I want to offer my family my deepest gratitude. To my parents, Stan and Virginia, whose lifetime of support I can never repay. To my beautiful wife Tara, who faithfully comforted me throughout the process by gently moderating my oscillations between vanity and inadequacy. To my daughters Beatrice and Josephine (the little monkeys), who gave me many needed smiles. In bringing purpose to my life, they enable me to bring purpose to my work. I love them all dearly.

Introduction

That the sure and certain defense of a free people is a well-regulated militia; and, as standing armies in time of peace are dangerous to freedom, they ought to be avoided as far as the circumstances and safety of the community will admit; and that in all cases the military shall be kept in strict subordination to the civil authority.
—1834 Tennessee Constitution, Art. I, Sec. 24

WAR OFFERS NUMEROUS OPPORTUNITIES FOR POLITICAL REALIGNMENT. And long, destructive wars can produce vicious and desperate peacetime political struggles. This is certainly true for the Reconstruction period in the South following the American Civil War. The former Confederate states may have conceded defeat on the battlefield, but in the postwar political arena, they proved astonishingly "unrepentant" and openly defiant toward their northern conquerors. As a result, the politics of Reconstruction increasingly became the politics of force as the contestants strove to instigate or obstruct the various plans for national reunification. Nowhere is this plunge into the politics of force more evident than in the state of Tennessee. Here, wartime Unionists who later styled themselves Radical Republicans briefly held the reins of power and, to the enduring infamy of their name, opted to wield their power through authoritarian force.

The main Radical weapon in this Reconstruction power play was the Tennessee State Guard. Following its legislative creation, Radical governor William G. Brownlow used this militia organization to uphold his administration and to provide some protection to the freedmen. In the process, the State Guard helped police elections and operated against a seemingly ubiquitous ex-Confederate opposition, particularly the emergent Ku Klux Klan. To its opponents, the Tennessee State Guard was the worst manifestation of a standing army as a danger to freedom. To its proponents, the State Guard was the epitome of a "well-regulated militia" necessary for the defense of a free people. Needless to say, the militia provisions of the state constitution took on profound significance for the Reconstruction period.

This resort to force in Tennessee (and throughout the South for that matter) should come as no surprise. Although the Civil War ended in 1865, Reconstruction was neither a time of peace nor one of normal relations between the North and South. Rather, as the word suggests, Reconstruction was a process that entailed substantial social and political restructuring. Consequently, Reconstruction was, in many respects, a militant continuation of the Civil War. Historian George Rable cleverly alters Karl von Clausewitz's dictum on politics and war when he states that "for the South, peace became war carried on by other means." The conduct of Tennessee's Radicals certainly suggests that many Reconstruction contemporaries felt that way. As men who had participated in a war fought to an unconditional surrender, the Radicals expected the vanquished Rebels to submit to whatever peace terms were presented, including Radical control of the government and civil equality for the freedmen. In pursuing these goals, the Radicals treated their state as if it was still within the "grasp of war," meaning that the victors monopolized formal power. To this end, the Radicals disfranchised their political enemies while trying to build up their party's apparatus throughout the state. When the state's ex-Confederates and Conservative Unionists— political allies hereafter referred to as the anti-Radicals—balked at these stern terms, the Radicals responded with coercion, most notably the Tennessee State Guard. Under the circumstances, it seemed to the Radicals a perfectly acceptable course of action.[1]

Political labels for the Reconstruction period can be confusing. White Tennesseans who supported Reconstruction went by many names, including Unconditional Unionist, Radical Unionist, and Radical Republican; their critics dubbed them "scalawags," a pejorative for white southerners who supposedly betrayed their region and their race. For the sake of simplicity, if not accuracy, I refer consistently to Tennessee's advocates of Reconstruction as "Radicals." It was a term they used routinely, even proudly, in describing themselves. Moreover, it is an appellation that effectively conveys the forceful nature of Reconstruction politics in Tennessee. The term "anti-Radical" is my construct, one used in referring to

the joint opposition to Reconstruction by so-called Conservative Unionists and ex-Confederates (a.k.a. Rebels). Most anti-Radicals would later
identify themselves as Democrats, but this party did not reorganize formally in the state until 1869.[2]

Historians have long debated the role of force in Reconstruction.
Could the nation secure its goals, namely, a readmitted South under sin-
cerely loyal governments and genuine civil equality for the freedmen,
with minimum force? For the most part, while sympathizing with the
North's frustration with southern intransigence, historians agree that
draconian force would likely have only further alienated an already hostile white South. Moreover, such a course of action would have required a huge, long-term military occupation that few Americans at the
time were willing to tolerate. If the Reconstruction state governments
of the South were to survive, they would have to do so without endless
infusions of federal power. Nevertheless, an articulate minority of historians insists that coercion was the most logical approach to Reconstruction. Because the North and South remained polarized after the
war, they say, Reconstruction should have been a time of dictation, not
negotiation. A more forceful Reconstruction, however unpalatable, was
essential in breaking white southern resistance and making Reconstruction work.[3]

The Tennessee State Guard offers a valuable case study of force politics in action during Reconstruction. If coercive control could have succeeded anywhere, that place was Tennessee. No other reconstructed state
contained so large a native, white Unionist element. No other state instigated sweeping disfranchisement of its Rebel opposition at the very beginning of Reconstruction. No other state possessed a Radical safe haven
like East Tennessee from which to draw strength. No other state had a
better claim to national legitimacy, thanks to Tennessee's early readmission. And in only a few other states did Republican governments employ
as effective an internal enforcing agent as the State Guard. For good reason then did William M. Connelly of Memphis declare in 1868 that
"Tennessee is really the place where southern Radicalism must make its
stand, or all will be lost."[4]

As interesting as Reconstruction in Tennessee was, there is relatively
little scholarly work on the subject. Most of the important monographs
are outdated and their treatment of Reconstruction and the Radical
party is highly slanted. Generally, the Radical Unionists are depicted as

petty, vindictive men who lacked political maturity. The heavy-handed gubernatorial leadership of William G. Brownlow is especially criticized. In the course of this harsh criticism, the Tennessee State Guard is typically discussed as merely one more example of despotic rule in the state. Its role in Reconstruction has never received detailed scholarly attention. (In fact, there have been few studies of any state militias during Reconstruction.) This is unfortunate, because the State Guard was a key component of Radical Reconstruction in the Volunteer State; it was the organization most responsible for carrying out the Brownlow administration's decrees. The importance of the State Guard is underscored when one remembers that Tennessee, having been readmitted to the Union in July 1866, did not come under the Reconstruction acts of 1867, which divided the former Confederacy into military districts. Therefore, the state neither experienced large-scale federal intervention nor had the kind of access to U.S. troops that other southern Republicans enjoyed. In other words, Tennessee Unionists had to effect Reconstruction largely on their own. A reliable, native coercive arm was imperative for Radical success—enter the State Guard.[5]

Generally speaking, scholars have simply described the Tennessee State Guard as a partisan military force that the Radicals used to suppress opposition, control elections, protect black voters, and uphold the governor's arbitrary power, or what was known as "Brownlowism." The earliest appraisal of the State Guard comes from the voluminous congressional investigations into the Ku Klux Klan. In the report on Tennessee, the Joint Select Committee branded the guard a pack of "ignorant and debased men" who spread "terror across the state." This view is contradicted in an obscure 1890 essay by Ira Jones. While regarding the Radicals as highhanded political opportunists, Jones offers a rather innocuous description of the militiamen as "licensed disturbers of the public-repose." The author goes on to state that Governor Brownlow enjoyed "carte blanche" power over the militia, but he insists that the State Guard itself was remarkably well behaved and generally respectful toward those Tennesseans over whom they watched. These would remain the last friendly words about the State Guard for the next half-century.[6]

In the 1930s, two books appeared in which Tennessee's Reconstruction figured prominently: James Patton's *Unionism and Reconstruction* and E. Merton Coulter's entertaining biography *William G. Brownlow*. Both say little about the State Guard specifically, and then only within the context of "Brownlow's Wars" for political power, but they concur that the performance of this organization was in keeping with the authoritarian style of its commander-in-chief. Coulter goes so far as to compare the State Guard to the New Model Army of seventeenth-century English dictator Oliver Cromwell—Brownlow's militia as "modern Ironsides."[7]

In 1950, Thomas B. Alexander presented the fullest study of Reconstruction politics in Tennessee. His observations on the State Guard are no different from those of his predecessors of the 1930s, but he does tie this militia body more closely to Brownlow himself. The State Guard is depicted as the governor's "personal possession" and his "private army." Not surprisingly, Alexander sees it as an instrument of tyranny.[8]

Negative observations about the State Guard culminate with the overtly anti-Brownlow commentary of Robert White, editor of several volumes of the *Messages of the Governors of Tennessee*. Invoking the Cromwell imagery again, he condemns the actions of the State Guard, with its "clanking swords and rattling militia musketry" and its "rampant Radical" leadership, as nothing more than legalized oppression. However prejudiced White's scholarship, the partisan nature of the State Guard, as well as its brethren in other southern states, should not be underestimated. Looking at the issue from the perspective of the U.S. Army, historian James Sefton contends that all Reconstruction militias more or less placed political allegiance above impartial law enforcement, making them in effect "worse than useless."[9]

Since the 1950s, no scholarly study of Tennessee Reconstruction has emerged beyond several articles, none of which addresses the State Guard. Nevertheless, some noteworthy monographs on the Reconstruction South as a whole have appeared which cast the State Guard in a more favorable light. Otis Singletary's *Negro Militia and Reconstruction* stands as the only published study specifically on Reconstruction militias. In this sympathetic work, the author aptly notes that "the need for the militia grew out of the stern dictates of political self-preservation." Although Singletary's main focus is on militia activities in Louisiana, Arkansas, and Mississippi, he does offer some interesting commentary on the Tennessee State Guard. His conclusion is that it "proved more annoying than overpowering." Overall, he judges the entire militia experiment a failure because Republican governors lacked the courage to "employ the militia forces to the full extent of their power."[10]

Another work that offers sympathetic treatment of the plight of southern Republicans is Allen Trelease's *White Terror*, perhaps the definitive study of the Ku Klux Klan during Reconstruction. The book includes detailed chapters on Klan activities in Tennessee and the state government's confrontations with this organization. Trelease says that the State Guard was created to suppress "an endemic spirit of lawlessness" that pervaded the middle and western portions of Tennessee. Although the organization was effective at controlling elections, its ability to defeat the Klan cannot be fairly measured due to its abrupt disbandment in 1869. In short, the State Guard's war against the KKK could have been decisive but proved "anticlimactic" in the end.[11]

Since *White Terror*, there has been no significant commentary on the Tennessee State Guard. While the old school—Patton, Coulter, and Alexander—appears to still hold sway on both this subject and their conclusions about "Brownlowism" as a whole, the truth about this particular militia probably lies somewhere within John Hope Franklin's brief and inadvertently contradictory appraisal of the State Guard. At one point in his book *Reconstruction After the Civil War*, Franklin claims that Governor Brownlow was "among the most vigorous defenders of Radical Reconstruction," a man who "did not hesitate to use [the militia]." However, at another point, he laments that the Tennessee militia "served more as a warning . . . than as an actual fighting force." Which statement is correct? Was the militia a genuine weapon or merely a threat?[12]

With all due respect to previous scholarship on Tennessee's Reconstruction, denouncing the Radicals as tyrants without examining in detail this group's mailed fist—the State Guard—is a serious deficiency. This book seeks to bring Tennessee's militia organization into the light and, in so doing, offer a reevaluation of supposed Radical tyranny and reopen the question of whether a more forceful military-style Reconstruction could have succeeded in Tennessee (and by extension in the rest of the South). To this end, a number of questions are addressed, all of which revolve around the central issue of the State Guard's effectiveness during Reconstruction: What was the precise mission of the State Guard? When did the situation justify its activation and for how long? Who served in the State Guard, and who were the leaders? Where exactly was it employed and what were the rules of engagement? What were the limitations of the State Guard as an instrument of force? Finally, how might the State Guard have been used differently?

With these questions in mind, I offer the following thesis: the Tennessee State Guard was remarkably effective at enforcing the Reconstruction policies of the Radical Republican government. Although it was a partisan law enforcement body—a Radical Army, in effect—the State Guard usually conducted itself with a marked degree of discipline and restraint. To be sure, the militia officers generally despised the "Rebel" majority, but the guard was never used to avenge the suffering of Unionists during the Civil War; it was not an instrument of tyranny. Rather, it operated fully within the laws of the state (however questionable the constitutionality of some of those laws). When it was used, in 1867 and early 1869, it successfully thwarted ex-Confederate resistance and ensured Radical success and safety. Its employment, however, was inconsistent. In 1868, a year that witnessed widespread Ku Klux Klan depredations, the State Guard was never called into service. And in the summer of 1869, the executive abruptly disbanded it before the Klan was sufficiently suppressed. By not maintaining an active State Guard presence throughout the Reconstruction period, the Radical Republicans forfeited perhaps the best means for preserving their hold on the state and completing their plans for a New Tennessee. Thus, Reconstruction failed in Tennessee, in large part because the Radicals were too cautious in their use of force.

Reconstruction in Tennessee has been lambasted by historians for far too long. The performance of the State Guard demonstrates that the Radicals were not that "radical" (if the term is used to mean despotic) and that Governor Brownlow, while certainly intemperate in his rhetoric, was usually levelheaded in his approach to governing. He did not recklessly engage in the politics of force, nor did any other important Radical for that matter. While rehabilitating the Radical image is beyond the scope of this book, a full discussion of the State Guard must bring the Radical record into consideration and thereby permit a qualified reconsideration. The unsavory Governor Brownlow is too often the focus of attention while the many other important leaders both in the Tennessee General Assembly and among the State Guard officer corps are ignored. This study looks at the more than two thousand militiamen who were simultaneously Radical leaders and followers. They played a larger role in Reconstruction than mere thugs marching to the governor's tune. To be sure, these militiamen, especially the officers, were all dedicated Radicals, but they had a vested interest in securing for the party not only power but also legitimacy. In this sense, the militiamen were active agents in making Reconstruction work for the Radical party and the Unionist populace. In the process, they made the State Guard an effective, and well-regulated, instrument of force.

Chapter 1

The Creation of a Radical Army

On January 11, 1867, a former Confederate guerrilla shot and killed Almon Case, a Radical state senator, near his home in Troy, Tennessee. Troy is in Obion County in northwestern Tennessee, a dangerous place for Radicals to live in the post–Civil War period. The majority of Obion's white males had voted for secession in 1861, and during the war the county was a haven for Rebel guerrillas. These whites did not like Senator Case, a wartime Unionist who firmly supported the Reconstruction administration of Governor William G. Brownlow. Case represented a small constituency that increasingly found itself the target of ex-Confederate harassment. In September 1866, an assailant murdered Case's son, Emmit. And at the time Case himself was killed, his assassin, Frank Farris, also wounded two Obion County deputy sheriffs. Although a reward of two thousand dollars was placed on his head, Farris enjoyed the protection of local Obion whites and was never arrested.[1]

Case's death sounded the political tocsin for the Radicals. After two years, their hold on power was still precarious in much of the state. Although the Radicals controlled all branches of the state government, their authority was routinely flouted by the state's large populace of ex-Confederates and a sizable group of Conservative Unionists—collectively, the anti-Radicals. The Tennessee General Assembly condemned the

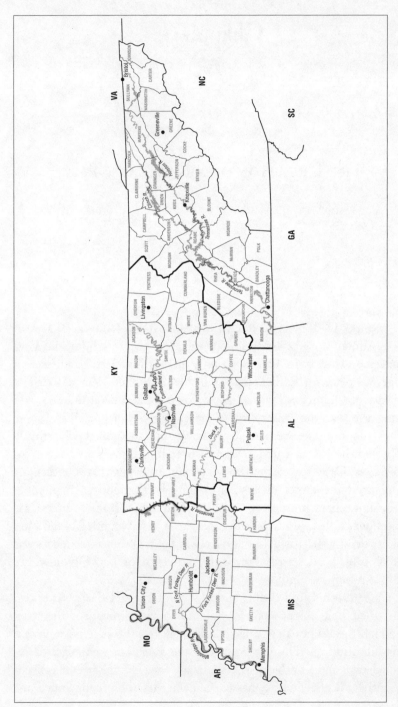

Tennessee in the late 1860s

assassination. Radicals, in particular, regarded it as another example of "the spirit of hatred, malice, and uncharitableness, the legitimate fruits of treason" that plagued much of the state. According to the Radical Samuel Arnell, "No explanation but political feeling could be offered for the act." The time had come, so it seemed, for the Brownlow administration to crack down hard on lawlessness. The Obion incident added impetus to Radical efforts to secure the passage of a militia bill, one that envisioned a powerful State Guard as a means of protection for the party and the Reconstruction process, and a new franchise bill, one that extended suffrage to blacks. (Both bills were then being debated in the second session of the Thirty-fourth General Assembly.) The Radicals viewed 1867 as a critical year for Reconstruction and for their hold on power. The first of August would mark the first peacetime statewide election since 1860 and the first time that southern blacks had ever voted. Case's death, however, marked an ominous start to that year.[2]

The Civil War had produced great enmity between those Tennesseans who supported the Union and those who advocated secession. As the sectional crisis unfolded in early 1861, most Tennesseans generally repudiated the idea of disunion. Public opinion changed, however, with the outbreak of war in April. In early May, secessionist governor Isham G. Harris and his allies in the general assembly effected a declaration of independence, subject to approval by the voters on June 8. Harris then entered into a "military league" with the Confederacy and began raising an army to defend the state against Federal invasion. Unionists from East Tennessee, the stronghold of Unionism in the state, gathered in Knoxville on May 30 and denounced Harris's fait accompli. Nevertheless, their efforts to halt the slide into secession failed. With aroused passions, West and Middle Tennessee voted overwhelmingly for secession on June 8. A second convention of East Tennessee Unionists gathered in Greeneville on June 17 and called for separate statehood, but the Harris regime ignored their application.[3]

Thwarted in their peaceable efforts to resolve the situation, many Tennessee Unionists resorted to violence. With the Civil War well underway, Unionist guerrillas in East Tennessee launched an uprising in November 1861. They burned five important railroad bridges and threw the region into pandemonium. The Confederacy countered with military occupation and martial law. Nevertheless, Unionists in East Tennessee as well as the other regions of the state continued to fight; at

Very Respectfully, &c,

W. G. Brownlow

William G. Brownlow. Courtesy of Special Collections Library, University of Tennessee, Knoxville.

least thirty thousand of them joined the Federal army, forming more than thirty regiments of Tennessee volunteers. These Unionists fought not only for their nation but also for the defense of their own homes and communities, which had been overrun by Confederate forces. For four years, Tennessee suffered a violent mixture of conventional and guerrilla warfare, along with political persecution and social and economic chaos. In many localities, the war descended to the level of personal vendetta and atrocity begot counter-atrocity.[4]

As the Confederacy collapsed in 1864–65, Tennessee Unionists quarreled over how to restore civil government. Two competing political factions emerged: the so-called Unconditional Unionists, men who wholeheartedly supported the Lincoln administration and the Republican party, especially the Radical wing, and the Conservative Unionists, men who opposed secession but also opposed emancipation. The Unconditional Unionists, who increasingly identified themselves as Radicals, viewed the ex-Confederate majority as "traitors" and "rebels" who deserved some kind of punishment for rending the Union and disrupting the lives of loyal men. Conservative Unionists urged a more conciliatory attitude toward ex-Confederates. At a convention in Nashville in January 1865, the Radicals, most of whom came from East Tennessee, dominated the proceedings and restored civil government on their terms. William G. Brownlow, a prominent Radical Unionist whose *Knoxville Whig and Rebel Ventilator* had waged a venomous propaganda war against the Confederacy, became the new governor on March 4, 1865. Intent on consolidating Radical power, this former circuit-riding Methodist preacher implemented a stern Reconstruction program.[5]

From the outset of Reconstruction, Governor Brownlow's main priority was to establish an electorate in Tennessee "that shall be thoroughly loyal." To this end, the Radical Unionists in the general assembly enacted a franchise law in June 1865 that temporarily forbade some eighty thousand ex-Confederates from voting. To the Radicals, such a measure seemed logical and justifiable. As state senator Samuel Arnell reasoned, "Rebellion had no right or privilege of citizenship whatever. This was the legal status brought about by secession. . . . To say that people conquered with arms in their hands are to be handed over to themselves for reconstruction is to talk absurdly, without sense." To the anti-Radicals, however, such thinking was spurious reasoning for what amounted to a naked power grab—the essence of "Brownlowism." The

The Creation of a Radical Army

fall congressional elections of 1865 proved a disappointment for the Radicals. In many instances, anti-Radical forces violated the franchise provisions, particularly the discriminatory loyalty oaths, and only three Radicals, all from East Tennessee, won their races. Arnell later prevailed in his Middle Tennessee district, but only after Brownlow tossed out thousands of "illegal" votes. Similarly, county elections held in March 1866 resulted in numerous victories for former Confederates in West and Middle Tennessee. In the eyes of the Radicals, Conservative opponents of the Brownlow administration, in league with their ex-Confederate partners, were manipulating the letter of the franchise act in order to pervert its spirit.[6]

In May 1866, a second, more severe, franchise law was passed. This new act created commissioners of registration for each county under direct executive control and permanently disfranchised all ex-Confederates. Brownlow, while admitting that this franchise amendment was "a terrible bill," insisted it was necessary under the circumstances. Resistance to this measure resulted in the resignation of twenty-one Conservative members of the state house in an effort to prevent a voting quorum. Once again, Brownlow resorted to makeshift countermeasures to thwart what the Radicals called the "little rebellion." He held special elections and then seated candidates of Radical proclivities who helped pass the revised franchise bill.[7]

These franchise restrictions were crucial to Radical Reconstruction in Tennessee. There was simply no other practical way to ensure that those who had ruptured the Union in 1861 did not regain power in 1865. Brownlow said as much in one of his first executive proclamations, when he declared that the Franchise Act of 1866 "IS THE SUPREME LAW OF THE LAND, and will be *rigidly enforced*." He said further that those who defied its precepts would be "dealt with as rebels." As events demonstrated, Radicals increasingly viewed even Conservative Unionists as "rebels." Unfortunately for the Brownlow administration, the Radicals were discovering that proscriptive legislative decrees, stringent loyalty oaths, and truculent gubernatorial proclamations were hollow measures without the coercive power to back them up. In the absence of an armed deterrent, these measures only inflamed the opposition and invited defiance. "Brownlowism" in 1865 and 1866 had spawned hatred, not fear.[8]

Hatred contributed to Senator Case's death. His assassination, however, was not an isolated event but the culmination of more than a year ex-Confederate audacity in violating the Franchise Act of 1865, managed to get federal troops deployed to Marshall County, where they prevented efforts to disrupt the voting. Brownlow even reluctantly acquiesced to the U.S. Army's continued presence in his beloved East Tennessee due to open resistance in that area. By the summer, conditions had deteriorated to such an extent that one army officer compared the disloyal lawlessness of Middle and West Tennessee to the ex-Confederate defiance he had witnessed in Mississippi. According to another officer, conditions in the rural parts of Tennessee were "most deplorable. . . . Outrages of all kinds [were] being committed without any effort on the part of the civil authorities to arrest the offenders."[13]

It was during these restless months that the Ku Klux Klan was spawned in Giles County. Originating as a fraternal organization, the infamous KKK soon developed into an unofficial paramilitary wing of the anti-Radical forces. Although its full terror would not occur until 1867, by the end of 1866 the nascent Klan frequently engaged in racial and political intimidation in Giles and its neighboring counties of Middle Tennessee. As one historian of the Klan has written, "If Giles County . . . was not the most lawless county in Tennessee in 1866 and 1867, it ranked high on the list."[14]

Beyond the Klan's activities, instances of political obstruction and violence increased as the year went on. In August, Chancellor J. J. Noah of Maury County complained to Governor Brownlow that outgoing chancellor David Campbell, a Conservative in league with local ex-Confederates, including Klan leader John C. Brown, had "contumaciously" refused to permit him to take office and had, in effect, shut down the court system. Noah believed that Campbell's "pow-wow" of "rebel friends" was trying to incite trouble. He requested assistance, but immediate relief was not forthcoming. Army general George H. Thomas corroborated Noah's allegations in his annual report to the secretary of war and added that local law enforcers throughout the region were basically "rebel sympathizers."[15]

Maury's neighboring counties in Middle Tennessee experienced similar disturbances. Discharged Union soldiers from Grundy County petitioned the governor for aid in their ongoing fight against local ex-Confederate outlaws. And one desperate farmer from Marshall County described an atmosphere of virulent hostility toward Unionists and blacks: "We cannot get justice here. . . . It is dangerous for us to go about, particularly a man who has served in the Federal army. . . . Here the civil law is a dead letter. . . . If the Governor and General Thomas don't send us some help, we are gone under. . . . We are in a worse condition than we had in 1861." While U.S. troops may have quelled disorder in March, during a special November election, with no troops in the vicinity, Marshall Conservatives violated the 1866 Franchise Act, ignored the registrar, and defeated a Radical candidate for local office. The Radical *Nashville Daily Press and Times* claimed that the situation in Marshall County was representative of that in many other parts of the state. To this newspaper, the "spirit which provoked secession and dragged the South into war is neither dead nor dormant, but a living and active feeling in the hearts of the reconstructed traitors."[16]

The *Daily Press and Times* was not exaggerating, for ex-Confederate lawlessness erupted elsewhere in Middle Tennessee. General Thomas reported that Unionists and blacks in Robertson County were "in constant danger of their lives." Sumner County proved especially troublesome. Under their old guerrilla commander, "King" Ellis Harper, a "gang" of about 150 ex-Confederates ruled the county like warlords, terrorizing Unionists and freedmen alike. The situation became so intolerable that the army sent a cavalry detachment under Capt. Edwin H. Leib to drive Harper's band out. Leib spent most of November and December hunting down these guerrilla outlaws, his efforts taking him throughout much of northern Middle Tennessee and into parts of Kentucky. Referring to the ex-Confederates as "barbarians," Leib informed his superiors that "if the troops are withdrawn . . . there will be no peace or quiet for the black man and the very few Union men in those counties." Leib's campaign was, in its essentials, indistinguishable from the dozens of such operations conducted in that region during the Civil War.[17]

Unfortunately for the Radicals, the withdrawal of U.S. troops was well under way in 1866. President Johnson, whom Governor Brownlow had recently dismissed as a "dead dog," saw no reason to maintain a large garrison in the Volunteer State. After readmission to the Union, troop strength in Tennessee dwindled from over seven thousand at the beginning of the year to less than two thousand by the end. Moreover, with the exception of Captain Leib's detachment, most of the federal troops were stationed in Nashville and remained in camp.[18]

Increasing anti-Radical defiance coupled with the decreasing presence of the federal garrison boded ill for the Radicals. The situation

The Creation of a Radical Army

prompted a delegation of twenty-two East Tennesseans to submit a petition to their congressmen. These Radicals proclaimed that "our prosperity as a people . . . depends almost entirely on the action of the loyal people of this section of the state." They urged their government to take decisive measures to subdue the opposition. Governor Brownlow and other Radicals believed a second civil war within the state of Tennessee was inevitable, perhaps imminent. A rumor of an assassination attempt against Brownlow himself circulated in October, charging certain ex-Confederates with trying to derail a train the governor had planned to use on a trip to Knoxville. In the autumn of 1866, Brownlow participated in the Convention of Union Loyalists, a group of southern Republicans who toured the North as part of a campaign to counter Andrew Johnson's anti-Radical stump of northern cities, the so-called Swing around the Circle. The Tennessee governor harangued his audiences about ex-Confederate efforts to restart the Civil War. He vividly described a condition of incessant hostilities and spoke of the need to march fresh armies into the South and finish off the traitors once and for all. Regardless of whether his assessment was accurate, it is notable that the key ingredient in his plan was military strength, something his own government lacked.[19]

On November 6, in an address before the legislature, Governor Brownlow formally condemned the growing anti-Radical agitation and violence. Describing what he called the "Threatened State of Revolution," Brownlow recited a familiar litany of political sedition, intimidation, and conspiracy, all designed to disrupt the state election of August 1867 and topple the loyal government. Explaining that "there is no military organization anywhere in the State," Brownlow implored the assembly to take "fearless action": "I recommend that you authorize the enlistment of a few regiments of loyal militia, to be armed and held as minute men, subject to the call of the Executive, to suppress insurrection or protect the ballot-box." He closed by promising to sustain the laws "be the consequences what they may." No doubt Brownlow exaggerated the threat of a second civil war and his own government's impotence, but given the unrepentant nature of many ex-Confederates, the Radicals were certainly confronted by an opponent who was both hostile and disloyal.[20]

Some three months after this address, on February 20, 1867, the assembly passed the Act to Organize and Equip a State Guard. Brownlow now had his much desired military strength. For all of the

11

criticism of Radical "tyranny" and "oppression," the Brownlow administration was remarkably slow to develop a reliable coercive instrument akin to a state militia. Not until two years after gaining power did the Radicals create this "loyal militia." A number of factors account for this delay. Cost was a primary concern for the state government. In the aftermath of the war, Tennessee was essentially bankrupt; many Tennessee legislators were loathe to add another expense, such as a militia organization, to the civil government's budget. State authorities preferred using the services of the free federal garrison in combating lawlessness, as long as it was available. Additionally, the issue of political legitimacy played a tacit, but crucial, role. Despite their suppression of ex-Confederate political liberties, the Radicals genuinely wanted a republican form of government. Cognizant of their minority political status, they were reluctant to create an armed force that would perforce be partisan. Only exigent circumstances could justify a standing army in peacetime. Besides, Conservative factions in the legislature were sure to oppose any militia bill that suggested the slightest political intent. To be sure, the anti-Radicals accused the Brownlow administration of tyranny anyway, but an arbitrary and excessive use of force would have confirmed it and possibly undermined Radical solidarity. Thus, Governor Brownlow adopted an incremental approach to the use of force. In this respect, the Tennessee State Guard marked the last resort, not the first choice, of Brownlow's "iron-glove regime."[21]

The Radical path to the State Guard Act of 1867 was circuitous and strewn with political obstacles. Tennessee legislators did debate the creation of a militia force from the time civil government was restored in the spring of 1865, but this early effort to augment executive power ultimately came to naught. Shortly after his inauguration on April 5, Governor Brownlow informed the legislature that armed bands of ex-Confederate guerrillas continued to roam the state and that the freedmen needed protection. Accordingly, he urged the creation of a "military contingent fund . . . confiding it under the control of the Executive." Unionists in the assembly agreed and soon presented several bills that went beyond a mere contingency fund and called for an actual militia. Roderick R. Butler of Johnson County, a leading member of the largely Radical state senate, presented on April 21 a bill titled "Amend the Militia Laws." Butler insisted that the militiamen be drawn from those Tennesseans mustering out of the army and believed that about three thousand would be sufficient. West Tennessean Fielding Hurst agreed and endorsed the militia bill as a law that would "inspire confidence in the people." Similarly, the Radical John Trimble of Davidson County, echoing the sentiments of President Johnson, stated that "the people must form home companies and protect themselves like men." Despite some concerns over cost and priorities, W. K. Hall of Dyer County believed that the militia bill was "about as good as we shall be likely to obtain." In the course of this debate, some Radicals even suggested conscripting secessionist clergymen into the militia as a means of punishment. Amid such support, Butler's militia bill easily passed its third reading, after only a few days of deliberation, sixteen to four.[22]

Meanwhile, in the state house, William J. Smith, chairman of the military committee, forcefully moved various pieces of militia legislation. At the time, Smith was probably the most zealous advocate for a state militia. A wartime Unionist and slaveholder from the West Tennessee county of Hardeman, Smith had been arrested by Confederate authorities in 1861 and charged with treason. Although he was acquitted, local secessionists threatened Smith's life. At this point, he joined the Union army, serving as a scout in West Tennessee and later as a cavalry commander. He finished the war with a brevet brigadier generalship. A staunch Republican by 1865, Smith was a loud proponent of Radical Reconstruction for whom a loyal militia force was second in importance only to a strict franchise law. From the end of April to the beginning of June, he directed efforts to move some four militia bills through the house. He replaced Butler's original senate bill with his own bill "to Organize a State Guard," but the substantial number of Conservatives in the state house defeated this piece of legislation. Perhaps angered, Smith resisted efforts to pass a revised version of Butler's senate bill. Eager to get something passed before the session ended on June 12, however, he readily supported a new senate bill for "the Military Discipline and Defense of the State." Nevertheless, this bill was defeated, as was the hasty reintroduction of the Butler bill on June 7. Smith's parliamentary inexperience coupled with his apparent stubbornness contributed to the assembly's failure to enact any militia laws in 1865.[23]

However attractive a state militia may have sounded to Tennessee Radicals, there was no sense of urgency about creating such an organization in 1865. Many elected officials, most notably James R. Hood, a house Conservative from Hamilton County who voted against all of the militia

William J. Smith, 1865. Courtesy of the Massachusetts Commandery Military Order of the Loyal Legion and U. S. Army Military History Institute.

bills, believed a state militia was fiscally impractical and unnecessary given the presence of a large federal garrison (over sixteen thousand soldiers were stationed in Tennessee at the time). Accordingly, the assembly petitioned the president for military aid, reminding him of his constitutional duty to "guarantee . . . a Republican form of government." President Andrew Johnson assured the Brownlow administration that Gen. George H. Thomas, the department commander, would furnish "whatever amount of military force is necessary to sustain the civil authority and enforce the law." Brownlow and most Radicals happily accepted this military force. As the defender of Nashville against Confederate general John B. Hood's invasion in 1864, Thomas was popular with Tennessee Unionists. Moreover, Thomas was sympathetic to the Radical cause in the state. Though content to rely on U.S. troops, the general assembly did offer some comfort to county authorities confronted with guerrilla bands left over from the war. In June, it passed the Act For the Protection of Sheriffs, which authorized the creation of County Guards, posses of twenty-five men that local sheriffs could employ to combat outlaws.[24]

By 1866, as political tensions mounted, these means of law enforcement proved inadequate. The Sheriffs Act was designed to combat leftover guerrillas, not enforce a Reconstruction political agenda. Brownlow was generally pleased with how sheriffs in East Tennessee suppressed ex-Confederate lawlessness, but sheriffs elsewhere were less interested in promoting Radical policy. As for the federal garrison, General Thomas, in accordance with President Johnson's final proclamation ending the war, scaled down U.S. Army operations (fewer than two thousand soldiers were stationed in the state for most of the year). Moreover, after Tennessee's readmission, the federal government properly expected the state government to solve its own problems.[25]

To this end, the Radicals enacted the controversial Metropolitan Police Act in May 1866. This law granted the governor significant control over the police forces in three of the state's major urban centers: Memphis, Nashville, and Chattanooga. (Knoxville, Brownlow's hometown, was considered secure for the Radicals, although it did have a self-appointed "secret" police to keep crime in check.) The disappointing results of the March elections and the horrors of the Memphis race riot seemed to justify this increase in the executive's coercive powers, but the Metropolitan Police was only partially effective in suppressing anti-Radical activities. In Chattanooga, police commissioners appointed by

George H.
Thomas, 1863–64.
From Miller's
*Photographic History
of the Civil War.*

Brownlow did help the Radicals win that city's December municipal elections, but most of the city's residents found this use of force distasteful and protested the partisanship of the police. In Memphis, the Metropolitan Police became mired in that city's complicated politics. The commissioners divided their loyalties between rival Republican factions, undermining Brownlow's influence in the process. In Nashville, the popular Conservative mayor Matt Brown, who habitually reminded people of his steadfast refusal to take the state's loyalty oaths, levied an injunction against Brownlow's commissioners that inhibited the organization of the Metropolitan Police for months. Not until October 1867, when the Radicals won mayoral power, would a viable Radical police force materialize in Nashville. Even when fully employed, however, the Metropolitan Police Act limited Brownlow's reach to the cities, leaving the majority of the state unpoliced.[26]

To achieve real and lasting power, the Radicals needed a strong, reliable force at the Governor's immediate disposal. Enter the Tennessee State Guard. Past elections demonstrated to the Radicals that the

Franchise Act of 1866 required vigilant enforcement, something only a militia force could provide. Furthermore, the necessity for the State Guard was decidedly urgent given the Radicals' pending efforts to enfranchise blacks. The Radical party was making a major effort in 1867 to implement its final version of Reconstruction—a Republican political hegemony that promoted public education, economic development, and a measure of racial equality. The potential for a second civil war, Brownlow's "State of Revolution," threatened to wreck these plans. The success of this Reconstruction venture, and the political survival of the Radicals, demanded a powerful militia to counter any armed resistance. By the autumn of 1866, the Radicals were on the verge of force politics.

Conservatives viewed with growing alarm both Brownlow's request for a militia force to prevent a rumored second civil war and the Radical party's gravitation toward black suffrage. Misperceptions concerning the creation of a large state militia circulated throughout the autumn. Edward H. East believed that the Radicals intended to "arm about 30,000 soldiers (white & negroes)." Alvan C. Gillem claimed that the recent political tension was the fault of the Radicals, who sought a "pretext to arm the militia, which in Middle & West Tennessee will be mostly *colored*." John S. Brien urged President Johnson to replace General Thomas with an army commander more favorable to the Conservatives, noting that "if Brownlow Sucedes in arming the negroes and organizing them as Malitia," then Conservatives would need white troops to maintain order.[27]

Governor Brownlow left the particulars of the militia to the discretion of his Radical cohorts in the legislature. Within weeks of the Governor's November "State of Revolution" address, they dutifully presented two militia bills for consideration. Words of encouragement came from the Radical *Daily Press and Times,* which declared "A Well Organized Loyal Militia" to be one of the party's principal objectives for the upcoming year. The sense of urgency notwithstanding, the state house military committee took a long time—nearly two months—to draft a single, suitable bill. The assassination of Senator Case, however, accelerated the process. Shortly after this instance of ex-Confederate violence, William J. Smith, the champion of earlier efforts to create a state militia, presented a lengthy, complex militia bill that incorporated ideas from all previous bills on the matter. Smith's bill—No. 727, "To Provide for Organizing, Arming, and Disciplining the Militia"—

contained twenty-nine sections dealing with every imaginable detail and contingency from personnel qualifications and recruitment procedures to training regulations and supply matters. Smith envisioned militia formations as large as divisions and volunteers who would serve for three years. The bill further stipulated that regiments would consist of an equal number of white and black troops. But the bill was plagued by extraneous details. Section 7 explained at length the adjutant general's responsibilities, although James P. Brownlow had already been performing quite ably in that capacity for two years. Section 10 described how soldiers were to dress and exactly what gear they would carry. Section 16 required so many days of military exercise per calendar year. Section 17 explained how and when subordinate commands were to report to higher headquarters. Section 24 provided instructions on employing artillery (a "four gun battery" was assigned for each brigade), even though there were no field pieces in the Tennessee arsenal. One portion of the bill even forbade the enrollment of "idiots and lunatics." A Conservative newspaper mockingly declared that this "lunatic clause" exempted the Radicals from participation in the militia altogether.[28]

However cumbersome Smith's bill, the Radicals passionately pushed for its "immediate passage." James A. Doughty of Campbell County reportedly exclaimed that "the loyal men intended to control the State; if they could not control her peaceably they would control her by blood-shed." As an afterthought, he added that "there had not been blood enough shed." James S. Mulloy of Robertson County echoed Doughty's statements. Accusing the ex-Confederates of "rape, robbery, murder and arson" throughout the state, he endorsed the militia bill, claiming that he "had rather be radically right that radically wrong." The Conservatives were appalled by such statements and attempted to postpone the bill's passage. John Lellyett of Davidson County warned that "armies and troops produced more murders and crimes than they suppressed." Nevertheless, Conservative delay tactics were defeated when William J. Smith forced a roll-call vote on the bill. It passed its second reading thirty-nine to twenty-three, but the tally reflected significant opposition.[29]

Outside observers took a keen interest in Smith's militia bill No. 727, and state newspapers weighed in on the legislative discussions. The Radical *Nashville Daily Press and Times* applauded the assembly's decisive action. It described the bill as the surest means to "exterminate the intolerable evil" of ex-Confederate violence, and it reminded readers that this bill limited Governor Brownlow to little more than eight thousand men, whereas Confederate governor Isham Harris had mobilized fifty-five thousand men in 1861. The Conservative *Nashville Union and Dispatch* condemned the militia bill as a "despotic scheme" engineered by the Radicals to secure their tyranny. Repudiating the Radical claim of Rebel lawlessness and ignoring the manifest political violence, the *Union and Dispatch* marveled that such legislation could be provoked by the death of a single man—Almon Case. This newspaper claimed that a state militia "will be a disgrace to the civilization of the age." In response to such criticism, the *Daily Press and Times* smugly retorted, "Let them wail." The *Knoxville Whig*, Brownlow's personal propaganda machine, offered a reasoned justification for the militia. It reassured Conservatives that "no very large number [of militiamen] will ever be called into actual service." It further insisted that the militia was not designed to control elections but to uphold the law where "a general spirit of defiance reigns supreme." Finally, it proclaimed that the Radicals would triumph "without brute force," and that with a militia, the governor could ensure that the Rebels also refrained from "brute force." Unconvinced, the *Union and Dispatch* rhetorically asked, "How much of republican government will there be left when these Praetorian bands are turned loose?"[30]

Realizing the seriousness of creating a standing army for the governor, even some Radical politicians urged caution. Smith's version of the militia bill ultimately proved too unwieldy, and other bills paraded the assembly floor in early February. In an effort to conciliate fellow Radicals and maintain his central role on the militia issue, Smith submitted a simplified version of his militia bill, but the house rejected it in a close vote (thirty to twenty-six). Conservatives consistently maintained that a militia was an excessive response to "the usual criminal outcroppings incident to every community" and recommended the cessation of debate on the topic. The Radicals, however, though still undecided on a final version, made the militia the "special order" of business for the house.[31]

As house legislators wrangled over the issue, Radicals in the senate crafted the militia bill that eventually passed into law. Alfred M. Cate, one of the Unionist heroes of the 1861 bridge-burning episode in East Tennessee, maneuvered a more succinct militia bill, An Act to Organize a State Guard, through the senate despite some reservations by several members. Conservatives presented two amendments which stipulated

The Creation of a Radical Army

that the militia could be deployed only after two-thirds of a county's civil authorities requested aid, and that the militia would be forbidden to assemble around polling places. Both amendments were defeated by a straight party vote. To further delay the bill's passage, Conservatives read a petition from Rutherford County stating that the residents there opposed the creation of any militia force. In the end, however, Cate's bill passed fifteen to seven.[32]

William J. Smith eagerly received the senate militia bill and moved its adoption in lieu of all other house versions. Successfully thwarting Conservative efforts to debate the merits of this new bill, the Radicals effected its passage, but only after the addition of a crucial amendment, presented by "bloodshed" James Doughty no less, which stipulated that "the militia is not to be armed until actually called up." On February 19, the house passed this latest militia bill forty-one to twenty-five. It became law the next day when the senate concurred with the newly amended bill, twenty-two to one, and the governor affixed his signature. Ignoring the many legislative objections, the *Daily Press and Times* cheered the "Union Phalanx" that brought the "loyal militia" into being. The Brownlow "regime" of Tennessee finally had at its disposal what could properly be described a Radical army.[33]

The final version of the militia law, An Act to Organize and Equip a State Guard, was short and to the point, containing only three sections. The militia force was to be known as the Tennessee State Guard and was to be "composed of loyal men." The governor was to serve as commander-in-chief. Each congressional district was permitted one or more regiments to operate in accordance with U.S. Army regulations. Given that there were eight districts in Tennessee and that an army regiment consisted of about one thousand men, the act authorized Governor Brownlow to raise at least eight thousand men.[34]

After weeks of heated debate, months of anti-Radical lawlessness and rumors of a second civil war, and almost two years of experimentation with alternative approaches to law enforcement, the Radicals of Tennessee had conceived a military force, the State Guard, that they hoped would finally bring peace and make Reconstruction work. The time involved reflects remarkable forbearance by the Radicals. To be sure, through the franchise laws, they implemented a hard Reconstruction policy toward the ex-Confederates, but they refrained, for as long as possible, from resorting to a standing army to enforce this policy. The process of enacting the militia act reveals that Governor Brownlow was not the sole power within the Radical party. Historian Robert H. White unfairly characterizes the Radical legislators as "a bunch of trained seals" who did whatever Brownlow ordered. But White overlooks the important role of several Radical leaders. In the house, William J. Smith, a former Civil War general, was a key figure behind the militia bill. Similarly, in the senate, Alfred M. Cate, another war veteran, helped make the State Guard a reality. These men were not dupes of the governor but confident, ambitious men with a Reconstruction vision of their own. At the end of February 1867, they had done their part. Now the party needed to find men who were militarily competent and politically reliable to command and serve in this new Radical army.[35]

Chapter 2

MOBILIZING THE STATE GUARD

FOLLOWING PASSAGE OF THE MILITIA ACT, RADICALS MET IN convention at Nashville on February 22, 1867, to prepare formally for the upcoming campaign. At this convention, the Radical party apparatus assumed full shape. Leonidas C. Houk, a leading East Tennessee Radical, fired up the gathering with a rousing speech. He warned the ex-Confederates not to interfere with the election or "we will get the Militia after you and whip you into the ranks of law and order, and execute you if necessary." Reminding his listeners of Confederate oppression during the Civil War, Houk closed his address with a firm promise that "red-hand rebels shall not rule." In keeping with such rhetoric, the delegates passed a platform resolution that reflected how the militia act instilled new confidence among the rank and file. Resolution No. 5 read: "Lawless violence, reckless disregard of the rights of person and property, murder, assassination, arson and kindred crime, must be put down by the strong arm of power, and be made to feel that law is indeed a terror to evil doers." To ensure the continued success of Radicalism, the convention unanimously nominated William G. Brownlow for reelection as governor.[1]

Inspired by the convention proceedings, Governor Brownlow threw down his executive gauntlet with a bellicose proclamation on February 25 stating his intention to mobilize the State Guard. He declared that the recent trend of lawlessness "*must* and *shall* cease," and that "the present State Government of Tennessee . . . will be sustained and preserved, despite all the efforts of disappointed traitors." Urging the citizens to obey the laws and keep the peace, he assured them that "prudent and experienced men will be placed in charge of the State Guard" and that militia units would be deployed only in selected counties. Although he claimed the State Guard was apolitical, Brownlow stated that "the number of troops called into active service will be increased or diminished as the good or bad conduct of the people shall be developed." "Old Proc," as the anti-Radicals often called Brownlow, had spoken.[2]

The boldness of the proclamation was indicative of the new, revolutionary momentum of Radical Reconstruction. On the same day, Brownlow signed into law the third franchise act, bestowing suffrage on the freedmen. For the first time in southern history, black men enjoyed the unqualified right to vote. In anticipation of this event, Radical leaders had already moved to mobilize, register, and indoctrinate the approximately forty thousand new black voters. The political vehicle by which these tasks were accomplished was the Union League. Formed by northerners during the war as a means of orchestrating support for the Union, this organization made an easy transition into a peacetime political club. In 1867, hundreds of Union League chapters sprouted over the state enrolling most white Radicals and thousands of freedmen. The secret meetings and political activities of this organization, known also as the Loyal League and the Radical League, alarmed many whites among the anti-Radical forces. Angry ex-Confederates in Wilson County, for example, posted warnings in February that they would kill any "Yankee" (i.e., white Radical) and burn out any freedman who engaged in political activity. To such men, in addition to imposing military tyranny, the Radicals had now perverted white supremacy by ushering in "the nightmare of the South": racial equality via the Union League.[3]

The provisions of the both the militia act and the Franchise Act of 1867 elicited a belligerent Conservative response. Referring to the militia act, in particular, as "that monster of iniquity," the *Fayetteville Observer* contended that, through armed force, Governor Brownlow would "execute the Franchise Act in defiance of any decision the Supreme Court might make on the subject." Other organs claimed that the militia act was simply a ploy to gain favor with the North by portraying ex-Confederates as bandits. The *Union and Dispatch,* citing "despicable demagoguery" on the part of the Radicals as the moving force behind the militia and black suffrage laws, desperately exhorted its readers: "*Radicalism must be hurled from power.*" The *Pulaski Citizen* unleashed a similarly damning assessment of this latest example of Radical Reconstruction: "Thus that immaculate conclave of scoundrels at the capital are drawing the cords more closely about our necks." To this newspaper, the State Guard and its eventual inclusion of black militiamen represented the end of white supremacy and an insult to southern honor. The *Citizen* sarcastically suggested that Tennessee be renamed "Miscegenia."[4]

Perhaps mindful of this anti-Radical outcry, many Tennessee politicians hoped that the militia would not have to be called into service. On March 1, the members of the general assembly unanimously resolved to petition General Thomas for military support in the upcoming election. One Conservative confided to President Johnson that no military force was needed at all but that he hoped that U.S. troops could at least keep Brownlow's militia of "thieves" from despoiling the state. The *Union and Dispatch* echoed such sentiments: "Of the two armies, we should infinitely prefer those of the regular service." Brownlow dutifully requested Thomas's cooperation in deploying troops to any county that proved unruly. General Thomas agreed to help preserve order but reminded Brownlow that since Tennessee was now back in the Union, "the laws can be enforced therein by proper civil authority." Accordingly, he stressed that his men would "act as aids only . . . and not assume control." Moreover, Thomas placed numerous constraints on his units, insisting that his troops would move only after a specific instance of disorder had been reported and corroborated by the civil authorities and only after a strict chain of command had been established between such authorities and the regular officer in charge. Although sympathetic to the Radicals' plight, Thomas was essentially telling Brownlow to use his own resources to enforce his own laws.[5]

Undeterred by General Thomas's understandable reservations about involving federal troops in a civil election, the governor committed to a state military buildup. On March 6, in accordance with the militia act, Brownlow issued his official call, known as General Order No. 1, for volunteer militia companies. Prospective company commanders would hold the rank of captain. These captains were authorized to enlist one hundred men for three-year terms "unless sooner discharged." Each company was permitted twenty-five mounted personnel. Two lieutenants would be elected by each company. All personnel, prior to muster, were required to take a franchise oath, one that required them to swear unconditional allegiance to the United States and swear that they had never voluntarily supported the Confederacy. After organizing, each company was to report to Nashville in order to draw equipment and arms. Under these instructions, a completed State Guard company would ideally have three officers, thirteen noncommissioned officers, and eighty-four privates.[6]

The Radical faithful throughout the state responded enthusiastically to Brownlow's call-up. Many prospective commanders emphasized politics and duty as their primary reasons for requesting a commission. East Tennessean Newton T. Beal went straight to the point: "Wishing the Radical Union Party to have every advantage of the Law is why I apply." John T. Rushing informed Governor Brownlow that the militia call-up "kindled anew the patriotic fire" within him, and that a commission in the State Guard would allow him "to live and die a soldier." Russ B. Davis of Warren County plainly stated that he would "proudly command anything you may give me." Other applicants stressed endemic lawlessness in their counties as reasons for wanting a commission. C. Underwood of Weakley begged for a commission lest the county fall to the "Rebills." He further stated, "If I was to Diclair for Brownlow in Company I Don't Believe I would Live 5 minuts." To Underwood, the militia mobilization was imperative, "the sooner the better." Robert Galbraith of Bedford County warned that "under the teachings of the *infamous traitor* Andy our section is beginning to assume the same aspect and attitude that it had in 1861 & 2 and I desire to be in a condition to combat Rebels, Copperheads, [and] Conservatives." John Enoch of Hickman County wanted to serve in order to "quell the riots that spring up." He believed a thirty-man company would suffice. William Bunker of Polk County promised Governor Brownlow that he would "hold in check the Treasonable portion" and "keep them from overthrowing your State government." With evident zeal, he added, "I would love very much to be one of its defenders. . . . Do not think that it is for money that I would enter your State Guard . . . but the love I have for my birth right."[7]

Whether motivated by partisanship or self-preservation, over sixty requests to form a militia company crossed the adjutant general's desk between March and June (twenty-seven from East Tennessee, twenty-four from Middle, and ten from West, with one from Kentucky). One Hawkins County Unionist, taking the militia act's passage for granted, requested permission to raise a company as early as February 2. James P.

Brownlow, the adjutant general and the governor's son, diligently went about administering the militia call-up (with his cousin Samuel Hunt serving as assistant). He sent all newly commissioned militia captains a copy of General Order No. 1, along with several blank muster rolls and morning reports with instructions to complete all forms in triplicate. He also ordered commanders to "proceed with as little delay as possible" in organizing their companies. Only when the adjutant general was satisfied with the paperwork would the unit be mustered into service.[8]

The difference between what Adjutant General Brownlow expected and what he often got made for some annoying administrative snarls. One prospective captain announced that he was recruiting volunteers although he did not have a signed commission, while twelve other men quit shortly after receiving their commissions. One such captain, W. O. White, explained that he had decided to run for the Tennessee General Assembly instead. Others, such as James M. Dickerson, cited personal or business reasons for their resignations. Although each applicant typically displayed a strong desire to raise a company, the actual work involved may have proved too taxing for many of them. Not lacking for volunteers, Brownlow gave their commissions to other worthy candidates, but company letter designations fluctuated throughout the spring as the adjutant general's office untangled the organizational jumble.[9]

Not surprisingly, the adjutant general's office expanded to meet the administrative challenge. To assist him in organizing the militia, James P. Brownlow commissioned William T. Cate and David M. Nelson to serve as mustering officers, both at the rank of colonel. Cate was the brother of Radical state senator Alfred M. Cate, one of the important architects of the militia act. The two brothers displayed their fierce Unionism early in the Civil War as participants in the Unionist bridge-burning operation of November 1861. W. T. Cate helped destroy two railroad bridges near Chattanooga. He spent the rest of the war in various irregular capacities for the army. Nelson, son of prominent East Tennessee Unionist T. A. R. Nelson, spent the war, in turn, as an artillery officer and a staff officer. The twenty-three-year-old Nelson hailed from Bradley County, where he pursued law. Both colonels greatly facilitated the militia call-up. Cate would supervise the swearing in of six companies, Nelson eleven.[10]

While the adjutant general mustered the volunteer companies, the quartermaster general provided logistical support. Horace H. Thomas, a

27

James P. Brownlow, 1863–64. Courtesy of McClung Historical Collection.

carpetbagger who also served as Governor Brownlow's private secretary, headed the quartermaster department. Assisting him was Capt. Albert E. Boone, a twenty-two-year-old from Benton County whom an associate described as "a gentleman familiarly acquainted with the [logistics] business." This reputed experience would prove invaluable, for unlike the U.S. Army quartermaster, the Tennessee quartermaster was responsible for ordnance, commissariat, and transportation, as well as uniforms and camp gear. Moreover, the Tennessee quartermaster was essentially starting from scratch: the state possessed virtually no military equipment. Throughout the spring, Thomas negotiated food contracts with various

Nashville distributors and uniform contracts with clothing warehouses in Cincinnati. In the meantime, company commanders were authorized either to make purchases locally using state vouchers or to forage, compensating private property owners as needed. Many companies also obtained supplies from sutlers, opportunistic vendors who followed the militia units from one campsite to the next.[11]

Although Thomas and Boone did their best, they were initially unprepared for the large-scale militia buildup. In ordering only thirty tents at the beginning of the mobilization, for instance, Thomas seriously underestimated the State Guard's campground needs. Even if the tents were Sibleys, a common Civil War tent that could accommodate twelve to twenty men, the requested number would not have provided shelter for more than five or six companies. The acquisition of uniforms also proved problematic and time consuming. State Guardsmen were supposed to be clothed in blue uniforms, complete with shoes, hats, and haversacks, but the quartermaster had to purchase these items from northern warehouses at a cost of more than sixteen dollars per uniform. Until these shipments arrived, many volunteer companies spent their first weeks on duty drilling in civilian clothes, albeit blue jeans in many cases. Supply delays left many units not only without uniforms but also without blankets. "Destitute" was a word commonly used by captains to describe their soldiers during the mobilization period.[12]

The importance of food, clothing, and shelter notwithstanding, the quartermaster's top priority in the first weeks of mobilization was ensuring an adequate supply of munitions. In this matter, it enjoyed quick and complete success. The Brownlow administration hoped that the federal government would furnish weaponry from its large stockpile of wartime armaments. As early as May 1866, in the wake of the Memphis race riot, the general assembly petitioned Washington, DC, for "five thousand stand of arms," a request that was ignored at the time. With the militia call-up of 1867, Brownlow tried again, asking the secretary of war for two thousand rifles. He justified this request by rightly stating that Tennessee's prewar arsenal had been "stolen by rebels in 1861." In the meantime, Horace Thomas looked into the purchase of firearms. He considered buying breech-loading carbines from a Philadelphia dealer, while a gun manufacturer in Connecticut offered to sell the state any number of rifles "cheaper than the same quality could bought elsewhere." In the end, the War Department agreed to make available as many as

10,000 rifles, free of charge, from its depots in Indiana and Michigan. On April 10, the first shipment—348 rifles, with accouterments, and over fifty-six thousand rounds of ammunition—arrived in Nashville. Denied permission to store these armaments in the federal garrison's Ash Barracks, the quartermaster converted the Nashville courthouse into a temporary magazine.[13]

As they mustered, the majority of militia companies were armed with what turned out to be used Enfield rifled muskets. This weapon had been a favorite during the Civil War, particularly among Confederate soldiers. With its .577 caliber, the eight-pound Enfield was powerful but not overly weighty. Throughout the spring and summer, the quartermaster received and distributed crate loads of Enfields, along with enough ammunition to equip each volunteer with at least sixty rounds. Thanks to the federal government's generous loan, the State Guard was always able to outgun its opponents throughout the Reconstruction years.[14]

Conservatives were dismayed by the growing reality of a standing army. Fanning the fires of anti-Radicalism, John Baxter, a virulent opponent of Brownlow, decried the mobilization of "8000 men in a time of peace." Addressing the state's anti-Radical majority, he explained that the militia would be "paid by taxes to be gathered from you and I." All the while, Baxter asserted that "a formidable military power is being organized, in violation of the constitution . . . for no other purpose than to control elections." The *Union and Dispatch* offered a similarly gloomy forecast: "It is evident that a terrible convulsion is anticipated. . . . A pall, terribly dark and threatening, hangs over the destiny of our people." As the militia units began to form, the *Republican Banner* predicted that the State Guard would cost the taxpayers $5–10 million annually, the free use of the federal arsenal notwithstanding. Some Conservatives found solace in the hope that assembling eight thousand men would prove too difficult for the Brownlow administration. The *Pulaski Citizen*, cognizant of ex-Confederate power in Giles County, smugly asked, "Who is to be captain of the militia in this county?" A local Radical took up the challenge and applied for a State Guard commission. Although this man purportedly had "extensive influence among the loyal men of Giles," he failed to raise a company. A similar result occurred in Marshall County.[15]

Such setbacks, however, appear to have been the exception rather than rule. The pool of militia applications was so large that Governor Brownlow expressed confidence in mobilizing a sizable State Guard. "I find no trouble in raising companies," he informed the people through one of his many proclamations. But it was never his intention to muster into service the entire force that was potentially at his disposal. When two would-be captains from Carroll and Marion counties informed the adjutant general's office that they could easily raise local units for the State Guard, the administration replied that it had found sufficient manpower elsewhere. Overall, the widespread response to the March call-up must have heartened Radicals everywhere.[16]

Eventually, the Tennessee State Guard would consist of twenty-one companies in two full regiments of ten companies and a third regiment with one company. More than eighteen hundred men enlisted. Most units came from East Tennessee, but all sections were represented. Moreover, Governor Brownlow, faithful to his new, if uneasy, alliance with black voters, encouraged the involvement of blacks in the militia. Seven companies contained black troopers, one of which was commanded entirely by black officers.

The first company raised under the new militia act was an all-white unit from DeKalb County. Twenty-four-year-old Joseph H. Blackburn served as its captain. Blackburn possessed excellent Radical credentials. At eighteen he enlisted in the Fifth Tennessee Cavalry (Union) and, despite his youth, was immediately elected a company commander. His war record was impressive. Serving mostly in Middle Tennessee, because "he knew the country perfectly," Blackburn participated in the Murfreesboro campaign and in numerous skirmishes with the troops of such Confederate cavalry raiders as John Hunt Morgan and Joseph Wheeler. He was wounded on more than one occasion and suffered the loss of his brother, Charley, who was killed in action in 1863. Known for riding into battle with a plume in his hat, Blackburn was praised for his "daring and efficient conduct" when on the attack and for his "stubborn and desperate resistance" when on the defensive. At the battle of Nashville, Blackburn, then a colonel commanding the Fourth Tennessee Mounted Infantry (Union), was instrumental in cutting off the retreat of some Confederate units attempting to escape toward East Tennessee. He finished the war clearing guerrilla bands out of Middle Tennessee, operations that led to his capture of the infamous Champ Ferguson, a Rebel guerrilla leader subsequently executed for wartime atrocities.[17]

Blackburn gained a small measure of notoriety among ex-Confederates shortly after the war when he paid an unfriendly visit on

Joseph H. Blackburn, 1870. Courtesy of McClung Historical Collection.

Confederate general Wheeler. Wheeler had just been released as a prisoner of war and was staying in a Nashville hotel when Blackburn, accompanied by a comrade, knocked at Wheeler's door. A brief altercation followed, including an apparent accusation that Wheeler had pillaged the homes of Middle Tennessee Unionists. At this point, Blackburn commenced beating the Confederate veteran about the head with "a club of considerable dimensions." A bloodied Wheeler staved off the assault and subsequently protested what he considered an attempt on his life. Blackburn received a stern letter of reprimand from Gen. George H. Thomas, but the incident only enhanced the young colonel's reputation among DeKalb County Unionists.[18]

Back home in Liberty, Tennessee, Blackburn joined the Republican party and pursued a career in law, but devoted much of his time to running his five-hundred-acre farm and raising his family. He was among the first to respond to Brownlow's March mobilization. Local ex-Confederates, reportedly veterans of Champ Ferguson's outfit, tried to thwart Blackburn's efforts by circulating a death list of prominent county Radicals. The circular promised a reward of four thousand dollars for the assassination of Blackburn. Undaunted, Blackburn recruited seventy-five men (later augmented to ninety-five) in a matter of weeks and mustered his company on April 1. In accordance with the militia act, two lieutenants were elected; both proved good choices. 1st Lt. William L. Hathaway, age twenty-five, had served in the war with Blackburn as one of his officers. He, too, displayed courage and ability on the battlefield. During a conventional engagement, Hathaway helped drive a Confederate unit from a ridge-line position as part of a general advance through Middle Tennessee. During a counterguerrilla operation, he personally killed Pomp Kersey, a DeKalb County Confederate and leader of a "gang of bushwhackers." 2nd Lt. William F. Cravens, age twenty-nine, had served as a private in Blackburn's Civil War regiment. Both lieutenants were DeKalb County farmers, as were most of this unit's enlisted men. Overall, the rank and file were middle- to lower-middle-class family men averaging twenty-four years of age.[19]

A month after the muster of Blackburn's unit, a second company from Middle Tennessee formed. The man in command was William O. Rickman, a thirty-three-year-old farmer from Franklin County. Wartime and Reconstruction experiences help explain Rickman's die-hard Radicalism. He spent the Civil War commanding a company in the same regiment as Blackburn. But while Blackburn was engaged in some of the more glamorous aspects of the war, Rickman was assigned mostly to antiguerrilla operations. Toward the end of the war, he received orders to pursue a band of Confederates who refused to surrender. The harsh and explicit terms of this assignment, namely to "exterminate" and "show no quarter," may have permanently colored his view of ex-Confederates. These punitive activities came back to haunt him after the war. In February 1867, a large band of ex-Confederates surrounded his farm, plundered his smokehouse, and destroyed various produce and farm equipment. All the while, Rickman single-handedly defended his home and family with steady fire from a Henry rifle. Rickman embellished the encounter for journalists, putting the number of attackers at several hundred "desperadoes." A skeptical *Union and Dispatch* sarcastically quipped, "Why don't Old Brownlow get four of five more 'cool and courageous' Rickmans and garrison the State?" Exaggeration or not, this episode undoubtedly contributed to Rickman's decision to raise a company for the State Guard only a few weeks after the incident.[20]

Whereas Blackburn raised a company from a single county, Rickman recruited volunteers from five—Bedford, Coffee, Franklin, Lincoln, and Marshall. Moreover, while Blackburn's recruitment was relatively painless and quick, Rickman's proved frustrating. He assured the adjutant general that he did not lack for recruits, but he noted growing ex-Confederate interference with his activities. For some time, local Unionists had been complaining of a "lawless band" of ex-Confederates who were acting "quite belligerent . . . making heavy threats." Many of Rickman's recruits reported being harassed, with some allegedly driven from their homes, by these "Rebel Gurilers." Accordingly, Rickman requested permission to establish a fortified encampment near Tullahoma in Franklin County and to muster and equip volunteers as he recruited. The adjutant general denied this request, probably because adequate ordnance was unavailable at that time. Perhaps desperate to increase his strength, Rickman refused to release one Private Tucker whose father claimed that the boy, being only seventeen, was too young to serve. Rickman accepted the boy's claim of being twenty years old and told the father to go home. Further complications arose in April when Rickman reported he was in bad health and needed at least one commissioned officer to assist him. Assistant Adjutant General Samuel Hunt arrived at the end of the month and helped Rickman complete his organization. On May 1, seventy-one white men were officially sworn into service.[21]

The election of lieutenants did not please Captain Rickman. In a close vote, only twenty-seven-year-old Jordan C. Holt received a majority. Acting 1st Sgt. G. W. Farnum believed that Holt, a small farmer from Bedford, was incompetent and he refused to serve under him. When Rickman ignored his request for a direct appointment to first lieutenant, Farnum protested to the adjutant general but received no relief. Instead, a falling out occurred between Farnum and Rickman, and before the month was out, Farnum quit, apparently without reprisal. Farnum's assessment of Holt ultimately proved accurate. Following a violent clash with local ex-Confederates at the end of May, Holt resigned his commission and returned to the ranks as a private, admitting his unfitness for the job. Rather than hold another election, Rickman elevated a trusted noncommissioned officer, John J. Mankin, to the first lieutenancy. The forty-two-year-old Mankin had served the U.S. Army as a scout and then enjoyed relative prosperity after the war as a farmer raising a large family. Rickman and Mankin worked well together and, with this harmony at the top, the company increased its strength to ninety-two enlisted personnel during June. Adjutant General Brownlow retroactively approved the selection of Mankin, however irregular its manner, and Rickman's company was fully functional two months before the state election.[22]

Rounding out the white militia companies from Middle Tennessee was one commanded by William S. Stuart, a resident of Putnam County. Only twenty-two years old, Stuart secured his commission thanks to the efforts of eighteen fellow Putnam residents who petitioned the governor in Stuart's behalf shortly after the mobilization proclamation. A former corporal (in Blackburn's regiment) during the Civil War, Stuart went about his recruitment duties with great purpose. Like Rickman, Stuart drew volunteers from five counties—Putnam, Smith, Van Buren, Warren, and White. Also like Rickman, he encountered obstacles. Stuart notified Nashville that a pronounced contempt for the militia act pervaded the entire region. He described one group of local ex-Confederates as the "worst men [who] threaten & carry arms & kepp the country in a confusion." Some would-be recruits feared that they would be "murdered some night" if they joined the militia. Others stated a willingness to serve but insisted on assurances of timely pay and a promise that they would be home for the autumn harvest (the militia act's stipulation of a three-year term was a disincentive to these men). Stuart further complained that local Rebels were falsely taking the required enlistment oath in an attempt to undermine his efforts. Adjutant General Brownlow warned Stuart that ex-Confederates throughout the state were perverting the concept of loyalty oaths, yet he urged Stuart to protect the integrity of the militia oath. Taking the adjutant general's concerns to heart, Stuart threatened scores of ex-Confederates with arrest if they persisted in defying his duty to raise a militia company. On April 11, Stuart made good his threat when he forcibly arrested two men in Sparta for an alleged breach of the peace. Anti-Radical residents in White County, one of Stuart's recruitment areas, lodged a complaint against the beleaguered militia officer after witnessing his heavy-handed methods. The petitioners resented what they called "military rule" and insisted that all was quiet in their county. They recommended Stuart's immediate replacement by an officer of their choosing.[23]

Stuart was not replaced but completed his organization on June 1, mustering in a small company of forty-eight men at Cookeville. By the end of the month, however, the unit's strength increased to eighty-six, at which point Stuart conducted officer elections and gained the services of two lieutenants. Edmund D. Pennington, age forty-one, became Stuart's first lieutenant. Pennington, a former Civil War captain from Carthage (Smith County), was described by his many friends as a "true man . . . a fighting man." David C. Patton, age thirty, became the second lieutenant. He had served as a private in Captain Blackburn's company in the Fifth Tennessee Cavalry (Union). For unspecified reasons, however, Patton would resign before the August election.[24]

During these same weeks, two companies of State Guard formed in West Tennessee. Despite the sizable black populace in the west, only one of these companies contained black militiamen. The region was heavily ex-Confederate and the adjutant general may have judged the enlistment of large numbers of blacks too risky. Unfortunately, white Unionists were few in number and still on edge following the assassination of Senator Case only a few months earlier; assembling sufficient volunteers for the militia posed a tremendous challenge. Moreover, ineffective law enforcement, as evidenced by the widespread intimidation of blacks by white regulators, made the peaceable registration of black voters nearly impossible.[25]

Conservative newspapers mocked Radical efforts to organize militia companies in the west, predicting that they would find few volunteers. Nonetheless, twenty-six-year-old John T. Robeson of Carroll County, formerly a captain in the Seventh Tennessee Cavalry (Union), embraced the opportunity to serve his state and his party in what promised to be an exciting peacetime military capacity. Anti-Radicals in Gibson denounced Robeson's activities, claiming that all was peaceful in their county. Elsewhere, however, Rebel intimidation of freedmen and white

Unionists increased as Robeson went about his duties. In neighboring Weakley County, for instance, nightriders fired on the home of a Republican official. Brownlow supporters in nearby Obion County received similar treatment at the hands of a vigilante band led by an "infamous villain" named Tom Hooks. A local Unionist opined that "any man attempting to raise a company here without protection would do it at the risk of his life." These obstacles notwithstanding, Robeson persevered, drawing on four counties for men—Carroll, Gibson, Obion, and Weakley. Like Rickman, Robeson took just about any loyal white man he could get, but unlike Rickman, he acquiesced when one irate father insisted on having his underage son's enlistment invalidated. Although he prematurely reported his command's readiness in mid-March (perhaps to receive arms and equipment with which to fend off Rebel assailants), Robeson did officially muster his all-white company, sixty-five strong, on May 8 at Huntingdon (Carroll County). Robeson continued recruiting, however, and increased his company strength to seventy-six within a month after muster. Both of his lieutenants hailed from Weakley County and both had served as privates during the war: 1st Lt. Charles B. Simpson, age twenty-five, and 2nd Lt. William G. Fuller.[26]

While Robeson was successful in raising an all-white militia company in West Tennessee, William C. Holt of Gibson County was not. A forty-nine-year-old farmer and a Civil War captain, Holt recruited volunteers from Gibson and Obion counties and even enlisted a few men from East Tennessee. Adjutant General Brownlow appears to have wrongly assumed that Holt would enlist more men. One of Holt's soldiers, Moses H. Kinman, a future lieutenant in the State Guard, claimed he could easily help his commander recruit seventy-five men. A former Union cavalry private, the thirty-one-year-old Kinman was one of the Obion County deputy sheriffs wounded by the outlaw Farris at the time Senator Case was murdered. Although the muster roll for this unit is cursory and ambiguous, it indicates that while Holt may have held a genuine commission, he recruited only thirty-three men, not enough for a separate State Guard company.[27]

Sometime in July, the adjutant general merged Holt's partial command with Captain Robeson's recently mustered company. Coupled with his ongoing recruitment efforts, this decision swelled the manpower under Robeson to at least 110, but it produced an awkward command situation, for Holt retained his commission. Thus, two captains ran the unit that would become Company E, First Tennessee State Guard. The adjutant general recognized Robeson as the overall commander (and would formalize this appointment with an eventual promotion to major after the election), while Holt either ran the day-to-day affairs of the newly combined company or served in a detached capacity with the men he had recruited. Neither Robeson nor Holt was ever quite satisfied with this peculiar arrangement, and events would demonstrate that the relationship between these two officers was one of rivalry. A perturbed Robeson tried throughout the campaign to gain a commission for his brother, Jeptha, but these efforts came to naught.[28]

The other militia unit formed in West Tennessee appears to have been racially mixed. On July 5, George Hamilton, who was white, mustered sixty-four men into service at Purdy in McNairy County. Information on this unit is sketchy, but census data confirm that at least three of these men were black. Ever since Brownlow's March proclamation, McNairy Radicals had begged the executive to take "speedy action in recruiting" a militia company in their county for the purpose of protecting free speech, among other liberties. Hamilton, a cavalry private during the Civil War, found recruitment slow and frustrating but managed to find an adequate number of men from McNairy and neighboring Hardin and Humphreys counties. Perhaps because of its size, the company elected only one lieutenant, Thomas Randolph, a former sergeant in the Sixth Tennessee Cavalry (Union).[29]

The Brownlow administration could not have been surprised at the dearth of white Radical manpower in West Tennessee, but it was apparently reluctant to employ blacks in the State Guard. Nevertheless, the governor was counting on the region's many blacks to help him win the August election. He was concerned, however, that the large number of ex-Confederates in the region would both intimidate these black voters and attempt to vote illegally themselves. To make matters worse, Brownlow's rival gubernatorial candidate, Emerson Etheridge, was a native of Weakley County. Although the governor would show no hesitation in deploying militia companies from East Tennessee to the west, the administration would have preferred a stronger local show of force.

The majority of the Tennessee State Guard's companies came from East Tennessee. Radical strength in this section was great and none of the twelve eventual company commanders had any difficulty in recruiting volunteers. One of the first companies of East Tennessee militia came from Bradley County and was commanded by Judge K. Clingan. Known as a "brave and gallant officer," Clingan had served as a company commander in the Fifth Tennessee Infantry (Union) in the early part of the Civil War. He later commanded a battery of six-pounders and participated in operations to capture Chattanooga. Gen. William S. Rosecrans commended Clingan for his "meritorious services" and placed him on the Army of the Cumberland's elite Roll of Honor, one of only ten officers from Tennessee so recognized.[30]

J. K. Clingan was the son of Alexander A. Clingan, a wealthy farmer and longtime sheriff of Bradley County. Family connections likely helped the younger Clingan win election to complete the term of Jesse Gaut in the Thirty-fourth General Assembly. Although a confirmed Unionist and Republican, Clingan was not an unconditional Radical. His family had maintained cordial relations with local Confederates during the war, and in the assembly, while ultimately voting for all major Radical legislation, particularly black suffrage, Clingan demonstrated that he was his own man. He initially opposed the Metropolitan Police Act, especially its centralization of power over Hamilton, a county neighboring his home in Bradley. He supported amendments to this controversial law that moderated executive influence. Similarly, during the controversy over the state's ratification of the Fourteenth Amendment, Clingan joined five other legislators in formally protesting the assembly's extralegal method of ratification. Finally, he resisted William J. Smith's efforts to push through the militia bill before the issue had received what Clingan considered adequate debate. He did vote aye in the end.[31]

Declining to run for a second term, the twenty-nine-year-old Clingan instead offered his services to the new State Guard that he had helped bring into existence. His conscientious devotion to constitutional procedures apparently did not earn the governor's wrath; the adjutant general's office commissioned him at the end of April. Captain Clingan went about recruiting his company with great alacrity, despite the loud threats of R. M. Edwards, a local Conservative, who howled, "If Gov. Brownlow dare call out any portion of the militia, the people . . . [will] rise and wrench their arms from their hands and *exterminate* them." On May 4, Clingan reported the election of his lieutenants—Robert A. Armstrong, age twenty-nine, and George W. Kelley, both enlisted men during the Civil War—and announced that his ninety-two volunteers (drawn from Bradley, Hamilton, McMinn, and Polk counties) were ready for muster.[32]

It was at this point that Clingan's otherwise smooth organizational effort suffered a needless complication. The mustering officer, Col. David M. Nelson, arrived and attended a local church service as Clingan readied his men for the swearing in ceremony. Something in the sermon offended Nelson and he publicly denounced the preacher for expressing treason in the pulpit. Local ex-Confederates then levied a lawsuit for slander against Nelson, who would not be acquitted of the charge until September. This awkward incident notwithstanding, Clingan's company mustered in Cleveland on May 11.[33]

Throughout May, Governor Brownlow, convalescing in Knoxville, personally involved himself in the organization of four militia companies. These four would muster within two weeks of one another. The first was Robert L. Hall's company of 109 white recruits from Knox County (a few came from Blount). Although there is no concrete evidence that either the twenty-eight-year-old Hall or his first lieutenant, Robert G. Miner, had served in the Civil War, Radical newspapers referred to them as veterans. The unit's second lieutenant, twenty-two-year-old Isaac H. Watson, had been a noncommissioned officer in the Fifth Tennessee Infantry (Union). Regardless of his military credentials, Captain Hall appears to have been a good organizer. His company was applauded, by Conservatives no less, for its impressive military bearing during muster.[34]

Another company that Brownlow took a special interest in was Shadrick T. Harris's all-white unit from Jefferson County. "Shade" Harris brought a unique perspective to his command. Like many other State Guard commanders, Harris had served as an officer during the Civil War, but his experience was markedly different from that of his colleagues. Conscripted by the Confederacy in 1862, he escaped to Union lines before reporting for duty. After a few months of service with the Third Tennessee Cavalry (Union), he was captured in January 1863, tried by Confederate military authorities for desertion, and sentenced to be shot. Jefferson Davis commuted the sentence, but Harris spent the next twenty-five months as a prisoner of war, much of it confined in "heavy chains" in South Carolina. According to an escaped Union officer, Harris was poorly treated, having "all the indignities heaped upon him by his brutal captors." Federal officials, moved by his plight, negotiated a prisoner exchange in March 1865, although Confederate officials steadfastly regarded Harris a criminal, not a soldier worthy of such consideration.[35]

After the Confederacy's defeat, Harris, described as "a zealous, high-spirited and gallant officer," returned to East Tennessee in an unforgiving mood. The prison shackles had so warped his legs that he limped about on the sides of his feet. In the summer of 1865, Harris assaulted an ex-Confederate named William Beard on the streets of Knoxville. Apparently, Beard had abused Harris while the latter was briefly imprisoned in Knoxville and had tried to summarily execute Harris after a failed escape attempt. Shaped by such an unusual wartime ordeal, "Shade" was just the kind of Radical the Brownlow government could count on. And Harris came through for his government, raising a company of 112 men from Jefferson and Cocke counties and gaining the services of two capable lieutenants. 1st Lt. Edwin R. Hall, age twenty-eight, was one of the few carpetbaggers among the State Guard's officer corps. And his military experience was quite varied: participation in the battle of Gettysburg as a private with the Twelfth Vermont Infantry; counterguerrilla operations in East Tennessee as a sergeant with the Tenth Michigan Cavalry; and service as a lieutenant in the First U.S. Colored Artillery (Heavy). Mustered out in 1866, Hall settled down in East Tennessee. Harris's other lieutenant, John W. Roberts, age twenty-two, had served as a private in the Sixth Tennessee Infantry (Union).[36]

On June 1, Harris mustered in his command at Dandridge (Jefferson County). Many of the men were small farmers and most of them were quite young. The average age of the recruits was twenty-one, and sixty-two of them were teenagers. A Conservative newspaper correspondent watched Harris's muster with disgust. "A harder looking gang I never saw in my life," he wrote. The correspondent criticized the company's youth and inexperience, and contended that the rank and file habitually harassed local blacks. This observer claimed—perhaps wishfully—that most of these militiamen were "opposed to Brownlow."[37]

The rapid recruitment of militia companies under Brownlow's supervision continued with the commissioning of James R. Evans of Claiborne County. The twenty-one-year-old Evans was a former noncommissioned officer in the Fourth Tennessee Cavalry (Union). A man of substantial wealth (he was worth nineteen thousand dollars in 1870), Evans presumably had a talent for organization and leadership. Operating out of Tazewell, Evans happily informed the adjutant general, "My boys are anxious," and he promised that he would have his company ready by April 15. This promise was not kept, for although Evans steadily recruited volunteers from Claiborne and neighboring Grainger County, he encountered considerable local opposition. Ex-Confederates made a habit of gathering outside of Evans's recruitment office and heckling prospective recruits. Evans twice extended his self-appointed muster deadline, citing growing "Rebel and Copperhead" interference. On one occasion, an alarmed Evans reported that an ex-Confederate had burst into the town firing a pistol and "swearing he was going to kill me." On another, ex-Confederates caused a disturbance when they blocked the efforts of "colored people" to register for the upcoming election. Adding to the tension was a rumor that Rebels from Grainger intended to burn railroad bridges to inhibit the deployment of Evans's men. Although he reassured the state government that Claiborne was loyal and would vote Radical, Evans insisted that unless it was provided with arms, his unit would be compelled to depart Tazewell.[38]

By mid-May, Evans's company had attained the impressive strength of one hundred men, but for the sake of civic peace he transferred his unit from Tazewell to Morristown in Grainger County. The young militia captain, however, could not resist a parting shot. En route to Morristown, his unarmed column marched past some road workers who were evidently anti-Radical. When Evans called on the workers to give a cheer for Brownlow, they refused. Evans's men then "arrested" the workers and herded them down the road for a few miles before releasing them. Local Conservatives were not amused by these militia antics and complained to President Johnson. Once in Morristown, Evans's official muster passed off without incident on June 3. His all-white company elected as first lieutenant forty-six-year-old John N. Ellis, a well-to-do farmer who had served as an officer in the Third Tennessee Infantry (Union). James A. England, age twenty two, a corporal in Ellis's wartime company, became second lieutenant. Difficulties notwithstanding, Evans was one of the few militia commanders to raise a full-strength company.[39]

The last company that Brownlow took a personal interest in raising was an all-white outfit under Silas L. Chambers. The twenty-nine-year-old Chambers was a merchant from Huntsville (Scott County) and had served as a first sergeant in the Second Tennessee Infantry (Union). Commissioned in April, Chambers drew on four counties—Anderson, Campbell, Morgan, and Scott—for recruits and soon had over one hundred men ready to enlist. Unfortunately, he experienced an embarrassing, and tragic, setback. When he and Col. D. M. Nelson attempted to muster the company in Huntsville on April 25, a "general melee" broke out among the recruits over the election of lieutenants. More than a dozen men were injured and one died. The incident prompted a Conservative correspondent to comment that "there is no telling what bad whiskey and Radicalism may do." Such blunt sarcasm was in some respects apt, for Chambers had a strong taste for whiskey, a vice that would cause problems during the campaign. The company reformed on May 15 with two ostensibly acceptable lieutenants: James W. Newport, age twenty-three, an enlisted veteran of Tennessee's wartime Civil Guards and a postwar farm laborer, and Alvin Parker, age eighteen, a wartime private and postwar farmhand. The unit then marched to Clinton (Anderson County) to muster. There, the town's anti-Radicals spread a rumor that the militia had arrived to supplant the civil court with its own military court. Chambers, however, was struggling to hold his own command together. On June 10, the day of official muster, 23 recruits were listed as "absent-without-leave" and eventually branded as deserters. Four more men deserted within the week. One Conservative derided Chambers's men as "the verry trash of the earth." In the end, only 83 of the original 106 volunteers were mustered into service.[40]

Brownlow may have busied himself with the administrative details of several militia companies, but most East Tennessee companies formed without his help. One was George W. Kirk's company from Greene County. Few other company commanders in the State Guard possessed as extensive a Civil War record as Kirk. Enlisting as a private, Kirk soon gained company command in the Eighth Tennessee Cavalry (Union). Most of his service took place in East Tennessee and western North Carolina, areas wracked by guerrilla warfare. There, Kirk helped "pilot" Unionists to a Federal recruitment center at Camp Dick Robinson, Kentucky. In 1864, he was commissioned to raise a regiment of loyal mountaineers and conduct raids into Confederate-held territory. In the process, he became a skilled guerrilla fighter. His most spectacular success came in June 1864, when his raiding party destroyed a Confederate supply depot at Camp Vance, North Carolina, and captured 277 enemy soldiers. He made several other forays into North Carolina, earning praise from Gen. John M. Schofield for the "gallant and successful manner" of his operations.[41]

Confederate authorities had regarded Kirk as a "renegade" whose commission was little more than a letter of marque. Confederate officers from North Carolina claimed that his unit was composed of deserters, Indians, and freedmen, and that Kirk himself was a "notorious tory and traitor, vagabond and scoundrel." As the war came to a close, Kirk, with a brevet colonelcy, was ordered to clear the mountains of Confederates. His orders contained the same harsh instructions to "exterminate" guerrillas that Captain Rickman received in Middle Tennessee. Kirk apparently did his job well, killing over one hundred Rebels and capturing an elusive guerrilla leader named Palmer. In the process, he allowed his men undue freedom to plunder. Federal authorities complained of his "excesses" and finally terminated his command in May 1865.[42]

After the war, "Colonel" Kirk became a thoroughgoing Radical. Governor Brownlow was anxious to gain the "valuable" services and "matchless heroism" of this twenty-eight-year-old Greene County Unionist. As the campaign of 1867 approached, Kirk publicly welcomed a showdown with the ex-Confederates: "If nothing else will do the rebels and copperheads but a fight, I say give it to them on all sides." Such audacity pleased Radicals and attracted many recruits from Greene County and its neighbors, Hawkins and Washington. On June 6, Kirk's company was mustered into service. In all, Kirk commanded eighty-five men, many of whom were barely out of their teens (the average age was 19.3 years). Francis Kirk, age 18, possibly a relative, was elected first lieutenant. Henry C. Sanders, a 22-year-old veteran of the Fourth Tennessee Mounted Infantry (Union), served as second lieutenant. In the days leading up to the activation of this militia company, a Radical newspaper confidently boasted that "Rebels and their despicable and despised sympathizers must 'lay low' when Col. Kirk comes round."[43]

From Roane County came a small company of State Guard under Joseph M Alexander, age twenty-three. Although Roane was a mostly Unionist county, Alexander suffered for his loyalty during the Civil War. During the first year of the war, he worked quietly in his father's general store in Loudon. In 1862 and 1863, however, he and his family were "molested in every conceivable way" by Confederate occupation forces. On one occasion, Rebel soldiers ransacked the elder Alexander's store. On another, they raided the Alexander home, where the intruders and occupants "had quite a fight." While his brother was conscripted into the Confederate army, Joseph avoided taking up arms and instead operated as a civilian informant for the Union army during Gen. Ambrose Burnside's occupation of the region. Evidently ready to serve in a military capacity in 1867, Alexander applied for a militia captaincy and assured the Brownlow administration of his patriotic devotion to the Radical cause: "I am making arrangements to protect the Loyal people of this dear old State of East Tennessee who sent forth her sons to protect the flag that we are supporters of." Commissioned in June, he recruited fifty-four men (drawn from McMinn and Monroe counties as well as Roane), and on July 6 his company was mustered into service. His only lieutenant was a man named E. R. Brown.[44]

The most eastern of the State Guard companies was Kemp Murphy's outfit from Johnson County. Murphy had been a nineteen-year-old delegate to the Greeneville Convention in 1861 and later served in the Fourth Tennessee Infantry (Union) as a private. At 25, he mustered his seventy-two white volunteers into service on July 19, a fortnight before the election. Like many of the other companies, Murphy's was basically made up of boys: 20.2 was the average age in his unit. His first lieutenant was William C. Arnold, a subsistence farmer in his early twenties who had been a first sergeant during the Civil War. His second lieutenant was Joseph A. Grace, age 26, who had been a private during the war. The two lieutenants had served together in the Thirteenth Tennessee Cavalry (Union).[45]

In the final week of the gubernatorial campaign, Governor Brownlow authorized the creation of two more white companies from East Tennessee. Little is known about these officers and men. William N. Purdy, age thirty-four, organized a half-strength company (fifty men) from Monroe County on July 22. A former hospital steward, Purdy commanded alone; he had no lieutenants. On July 26, twenty-one-year-old A. M. Clapp, a Knox County farmer, hastily mustered into service an indeterminate number of men from Grainger, Hawkins, Jefferson, and Knox counties. The company roster lists two lieutenants, R. M. Stone and twenty-year-old James S. Clapp, but only forty-one enlisted men are on the muster roll. Probably, there were more men in this unit.[46]

The majority of the Tennessee State Guard was white. Significantly, however, seven militia companies contained blacks, including the previously discussed West Tennessee company under George Hamilton. Having enfranchised the freedmen, the Brownlow administration saw no reason not to employ them as militiamen. Presumably, the Radicals hoped that the black electorate would respond to the political campaign more enthusiastically knowing some of their own were in the ranks of the State Guard. Several commission seekers informed the state government of their willingness to organize and command a black company. One applicant used political alliteration to make his case: "Lincoln, Liberty, Law, Loyal, League." Nevertheless, the decision to recruit black militiamen was controversial and not taken lightly. White southerners had long trembled at the idea of blacks with guns. The praiseworthy performance of black Civil War soldiers (twenty thousand of whom came from Tennessee) did not allay these white supremacist concerns. Anti-Radical whites blamed black soldiers for the Memphis race riot. Other incidents, such as a shoot-out between white youths and black troops in Montgomery County on Christmas Day 1865, only exacerbated race relations. In the aftermath of the Civil War, President Johnson urged General Thomas to exercise tight control over his black soldiers in Tennessee: "In the event of an insurrection it is feared that the colored troops, so great in number, could not be controlled." Thomas dismissed such concerns as unfounded, but Governor Brownlow also worried about the possibility of race war, although he may have privately delighted at the prospect of covering West Tennessee with black troops. In the end, he prudently kept black numbers in the militia small.[47]

The first blacks to join the State Guard came from Washington County. They would serve in a racially mixed company under white officers, most notably George E. Grisham, who issued a call for militia volunteers shortly after receiving his commission in April. At thirty-three years of age, Grisham was a rising star among the Radicals of East Tennessee and a seemingly good choice to command black militiamen. During the Civil War, he served as a company commander in the Eighth Tennessee Cavalry (Union) and later as a staff officer under Maj. Gen. Alvan C. Gillem. Local ex-Confederates tried to disparage his character by claiming he was a Confederate deserter, but Grisham served the Union with distinction. Following the war, he became the postmaster of Jonesboro, but his primary activity was running his newspaper, the *Jonesboro Union Flag*. Initially a moderate in politics, Grisham grew enamored with Brownlow's leadership and his news organ became increasingly radical. In October 1865, Grisham ran unsuccessfully for an open seat in the Tennessee General Assembly. His simple platform called for public education, compensation for Unionists, and tax reforms. Throughout his campaign, Grisham denounced the ex-Confederates. To him, Reconstruction meant "Union construction and Rebel destruction."

46

The following year, Grisham coauthored a petition to Radical leader L. C. Houk that urged an uncompromising stance toward the growing anti-Radical forces in the state: "We must fight the enemies of our country, and fight them everywhere and in every way. We are on the tower watching and must do all we can to save ourselves." County conservatives, dismayed by such hard-line sentiments, persuaded President Johnson to remove Grisham from his postmaster position. Local ex-Confederates employed more violent measures. In October 1866, two attempts were made to burn the office of the *Union Flag* to the ground, both while the printing staff was on duty.[48]

Grisham eagerly responded to Governor Brownlow's militia proclamation. When applying for his commission, Grisham oddly requested assignment to the Middle Tennessee county of Franklin in order "to keep the Rebs straight [and] hold that line of communication open for yours." As he recruited loyal volunteers, the energetic Grisham helped get Washington County on a solid political footing. He was instrumental in forming Union Leagues throughout the county, and he served as secretary to the county's Radical nominating convention. In the process, Grisham described the upcoming political campaign in do-or-die terms: "The man that does not understand that this State is to remain under the control and management of *its friends at any cost or sacrifice,* is certainly too far behind the times. . . . The Radicals will rule this State peaceably, if they can; forcibly, if they must." Conservatives were appalled at such militancy and regarded Grisham's commission in the State Guard as a prime example of partisan politics—a militia captain, Radical politician, and newspaper editor rolled into one.[49]

On April 13, Grisham reported that his company of approximately 114 men was fully organized. About half of Grisham's command was black, quite likely members of the new Washington County Union Leagues. Additionally, many of these men claimed to have served in colored regiments during the war. How blacks voted in the election for lieutenants is unknown, but both junior officers were white men. 1st Lt. Nelson McLaughlin, age forty, was a well-respected Washington County farmer. Additionally, McLaughlin was a veteran of both the Mexican and Civil Wars, serving in the latter as a company commander alongside Grisham in the Eighth Tennessee Cavalry (Union). The twenty-one-year-old Joseph A. February won the second lieutenancy. Affectionately referred to as "Jo," February was a veteran of the Fourth

George E. Grisham, 1864–65. Courtesy of Tennessee State Museum Collection.

Tennessee Infantry (Union). In the forthcoming campaign, Grisham usually commanded the black contingent of his company, while McLaughlin often commanded the whites on detached assignments.[50]

Using his printing office as a command center, Grisham issued orders through the *Union Flag* for his recruits to muster on May 1: "Every volunteer is required to be punctually present." The swearing-in ceremony was a prominent part of a grand political rally in Jonesboro that included speeches by various Radical politicos, all of whom denounced President Johnson. Some three thousand people attended, including Governor Brownlow. At the end of the day, Grisham's company led a parade procession through the streets amid great cheering. "The measured tread of the soldiery, the bristling array of gleaming bayonets, and the martial music of fife and drum" entertained the crowd. Fellow militia officer George W. Kirk served as marshal. One Radical correspondent expressed delight over the mustering of Grisham's company: "They again go forth to protect Union men from the violence of resuscitated treason." The next day, Grisham's unit deployed to the East Tennessee county of Sullivan, most of whose residents had supported the Confederacy during the war and defied the Radicals afterward. The duty was temporary and the mission was simply to "regulate these bad men."[51]

Not long after Grisham's unit embarked on its first assignment for the State Guard a second mixed militia company began forming in East Tennessee. The officer in charge was John L. Kirk of Greene County. It is unclear whether John Kirk was related to George Kirk, but both came from Greene County and served together as company commanders in the Eighth Tennessee Cavalry (Union). Like G. W. Kirk and Grisham before him, J. L. Kirk recruited volunteers from Greene and Washington counties, land rich in Radical manpower. On June 6, he mustered his 68 recruits (race ratio unknown) who then elected two white lieutenants: David E. Burchfield and Joseph S. Lawrence, the latter a veteran enlisted man. Several weeks later, while deployed in Montgomery County in Middle Tennessee, Kirk apparently recruited another 61 men. Many of these new volunteers were black. Moreover, his command added a third lieutenant, Page McKinney, about whom little is known. Overall, by the time of the election, Captain Kirk appears to have commanded as many as 129 men.[52]

While the two "Negro" militia companies from East Tennessee were racially mixed and under white officers, four companies from Middle

Tennessee were virtually all black. At the end of March, Thompson McKinley, a thirty-five-year-old white Radical from Sumner County, was commissioned explicitly "to organize a company of Colored Troops" as a reward for black loyalty and as a means of self-protection in that strife-ridden part of the state. One of the few carpetbaggers in the State Guard, McKinley was an unsavory character to many Sumner County whites. The Conservative press described him as "a dirty trickster" and a "second Brownlow," while former guerrilla leader Ellis Harper "vowed his inten-tion to blow Mr. T. McKinley's d—d brains out." In addition to becom-ing a militia captain, McKinley was the county's commissioner of regis-tration and he ran as the county's Radical candidate for the Tennessee General Assembly in 1867. He may also have been involved in the for-mation of a Union League in Gallatin. Conservatives believed his per-formance as registrar was crooked and self-serving and that his political aspiration was wholly dependent on black votes. They understandably protested his acceptance of a captaincy in the State Guard, a position that would allow him considerable control over the polling places, as a flagrant conflict of interest. Moreover, they insisted that Sumner was safe and peaceful, and they resented the arming of blacks in their midst. Memories of Union occupation in 1865, when black soldiers allegedly committed several felonies, including rape, haunted this white community.[53]

Undaunted by local animus, Thompson McKinley accepted the dual role of candidate and captain and proceeded to assemble his command. Ex-Confederates hampered recruitment, just as they had disrupted an election for constable of Gallatin in February, but McKinley and his fel-low Radicals were assured by the Brownlow administration that "the dis-regard of law evinced by many of the people of Sumner Co. may invite some very unpleasant consequences in the future." McKinley's command would give this threat genuine punch. He mustered in one hundred black volunteers on June 10 in Gallatin. Many of these men may have served in the Fourteenth U.S. Colored Infantry, which formed in Sumner in 1863. The average age of the enlistees was 22.3, but the com-pany roster reflects a couple of irregularities. One soldier is listed as 16 years of age, and one of the unit's sergeants is listed as 14.[54]

Although no one appears to have objected to McKinley's recruit-ment of adolescents, many black volunteers challenged the captain's decision to appoint white lieutenants instead of conducting an election. Led by 1st Sgt. Nelson Turner, the enlisted men flatly refused to serve under McKinley's choice for first lieutenant, a reputedly unsavory fellow named George Weaver. They did agree, however, to serve under McKinley's other appointee, Lt. I. N. Phillips. Phillips was a twenty-two-year-old schoolteacher from Vermont and was apparently well liked by the men and by Sumner's black community. In 1866, the Freedmen's Bureau sponsored his journey to Sumner County, where Phillips became an education superintendent and later an active member in the Gallatin Union League.[55]

Governor Brownlow took a bold step toward racial equality in the State Guard when he commissioned James H. Sumner to command an all-black company. A free, native black before the war, and an active Nashville Radical and saloon keeper after the war, the twenty-seven-year-old Sumner was the only black captain in the State Guard. As a result, he endured particularly scathing scrutiny from Conservative newspapers. The *Pulaski Citizen* mocked Sumner's commission, claiming that "he now carries [it] in his breeches pocket" in order to be ready to prove his title to a skeptical world. The *Union and Dispatch* dismissed Sumner as a "mere civilian" while extolling the virtues of a Conservative black veteran, Joseph Williams, a man who campaigned with the Conservative Emerson Etheridge in 1867. This newspaper challenged Brownlow to commission Williams. Brownlow, of course, did not commission Williams, but Sumner did engage his Conservative counterpart in debate during the campaign.[56]

Conservatives predicted that Sumner would fail to recruit enough men for a company. They were wrong. Sumner organized one of the largest companies in the State Guard, 113 black men drawn from Davidson and Williamson counties, and mustered them into service on June 27. The average age of his command was 24.2 years. His lieutenants were George Sumner, age 23 (relation to James unknown), a veteran of the Fifty-first U.S. Colored Infantry, and 24-year-old Henry H. Mitchell, who also served in the U.S. Colored Troops.[57]

Sumner's company remained stationed in Nashville for several days after muster and became the target of Conservative abuse. The anti-Radical press branded these militiamen a "band of cut-throats," while the white community ostracized Captain Sumner. In one telling incident, Sumner boarded a Nashville streetcar while in uniform, but was told by the driver that he had to leave. When he refused, the white passengers got off in protest. Sumner then got off himself, but when the driver then called the white passengers to return, Sumner hopped back on. Again the passengers left, and after a brief standoff, the driver reluctantly transported Sumner, the lone passenger, to his destination. A Conservative correspondent concluded that "it was the intention of this militiaman to provoke a difficulty, no doubt."[58]

The last two black militia companies and the last two companies recruited in 1867 were both from the Nashville area. Philip J. Flemming (white) mustered sixty blacks from Williamson County on July 29, likely from the politically active Union League of the county seat, Franklin. Michael Houston, a white officer, mustered ninety-one blacks from Davidson County on July 30. At least one of his two lieutenants was black and a veteran: 1st Lt. Alexander Gleaves, age thirty-five, served as a sergeant in the Thirteenth U.S. Colored Infantry, a unit that saw intense action at the battle of Nashville. Houston's second lieutenant was John S. Durham. Described by the anti-Radical press as "a certain Tueton," Durham appears to have been a German American. If true, then Gleaves's seniority may mark one of the first instances in American military history where a white man served under a black. Both of these companies, about which little is known, were organized a few days before the August election.[59]

In all, twenty-one companies of State Guard were mustered into service between April 1 and July 30, 1867 (see Appendix A). Many units failed to attain the 100 men desired by Brownlow, but all were considered fit for duty. Two companies came from West Tennessee, one white and one mixed, totaling 175 men. Seven came from Middle Tennessee, three white and four black, totaling about 707 men (366 blacks, plus as many as 61 more who joined John Kirk's East Tennessee command). Twelve companies were organized in East Tennessee, ten white and two mixed, totaling at least 993 men (A. M. Clapp's extant muster roll seems incomplete). Due to lack of information on the racial makeup of the companies of George Grisham, John Kirk, and George Hamilton, the exact figures on black personnel are estimates only. Sources indicate that about half of Grisham's 114 militiamen were black (about 57 men). Kirk recruited blacks from East Tennessee and more while stationed in Montgomery County. If half of his original 68 enlisted volunteers were black (34 men), then approximately 91 blacks from East Tennessee served in the State Guard. Using the same methodology for Hamilton's company of 64 men, it can be estimated that 32 black militiamen came from West Tennessee.

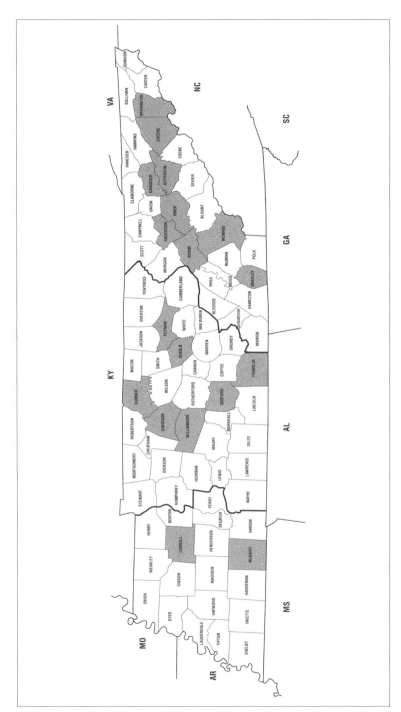

Tennessee State Guard muster points in 1867.

Overall, at least 1,875 men (not counting staff personnel) served in the Tennessee State Guard of 1867: between 1,331 and 1,392 whites and between 483 and 544 blacks. Thus, some 25 to 29 percent of the State Guardsmen were black, most of them from Middle Tennessee.

There has been a good deal of misinformation in the scholarship on the Tennessee State Guard, which the above statistics should help correct. E. Merton Coulter claims that there were nineteen companies comprising fifteen hundred men. Allen Trelease states that there were only twelve comprising nine hundred men. James Patton and Robert White correctly report twenty-one companies, but offer no specific figures on manpower. With regard to race ratios, Coulter and Thomas Alexander state that the units raised and stationed in Middle and West Tennessee were mostly black. While this is true, these scholars neglect to address the overwhelmingly white companies from East Tennessee. Allen Trelease rightly asserts that the State Guard throughout Tennessee was mostly white, but, like Coulter and Alexander, he is vague about exact numbers. Robert White erroneously insists that black militiamen were in the majority. Otis Singletary, who acknowledges that the Tennessee militia was racially mixed, notes that the fixation, during and since Reconstruction, on "Negro militia" overlooks the significant role native whites played in upholding the Republican party and reflects "the longstanding Southern [white] indifference to logic when considering questions involving race."[60]

Sixty-one men served as company officers in the State Guard, four of whom were black. At least forty-four of these men (72 percent) possessed Civil War experience, all in the Union army, sixteen as officers. Moreover, fifteen company commanders were veterans, nine as officers. Several militia officers, such as Blackburn, Hathaway, Rickman, G. W. Kirk, and E. R. Hall, were skilled in antiguerrilla fighting, a useful talent given the persistence of ex-Confederate lawlessness in rural areas. The average age of the officer corps was 27.5 years. Additionally, 1870 census data on twenty-two company officers suggest that these militia leaders were for the most part married farmers with children whose property value averaged more than three thousand dollars. Overall, the officers of the State Guard were battle-hardened, vigorous, mature men. Furthermore, their settled, moderately prosperous status militated against politically reckless conduct, an important consideration in the volatile election atmosphere of 1867.

In general, this State Guard officer corps represents a fair profile of the Radical mindset. They joined because the party and its Reconstruction program were important to them and because they believed that the survival of both were at stake in 1867. Such political partisanship, however, was tempered by a military devotion to duty. While the backgrounds of William Rickman and Shadrack Harris suggest a potential for vindictiveness, the background of Judge Clingan reveals a preference for moderation. And despite the Rebel-bashing rhetoric of such captains as George Grisham and G. W. Kirk, the State Guard was hardly an instrument of repression, at least during the mobilization phase. In fact, the reverse was often the case in Middle and West Tennessee, where many prospective militiamen found themselves assailed by an angry ex-Confederate populace. Nevertheless, the State Guard officers, through their public recruitment activities, acted in effect as political agents and helped invigorate the white and black supporters of Radicalism at the grass-roots level. As the campaign unfolded, the Brownlow administration was confident that it had assembled a militia leadership that was both dedicated to the Radical cause and professional enough to uphold the law and prevent open warfare.

The political proclivities of the 1,816 enlisted men are less clear and for the most part can only be assumed. Many of the rank and file were Union Army veterans, but a substantial number were teenagers who never served in any regular military forces. Interestingly, considering that they were members of an organization designed in part to protect the ballot box, hundreds of militiamen were under the legal voting age of twenty-one. The socioeconomic status is hard to determine, but many were small farmers who presumably had lived in Unionist households during the war. Why they joined the State Guard is unclear. They probably wanted to help Radicalism triumph, and a few no doubt saw the uniform as an opportunity to exact revenge, but many may have simply wanted a steady monthly wage. Black recruits, in particular, believed that service in the militia (like service in the Union army) would grant them the power and respect needed to secure their new status as citizens. Lastly, many volunteers may have enlisted simply for adventure. Sociologist Eric Hoffer argues that in the aftermath of great struggles, many of the youths who missed out on the conflict eagerly seek equivalent experiences. For those Unionists too young to fight against the Confederacy, the State Guard promised a measure of martial glory.[61]

By the beginning of June 1867, the Tennessee State Guard consisted of twelve companies already deployed, with several others in the process of mustering. At this point, Governor Brownlow believed it was time for an overall militia field commander. On June 7, he placed Joseph A. Cooper in charge with the rank of brigadier general. It proved an excellent choice. Cooper was a dedicated Radical and, as a veteran of the Mexican War and the Civil War, a distinguished military officer. Like most other leading Radicals, he was from East Tennessee. He was a respectable and relatively prosperous farmer with a large family. During the secession crisis, he attended the Greeneville Convention as Campbell County's lone delegate. Throughout the proceedings, he maintained a hawkish stance toward the Confederacy, and at the convention's close, he was one of the first Tennessee Unionists to raise volunteers for the Federal army. He rose quickly through the ranks, ending the war with a brevet major generalship. He fought in some of the western theater's grimmest battles: Murfreesboro, Lookout Mountain, Resaca (where his brigade suffered 30 percent casualties), and Nashville. In this last battle, Cooper's division helped crush the left flank of Gen. John B. Hood's besieging Confederate army.[62]

General Cooper never received any formal military training, but was, by all accounts, a natural leader. Contemporaries noted his "modest" yet "imperious" style of leadership. During Hood's campaign, for example, Cooper was anxious to link his detached unit with General Thomas's command at Nashville. Marching through the night, he reportedly "forced a countryman who knew all the roads to guide him under penalty of death in case of betrayal." Discipline and training were his constant priorities, and Cooper expected his men to face such wartime trials as poor supply, inadequate pay, and miserable camp conditions with stoic calm. Years after the war, at a reunion, Cooper gave his men laconic praise: "All that I am, you made me, by obeying my orders."[63]

A Whig before the war, Cooper was one of the 521 Unionists who gathered at Nashville in January 1865 to restore civil government to the state. Like many other Unionists, he initially applauded President Andrew Johnson's Reconstruction policies. In a letter to the president, Cooper expressed his support of Johnson's plan for Reconstruction but pointed out that "the rebels are verry bold and defiant." He then related to the president the essence of his political views: "I still hold to the old doctrin the Union the constitution the enforement of the law." He soon

Joseph A. Cooper, 1865. From Miller's *Photographic History of the Civil War.*

gravitated into the Radical fold, however. When Brownlow and the Radical party broke with Johnson over his increasing obstruction of congressional Reconstruction and his alignment with Conservative Democrats, Cooper followed suit. East Tennessee Conservatives noted with alarm Cooper's public denunciations of Johnson. One observer described Cooper as "one of [Johnson's] most violent enemies" and urged his dismissal as Knoxville's collector of internal revenue. When Cooper's friends warned him that his employment was in jeopardy, the general reportedly boasted, "I will split rails . . . sooner than desert the Union party . . . and turn rebel." Cooper shortly thereafter lost his post and its annual salary of four thousand dollars.[64]

The tempo of political events in Tennessee seemed to excite Cooper. After moving his family to Knox County, he entered politics. Unfortunately, in seeking nomination for Congress in 1865 and 1867, he was defeated by the politically savvy Horace Maynard. Although he had a "sharp, quick voice," Cooper lacked the oratorical skills of his opponent as well as his political experience. Perhaps dejected, Cooper declined calls to run for the general assembly.[65]

Out of a job and frustrated in his bid for elected office, the forty-four-year-old Cooper probably welcomed the opportunity to serve as commander of the newly created Tennessee State Guard. It would mark a return to an environment where he had previously enjoyed success and prestige. And it would reunite him with many of the officers he had commanded. Radical newspapers hailed his appointment, describing Cooper as "brave as a lion" and "preeminently the officer for the post." The *Knoxville Whig*, in particular, interpreted his failed political career in a positive light, declaring that "Gen. Cooper has shown himself unwilling to sacrifice the good of the cause to his personal ambition." Most Conservative newspapers withheld their judgment of Cooper at the time, but the *Republican Banner* did tersely note that the new militia general "may prove as good a cat's paw as the next." Given the political stakes involved, as well as Governor Brownlow's manifest decline in health, the campaign of 1867 posed a challenging test of Cooper's leadership skills.[66]

On June 19, General Cooper established his headquarters in Nashville and completed the organization of his staff, which included colonels Cate and Nelson, and his newly appointed aide-de-camp, 1st Lt. Larken B. Gamble, yet another Civil War officer. Gamble helped muster in the final companies during the closing weeks of the campaign. On Governor Brownlow's recommendation, Cooper also accepted the services of Dr. Fredrick W. Sparling as the chief surgeon of the State Guard.[67]

At the beginning of July, Cooper helped ameliorate the State Guard's early difficulties with supply. He instructed company commanders to pay closer attention to proper procedure (i.e., army regulations) and to cooperate more closely with the quartermaster. For several weeks, many officers had unwittingly contributed to their own supply deficiencies through their ignorance of, or indifference to, logistical matters. For example, Capt. James Evans neglected to keep an inventory of his supplies, while Capt. George Grisham lost copies of his requisitions during a movement. Capt. William Rickman occasionally failed to report his voucher purchases, while Capt. Joseph Blackburn submitted vouchers with mathematical errors. And Capt. Robert Hall apparently entrusted his unit's supply to "an old Q. M." named J. K. Woodard, an agent not affiliated with the Quartermaster Department. Virtually all of these men at one time or another forgot to sign the appropriate forms for goods requested or received. With General Cooper's help, however, supply improved, and as the numerous transactions recorded in the State Guard's ledger indicate, each company eventually received everything it needed.[68]

With his staff organized and the militia's supply problems presumably solved, General Cooper formalized the structure of the State Guard and finalized the company letter designations that had fluctuated during the mobilization period (see Appendix A). Perhaps by intention, the two full regiments had an equal number of companies from each section of the state. Oddly, the State Guard of 1867 never had any regimental commanders; all company commanders reported directly to either Cooper or the adjutant general. Less than a week before the election, Cooper informed the adjutant general that the State Guard was ready and that no new companies were being formed. All the while, Cooper judiciously deployed his twenty-one companies so as to cover as many potentially troublesome counties as his relatively small force would permit.[69]

The mobilization of Tennessee's Radical army had taken much time and effort, but the product was satisfying. Comprised of nearly two thousand men under seasoned leadership, the State Guard served as the spearhead of a Radical party that claimed approximately forty thousand white Unionists and about as many newly enfranchised freedmen. Pitted against this array of Radical power was an indeterminate number of legal and illegal Conservative voters (perhaps twenty thousand) and over eighty thousand disfranchised ex-Confederates. Franchise restrictions notwithstanding, the anti-Radical forces fully intended to defy "Brownlowism." The performance of the Tennessee State Guard would largely determine whether law and order or civil strife prevailed during the campaign.

Chapter 3

The Opening Shots of the Campaign of 1867

ANTI-RADICALS THROUGHOUT TENNESSEE WERE ALARMED BY THE creation of "Brownlow's Melish." The *Union and Dispatch* declared that the State Guard had transformed Tennessee into a "military republic, a government founded on mock elections, and supported only by the sword." A few days after Governor Brownlow promulgated his General Order No. 1, twenty-four Conservative members of the Tennessee General Assembly issued a call for "a Convention of all who oppose the tendencies and ruinous policy and practices of the dominant party." Declaring that they were "deeply impressed with the dangers which imperil our beloved country," these men demanded the formation of a Conservative Unionist Party and the nomination of a full slate of candidates to run against the Radicals.[1]

On April 16, Conservative delegates gathered in Nashville, formulated a platform, and nominated a candidate for governor. Notable among the party's resolutions was a promise to restore the suffrage to those disfranchised by the Brownlow administration. The convention also denounced the State Guard: "The establishment of a standing army in our state in times of peace, is a flagrant and dangerous encroachment on the rights and liberties of the citizens, violent and oppressive to the taxpayers, and evidently designed to over-awe the voters at the ballot-box." For governor, the convention selected Henry Emerson Etheridge, a powerful stump speaker, as the man best suited to enter the political arena against Brownlow.[2]

The forty-eight-year-old Etheridge was a prominent Conservative Unionist from Weakley County in West Tennessee. Vilified by the Confederacy for staying loyal to the Union, he later incurred the wrath of both the Republican party for opposing emancipation (he was a former slaveholder) and the Tennessee Radicals for opposing the franchise acts, especially black suffrage. In 1865, he was briefly arrested for sedition against the Brownlow government, although the charges were subsequently dropped. In May 1867, as gubernatorial candidate, he condemned the Tennessee State Guard, particularly the arming of black militiamen, and claimed that one of its main functions was to force freedmen into the Radical-controlled Union Leagues. At one point, he allegedly declared that anyone encouraging black citizenship should be shot. Nevertheless, he officially urged his followers to refrain from violence. His racism notwithstanding, Etheridge predicted that he would defeat the incumbent Brownlow by winning over the new black electorate.[3]

Etheridge opened his canvass of the state on May 11 with a speech in Union City in Obion County, only miles from the site of Senator Almon Case's assassination. Given the strong anti-Radical feeling in West Tennessee, Etheridge rightly expected large receptions at each of his stops in that part of the state. Most of his summer campaigning, however, was in Middle and East Tennessee. His speeches were pure billingsgate, with "Brownlowism" the target. In his efforts to convert blacks to his banner, Etheridge added Joseph E. Williams, a Conservative black war veteran, to his speaking tour. Etheridge's dubious tactic of portraying Brownlow's racism as worse than his own, however, earned little black applause. Governor Brownlow, no amateur when it came to mudslinging rhetoric, was too ill to participate personally in the canvass. However, several leading Radicals, such as Samuel Arnell, William B. Stokes, L. C. Houk, and Horace Maynard, made a point of attending Etheridge's meetings and "dividing time" whenever possible.[4]

Governor Brownlow was incensed by the nomination of Etheridge, claiming that it "was not made in the expectation of electing him, but to produce mischief." Branding Etheridge a disloyal demagogue, he warned the Conservatives through one of his proclamations that "wherever . . . violent speeches are made, inflaming the bad passions of bad men, I deem it my duty to station troops." Though insisting that he had no intention

The Opening Shots of the Campaign of 1867

of suppressing free speech, he did "not conceive it to be the duty of the State Guards to stand quietly by and hear any man excite the mob spirit." Alarmed by this threatening language, East Tennessean John P. Holtsinger asked the governor whether the Conservative party would be permitted to canvass the state "without being overawed or intimidated by the State troops." In reply, Brownlow assured all Conservatives that "however severe the speakers may be, no State Guards will be allowed to interrupt them, or be upheld in doing so." Nonetheless, the governor reiterated his desire to maintain law and order: "If bad men, from disloyal motives, shall venture to deliver incendiary speeches, and advise the overthrow of the State government by mob violence, I should think the State Guards . . . greatly at fault to tolerate such men."[5]

Given the tenor of Brownlow's comments and his "extreme activity" in organizing his Radical army, distrustful Conservatives feared Brownlow would use any anti-Radical speech or meeting as a justification to cover the state with militia. The *Fayetteville Observer*, in a sensational editorial titled "Brownlow Counselling Murder," declared that a Radical victory at the polls was possible only through the "bullying intimidation of that 'loyal militia.'" To anti-Radicals from Henry County, the mobilization of the militia "look[s] like preparations for another war." The editor of this county's principal newspaper, the *Paris Intelligencer*, believed that the militia would quash free speech and prevent an honest election. "Brownlow had better declare himself King," this paper exclaimed. "If you want Peace, vote for Etheridge—if you prefer to go to war, then vote for Brownlow." In a letter to President Johnson, Conservative John C. Gaut presented a similarly frightening picture of oppression. Defining "Brownlowism" as "despicable tyranny," Gaut informed Johnson that the governor had perverted democracy while "organizing his malitia & arming them . . . as fast as he can." According to Gaut, "Brownlow and faction intend to carry the August elections, by force, and intimidation." He beseeched the president "to take charge of Brownlow's malitia."[6]

These anti-Radical statements expressed fears, not reality, for at the time they were uttered, barely half a dozen companies of State Guard had been mustered into service, and only a few had been deployed. Far from terrorizing the state, these units were drawing equipment and training within the confines of their encampments (when not fending off hostile ex-Confederates in West and Middle Tennessee). Governor Brownlow had made it clear to his militia officers that they were to conduct themselves and employ their commands in accordance with U.S. Army regulations. To this end, Capt. J. K. Clingan, shortly after mustering in his Company D, First Regiment, requested a copy of Hardee's drill manual, *Rifle and Light Infantry Tactics.* Like his fellow company commanders, Clingan wanted to instill a modicum of discipline and uniformity among his men before undertaking his mission. While the anti-Radical press was portraying the militia as a band of armed thugs, the State Guard leadership was taking time to transform its raw recruits into trained soldiers who would obey orders during the forthcoming political battles.[7]

Although the suppression of Rebel vigilantism would rank high as a militia priority, the Brownlow administration's most immediate concern in the spring of 1867 was the registration of black voters, whose numbers were crucial for Radical success at the polls. Unfortunately, registration difficulties occurred throughout the state. Anderson H. Walker, the registrar of Weakley County, bluntly informed the governor that "it will be dangerous to attempt to register voters in this county without some protection." Similar complaints came from Sumner County, where ex-Confederates were obtaining phony certificates; from Perry County, where "villainous Rebel papers" were warning blacks not to register; from Bedford County, where the poll books were "wickedly stolen" by unidentified thieves; and from Stewart County, where Registrar Russell A. Salisbury felt compelled to reregister all eligible voters in an effort to make sure he certified only loyal men. Such reports led the governor's office to conclude that "in counties where the disloyal element is largely in the majority all sorts of obstacles are placed in the way of colored men being properly registered." Reminding these correspondents that "the office of Registrar is really the most important one politically," the executive department urged them to execute their duties faithfully and await the deployment of the State Guard.[8]

No single, complete mission statement for the State Guard of 1867 exists, but its task, as suggested by the militia act and various executive proclamations and general orders, was apparently threefold. First, the State Guard was to preserve the integrity of the electoral process through the rigid enforcement of the franchise acts. To this end, militia commanders were instructed to assist county registrars in compiling rosters of loyal voters and then protecting the polling sites on election day to prevent interference or illegal voting. (Arguments against the constitutionality of disfranchisement are thus irrelevant in judging the State Guard. The organization was duty-bound to enforce laws, not interpret them.) Second, the State Guard was to defend the lives and property of the recently enfranchised freedmen, whose right to vote was an affront to the ex-Confederate majority, which could not vote. Radical whites in West and Middle Tennessee, where the loyalty of local sheriffs was often suspect, also required protection. Third, the State Guard was to ensure that no anti-Radical conspiracies or insurrections threatened the state. Accordingly, company commanders were authorized to patrol the hinterlands of counties with strong Rebel sympathies and to monitor the Conservative canvass of the state. In this respect, the State Guard would serve as a super-sized constabulary. Indubitably, the State Guard was also a partisan, political army, whose broader Reconstruction mission, as enunciated by Horace Maynard, was "bringing the unruly opposers of Radicalism to terms."[9]

The nature of the State Guard's mission, coupled with the animosity of the ex-Confederate populace toward Radicalism, required that the new company commanders carry out their assignments as if they were occupying enemy territory. The anti-Radicals closely watched militia movements throughout the campaign, anticipating, even hoping for, a flagrant abuse of power that would confirm their allegations that the State Guard was nothing more than an instrument of military oppression. They would not have to wait long. Toward the end of May and into June 1867, the activities of six companies of the First Regiment—Rickman (Company H), Blackburn (Company A), Clingan (Company D), Robeson (Company E), Grisham (Company B), and Evans (Company I)—would stir up controversy in all three sections of the state. Although some of their activities would tarnish the Radical campaign, their performance was precisely the show of force that the Brownlow administration wanted from its Radical army.

Capt. William O. Rickman's initial area of operations was Franklin County in Middle Tennessee. In 1861, Franklin whites had voted unanimously for secession. In 1867, the county was, according to one local Radical, a den for the "Hell Hounds of Rebellion." These "hell hounds" were reportedly ordering blacks who had registered to vote to leave the region or face some terrible reprisal. This ex-Confederate activity likely explains why no Union League formed in Franklin and why the Freedmen's Bureau agent in neighboring Bedford County rarely visited.

The few white Radicals in the county feared to campaign openly for their party lest they be shot down by "midnight assassins." Efforts to form a local Radical defense force fell short due to lack of weaponry. Captain Rickman moved aggressively to rectify the situation.[10]

Shortly after muster on May 1, Rickman established a base of operations, Camp New Hope, in the Franklin countryside. This encampment was eleven miles from the county seat, Winchester, the "Rebel City." On May 10, Rickman issued a proclamation "to the Citizens of Franklin and adjoining counties" acknowledging the "great excitement" that his deployment had caused but reminding his readers of his lawful mission to preserve order. "No citizen that is obeying the laws of Tennessee will be molested by my command, but protected regardless of past political sentiments." Noting that "parts of this county are overrun by robbers and assassins," he expressed his disappointment that these criminals, in addition to receiving aid and comfort from the citizenry, were seen as heroes for having fought against the Union. Rickman explained that his intention was "to bring to justice all violators of the law" and vowed that "as long as these outlaws are allowed to run at large . . . you will have the Tennessee State Guard."[11]

Anti-Radicals were appalled by the "vile slander" of Rickman's proclamation. The *Fayetteville Observer* protested that Rickman's statements were more applicable to the Radical stronghold of East Tennessee than to the peaceful citizens of Middle Tennessee. Nevertheless, Rickman soon commenced a series of mounted patrols throughout the county. One such patrol reported that several "rebel citizens" in Winchester carried sidearms in public and that the townspeople displayed open contempt for the militia. Demonstrating sound tactical judgment, Rickman tried to dissuade the adjutant general from dividing Company H into small squads to be stationed in the county's towns and villages. He reasoned that by keeping his infantry together in a central location he could respond to crises more effectively and protect his troops from ambush. Moreover, by staying in the countryside, Rickman believed that he could keep the ex-Confederates in the dark about his activities. Although sympathetic to Rickman's concerns, Adjutant General Brownlow ordered him to post a twenty-man detachment in Winchester. A recent Radical meeting in that town, attended by many blacks, had been disrupted by "an armed mob." Moreover, Registrar Daniel E. Davenport complained that he was heckled whenever he left his office. The adjutant general felt that a display of strength was needed to encourage these local Radicals.[12]

Toward the end of May, after about two weeks of deployment, Rickman sensed that the county's "hell hounds" were preparing for a showdown. On May 21, a white Radical was murdered near his home. Rickman sent out a mounted detachment in a fruitless pursuit of the killer. A few days later, a black man was "brutally shot down" for no apparent reason. Rickman learned that the perpetrators were all members of a band of ex-Confederate outlaws under former guerrilla leader Joe Rodgers. It was the expressed intention of this group "*to clean out Rickman's command.*" On May 25, in a preemptive move, Rickman ordered Lt. Jordan Holt to search the homes of all suspected members of Rodgers's outfit and confiscate their firearms.[13]

Lieutenant Holt carried out his orders enthusiastically. Over the next few days, his mounted detachment moved from residence to residence and confiscated several weapons. In the process, however, Company H overstepped the bounds of its authority. In several instances, Holt's men needlessly insulted the family members of the accused and, in some cases, allegedly threatened to kill the adult males. When the militia arrived at the home of Dr. J. J. Abernathy, a well-respected citizen whose association with Rodgers's band was never established, the doctor insisted on seeing a search warrant. Lieutenant Holt reportedly put his hands on his holsters and said, "This is my authority." Later, at the home of ex-Confederate E. H. Poe, the militiamen encountered an armed Mrs. Poe and her intoxicated fifteen-year-old son. When the younger Poe brazenly threatened to kill Captain Rickman, Holt's men wrested the rifle from Mrs. Poe and then arrested her son. Lieutenant Holt then returned to camp on May 28, leaving the Franklin countryside in an uproar.[14]

Although Registrar Davenport worried that Holt's recklessness would undermine his efforts to get out the Radical vote, Captain Rickman seemed satisfied with the dragnet. As for prisoner Poe, Rickman did not take seriously the teenager's threats and, after talking "very kindly" to him, sent the boy home. Rickman did, however, take seriously some intelligence he had received during Holt's absence. One of his scouts, Pvt. Samuel Heath, in searching for his bolted horse, had struck up a conversation with a local man named James Brown. Brown foolishly confided in Heath his membership in Rodgers's "company of bushwhackers," and he identified a James Simmons as a fellow member. Brown further boasted that he "had never surrendered" and regaled Heath with his wartime exploits, including the killing of two Union soldiers, whose bones apparently still lay nearby. Rickman acted decisively on this fresh information, making plans to apprehend both Brown and Simmons.[15]

In the early morning hours of May 29, an infantry squad marched to the home of Simmons, while Lieutenant Holt and a cavalry squad raced to Brown's. Holt was under orders to compel Brown to disclose the location of "his graveyard." Simmons caught wind of the raid, and managed to evade the infantry squad, which fired on him as he fled into the woods. Brown was not so lucky. Holt's men arrested him, but at this point tragedy occurred. While leading his captors toward the grave site of the Union soldiers, Brown reportedly "broke and run" toward a ravine but was shot fatally through the head before he could escape. Captain Rickman matter-of-factly related the particulars to Adjutant General Brownlow, his letter beginning, "I have the honor to report that my men this morning killed a man by the name of James Brown."[16]

The killing of Brown and the general conduct of Company H on May 25–29 sparked an outcry against the Brownlow administration. Over the next several days, the residents of Franklin held anti-Radical rallies. Led by Arthur S. Colyar, a former member of the Confederate Congress, Franklin whites drew up a list of grievances against the State Guard. The somewhat exaggerated petition accused Rickman's company of having, "in a most violent manner," conducted illegal searches and seizures; of having frightened women and children; of having jeopardized the economic prosperity of the county; of having arrested Poe, "an inoffensive boy," trying him by drum-head court, and sentencing him to be shot; and of having murdered James Brown, "a peaceable, quiet citizen . . . in a most heartless and cruel manner." In short, as the *Union and Dispatch* declared, Rickman had instigated a "Reign of Terror." The Winchester petition, which was transmitted to President Johnson, concluded with a warning aimed at the Brownlow administration: "If the depredations of this militia are continued . . . we recommend that the people combine and protect themselves."[17]

The rabidly anti-Radical *Republican Banner* devoted space in ten of its issues to the militia in Franklin. Every local white seemed to have an exciting story to tell about Lieutenant Holt's rampage and the Brown killing. Mixing fact with fiction, they all related a tale of "pillage and violence unrestrained." Some accounts stressed that several militiamen were Franklin natives who exploited their uniform to exact revenge on their secessionist neighbors. Others elaborated on the manner in which Brown was killed, until his death took on grotesque proportions. It was stated that the militia took Brown "into the woods, tied him to a tree with thongs of bark and literally riddled his body with balls." In all, nearly twenty affidavits were printed for public consumption. The *Banner* damned the Radicals: "The blood of poor Brown is on the hands of every man who voted for the militia bill." Surprisingly, despite the propaganda capital of Brown's death, Etheridge rarely mentioned the incident in his stump speeches.[18]

As the Conservative press built Brown's death into "the worst, unprovoked, dastardly and cruel murder ever perpetrated in the country," Radical editors engaged in damage control. They predictably portrayed the anti-Radical newspaper versions as gross exaggerations. They further denounced the Winchester petition as "inflammatory," an irresponsible call for "armed resistance against the state authorities." Captain Rickman himself dismissed the Winchester accusations as sheer hyperbole: "This County is full of Bushwhackers, and if wee go to arrest one of them thare is a big hue and Cry rased by the Rebels." Determined to continue his mission, he arrested six more men in the days following Brown's death, presumably members of Rodgers's band, and turned them over to the civil authorities.[19]

The outcry over the killing of Brown prompted two official investigations into the conduct of Company H. Assistant Adjutant General Samuel Hunt represented the state of Tennessee, and Gen. William D. Whipple represented the federal authorities. On most matters, Hunt and Whipple were in agreement. Both men acknowledged ex-Confederate animosity as a mitigating circumstance for all of the alleged militia transgressions. Furthermore, both rejected the charge that Poe was unfairly tried and nearly executed. Poe, it was noted, later stated that Captain Rickman "had treated him well." Overall, Rickman was judged a capable officer (Hunt especially expressed confidence in his leadership). However, both reports cited instances of "bad conduct." Hunt stated that "some of the men . . . have been imprudent . . . and guilty of trespasses, which they were not guaranteed in doing." Whipple was more critical, particularly in his evaluation of Holt's performance. He chastised the militia lieutenant for excessive use of force. He also noted that the cavalry squad under Holt prevented Brown's father from participating in the trek to the grave site. To Whipple, this fact "is perhaps sufficient to excite suspicion of intent to murder on the part of the militia." In the end, however, both investigations exonerated Captain Rickman and his men of any major wrongdoing. Whipple, in particular, expressed satisfaction that both Rickman and Holt regretted the whole affair; he saw no reason for any federal intervention. Department commander Gen. George H. Thomas endorsed his subordinate's findings and explained to President Johnson that "the terror among the people of Franklin County . . . is very much magnified for political purposes." As for the killing of Brown, Thomas assured the president that "there is no danger whatever of a repetition of a similar offence."[20]

As the story unfolded, Captain Rickman, unflappable in the face of anti-Radical criticism, privately expressed disappointment in Holt. He rebuked his lieutenant for harassing Dr. Abernathy and for not exercising tighter control over his men during the arrests of Poe and Brown. The reprimands and the stress of command proved too much for Holt; he resigned his commission of his own volition and returned to ranks as a private. Sgt. John Mankin replaced him as first lieutenant. In mid-June, Rickman reported, "I have got my men under tolerable good discipline."[21]

While the investigations were underway, Governor Brownlow announced that he was placing Rickman under arrest and that the captain would stand trial for his misdeeds. This arrest, however, never occurred, and the Conservative press depicted Brownlow's order as a hoax. "We have heard of no arrests," exclaimed the *Union and Dispatch*, "no dismissal of [Rickman] from the State service." In fact, later in June, Rickman was seen "swaggering through the streets" of Nashville. These newspapers further ridiculed the "official" investigations, claiming that Samuel Hunt "hunted" evidence only from the militia while ignoring the *Republican Banner*'s large collection of affidavits. Rather than arresting Rickman, the executive department transferred his company to Marshall County. Franklin, however, was not spared the presence of a militia force. At the secret urging of General Whipple, who advised "against backing down" in the face of anti-Radical opposition, the adjutant general deployed Capt. George W. Kirk's newly mustered militia company from East Tennessee to Franklin.[22]

In contrast to affairs in Franklin, the militia activities of Capt. Joseph H. Blackburn in DeKalb, a few counties to the north, drew very few headlines. In accomplishing his mission, Captain Blackburn preferred a less confrontational approach than Rickman. For several weeks

70

after mustering in his Company A on April 1, Blackburn methodically helped solidify Radical control over DeKalb County. In this task, he was greatly assisted by his first lieutenant, William L. Hathaway, who was also sheriff of the county. Although DeKalb had a majority for secession in 1861, more than 40 percent of the voters rejected it. Many of these Unionists had served in the Federal army, and most of those who did so embraced the Republican party after the war. In an effort to mobilize this significant white Radical strength, Blackburn sponsored efforts to raise two additional State Guard companies from DeKalb. He and fellow militia captain, William S. Stuart (Company K) of neighboring Putnam County, even suggested to the adjutant general that their separate commands be combined into a super-company under Blackburn. The state government disapproved the raising of additional companies from DeKalb, but was nevertheless grateful to Blackburn for his contributions in transforming the county into a Radical stronghold where racial violence and ex-Confederate agitation were minimal.[23]

Blackburn's command was unique in that it was essentially a cavalry company. While many State Guard captains were fortunate to have a full mounted section of twenty-five men (as authorized in General Order No. 1), over sixty men in Company A were mounted. This advantage in mobility enabled Blackburn to project militia power into all counties adjacent to DeKalb: Cannon, Putnam, Smith, Warren, White, and Wilson. Throughout May and June, using the DeKalb towns of Alexandria and then Liberty as his headquarters, Blackburn dispatched squad-sized detachments (ten to twelve men) to such towns as Lebanon (Wilson County), Sparta (White County), and McMinnville (Warren County). This last county was particularly troublesome to the Radicals. In early June, Registrar William Baker discovered that several dozen ex-Confederates possessed bogus voting certificates. When he initiated a complete reregistration of the county, anti-Radicals resisted his efforts. Baker beseeched the governor: "A detachment of the State Guard is urgently needed . . . not only to insure a safe and correct reregistration . . . but also to protect the persons and lives of loyal citizens from conservative and rebel violence. . . . Without military protection there is danger of an outbreak, which may result in the killing of some of our best citizens." On June 21, Blackburn sent 2nd Lt. William Cravens with fifteen soldiers to assist Baker.[24]

Although an implacable foe of the rebellion during the Civil War, Blackburn was commended, by Conservatives no less, for his moderation as a militia captain. When White County residents protested Captain Stuart's peremptory treatment of local troublemakers (he had forcibly arrested two ex-Confederates in April), Blackburn played the peacemaker. He first persuaded Stuart to tone down his pugnacity and then assured local whites that the militia was not an enemy but merely a law enforcer. Stuart, who had served as a noncommissioned officer under Blackburn during the war, appears to have deferred to his former commander without resentment. Blackburn's Reconstruction diplomacy may have been effective because of his wartime reputation for ruthlessness toward Confederate guerrillas. On one occasion during the war, he was alleged to have tortured and hanged one White County Confederate for withholding information about enemy movements, and on another to have summarily executed two guerrillas after they surrendered to his men. Adding to his fearsome persona was a rumor, reported by the *Republican Banner*, that Blackburn's Company A had killed eleven ex-Confederates since its muster. For Captain Blackburn, the mere threat of force seems to have been effective.[25]

In addition to neutralizing anti-Radical opposition in DeKalb and the surrounding area, Captain Blackburn served as a bodyguard for William B. Stokes, Radical candidate for Congress. Stokes apparently feared assassination, ex-Confederates having earlier in the year advertised a reward of five thousand dollars for his murder. As he stumped the Third Congressional District, Stokes called on Blackburn to provide security, a service few other Radical candidates enjoyed. Blackburn could hardly refuse his old commander (he had served under Stokes in the Fifth Tennessee Cavalry, Union). As a result, a portion of Company A frequently accompanied Stokes during his canvass. In one instance, Blackburn's men not only protected Stokes's life but also defended his honor. On June 22, during a joint political debate in Lebanon (Wilson County), a Conservative speaker implied that Stokes was either a coward or a woman. Incensed by this insult, Lieutenant Hathaway, "who had come to protect William B.'s precious person," moved to strike the offender. In self-defense, the man produced a pistol and fired at Hathaway, missing the militia officer but hitting a black onlooker in the leg. A general scuffle ensued, but Captain Blackburn barked out some commands and quickly restored order. The shooter was disarmed and "pitched headlong" out of the speaking hall, though he was not arrested. The *Republican Banner* reported that the affray had left Stokes "pale as death."[26]

Early militia activities in West Tennessee lacked the drama of Rickman's experience in Franklin and Blackburn's in Wilson, but they too proved controversial. On or about May 22, Capt. Judge K. Clingan, commanding Company D, deployed to Haywood County in response to a recent disturbance. Haywood had been a hotbed of secession in 1861, with 87 percent of the electorate voting to leave the Union. In 1867, the white populace was no less opposed to Radical Reconstruction. On May 13, a group of "young white men" broke up a Radical rally in Brownsville, the county seat. According to reports, when the several hundred blacks in attendance commenced cheering for Governor Brownlow, the youths dispersed the crowd with pistol fire. Radicals referred to the perpetrators as "Etheridge's guerrillas" and intimated a connection between the incident and the Conservative gubernatorial candidate's concurrent stump speech in neighboring Gibson County and his speech in Haywood scheduled for May 15. Whether this was true or not, it was clear that protecting blacks in West Tennessee was going to be a difficult task for the Brownlow administration.[27]

Company D had no sooner set up camp on the Brownsville fairgrounds than it became the target of anti-Radical abuse. Ex-Confederates mocked Clingan's men as a "lazy, shiftless class who hang around the groggeries of small county towns." Some of the citizens tried to get the militiamen to make bets on who would win the election. One Conservative newspaper even portrayed the militiamen as Negrophobes who devoted most of their time to disrupting black meetings, harassing black men, and making "indecent advances to colored women." This source claimed that one of Clingan's soldiers had killed a black man in East Tennessee "and would just as lieve as not kill another one." The Radical press countered these aspersions, describing Clingan's troops as "quiet, civil men [who] are commended by all good citizens in the county." The militia officers themselves urged the residents to promptly report any misconduct by their soldiers.[28]

Captain Clingan ignored the propaganda battles. Instead, he spent the first few days in Brownsville drilling his men and planning security for a second Radical meeting scheduled for May 28–29. These dates appear to have been cursed for the Tennessee State Guard, for as Rickman clashed with former Confederates in Franklin, Clingan earned notoriety of his own in Haywood. The militia's performance during the convention started out well enough. When a large body of armed blacks arrived, probably in anticipation of another row with local whites,

Clingan calmly informed them that his unit would keep order "and that their services were not required." The following day, Clingan closed all liquor establishments during the convention's closing ceremonies. Thanks to Company D, Haywood's second Radical rally passed off quietly.[29]

Unfortunately for the Radicals, an incident outside the convention hall tarnished the day's success. An elderly ex-Confederate approached some militiamen and promised them horses, clothing, money, and sanctuary if they would desert "the d—d militia." One enlisted man did accept the offer and absconded. On learning of the matter, Clingan arrested the old man, charged him with willful interference, and implemented a bizarre punishment. He "ordered the gentleman to be ridden upon a rail through the town of Brownsville." In a letter to the *Union and Dispatch,* Clingan justified his action on the grounds that he had a duty to protect his men, and that he believed the punishment would deter other residents from future attempts to induce desertion. He declared that "if any other man, Radical, Conservative, or Rebel, is found guilty of the same offence, he may expect to receive what we think is just."[30]

The incident lacked the explosiveness of the Brown affair in Franklin, but Conservatives still tried to exploit it as another example of "Brownlowism." Decrying the "absolutism of military power," the *Union and Dispatch* objected to the fact that the old man in question had received no trial, only the summary infliction of "gross cruelties." Local people claimed the old man was simply trying to persuade his sons, who had apparently joined the militia, to come back home. Clingan firmly denied this last assertion, stating that none of his men were kin to the perpetrator. Conservatives demanded an investigation into the "Dare Devil Doings of the Brownlow Melish" in Haywood, but the executive branch took no action.[31]

In the weeks following the rail-riding incident, Haywood was quiet and orderly. In mid-June, Captain Clingan reported that he and his men had settled into a comfortable routine of peacekeeping. While mounted detachments regularly patrolled the countryside, Clingan oversaw the formation of a Union League in Brownsville, one largely run by blacks. Noting that "the boys are . . . very well pleased and enjoying themselves," the militia captain reiterated his commitment to drill: "Our discipline is as severe as practicable for recruits." For exercise, the men often wrestled and sometimes challenged the officers to a friendly match. Clingan, manifestly proud of his company, noted, "I can say without boasting that

The Opening Shots of the Campaign of 1867

the men of this command can not be excelled in trying to do what is right and what they think is their duty." They evidently did their duty well, for during a visit through the county in early July, Tennessee secretary of state A. J. Fletcher found Haywood "a perfect blaze of enthusiasm for Brownlow."[32]

This favorable assessment notwithstanding, some of Clingan's men were unhappy with life in the State Guard. Pvt. James Kelley, for instance, penned a petition to the governor complaining about the poor supply of food: "We have never had a change in diet, which you know is contrary to the laws of hygiene, nature, and Army regulations. We draw meal, bacon, sugar, and coffee . . . all of which is deficient in quantity and inferior in quality." Foraging for chickens and other foodstuffs helped offset some shortages, but mess in Company D apparently left much to be desired. Illness or injury dampened the enthusiasm of other volunteers. When fifteen-year-old Cpl. Charles Fry became sick, he used his mother's influence to gain a discharge. Pvt. Joseph H. Bailes, who accidentally shot himself in the hand, and at least four other enlisted men were not as lucky as Fry. They spent most of their time in the militia laid up in makeshift field hospitals.[33]

On June 16, a squad of regular army troops marched into Brownsville, evidently at the behest some of Haywood's citizens. These petitioners claimed that the officers of Company D had threatened to "lynch those who offend them." According to Clingan, the "rebels rejoiced exceedingly when the U.S. troops arrived." After their arrival, he added, these ex-Confederates became "considerably bolder." Clingan considered his further presence in Haywood superfluous now that federal troops had appeared. General Cooper, having recently assumed command of the State Guard, agreed and ordered Company D to neighboring Madison County, a decision that not only projected power into that troublesome region but also avoided potential clashes over authority in Haywood. As his men prepared to march out of Brownsville on June 19, Clingan noted with amusement how several ex-Confederates heckled his men from afar, boasting that any one of them "could whip any three of Brownlow's malitia." The ex-Confederates had had a month to put that claim to the test, but the militia departed with injuries to none (except the "old man").[34]

Madison whites would come to resent Clingan's command as much as those of Haywood, but militia captain John T. Robeson welcomed the presence of his compatriot from East Tennessee. Prior to Clingan's arrival, Robeson's Company E had constituted the only Radical force in the entire western section of the state (save the Memphis Metropolitan Police). Robeson's principal area of operations was the northwest corner of Tennessee (Dyer, Gibson, Obion, and Weakley counties). With the exception of Weakley, which boasted six chapters of the Union League, this region was overwhelmingly ex-Confederate. Toward the end of May, Captain Robeson moved his company into Obion County and set up camp in Troy, the site of Senator Almon Case's assassination. On June 15, he relocated to Union City, in part to counter the political effects of Etheridge's inaugural campaign speech, but more importantly to take advantage of the town's railroad nexus.[35]

Robeson was dismayed to find that the Radical party was virtually nonexistent in Obion and Dyer. His arrival did encourage local Radicals, but loyal whites were scarce and the freedmen were politically inactive. Robeson did have a valuable ally in James W. Tarkington, the sheriff of Dyer County and "a strong Radical," but the county registrars appear to have done little to enroll blacks as voters. The militia captain further discovered that there had been no Freedmen's Bureau agent in Obion or Dyer for some time. Under the circumstances, Robeson realized that he was going to have to assume political leadership. In mid-June, he organized a chapter of the Union League in Obion County and "initiated quite a number of men both white and black." Presumably, he also took steps to get them registered to vote. Proud of his initiatives, Robeson assured the adjutant general that Obion blacks would all vote the Radical ticket, and he predicted Brownlow would take the county by a three-to-one margin. His confidence in the freedmen notwithstanding, Robeson closed one of his reports with an ominous forecast: "I look for trouble on the day of the election."[36]

Robeson had good reason to be worried about election difficulties. Obion's ex-Confederates harassed his men daily. "The Rebs are very bitter," he observed the day after his arrival in Union City. When they were not trying to induce the militiamen to desert, the "Rebs" tried unsuccessfully to incite conflict between Company E and a small detachment of federal troops stationed in Obion. On one occasion, while Robeson was scouting the area around Obionville (along the Mississippi River), four militiamen, including a corporal, did desert the Union City encampment. Evidently, some ex-Confederates falsely told them that the army was

The Opening Shots of the Campaign of 1867

going to arrest all members of the State Guard. Robeson reprimanded 1st Lt. Charles B. Simpson for being inattentive in his absence. Two of the deserters eventually returned, and thereafter desertion in Company E was infrequent. Robeson informed State Guard headquarters that all was "write" with his command and that discipline was "Good."[37]

Toward the end of June, Captain Robeson became concerned about a rumor of a planned insurrection in West Tennessee. A Rebel named Day was reportedly organizing and arming a band of five hundred men with which to combat the militia. Day vowed that if he and his men were prevented from voting on election day, they would seize control "by the Bayonet." Robeson refused "to be alarmed by the threats of Johnnie Reb," but he requested more men and horses so that he could better patrol the open country and thereby "ceep the Rebs and the bad men quiete." Until the end of June, when General Cooper deployed reinforcements to northwest Tennessee, Robeson defended the Radical banner alone in that part of the state. Nevertheless, he was optimistic: "I intend to take a Straightforward course. My men shall respect every citizen and I expect the same in return."[38]

As the militia companies stationed in Middle and West Tennessee subdued the opposition with varying degrees of success, two companies in East Tennessee earned their own peculiar notoriety. Following the festivities of his unit's muster in Jonesboro on May 1, Capt. George E. Grisham transported his oversized Company B (115 men) to Sullivan County. Tucked away in the remote northeast corner of the state, along the Virginia border, Sullivan was one of the few East Tennessee counties to vote for secession in 1861 (by over 70 percent). These isolated ex-Confederates banded together tightly. Conservatives were perplexed by the Governor's decision to station militia in Sullivan, but according to local Radicals, "most of the rebel desperadoes of this section have taken refuge in [the Sullivan vicinity], and occasionally make raids on our farmers, and take their fine horses." Prior to his deployment, Grisham appears to have sent "spies" into Sullivan. From these individuals, he discovered that the white populace was ready to "rise up against him to a man" if he overstepped his authority. This intelligence notwithstanding, Grisham, who reportedly described Sullivan as "the worst Rebel hole in the State," established a firm presence there during the first weeks of May 1867. He and part of his command camped in Bristol, while 1st Lt. Nelson McLaughlin led a detachment to Kingsport.[39]

About half of the men in Company B were black and this unit's deployment to Sullivan County marked the first use of "Negro militia" in the Reconstruction South. The significance of the occasion was not missed by the anti-Radical press, which scowled at this experiment in racial equality. The *Republican Banner* circulated a story about the "boisterous" behavior of Grisham's black recruits during the unit's movement by rail. At some point on the journey, four black militiamen supposedly forced their way into a passenger car, "made themselves very obnoxious to the lady passengers," and bullied the white conductor with a bayonet, all the while shouting, "Brownlow!"[40]

Sullivan whites vilified Grisham's men as "the meanest negroes in the country and the meanest of the poor white trash of East Tennessee," but the unit's performance in Sullivan proved more humorous than repressive. After informing Registrar A. C. Shipley of his arrival, Grisham began his "perfect reign of terror" on May 27. Inexplicably, Grisham involved himself in a domestic dispute. Evidently, a recently divorced local woman came to his encampment with a complaint that her former husband had seized their seven-month-old daughter and forbade her any contact with the child. Grisham decided to hold a hearing in his camp and ordered three Bristol magistrates to attend and help him arbitrate the case. Conservatives sarcastically commended "the valiant" Grisham for calling on local authorities for assistance, but proclaimed that his "uncivil" action was "without precedent in legal or military history."[41]

The ruling in the child custody hearing is unknown, but one of the magistrates, J. S. Shangle, was infuriated by the whole affair. In a letter to President Johnson, he denounced the State Guard as a "rag-tag-&-bob-tail-malitia" and accused Captain Grisham of suppressing free discussion of politics in the county. Anti-Radical newspapers tried to corroborate Shangle's statement but presented nothing more than vague references to various "depredations." A visiting northern correspondent refuted the libel and insisted that Company B behaved with "perfect decency, propriety and order." Although this observer admitted that Grisham "did make rather a fool of himself" by getting involved in a domestic dispute, he considered the militia captain a "peaceable, good-natured, sensible fellow."[42]

Company B performed its mission without further controversy until the beginning of July, when Captain Grisham got involved in another dispute. On July 1, county Radicals and Conservatives held a joint political discussion in Blountville. Grisham provided security and everything

The Opening Shots of the Campaign of 1867

went smoothly. According to the *Union and Dispatch*, however, in the course of the day, two black militiamen accosted a local black named Billy Murray and reprimanded him for addressing a local white as "Massa." Dragging him before Grisham, who seemed to enjoy his self-appointed role as provost marshal, the black militiamen further dressed down the defendant: "You are a pretty d——n fool to be calling a white rascal master; don't you know that's treason?" Grisham reportedly fined the hapless Murray ten dollars. His judicial misadventures aside, Grisham apparently did a good job of neutralizing local ex-Confederate vigilantism. Later in July, Governor Brownlow felt comfortable in permitting Company B's redeployment to Middle Tennessee. Sullivan whites expressed elation when the "Brownlow-Grisham Melish" departed after two months of occupation.[43]

The State Guard was active elsewhere in East Tennessee as well. In the first week of June 1867, Capt. James R. Evans of Company I was planning for an imminent assignment in Claiborne County, one similar to Grisham's in Sullivan. Although Claiborne cast a majority vote against secession in 1861, the county had recently become a haven for ex-Confederate guerrillas. At the end of May, Evans had been forced by local animus to leave Claiborne before mustering in his men, but he was looking forward to a second crack at the county's "bushwhackers." His opening shot of the campaign, however, was not aimed at bushwhackers but at Governor Brownlow's archrival, Emerson Etheridge. Mustered into service at Morristown in Grainger County on June 3, Evans's company barely had time to draw equipment and get some rudimentary training before the Etheridge cavalcade arrived on June 8. Morristown was the sixth of eight campaign stops in East Tennessee for the Conservative gubernatorial candidate (who was on the first of two swings through the heart of Tennessee Radicalism). Having heard that some anti-Radicals had caused a disturbance during Etheridge's stop in Greeneville on June 3, Evans decided he would forestall any similar outbreaks by posting Company I conspicuously near the Morristown festivities.[44]

The Conservative rally at Morristown was held in a church, but there was nothing reverent about Etheridge's speech there. Radicals, led by Judge L. C. Houk, showed up at the church and requested a division of time with Etheridge, but the Conservative candidate refused. Houk and his followers then moved to a nearby grove, "yelling and howling" all the way, and held an outdoor meeting. The proximity of the antagonists led to some heckling and a few cases of fisticuffs. Into this volatile atmosphere marched Company I, in full military array. According to the Conservatives, Captain Evans deployed his company into a line of battle just outside the church and ordered his men to "fix bayonets." Not surprisingly, as one eyewitness explained, "this caused a panic among the people inside, who feared they were going to be shot into and the meeting broken up." All the while, Etheridge coolly continued his excoriation of "Radicalism." Company I did not attack and the day passed without incident.[45]

Conservatives added Evans's conduct at Morristown to a growing list of complaints against the State Guard. A petition to Andrew Johnson claimed that the episode proved that the militia was "engaged in overawing, insulting, and oppressing the people." Characterizing all militia companies, not just Company I, as "lawless bands of armed men," the petitioners further declared that the State Guard made a free canvass of the state impossible. John Williams, a Conservative from Knoxville, described the situation as desperate and implored the president for help: "If this Militia is not disbanded, or sent out there will be actual war in East Tennessee. . . . We cannot much longer submit to Brownlowism. . . . For *Gods sake* come to our relief, & spare an effusion of blood."[46]

This outcry prompted another federal investigation into militia affairs, this one headed by Col. Alfred L. Hough. When questioned, Captain Evans denied having threatened the Conservatives in the church in any way. He stressed that he stationed his men visibly in the area of both party rallies, and he further insisted that "the presence of the militia had prevented a riot." Conservatives reiterated the material cited in their petition, but admitted to Colonel Hough that Captain Evans exercised firm control over his men at all times. On further inquiry, Hough determined that many of the complaints about militia "outrages" in East Tennessee were unfounded. In addition to absolving Evans of any serious misconduct, Hough dismissed Captain Grisham's improprieties in Sullivan as "small grievances." He further discovered that most Conservatives had "only praise and compliments" for the conduct of Capt. Robert L. Hall's recently mustered Company C, which was stationed in Knoxville (possibly as a bodyguard for Governor Brownlow).[47]

The day after his Morristown demonstration, Captain Evans marched his command to Claiborne County. Evidently, while he was monitoring the Conservatives in Grainger County, a band of mounted ex-Confederates had "made a rush into Tazewell," where they threatened local Radicals and warned blacks not to register. For the rest of June and into July, the "vigorous, active and efficient men" of Company I endeavored to keep the peace in yet another county Governor Brownlow had labeled "rebellious."[48]

While stationed in Claiborne, Company I discovered the limitations of supplying itself through the voucher system. Charged with procuring victuals, Lt. John Ellis could find only one general store willing to do business with his company. Anti-Radical merchants either refused to sell goods to him or demanded cash payments, often at inflated prices. The one friendly merchant proved unable to meet Company I's daily food requirements. Fortunately, as the summer wore on, Nashville grocers began delivering commissary goods in sufficient quantities to satisfy most company commanders. W. W. Totten & Brothers ultimately became the State Guard's largest food distributor, providing about one-third of the militia's subsistence before the deployment ended. Totten not only shipped a variety of foodstuffs, but also regularly furnished such basic items as tobacco, candles, and soap. In the process, the dealer grossed over eighteen thousand dollars from its business with the State Guard.[49]

Many scholars of Reconstruction in Tennessee readily accept the Conservative claim that the State Guard repeatedly disrupted Emerson Etheridge's canvass of the state. In actuality, the only direct encounter between Etheridge and the State Guard occurred at Morristown on June 8. Militia recruitment was well underway when Conservatives established their gubernatorial candidate's campaign itinerary. Inevitably, many of Etheridge's campaign stops, especially in East Tennessee, were also State Guard muster points. Militiamen, armed or otherwise, were undoubtedly in the vicinity of several of his speeches, but with the exception of Captain Evans's men, they generally gave Etheridge a wide berth. When he spoke in Greeneville on June 3, over 150 militia recruits were gathering to form two companies of State Guard (those of the two Kirks), but they in no way interfered with the Conservative rally. Far from wanting to suppress a free canvass, Radical leaders welcomed all opportunities to spar with the combative Etheridge. When the *Knoxville Whig* claimed that Horace Maynard "literally demolished" Etheridge in a rare face-to-face debate at Greeneville, it meant through the power of oratory, not through the discharge of militia gunfire.[50]

By mid-June, Radicals throughout the state were fed up with the criticism of their "loyal militia." When the ex-Confederate *Republican Banner* speculated about whether the newly appointed Gen. Joseph A.

Cooper intended to start burning homes and shutting down the press, the Radicals replied vehemently. Andrew J. Fletcher, Tennessee's secretary of state, went on the stump to justify the call for a State Guard. "It is a matter of profound regret," he explained, "that a necessity should exist for the active organization of the militia . . . but the responsibility rests . . . upon the turbulent leaders of the rebel party in this State." Similarly, the *Daily Press and Times* placed the blame for a standing army squarely on the Conservatives: "If a thousand quiet rebel sympathizers in any county choose to let fifty violent rebels commit outrages, they must not be surprised to see a company of militia sent to bring the ruffians into subjection." Finally, the *Knoxville Whig* defended the record of the militia captains: "No soldiers were ever in Tennessee, Union or rebel, who were kept under as strict discipline as the State Guard." To this newspaper, the only legitimate charge that the anti-Radicals could bring against the militia was the killing of "the notorious guerrilla, Brown."[51]

For all of the anti-Radical criticism, the Brownlow administration had imposed its authority over the state with a relatively small militia force. Although fifteen units were officially in the field by July 1, from the beginning of May to the end of June, the Radical army of Tennessee basically consisted of six companies. As they awaited the deployment of their brethren officers, Captains Rickman, Blackburn, Clingan, Robeson, Grisham, and Evans interpreted and executed the mission of the State Guard in a variety of ways. A common denominator in the experiences of the six men was boldness. Timidity in the face of the numerically superior anti-Radicals, who were going to howl in protest over any use of force, might actually have invited trouble. From Rickman's punitive operations in Franklin County to Evans's martial display in Morristown, these six commanders proclaimed to those ex-Confederates who dared test its resolve that the militia was a force to be reckoned with. In the process, through such accomplishments as Blackburn's establishment of Radical hegemony around DeKalb and Robeson's development of a party apparatus in Obion, the State Guard helped get the campaign off to a strong start for the Brownlow administration.

Unfortunately for the Radicals, there were instances when the State Guard crossed the boundary between reasonable and unwarranted force. However gratifying his domineering presence in Franklin must have been for the Radicals, Captain Rickman was arguably too aggressive.

Franklin whites were not pacified by his tactics; they only became more enraged. To a lesser extent, Captains Clingan and Grisham also exceeded their authority. Clingan hardly followed due process in riding a Haywood resident on a rail. And Grisham certainly had no business extending his jurisdiction into domestic affairs. Moreover, Evans's drill and ceremony during the Morristown rally was certainly designed to "over-awe" the Conservatives (although in the end it proved ineffectual). To its credit, the Brownlow administration tried to rein in the worst abuses, acceding to two federal investigations, but missteps were made and controversy was unavoidable.

The State Guard's somewhat inconsistent application of force early in the campaign may be attributable, in part, to an inchoate chain of command. Although the militia captains usually maintained regular communications with headquarters, the executive branch could often offer them only perfunctory instructions. Governor Brownlow was virtually bedridden in Knoxville, while Adjutant General James P. Brownlow was distracted by the ongoing militia mobilization. In addition to directing the efforts of those units already deployed (in all three sections of the state, no less), the adjutant general was supervising the organization of almost a dozen new companies, and overseeing the procurement of arms and supplies for them all. To be sure, Governor Brownlow ameliorated these command difficulties when he appointed General Cooper to manage the State Guard on June 7, but Cooper would not appreciably affect militia operations until the latter half of the month. In the meantime, the militia captains operated largely on their own initiative. With the exception of Rickman, who must bear the ultimate responsibility for his company's temporary breakdown in discipline, the captains applied force responsibly as well as effectively.

Such were the opening shots of the campaign of 1867, which historian Philip M. Hamer describes as "probably the most bitterly contested one in the history of Tennessee." For the Radicals, it was certainly an auspicious start, and one that boded ill for the Conservatives. By July, with General Cooper coordinating the efforts of three times the number of State Guard companies that had operated in May and June, the Radicals were ready for the final stage of the campaign and confident of victory.[52]

Chapter 4

The State Guard in Full Blast

IF THE POLITICAL CAMPAIGN OF 1867 RESEMBLED A MILITARY skirmish in May and June, it took on the character of an all-out war in July. With more than one thousand militiamen in the field at the beginning of the month and several hundred more mustering into service, the Tennessee State Guard was rapidly taking on formidable size. Earlier in June, the *Republican Banner* expressed the attitude of many anti-Radicals when it wailed, "We have now a standing army in full blast." Brig. Gen. Joseph A. Cooper deployed this "standing army" with great alacrity, concentrating his forces in Middle and West Tennessee. Throughout the final month of the campaign, he steadily reinforced companies already in those sections with most of the units raised in East Tennessee and with the newly mustered and highly controversial all-black companies of Middle Tennessee. After a Radical meeting in Nashville toward the end of June, at which Cooper reportedly exclaimed, "I am the organ of the Radical Party," Conservatives accused him of taking on the mien of a modern-day Caesar. Conservatives further claimed that the "Generalissimo" had threatened to shut down what he termed the "rebel sheets"—the anti-Radical press. Daniel A. Carpenter, a disgruntled Conservative from East Tennessee, told Andrew Johnson that he was not going to submit to the Radicals' military tyranny. He ominously informed the president, "There is plenty of

Enfield rifles scattered through this country. . . . If you cant help us we will help our selves."[1]

Many white Tennesseans shared Carpenter's rage. In response to the growing militia power, and in an effort to infuse additional vigor into its canvass, the Conservative party launched a bold political counterattack. During the last week of June, party chairman John C. Gaut issued a provocative circular, one that exploited an apparent loophole in the 1867 Franchise Act. Gaut contended that while Brownlow's commissioners controlled voter registration in the counties, they did not have exclusive control over the appointment of election judges. Accordingly, Gaut urged county authorities (most of whom in Middle and West Tennessee were Conservatives) to take speedy action: "Do not fail to appoint Judges in all the precincts." In doing so, the Conservatives clearly hoped to have some influence over how votes were cast.[2]

On July 1, an enraged Governor Brownlow moved to crush what he considered a blatant attempt to circumvent the 1867 Franchise Act. He condemned Gaut and his "audacious authors" for their "false and rebellious construction" of the franchise clause pertaining to election officials, an interpretation the governor insisted demonstrated a "wicked and revolutionary purpose." Proclaiming that his registrars had absolute control over all aspects of the election, he warned the county officials to ignore the Gaut circular or find "themselves liable to be punished." He closed his proclamation with another threat: "Order must be maintained, and the law executed, if it require that I shall call into the field the whole available force at my command to do so."[3]

Conservatives were indignant at this gubernatorial fulmination and pressed ahead in their defiance of "Brownlowism." Chairman Gaut publicly defended his circular and criticized Brownlow's "extraordinary" proclamation as one designed "to incite his militia and partisans to acts of lawless violence and bloodshed." In this he was echoing President Johnson, who had stated, in a recent interview with the *Cincinnati Commercial,* that "BROWNLOW'S militia would provoke riot and bloodshed." On July 4, the Conservative Executive Committee of Middle Tennessee issued aggressive marching orders. The committee compared the current political "crisis" to that of 1861 but encouraged its followers to show no fear in the face of "a mercenary militia of outlaws." Though ordering the people to obey the laws and refrain from violence, the committee unveiled a compelling, and lawful, campaign strategy. While all

The State Guard in Full Blast

Conservatives who could take the franchise oath were instructed to vote, even the disfranchised were enlisted into the service of the party. Ex-Confederates were asked to attend party rallies and be present on election day as a show of white, anti-Radical solidarity. Additionally, the committee promoted social ostracism of Radical voters and urged its followers to "induce those [blacks] within your influence to withdraw from the treasonable [Union] leagues." Conservative leaders assured the white majority that "Brownlow and his militia . . . dare not confront a determined people."[4]

On July 5, Governor Brownlow again demanded that the Conservatives desist in their efforts to subvert the Franchise Act of 1867. He ordered "all officers commanding the State Guards . . . to arrest the said John C. Gaut, or any of his committee or agents wherever found, if they shall persist in their effort to defeat the execution of the laws." The Radical press reflected the governor's exasperation with the Conservatives. The *Daily Press and Times* marveled at Gaut's "sophistry" while the *Whig* castigated the Conservatives for their "blind" alignment with the ex-Confederates. Brownlow's tactics gained a significant victory for his administration. Chairman Gaut instructed his party to concede the franchise question and devote its energies to other campaign matters. For his part, Gaut made the cost of the State Guard his new political issue. At a Conservative rally later in July, he warned his listeners that the force then mustered would cost at least $1 million, "with chickens, roasting ears and watermelons, to boot."[5]

In addition to combating the Conservatives' legal challenge, the Brownlow administration warily monitored the developing ex-Confederate paramilitary movement. Throughout the summer of 1867, former Confederate general Albert Pike of Memphis called on Tennessee whites to "arm and organize" against the Radicals and the State Guard. "Are a few ragamuffins and a mob of miscreants," he asked, "to overawe and ride over a whole state?" He urged the formation of so-called Civic Guard companies of "sixty or eighty men." In doing so, he probably had the Ku Klux Klan in mind as a ready source of manpower. Though largely confined to Giles County for most of 1866, the Klan began expanding its operations in the spring of 1867. Distinguishing the Klan from the many other bands of ex-Confederate vigilantes is often difficult, but most scholars agree that at about the time the Conservative party convention met in April, delegates from the Giles Klan and neighboring affiliates held a clandestine meeting in Nashville. There, the Klan formally organized as a counterforce to the State Guard and the Union Leagues. Sometime in May, the Klan elected Nathan B. Forrest its Grand Wizard. Never more than a titular leader, Forrest always maintained that the Klan was a defensive organization. Its only overt act of defiance during the campaign of 1867 took place in Pulaski (Giles) on June 5, when seventy-five members held a parade in full costume. Nevertheless, Governor Brownlow regarded the Klan as a "secret guerrilla army," and dens did exist in several counties occupied by militia: Bedford, Davidson, Franklin, Giles, Maury, and Williamson in Middle Tennessee, and Dyer, Hardin, Haywood, and McNairy in the west.[6]

In the midst of all this political and militaristic posturing, a violent clash between white anti-Radicals and black Union Leaguers occurred in Franklin in Williamson County. The Union League of Franklin was one of the more active chapters in the state and was largely run by black Civil War veterans. Local Conservatives denounced its public activities, especially its daily parades through the town during the week of July 4. On July 6, Joseph Williams, the black Conservative stump speaker, arrived and tried to address a Radical party rally. The Union Leaguers, however, disrupted much of his impromptu speech with catcalls. In response, an ex-Confederate officer appeared at the head of a group of armed whites and began insulting the black Leaguers. Sensing the hostility of a gathering crowd of white Conservatives, Radical leaders persuaded their black friends to leave the area, but the Leaguers, also well armed, staged a defiant exit. Moments later, several whites attacked the departing black procession and shooting soon erupted from both sides. By the time the riot was over, twenty-seven black Leaguers and fourteen whites had been wounded; one of the whites later died.[7]

Recriminations followed. The *Daily Press and Times* declared that the Franklin "outrage" had instilled the Radical party with "fresh zeal" in its fight against the "treachery and malignity of the Conservative faction." William Mills and Horace H. Thomas, Tennessee delegates to a July meeting in New York City of the Union League of America, exploited the occasion to garner financial support for their party's campaign. Emphasizing the seemingly incessant anti-Radical violence in their state, Mills and Thomas defended the mobilization of the Guard: "Were it not for the militia there could be no election. The 50,000 black men who have been enfranchised would be shot down by rebels if they dared to vote." To the Brownlow administration, the riot, combined with the Gaut circular, the Conservatives' strategy for Middle Tennessee, and Pike's exhortations from the west (dubbed a "bastard rebellion" by the Radicals), was proof that a counterrevolution of some sort was underway. Consequently, for the rest of July, the anti-Radicals would feel the "full blast" of the Tennessee State Guard.[8]

General Cooper identified Middle Tennessee as the principal battle-ground. Thirteen companies of the State Guard would eventually be deployed there before the August election. Two of them, Capt. Joseph H. Blackburn's Company A and Capt. William S. Stuart's Company K, were already actively engaged. The Conservative party's aggressive stance in early July threatened the Radical control these two units had helped establish in June. Warren County continued to prove especially troublesome. There, W. J. Clift, a former colonel in the Union army and a Conservative candidate for the Tennessee General Assembly, spear-headed a strong effort to defeat Radicalism. For weeks, Clift had been lambasting the Brownlow administration, urging local Conservatives to permit ex-Confederates access to the ballot. When McMinnville's Conservative civil authorities, emboldened by the Gaut circular, attempted to halt Registrar William Baker's activities, Clift eagerly joined the battle. Accusing Baker of various improprieties, Clift obtained an injunction against the registrar, which effectively halted voter registration while Baker defended himself in court. Lt. William Cravens, who had arrived with a squad of militia at the end of June, warned Clift and his fellow Conservatives that they had no authority to interfere with registration. At Clift's prompting, the chairman of the county court replied that "the restraint of the military would not be regarded." With the county sher-iff providing armed support, the Conservative court fined Baker $150 and dared Cravens to intervene.[9]

Captain Blackburn was quick to aid his lieutenant. With orders to "*watch* Cliffe," Blackburn arrived at McMinnville on July 12 with twenty men (bringing the State Guard forces in that town to thirty-five soldiers) and took command. The adjutant general certainly wanted to quell the political defiance in Warren, but he cautioned Blackburn to handle Clift with care in order to avoid charges of military despotism: "Have him arrested by civil process under the Sedition law not by the military." Blackburn's presence appears to have broken the Conservatives' resolve: Clift backed down without being arrested, registration resumed, and

Warren County remained relatively quiet for the duration of the campaign. This outcome prompted the Radical *McMinnville Enterprise* to exclaim that the militia was "the best prescription for disloyalty ever yet discovered."[10]

As Blackburn neutralized Conservative opposition in Warren County, Capt. William S. Stuart encountered renewed troubles in White. On July 1, an ex-Confederate approached the perimeter of Stuart's command at "Camp Stokes" (named after Radical congressman William B. Stokes) near Yankeytown. From a distance, the Rebel unleashed a fusillade of profanity, calling the men of Company K "d—d horse thieves" and swearing that the "white men was going to bust up the d—d militia and . . . whip out the D—d negro." Pickets apprehended the man and Stuart confined him under guard until the following day. As this incident transpired, three ex-Confederates attacked the farm of a white Radical named Rigsby. The assailants fired their pistols at Rigsby's house, insulted the females inside with language so shocking that one reportedly "fainted," and, before riding off, threatened to kill Rigsby himself. Stuart sent a detachment in pursuit, but he doubted whether the civil authorities would prosecute the perpetrators if he caught them. Exasperated by ex-Confederate harassment, Stuart exploded to General Cooper: "If we have to take such abuse as they have been giving us we are going to quit & git to killing them catch us if they can for I had rather die and go to hell as to be run over by a set of rebels."[11]

A short time after submitting this fiery report, Captain Stuart carried out his threatened violence in an unexpected way. On the night of July 15, an intoxicated Pvt. W. B. Davis surprised his comrades by cursing the State Guard as "the d—d militia." Davis then entered Stuart's tent and provoked a fight with the captain. Stuart, however, twice knocked his assailant to the ground before placing him under arrest. As the company soon learned, Davis had been a bounty jumper during the Civil War, deserting from several regiments, Confederate and Union. In Stuart's view, Davis was a Confederate who "swore a lie" when he took the oath to join the State Guard. In any event, Davis escaped from the stockade later that night, but was shot through the bowels by pursuing sentries. According to the *Union and Dispatch*, Stuart then staked his wounded captive to the ground leaving him to bleed to death. Stuart's report, however, indicates that Davis received medical attention, despite his protests and incessant cursing, but died the following day. Anti-Radicals branded

Davis's death "a Fiendish Murder," but Stuart placed the blame and outcome squarely on the disloyalty of the deceased militia private.[12]

In addition to combating these various anti-Radical challenges, both internal as well as external, Captains Blackburn and Stuart continued to provide security for William B. Stokes's congressional campaign. Blackburn's men typically served as escort in the southern half of the Third Congressional District, Stuart's men in the northern half. General Cooper never forbade this overtly partisan duty provided it did not interfere with the primary mission of protecting voter registration. When ex-Confederates killed the brother of Fentress registrar Perry O. Dowdy on June 15, Cooper ordered Stuart to investigate. Evidently, the situation required the deployment of militia. On July 9, a forty-man detachment from Company K set up camp in neighboring Overton County and remained there for the duration of the campaign.[13]

Traveling with Stokes produced additional controversies for the State Guard. Running against Stokes was Eli G. Fleming, a former captain in Stokes's Civil War regiment (W. J. Clift served as Fleming's unofficial campaign manager). Bad blood existed between the two opponents. Stokes had been instrumental in getting Fleming dishonorably discharged for disobedience and incompetence at the battle of Murfreesboro. During the campaign of 1867, Stokes accused Fleming of trying to assassinate him at a Van Buren County rally, and attributed his survival to the presence of Blackburn's militia. Fleming, in turn, accused the militia of trying to kill him on at least two occasions. On July 5, "five ruffians" waylaid the Conservative candidate's buggy. Furious at not finding Fleming, but rather his black servant, they vandalized the buggy and chased the driver into the woods. Fleming claimed that Lt. William L. Hathaway, who had described Fleming as a "liar, scoundrel and coward," commanded the assailants. On July 15, Conservatives in McMinnville persuaded Fleming not to make a speech there as Captain Blackburn had supposedly declared that he would not tolerate Fleming's presence. To counter Stokes's militia escort, Fleming petitioned the federal garrison for a bodyguard of U.S. troops, but his request was denied.[14]

The *Republican Banner* sympathized with Fleming. In the final weeks of July, it described a scene of almost daily militia atrocities in the state's Third District. Without identifying specific State Guard officers or companies (which this newspaper usually did), the *Banner* charged that the militia "rob, burn, threaten and even kill their enemies with impunity. . . .

They spare no one." This newspaper alleged that the militia plundered the home of a "poor widow" in Van Buren County. It reported that the militia whipped several ex-Confederates in White County and prevented them from tending to their crops. Finally, it claimed that the militia vowed to "kill every man who put his pen" to a Warren County petition calling for relief from "Brownlow's terrible carniverous militia." How General Cooper managed to "terrorize" an eighteen-county district with a total force of 180 men, the *Banner* did not explain.[15]

As Captains Blackburn and Stuart worked to preserve Radical control in their respective areas of operation, Capt. William O. Rickman brought his maligned brand of law enforcement to Marshall County. He and his Company H arrived in Lewisburg in Marshall County on June 22, after a forty-two-mile march from Franklin County, and set up camp on the local fairgrounds. Two days later, he dispatched Lt. John J. Mankin and twenty-five men to neighboring Giles County to facilitate registration there. Marshall's Radicals welcomed Company H "with glad hearts." Registrar Robert Wiley, in particular, was thankful for the militia's presence, for according to Rickman, "the colored men were afraid to register until we came to this place." Perhaps cognizant of Rickman's treatment of Franklin's white populace, Marshall whites accorded the militia captain noticeable respect. In a county that had voted for secession by more than 90 percent, Rickman reported that even "the Rebels meet us friendly," and he predicted that he would "get a long smoothely."[16]

All did go well for Captain Rickman throughout the final month of the campaign. Although Conservatives protested the "partisan" registration of voters, they commended Rickman's unexpected professionalism. After watching the militiamen for a few days, a correspondent for the *Union and Dispatch* noted that "the troops are very quiet and orderly, and in justice of Capt. R., he has so far, disavowed any intention of interfering in the election." Rather than prowling the countryside for ex-Confederate renegades, as he did in Franklin, Rickman devoted his energies to providing security for the political canvass. In one instance, a squad of twelve men stood silent watch over a joint debate between Radical James Mullins and Conservative Edmund Cooper at Cornersville. The only notable incident involving Rickman's command occurred during a Fourth of July celebration in neighboring Lincoln County. General Cooper had ordered Company H to oversee Radical rallies in four counties—Marshall, Lincoln, Giles, and Lawrence. At Rickman's request, a black Radical named Dr. Wood addressed large black audiences in Lewisburg and Fayetteville in Lincoln County. During the Fayetteville rally, an ex-Confederate broke through the crowd and threatened "the nigger speaker" with a pistol. Rickman's militiamen quickly "seized the ruffian and quieted him in a very summary manner." The celebrations in Giles and Lawrence, for which Lieutenant Mankin was responsible, passed off without any disturbances. In contrast to its reprehensible conduct in Franklin County, Company H was a model of restraint in Marshall and Giles, and the Radical party prospered in those counties as a result. Captain Rickman later gloated to headquarters, "I won the confidence of all Loyal men and the Rebels say that we have Conducted our selfs well."[17]

Replacing Rickman in Franklin County was Capt. George W. Kirk, whose Company A, Second Regiment, arrived toward the end of June. Franklin whites greeted their new militia commander with scorn. Kirk was told that "he had better watch out." Some of the locals even threatened to poison any well used by the State Guard. Adding to the hostile reception was the murder of two Franklin blacks during Company A's first two weeks in the county. Undaunted, Kirk carried out his mission with aplomb, picking up a few local whites as recruits in the process. He established his headquarters at Tullahoma with his company in bivouac on the grounds of the town's private academy. When white residents insisted that he move his camp elsewhere, Kirk refused, whereupon the school closed in protest. On June 21, Kirk moved half of his men to Winchester under Lt. Francis Kirk.[18]

Captain Kirk devoted much of his time to revitalizing the county's Radical party. On July 1, acting on the governor's condemnation of the Gaut circular, Kirk ordered Conservative leaders in Winchester to halt their efforts to appoint election judges. The Conservatives reluctantly complied, and Registrar D. E. Davenport completed his duties without further interference. On July 4, a detachment of militia provided security for a Radical rally in Winchester attended by some eight hundred blacks. At the request of the black leaders, Captain Kirk personally hoisted an American flag with appropriate pomp and ceremony. After castigating some ex-Confederate hecklers, Kirk headed a parade of "loyal colored men," under a militia escort, through the streets and out of the town toward Decherd. En route, several hundred more supporters joined the throngs, including some black women who carried a large portrait of

93

Abraham Lincoln. The procession, now more than thirteen hundred, halted at intervals to listen to impromptu speeches by Radical office seekers. A rain shower eventually dispersed the crowd, but Jacob W. Brown, a Radical candidate for the general assembly, was so delighted by the event, and by Kirk's performance, that he boasted to the governor that troublesome Franklin had become "the Banner County of the State."[19]

The killing of one of Kirk's men only a couple of days later abruptly shattered the Radicals' newfound mood of confidence. On July 6, Pvt. Martin Jones and a comrade entered the Tullahoma general store of ex-Confederate DeWitt Bennett in search of tobacco. When Bennett handed them a package, the two men, who apparently had no money, pretended to make off with the tobacco "in a sort of playful manner." Bennett was not amused, and after grabbing the package from the two pranksters, he ushered them out of his store and locked the door. For some reason, Private Jones, accompanied by Sgt. John Hughes, returned. An apprehensive Bennett then fired a pistol at the men, killing Jones instantly with a shot to the head. According to Conservative accounts, the two militiamen were "tipsy" and tried to batter their way into the store. According to the Radicals, Bennett was a vindictive, splenetic man who opened fire after the militiamen merely "knocked" on his door. A coroner's jury ruled that the death of the twenty-four-year-old Jones was the result of a "malicious shooting."[20]

In the furor that followed, Captain Kirk remained calm, and he restrained his outraged men from exacting revenge. The Conservative press depicted Jones's death as the consequence of a policy that permitted the State Guard to "plunder 'rebels' at will." The Radical press intimated that the killing of Jones was retribution for the death of the ex-Confederate Brown a month before. Kirk, however, avoided making accusations and concentrated on defusing the situation. Militia efforts to arrest Bennett failed, he having apparently found refuge with local ex-Confederates. He later notified the public via the *Republican Banner* that he would surrender himself only to civilian authorities. Kirk suspected that the *Banner's* correspondent knew of Bennett's whereabouts and demanded, in vain, that that organ's editors cooperate with his efforts to uphold the law. As late as November 1867, Bennett was still at large, while his lawyer negotiated terms for surrender. Significantly, Kirk arrested Sergeant Hughes for his role in the tragedy and remanded him to the state penitentiary. A court-martial later found Hughes guilty of intoxication while on duty and of illegal entrance into Bennett's store. Hughes was reduced in rank with forfeiture of two months' wages.[21]

Kirk's impartiality appears to have mitigated Franklin's anti-Radical antipathy. In mid-July, Kirk reported that "all is going smooth here," a painful, personal bout with diarrhea notwithstanding. However, Edmund Cooper, Conservative candidate for Congress, frowned on Kirk's public advocacy of the Radicals and his increasing proclivity to attend joint debates with his men standing near the speakers. At a joint debate in Salem, for instance, anti-Radicals claimed that Kirk surrounded the platform with one hundred militiamen. Fearful that General Cooper had plans to reassign Kirk's command, the formerly optimistic Jacob Brown begged the general to keep the entire company in Franklin to ensure "the *fair expression* of the *Public Voice.*" Company A remained, and the county was relatively quiet in the final weeks of the campaign.[22]

Following Kirk to Middle Tennessee was Capt. James R. Evans and his Company I, fresh from its encounter with Etheridge in Morristown. Leaving a detachment of forty men under Lt. John N. Ellis in Claiborne County, Evans reached Humphreys County on June 28. Humphreys's whites had voted unanimously for secession in 1861 and Registrar William Welch wanted to ensure that these "persons" did not go to the polls in 1867. To aid Welch, Evans stationed twenty-nine men under Lt. James A. England at Johnsonville, while he commanded thirty men at the county seat of Waverly. On July 13, Evans concentrated his forces at Johnsonville, where Registrar Welch was completing his duties. With the militia at his disposal, Welch brushed aside a timid Conservative effort to execute the Gaut circular, registered over three hundred blacks and whites, and a fortnight before the election confidently informed the governor that Humphreys, "Rebel as it is," would vote the Radical ticket.[23]

Only one incident disturbed Company I's occupation of Humphreys. The day after his arrival in Johnsonville, Lieutenant England provided security for a Radical rally, one that featured General Cooper as a guest speaker. In the crowd was a "fool drunk" ex-Confederate named Thomas J. Warren. Bored by the "Radical harangue," Warren staggered off toward a dry goods store babbling that he wanted to kill a "d—d Yankee." When storekeeper Dan Rice tried to calm Warren down, the inebriated Rebel brandished a pistol and shot Rice through the chest. England and his men rushed to the scene and arrested Warren. Newspapers roundly condemned the shooting—even the *Republican*

Banner, which had only that morning denounced the militia's presence in Humphreys, presciently quipping that "a few murders of unoffending 'Rebels' are needed to fire the Radical Party." The Radicals were fired up, but not by murder, rather by Lieutenant England's swift law enforcement.[24]

Due to logistical problems, Company F, First Regiment, under Capt. Shadrick T. Harris marked time in Jefferson County for nearly a month after its muster. Not until July 3 did the unit finally get into the action. General Cooper decided to split the oversized company (113 men) into three detachments in order to cover more territory. Harris proceeded to West Tennessee with over 50 men, while his first lieutenant, Edwin R. Hall, went to Cheatham County with 30 men and his second lieutenant, John W. Roberts, went to Stewart County with about 20. Stewart was heavily ex-Confederate, but with the exception of an episode back in April, involving the desecration of some Union graves, nothing controversial had occurred there, and after Roberts's arrival the county remained "tolerby quiete," as he reported. Roberts developed a good working relationship with Registrar R. A. Salisbury and the registration of voters proceeded speedily.[25]

In contrast to Roberts's experience, Lieutenant Hall's assignment in Cheatham was marked by tension. The county had cast its lot with the Confederacy by over 90 percent in 1861. In 1867, Cheatham's whites were no less united in their opposition to Radical rule. Earlier in June, local Radicals beseeched the governor for protection following the rancorous disruption of a party meeting in Ashland City. According to their petition, a group of ex-Confederates rejected an offer to divide time "politely" and instead cursed "the Brownlow *clique* and nigger Leagues" of the county. Registrar E. B. Harris, in particular, endured scathing verbal abuse. Later that night, these Rebels "prominaded the streets, hurrahing for Davis and the Confederacy and . . . discharging their pieces." These aggressive displays succeeded in cowing Cheatham's freedmen, who, although organized into a Union League of 150 members, made it clear that they would rather "yield and remain neutral . . . than . . . be murdered and bushwhacked by rebels for supporting a party that [was] either unable or unwilling to afford them the promised protection."[26]

Two days before Lieutenant Hall arrived with the "promised protection," Registrar Harris took matters into his own hands with tragic consequences. According to the *Daily Press and Times,* after rebuking county Conservatives for trying to appoint election officials in violation of the Franchise Act of 1867, Harris encountered an armed and angry Hardy Brinkley, one of the "ruffians" involved in the Ashland City fracas. "In self-defense," Harris drew his own pistol and shot Brinkley dead. According to the Conservatives, however, Brinkley's death was the culmination of a daylong rampage by Harris and his friend, Stephen Martin, a white member of the Union League. After supposedly disrupting a Conservative meeting, the two men ambushed Brinkley with shotgun fire.[27]

Harris and Martin were arrested and arraigned in Ashland City on July 6 before a bipartisan court. Lieutenant Hall spent the next couple of weeks providing security for the trial, worrying all the while that he might have to combat an ex-Confederate lynch mob. Whether in jail, in court, or traveling in between, the two defendants received round-the-clock protection from a squad of militia. Radicals publicly lamented Brinkley's death, while Conservatives exploited it. Dubbing the killing "another Brownlow murder," the *Republican Banner* tried to implicate the militia, claiming that Stephen Martin was a commissioned officer in the State Guard. (Martin was not in the militia, and no record exists of any application by him for a commission.) Other Conservative newspapers argued that Brinkley's death was part of a growing pattern of Radical vigilantism, one emboldened by the activation of a partisan militia under a "fiend-like Governor." Predicting more atrocities, the *Union and Dispatch* bellowed, "How long will the God of Heaven look down upon such crimes and withhold His terrible vengeance?" In mid-July, the Harris-Martin trial was moved, for reasons of safety, to Nashville, where both defendants were released on August 2, the judge ruling that the men had acted in the "heat of passion." For the rest of the campaign, Lieutenant Hall avoided further publicity, provoking Conservative ire on only one occasion. On July 27, his men caused a "disturbance" when they marched past a Conservative rally en route to their camp.[28]

In the weeks prior to the election, four all-black companies and two racially mixed companies also made their presence felt in Middle Tennessee. Their deployment was undoubtedly the most "radical" feature of the Radical campaign. If white militiamen elicited bitter complaints from the anti-Radicals, then black militiamen were sure to send them into paroxysms of protest. Nevertheless, General Cooper made full use of the militia forces at his disposal, regardless of their race. After all, he could point to the solid performance of Capt. George E. Grisham's mixed company in Sullivan County, the *Republican Banner*'s racial caricatures notwithstanding, as an indication of how uniformed blacks behaved.

Capt. Thompson McKinley's Company B, Second Regiment, operated throughout the campaign in Sumner County, where it had mustered. From the perspective of the county's whites, this "colored militia" wasted no time before making a nuisance of itself. According to the anti-Radical press (from which comes most of the information on this company's activities), one of McKinley's "very first acts of lawlessness" was his selection of an abandoned lot near Gallatin's Female Academy to set up camp. Given contemporary phobias about black men and white women, the site was a poor choice. There is, however, no record of any contact between the black militiamen and the students. There was contact between black militiamen and the white male residents of Gallatin. According to Conservative accounts, on June 14 a militia private "insolently pushed" a Dr. Tompkins off a sidewalk. Tompkins, in turn, "knocked the black rascal down." The doctor fled the scene when more militiamen arrived, but black rage had apparently been aroused. The militiamen reportedly gathered at a black saloon, where "liquor began to circulate freely and the fear of a riot became general." Conservative newspapers claimed that only the timely intervention of U.S. troops averted a disaster, but not before some of "Brownlow's pets" exchanged blows with the regulars. Army captain Edwin H. Leib vehemently denied that his men brawled with the militia and expressed no knowledge of any threatened riot. In a remarkable instance of editorial contrition, a chastened *Republican Banner* apologized to Leib and admitted that "our details were imperfect. . . . Our informant had got them second hand."[29]

By the end of June, Company B was ready for active duty. Captain McKinley, Sumner's Radical candidate for the state legislature and its voting registrar, made good use of his militia command to canvass the county. On one occasion, his men went about the countryside posting campaign signs and promoting the Radical party. On another, the men of Company B stood by in formation during their captain's address to a black crowd in Saundersville. Whites objected not only to McKinley's abuse of power but also to his troops' behavior. Those in Gallatin complained that black troopers "have a practice of firing their guns near the turnpike . . . to the great terror of passersby."[30]

On July 1, General Cooper ordered the unit to Hartsville, a town along the Sumner-Smith county line. The ex-Confederate guerrilla leader

Ellis Harper was reportedly in the vicinity, and Cooper wanted McKinley's militia to stand watch. (Cooper may also have wanted to remove Company B from Gallatin prior to Emerson Etheridge's scheduled July 2 speech in that town.) Although he later stumped the eastern part of the county, McKinley did not accompany his unit to Hartsville "being busily engaged in filling out certificates for colored voters." Instead, Lt. I. N. Phillips commanded the company on its first genuine mission.[31]

Described by Conservatives as "a little upstart," Phillips displayed zealous leadership. On completing a sixteen-mile road march, Phillips rested the company on the outskirts of Hartsville. He then reminded his men that they were in "the enemies' country" and ordered them to keep a sharp lookout for Harper and his "blood-thirsty gang." After ostensibly avoiding the Etheridge cavalcade as it passed through Hartsville on July 3, Phillips scouted the surrounding area. He made several attempts to question the locals, presumably about Harper's whereabouts, but received mostly cold silence. The *Republican Banner* later claimed that Phillips was really going around looking for room and board so that he would not have to share outdoor quarters with his "dusky warriors." Fearful of a clash with Harper's ex-Confederates, Phillips ordered his sentinels to shoot without hesitation if they suspected intruders. Unfortunately, these instructions contributed to the killing of seventeen-year-old Pvt. John Apples. On the night of July 6, Apples, who was absent without leave at the time, tried to "force the guard" and was shot dead. The *Republican Banner* smugly noted that the incident had resulted in "a dead negro—one less of the Brownlow's State Guard." Shortly after this tragedy, Company B returned to Gallatin (and to Captain McKinley), where the men constructed a makeshift "fort" on a hill near the town's railroad station and then awaited election day.[32]

Arguably the most controversial militia unit deployed during the campaign of 1867, and the one most detested by the anti-Radicals, was Company G, Second Regiment. This company was all black, including its captain, James H. Sumner. In the first week of July, General Cooper planned to send Sumner to Williamson County in response to Registrar D. M. Cliffe's request for protection against alleged ex-Confederate "proscription" of local Radicals. Before Company G was ready to depart, however, the Franklin race riot erupted and Adjutant General Samuel Hunt called on the federal garrison to restore order "for the time being." Gen. Thomas Duncan, post commander in Nashville, complied, and on July 7 a company of federal troops arrived in Franklin and began an investigation into the violence. Duncan, however, apparently failed to understand that Hunt's request was for temporary assistance only, and he was unaware that militia was en route. Despite the potential for a conflict over authority, General Cooper dispatched Company G as scheduled. Captain Sumner's orders reflected awareness of the racial hostility his unit was likely to encounter. He was to "preserve strict order and military discipline among his men and see that they offer insults to no one."[33]

For the next several weeks, the anti-Radical press maintained a steady barrage of vituperation against Captain Sumner. The *Republican Banner* professed incredulity over General Cooper's decision to send "an infuriate negro," commanding a company of "irresponsible and excited negroes," to the site of a "negro riot." Prior to his unit's departure by rail, Sumner had marched his newly outfitted command through the streets of Nashville, pausing outside of a saloon (possibly his own) to address his men. Radical observers noted the captain's gratitude for the chance to serve his state and commended his exhortation to his men to "never dishonor the flag." Conservative witnesses, however, claimed that the speech was inflammatory and that the militiamen were thoroughly drunk. Sumner supposedly reminded his men of the Fort Pillow massacre, and declared that if the ex-Confederates of Franklin defied his authority, "he would order his company to shoot them down like dogs." Nashville mayor Matt Brown proclaimed Sumner's conduct "coarse, violent, seditious and menacing." The *Daily Press and Times,* however, refuted the mayor's charge, stating that the militiamen's only "crime is that they march under the Stars and Stripes."[34]

Company G arrived at Franklin on the evening of July 8, like "a conquering army," according to local whites. Etheridge was scheduled to speak in the town on the tenth, and many Conservatives feared that "the sable" Sumner would exploit the occasion to "clean out the secesh." Although Captain Sumner marched his company through the streets of Franklin on July 9 as a demonstration of State Guard power, he kept his men in camp on the outskirts of town during the Conservative rally the following day. Federal troops under Capt. Dan M. Burke provide security for the event. The Etheridge visit passed off without incident and Radicals applauded Sumner's leadership: "There has been no intoxication, no insubordination, no outrages, nothing of the sort."[35]

The dual command structure in Franklin afforded the Conservatives an opportunity to depict discord between the State Guard and the U.S.

Army. According to them, both Captain Burke and General Duncan were unhappy with Sumner's presence in Franklin. The *Union and Dispatch* claimed that Duncan wanted the black militiamen arrested for their "mischiefs." One such instance apparently occurred on July 14, when Company G marched double-time through the streets in response to a call from Registrar Cliffe. Army sergeant M. V. B. Hazen intercepted the militia column and ordered the men back to their camp. The militiamen, again described as drunk, complied only after learning that the whole commotion was a false alarm. Incidents like this supposedly undermined the army's respect for the black militia. White enlisted regulars refused to salute Captain Sumner and his lieutenants. The *Republican Banner* printed a crude, and likely apocryphal, anecdote that illustrated the army's contempt for the "bold Othello." One day, so the story began, Sumner approached an army sergeant on the streets of Franklin and declared, "I out rank you." "Yes," replied the sergeant, "in smell."[36]

To the *Daily Press and Times,* stories depicting rancor between Company G and the federal garrison were part of a Conservative effort to divert attention from the real problem—the anti-Radical animus that provoked the Franklin riot. This newspaper countered its rivals' allegations with articles that described a harmonious relationship between generals Cooper and Duncan. It quoted a black militiaman, who insisted that a "perfect good feeling" existed between the regulars and the militia. Nevertheless, General Cooper disapproved of the redundant assignment of forces in Franklin. On more than one occasion, he was compelled to go in person to Franklin to sort out jurisdictional confusion. Toward the end of the month, he employed detachments from Company G in more useful tasks. On July 22, one of Sumner's lieutenants embarked with fifty men on a three-day patrol through the countryside around Triune in Williamson County. It was hoped that this show of force would encourage the area's eligible blacks to register and vote. Similarly, on July 29, 1st Lt. George Sumner headed with half of Company G to Columbia in Maury County in response to various registration difficulties and to provide security on election day. All the while, Captain Sumner remained in Franklin, as much for the sake of Radical pride at that point as to enforce the laws. To the dismay of local whites, he and his half-strength company participated in a Union League parade on July 29 and later forced a white employer to compensate a black worker who took time off to attend the political festivities. Such actions prompted the *Daily Press and Times* to declare that "the spirit of riot . . . has been most effectually quenched in Franklin." Cooper, however, ultimately conceded full authority to the army; he placed Sumner (and elements of the recently mustered black Company K, Second Regiment) under Captain Burke's command for the day of the election. The *Republican Banner* rejoiced at this final development: "So the black man will be taught subordination for the future."[37]

If racial slurs and professional humiliation were not enough, Captain Sumner also endured some aggravating complications with logistical support. Only a few days before the election, many of his men still lacked a complete set of uniforms, among other basic issue items. "One third of the men are preatty in need," he informed the quartermaster, "they are hard laying over the ground at night in the dew,—I want Blankets Coats Tents Drawers and Shirts." Perhaps Sumner found solace in the fact that at least it was summertime.[38]

While his all-black companies pressed on under an implacable propaganda assault, General Cooper deployed the rest of the State Guard. Over the final two weeks of the campaign, he stationed three additional companies in Middle Tennessee. As far as the Brownlow administration was concerned, there were plenty of "rebellious" counties in need of State Guard pacification. Moreover, Cooper decided that Captains Blackburn and Rickman were overextended, both being responsible for four or more counties, and in need of some relief. Enter the racially mixed units of George E. Grisham (Company B, First Regiment) and John L. Kirk (Company C, Second Regiment) and the all-white command of Robert L. Hall (Company C, First Regiment), all from East Tennessee.[39]

Grisham and Hall arrived together in Nashville on July 18–19. City Radicals were jubilant at the presence of over two hundred loyal militiamen. They described Grisham as mentally "whole-souled" and physically in "fine trim," affectionately referred to Hall as "Friend Bob," and praised the enlisted men on their disciplined military bearing. Conservatives were less impressed. The *Union and Dispatch* conceded that Hall's all-white company, decked out in distinctive Burnside hats, "made a better show" than any other militia unit it had thus far observed, but declared that Grisham's mixed command was "as ragged and dirty a set of green looking bumpkins as ever went barefoot." Company B's flag, inscribed with "Tennessee Vol's," was ridiculed as "bogus." Unfortunately for the

Radicals, at some point during these companies' stay, three or four militiamen wandered into a saloon, got drunk, and started a row. After knocking down the barkeep, they stumbled onto the street and fired a gunshot into a neighboring building. A passing constable sounded the alarm, but the militiamen fled the scene. Civilian witnesses magnified the incident into a street riot, but no arrests were made and the militia companies soon headed for their final destinations, leaving in their wake yet another "outrage" for the anti-Radical press to exploit.[40]

Captain Hall moved his men to nearby Buena Vista Springs, where they would act as a State Guard reserve. Captain Grisham's company, however, was split into two forces. 1st Lt. Nelson McLaughlin commanded one of them, a forty-man detachment, which he marched to Lebanon in Wilson County on July 20 to protect the Radical minority there. Previously, Wilson had been part of Captain Blackburn's rather large militia bailiwick. In early July, however, new priorities compelled Blackburn to withdraw his squad from Lebanon. As a result, Wilson Conservatives renewed their challenge to Registrar W. H. Goodwin's control over the election. Simultaneously, ex-Confederate landlords threatened their black field hands that they would "be turned out of employment if they vote the Brownlow ticket." After setting up camp, McLaughlin publicly warned the Conservatives that he would not permit them to interfere with Goodwin's duties. He tempered his address, however, by assuring them that his men would remain quietly in camp "unless a conflict is forced." The Conservatives did not challenge McLaughlin.[41]

Captain Grisham took the rest of his Company B to Fayetteville in Lincoln County. Captain Rickman had temporarily occupied that town during the Fourth of July celebration. Registrar John Carey, however, desired a full-time militia force. "I have been cursed and threatened," he complained to Governor Brownlow, adding that ex-Confederate harassment inhibited Radical efforts to organize blacks into a Union League. A militant speech by Emerson Etheridge on July 8 exacerbated Carey's plight. Along with his typical denunciations of the governor, Etheridge declared the militia a violation of the Bill of Rights and insinuated that the "Caries" of Tennessee were thieves deserving to be overthrown. Grisham was sent to the rescue. Before he departed Nashville, however, Grisham paid a surprise visit to the office of the anti-Radical *Republican Banner*, where he told the staff that he felt "no spirit of hostility to the people" of Lincoln County. Grisham, an editor himself, believed that this

Nelson McLaughlin, 1864–65. Courtesy of Tennessee State
Museum Collection.

face-to-face meeting might change the *Banner*'s opinion of the State Guard. The editors did, indeed, acknowledge Grisham's sincerity and deemed the unusual dialogue "a cheering indication" that some of the militia units could actually be respectable. From that point on, the *Banner* spared Company B negative press coverage.[42]

From Grisham's perspective, his deployment to Lincoln was a resounding success. After arriving in Tullahoma by rail on July 22 and drawing additional equipment, he commenced a march to Fayetteville on the evening of the twenty-fifth. As a hot summer sun rose on the morning of the twenty-sixth, Grisham and his men beheld a beautiful rolling countryside laced in fields of cotton and corn. Throughout the trek, Grisham rode up and down his column conversing with the men and dispelling rumors that three thousand armed ex-Confederates awaited them to give battle. When the company entered Fayetteville, Mayor Robert Farquharson, a former Confederate colonel, commended its orderly deportment. Grisham thereupon proclaimed, "our whole mission among you is peace, quiet and the enforcement of the laws." After paying a friendly visit on the local newspaper editor, Grisham helped his men establish a "good & healthy camp." Conservatives were generally impressed by Grisham, whose militiamen were described as "delightful electioneering wheelhorses."[43]

Although Grisham apparently enjoyed his Guard duty in Fayetteville, there was cause for concern in the last few days before the election. The Lincoln County sheriff was an ex-Confederate. Moreover, he was dubious of Grisham's goodwill and pointedly warned the militia captain that if the Radicals tried to attend the polls in procession, he would call out some five hundred armed "police" to disperse them. Grisham informed General Cooper that he would not hesitate to meet force with force: "I will fight them with ball cartridges and bayonets until ammunition and men are exhausted." Determined to protect the polls and the county's five hundred registered black voters, Grisham ordered all saloons closed on election day. Furthermore, on the advice of the registrar, he stationed ten men under Lt. Joseph February at one of the county's more remote polling sites.[44]

The final addition to the State Guard presence in Middle Tennessee came on July 24, when Capt. John L. Kirk and his racially mixed command arrived in Nashville en route for Montgomery and Robertson, counties with strong Confederate sympathies. Montgomery whites had recently petitioned the federal garrison for some soldiers to maintain order on the day of the election. The request may have been a compromise between local Radicals who wanted militia and local Conservatives who wanted no troops at all. General Duncan, however, referred the matter to General Cooper, who ordered Kirk to fulfill the task. On July 25, Kirk entered the county seat of Clarksville with forty men, whom the *Republican Banner* characterized as "colored warriors . . . panting for military glory." Their presence was like a surge of electricity through the ranks of the Radicals. "The Negroes are jubilant [and] the Reb citizens are more fearful," noted Registrar John L. Roberts. Many county blacks volunteered to join Kirk's company and over the next several days he mustered in over sixty additional recruits, bringing his force in Clarksville to about one hundred militiamen.[45]

While Kirk headed for Clarksville, his first lieutenant, David E. Burchfield, took a thirty-man detachment to Springfield in Robertson County. Given that Kirk's force was predominately black, most of Burchfield's men were probably white. The distinction was significant, for Robertson County was a hotbed of ex-Confederate outlawry. Registrar H. D. Featherston was undoubtedly relieved when Burchfield's contingent arrived, but his prediction that all would thenceforth be "peaceable and quiet" proved wrong. On the night of July 30, unidentified raiders fired rifle shots into the militia camp. Burchfield reacted decisively: "My men raleyed and gave a furius voley in the same direction." For the next ten minutes the militiamen anxiously stared into the darkness. Then, another shot rang out from the woods, followed by a shotgun blast. None of the troops was hit, however, and Burchfield was content merely to return fire until the attackers withdrew. The *Union and Dispatch* dismissed the State Guard's official report of the incident. According to this newspaper, one of Burchfield's few "colored" militiamen accidentally fired his weapon, "creating a temporary stampede, and setting the musketry to popping in all directions."[46]

Although General Cooper distributed most of his units in Middle Tennessee, the west was not neglected. Five militia companies plus one detachment would see action in West Tennessee. One of Cooper's main priorities was reinforcing Capt. John T. Robeson's hard-pressed forces in the northwest corner. For over a month, Robeson had been trying single-handedly to regulate political affairs in Obion, Weakley, Dyer, and Gibson counties. During a tour through several western counties in early

July, Secretary of State Andrew J. Fletcher observed that in spite of potential militia reprisals, "the rebels are brow-beating and threatening the negroes with all manner of punishment." He concluded that "the strong arm of military power is needed to keep them in check." Accordingly, on June 21, Cooper ordered Company G, First Regiment, under Capt. Silas L. Chambers, into the region. When the unit passed through Nashville, the anti-Radical press mocked it with typical venom: "The 'volunteers' [were] . . . armed to the teeth with rusty old shooting irons of uncouth finish and ancient make . . . some of them barefooted, and all of them notoriously ugly." The *Daily Press and Times* contradicted its rivals, describing the militiamen as "entirely worthy of the uniform" and promising that Chambers would "neither oppress or insult any man."[47]

The anti-Radicals were closer to the mark in their assessment; Company G's performance proved embarrassingly "ugly." While Lt. James W. Newport went to Dresden (Weakley County) with forty men, Captain Chambers headed for Trenton (Gibson County) with forty-five. Chambers arrived on June 28 and found everything "all rite." But the leadership and morale problems that marred his company's muster soon reemerged. Sometime during the first week of July, Chambers took one too many shots of whiskey and proceeded to make a jackass of himself before the citizens of Trenton. According to witnesses, the intoxicated Chambers "made some very Severe Threats to Burn the Town." All the while, the militia captain "flourished his pistol, Threatened to Shoot any one who interfered with him and used very obscene language." 1st Lt. Larken B. Gamble, the state's investigating officer and a member of the Knoxville Sons of Temperance, corroborated the charges. On Larken's recommendation, General Cooper, himself a teetotaler, punished the "disgraceful" company commander. Chambers was arrested and dishonorably discharged. Calling on the governor for clemency, Chambers meekly confessed, "It is true that I drink a little whiskey." He begged in vain for a second chance. The *Republican Banner* snickered at the episode: "He must be a wretch indeed who is not deemed worthy to hold a commission in Brownlow's militia."[48]

Captain Chambers's dismissal did not prevent the decline of Company G as a reliable militia unit. General Cooper placed Lieutenant Newport in command, but this officer evidently lacked what the general was looking for. Some time in the middle of July, Cooper promoted Pryor Adkins, one of the company's noncommissioned officers, to the captaincy. Adkins was a twenty-five-year-old Scott County farmer and a Civil War veteran. Under his direction, Company G provided protection for Gibson County registrar Robert E. Bogle, who added 350 blacks to his voting roster. At the end of July, however, Company G suffered another humiliation. For several days, local whites had been spreading rumors that a large ex-Confederate force was massing for an attack. When a group of boys fired off some skyrockets on the night of July 28 and then screeched an imitation of the Rebel yell, a jumpy Captain Adkins reportedly telegraphed for help, while his men "set to work with desperate energy to dig a ditch." The *Republican Banner* exaggerated many of the facts surrounding this "terrible scare," but Adkins's overreaction earned him the sobriquet "Captain Shirttail." Adkins appears to have lost the respect of some of his men as well, for he was forced to reduce three corporals to the rank of private for "mutinous conduct." An exasperated General Cooper authorized Adkins to use any means necessary to instill better discipline.[49]

Company G failed to provide Captain Robeson much relief. Fortunately for the Radicals, Robeson was one of the most able officers in the State Guard. In the first half of July, he led patrols through Obion, Dyer, and Weakley counties in his ongoing effort to establish Radical control. He was pleased "to find the Freedmen all for Brownlow," but he also reported that "the Rebels are verry bitter." Wherever he went, ex-Confederates vowed their intention to "vote or die." While scouting in Weakley County (where Lieutenant Newport was ostensibly in charge) on July 13, Robeson captured Martin Vowell, "a verry bad man." Vowell was part of an ex-Confederate band that boasted that it could "whip the State Troops." The prospect of clashing with Rebel vigilantes evidently excited Robeson. "I think I will have some fun," he confided to the adjutant general.[50]

The difficulty of bringing law and order to four large counties eventually discouraged even the doughty Robeson. Try as his did, he could not be everywhere all of the time. Leaving his foot soldiers in Obion County, Robeson kept his mounted section in motion. Beginning on July 19, he embarked on an ambitious eight-day patrol through Dyer, Gibson, and Lauderdale counties, the last one an extension of his already vast area of operations. Ex-Confederates in Dyer County took advantage of his absence to try to roll back Radicalism. On July 24, they disrupted a Union League meeting in Dyersburg with brickbats and pistol shots.

As a result, many blacks opted not to register. Only twenty-eight blacks received voting certificates from Registrar James McCoy during Robeson's excursion. On his return to Dyersburg, Robeson arrested several whites accused of perpetrating the attack. Nevertheless, he realized that he did not have enough men to garrison Dyer effectively. Moreover, he determined from his patrol that Lauderdale County needed militia and that Trenton, though occupied by a detachment from Company G, was essentially "controlled by the Rebels." General Cooper did augment Robeson's forces by attaching Capt. William C. Holt's thirty volunteers to Company E, but given the political challenges elsewhere in West and Middle Tennessee, no substantial reinforcements were available.[51]

As Robeson orchestrated State Guard activities in four counties, Capt. Judge K. Clingan had his hands full in one—Madison. Having ostensibly secured Haywood County for the Radicals, Clingan arrived at the town of Jackson in Madison in the last week of June. More than 99 percent of Madison's white electorate had voted for secession in 1861. In 1867, the county's whites were in no mood for the presence of a company of "Melish." Two years after the Civil War, Jackson still showed the effects of wartime devastation; entire blocks were little more than charred ruins. Local whites complained that business was poor and that many freedmen seemed to hang around doing nothing. Into this dismal setting came Company D, First Regiment, "without the slightest provocation," according to Conservatives.[52]

Clingan found the anti-Radicals of Madison far more truculent than those of Haywood. Shortly after his arrival, he earned the locals' ire when he forbade the carrying of firearms in public. Whether all complied or merely concealed their weapons is unclear, but the white townspeople did not hide their contempt for the militia. "They . . . scorn us as we pass," Clingan noted, and appear to have closed their shops to his men compelling the militia captain to rely exclusively on the quartermaster for supplies. On one occasion, a group of ex-Confederates confronted Clingan personally, cursing the captain and his "god damned Yankey and Brownlow militia." Toward the middle of July, Clingan reported that "there is something misteriouse going on in this place." For weeks, Madison whites had been creating a climate of fear, "doing all in their power to demoralize" Clingan's men. During the night, sporadic gunfire kept militia sentries on edge, while false alarms of murder had militia details chasing phantoms. During the day, Jackson residents tempted the militiamen to leave their posts with offers of clean clothes and home-cooked meals. Company D's morale suffered: sixteen men deserted during one ten-day period. While riding a man on a rail had quelled the harassment of his men in Haywood, Clingan proved reluctant to employ similar tactics in Madison. Instead, he appears to have holed up with his entire command in an encampment on the outskirts of town, leaving the countryside to the Rebels, except for an occasional mounted patrol.[53]

Clingan's defensiveness was a wise precaution. His scouts discovered the existence of several caches of regular army rifles (some stored in one of Jackson's banks). Additionally, they reported that a group of some five hundred ex-Confederates, whose "looks shows vengeance," had standing orders to assemble quickly should conflict with the militia arise. Clingan told General Cooper that "if it was not fear of more soldiers, the citizens would not allow us to remain here." Further complicating Clingan's task was a political circular distributed by county Conservatives urging ex-Confederates to participate in the election and chastising them for not trying to register. Evidently, the Conservatives hoped that a swarm of illegal certificate seekers would overwhelm Registrar Robert Medlin and inhibit his registration of blacks. One of Clingan's lieutenants overheard a Rebel exclaim that if whites were not allowed to vote, then "no d—d nigger should vote." Clingan concluded that Madison was "the worst place without any doubt in West Tennessee."[54]

As unnerving as all of this anti-Radical opposition must have been, Captain Clingan persevered in his duty. He requested permission from General Cooper to confiscate all weapons until after the election. He also maintained order, albeit with difficulty, during a mid-July Radical rally, one attended by several Rebels who mercilessly insulted the speakers. Finally, he remonstrated against the racial "hatered" of Madison's whites, particularly their maltreatment of a mentally and physically handicapped black man. Apparently, this former slave had recently become a ward of the county, costing the residents about twenty-five dollars for three months of care. Sometime in the first week of July, city officials cast the man into the streets outside the courthouse, where he lay virtually naked for over an hour. When Clingan demanded an explanation for this appalling act, one Conservative retorted that since "Brownlows malitia was the friend of the negro . . . let them take care of him." Clingan helped some locals blacks get the man into shelter, giving them five dollars out of his own pocket for food and clothes. Unfortunately, the man later died.

Clingan was disgusted by Madison's attitude toward the freedmen: "This is the feeling of the flower of the lost cause."[55]

Capt. Shadrack T. Harris of Company F, First Regiment, joined his militia compatriots in the west on July 4. Half of the company was on detached service in Middle Tennessee, but General Cooper assigned Harris and his remaining fifty men to Henry County. The unit's trip by rail was uncomfortable from start to finish. Through a scheduling miscommunication with the Edgefield & Kentucky, the company left Nashville in boxcars instead of passenger cars. An apologetic superintendent later installed some couches for the militiamen, but Captain Harris arrived at his destination in an irascible mood. Henry County had supported secession by nearly 85 percent in 1861, and its "rebellious" mindset had not diminished much by 1867. Registrar James B. Guthrie, whom local whites branded "an unfeeling brute, a faithless cur," had so far failed to register any blacks. Harris's arrival in the county seat of Paris on American independence day elicited a grim comment from the county newspaper: "Despotism fastened one of its armed heels on this quiet community. . . . We are overawed by the surveillance of an irresponsible body of armed men." Conservatives feared the worst from Harris, the man who had languished in a Confederate prison for over two years. White residents scrutinized every move by his men for signs of "drunken, indecent and lawless conduct." The *Republican Banner* even claimed that Harris had given his men orders to "burn the town and kill every rebel in it" if the election went against the Radicals. Harris hardly deserved the abuse. His occupation proved relatively uneventful and, in some respects, ineffective. Perhaps unable to act more forcefully because of his crippled condition, Harris submitted his letter of resignation one day before the election, citing "private business." Leaving the company first sergeant in charge in Cheatham, Lt. E. R. Hall rushed to Paris to take over, only to discover that Guthrie had managed to register just a few dozen voters.[56]

In contrast to Harris's, Capt. George Hamilton's experience in McNairy County was nerve-wracking. After mustering in his racially mixed Company E, Second Regiment, in mid-June, Hamilton established his base at Purdy, the county seat, and remained there for the duration of the campaign, the men possibly enjoying the comforts of wooden barracks constructed from lumber purchased by the quartermaster. For about a month, all was calm in the county, which had voted for secession by just under 70 percent. Hamilton and Registrar Levi Hurst appear to have quietly prepared the loyal voters for the upcoming election. In July, however, ex-Confederates mounted a serious challenge to Radical authority. On the night of the fifteenth, a small group of "bushwhackers" fired several gunshots into the militia encampment and then galloped off before the militiamen could return the fire. Having few horsemen, Captain Hamilton could undertake no pursuit. The *Daily Press and Times* condemned the sneak attack, proclaiming that "the Purdy guerrillas . . . richly deserve to dangle on the gallows."[57]

Less than two weeks later, a much larger group of ex-Confederates attacked. On the night of July 26, some fifteen to twenty men, heavily armed and with blackened faces, commenced firing on the militia encampment. This time, the assailants did not flee but instead made sporadic attacks throughout the night. The militiamen fired back as best they could from their position. With the light of dawn, however, Captain Hamilton went on the offensive. Placing his company in assault formation, he "charged the guerrillas and drove them pell-mell through the town to the woods." Three Rebels were reportedly wounded, while Company E miraculously suffered no casualties. Conservatives downplayed the incident as a "desultory skirmish."[58]

The following day, black Union Leaguers held a flag-raising rally in Purdy with Company E providing security. Several speeches were made, some apparently in honor of the militia's nighttime heroics, before three "pestiferous rebels" interrupted the proceedings with loud insults. When militia Sgt. James Hardin attempted to silence the men, he was shot through the shoulder. More shots were fired and more injuries were sustained before the militia restored order. Ex-Confederate Samuel Lewis was among the wounded. When he died two days later, McNairy's Conservative authorities tried to indict Captain Hamilton's black militiamen for murder. It is not clear what became of this legal action nor whether Sergeant Hardin recovered from his own wound. What is clear is that Hamilton faced a determined enemy in McNairy County. Few other militia companies expended as much ammunition as Company E appears to have discharged. Still, Hamilton held the field, and the anti-Radicals knew that he would not give up without a hard fight.[59]

Hamilton's lack of cavalry horses was a common deficiency in the State Guard. The militia act permitted a twenty-five-man mounted section for each company, but militiamen apparently had to provide their own steeds. With good quality horses often costing more than one hundred dollars, few volunteers owned one. As a result, many companies failed to field a complete complement of horsemen. This loss in mobility hindered the performance of some units, such as Hamiliton's. Some companies appear to have pooled their horses for joint use. Captains Grisham and G. W. Kirk, for example, occasionally borrowed extra mounts from Rickman's unit during the last half of July. (Much later in the deployment, General Cooper would implement an equitable redistribution of horses.) For those militiamen who did join with their own horse, the state compensated them forty cents per day for feed and grooming, but it is unclear if it reimbursed soldiers for horses that died in the line of duty. There is no indication, for instance, that the quartermaster ever settled a claim entered by Pvt. Joseph Law (Company I, First Regiment), who lost his mount, valued at one hundred dollars, while on patrol. For better or worse, the Brownlow administration avoided most of the costs that horses added to nineteenth-century military operations.[60]

The last State Guard unit to deploy to West Tennessee was Company F, Second Regiment, 1st Lt. Joseph M. Alexander commanding. In the second week of July, while waiting for orders, Alexander imposed quasi–martial law on the town of Loudon (Roane County). Claiming that the town was controlled by a "rebel dynasty" (although the county had voted against secession by over 70 percent), Alexander issued some strict decrees, such as nighttime curfews, restrictions on the sale of liquor, and a requirement that certain individuals (i.e., ex-Confederates) carry travel passes while in town. The anti-Radical populace vehemently protested these infringements on their civil liberties. Referring to Alexander as "the great Mogul," residents called for his dismissal. The militia lieutenant ignored all remonstrance.[61]

Infuriated by Alexander's "officious" conduct, ex-Confederate S. "Bob" Viars tried to stir up trouble. Denouncing the militiamen as "low-flung," he called for volunteers to help him "run the State Guards out of Loudon." On July 15, he stormed alone into the militia encampment, hurled insults at Alexander, and threatened to tear down the American flag. The men of Company F pounced on him. Alexander later commented that "it was with much difficulty [that] I could restrain the men from putting him through." Alexander then held a drum-head court where the battered Viars was charged with insurrection and treason, and reportedly "sentenced to *eat grass* or go hungry." Though coerced with bayonets, Viars "refused to nibble." After a few more indignities, the "malignant scoundrel" was released.[62]

Civil authorities brought a lawsuit against Alexander and his men, but it never reached court, for Company F headed for West Tennessee on July 22. Probably influenced by Captain Robeson's report on conditions in Lauderdale County, General Cooper ordered Lieutenant Alexander to set up camp in the county seat of Ripley. The unit's cross-state journey was quite eventful. Its passage through Nashville was something like a Roman triumph. "With colors flying, a clanging snare drum sounding, and the bayonet of every musket fixed," Company F proceeded toward its rail connection. The *Union and Dispatch* described the march through the city as one of "glistening intimidation."[63]

On July 25, Company F briefly halted at Humboldt (Gibson County). From the Radicals' standpoint, Gibson was in political disarray, the presence of a detachment from Company G, First Regiment, notwithstanding. While Lieutenant Alexander went to Trenton, presumably to consult with Captain Adkins, 2nd Lt. E. R. Brown remained in Humboldt with the main body. Brown observed firsthand the ex-Confederates' domination of the county. According to the lieutenant, the "Rebs" brazenly congregated near his bivouac and taunted his men. One ex-Confederate sneered that the Radicals "had better send more men . . . if they expect the *d—d* nigger to *Vote*." Another ridiculed the militiamen as dupes of "Brownlow's Bogus *State Govt.*" and vowed to send the "*Ignorant* niggers" back to slavery regardless of the outcome of the election. Brown ordered his men to ignore the catcalls. Several freedmen braved the gauntlet of ex-Confederate loiterers and informed the lieutenant that barely half of the eligible black voters had been registered. Moreover, they intimated that the militia detachment in Trenton had done very little to suppress ex-Confederate lawlessness. Some Gibson blacks had actually formed their own vigilante groups, inflicting three casualties on a band of ex-Confederates in one clash. Brown requested permission from General Cooper to stay and register the freedmen personally, but a couple of days later Alexander returned from Trenton and Company F proceeded to Ripley. Arriving on July 31, Alexander reported that the blacks in that region turned out in large numbers to welcome his command.[64]

Alexander's relatively rapid movement from Loudon to Ripley (a distance of about 350 miles) highlights the importance of rail transportation to the militia deployment. Given that most lawless counties were located in Middle and West Tennessee and that most of the militia units came from East Tennessee, trains were indispensable to the politics of force. Shortly after mobilization, the major railroad companies agreed to a "special arrangement" with the Tennessee quartermaster, whereby militia personnel and freight could travel at a 40 percent discount. Moreover, H. H. Thomas persuaded some of these companies to conduct business on credit, assuring them that the state was good for all fees. In return, the State Guard received timely transport and courteous treatment from many superintendents. J. L. Williams of the Mobile & Ohio, for example, intervened in behalf of the quartermaster when one of his conductors refused to accommodate an unscheduled shipment of munitions. Williams ordered the conductor to readjust his plans or face discharge. Captain Harris's bumpy ride to Henry County was an aberration in an otherwise efficient mode of travel. The railroad companies also presumably turned a profit, grossing $27,347 over the course of their business with the State Guard.[65]

General Cooper might well have deployed the balance of his State Guard, three companies from East Tennessee, to other trouble spots in the middle and western sections had it not been for some unexpected anti-Radical challenges in the mountain counties. On July 23, a political riot broke out in Rogersville (Hawkins County). The Radicals and the Conservatives had staged competing rallies in close proximity, the latter's featuring one of Emerson Etheridge's stump speeches. At some point, shots rang out and a melee ensued, leaving one black Union Leaguer dead and two wounded and one white Conservative dead and another wounded. Radicals blamed the Conservatives for opening fire, while Conservatives accused the Radicals of trying to assassinate Etheridge. The day after this incident, an ex-Confederate shot a black Radical in the face during a Knoxville party rally. This violent turn of events in East Tennessee compelled Governor Brownlow to retain the remaining militia companies in that section. He stationed Capt. Kemp Murphy's Company D, Second Regiment, in Knoxville (probably as a personal bodyguard as well as a law enforcer). Capt. A. M. Clapp's Company H, Second Regiment, went to Hawkins County to restore order there. Clapp may have detached some men to neighboring Sullivan, for Conservatives in that county claimed that his "rabble" made a habit of marching "up and down the country, threatening and terrifying all they meet." Finally, 1st Lt. William N. Purdy's newly mustered Company I, Second Regiment, was ordered to Monroe and Polk, counties that had voted for secession.[66]

Unable to get more men from East Tennessee, General Cooper committed his reserve unit, Captain Hall's Company C, to Rutherford County on July 30. Radicals there had long insisted that they could handle voter registration and the election itself without militia troops. The Etheridge camp, however, had heated up the political climate and frightened many registered freedmen in the process. Toward the end of July, county Radicals requested militia, and Hall encamped his men in the county seat of Murfreesboro. Cooper replaced Hall's company as a reserve by hastily mustering in the all-black Company A, Third Regiment, a mere two days before the election. The *Republican Banner,* always on the look out for military despotism, found the general's abrupt "augmentation of the Brownlow army . . . rather mysterious." As far as Cooper was concerned, however, even the capital county of Davidson needed some State Guard. One day before the election he ordered the white Capt. Michael J. Houston to deploy his black militiamen throughout the county.[67]

Except for a few last-minute adjustments, the twenty-one companies of the State Guard were all in place by July 31. In looking back at this political campaign, Conservative candidate for Congress Edmund Cooper grumbled, "My district [the Fourth] was, just before the election, flooded with troops—Tennessee militia." In some respects, "flooded" was not an exaggeration. Six of the eight counties in Cooper's Middle Tennessee district were occupied by three full companies of militia and detachments from three others. Some 1,210 militiamen (including most of the black volunteers) from thirteen companies had either patrolled or physically occupied at least twenty-four of Middle Tennessee's thirty-five counties. In West Tennessee, approximately 460 militiamen from six companies occupied at one time or another at least nine of the section's nineteen counties. And in East Tennessee, some 205 militiamen from four companies exercised authority over six of that section's thirty counties (see Appendix B). The "full blast" of the Tennessee State Guard was indeed a dramatic display of Radical power.[68]

The conduct of this Radical army was a major issue throughout the campaign. John P. Holtsinger spoke for many Conservatives when he complained to President Johnson that "the presence of Brownlow's

Tennessee State Guard dispositions during the election of 1867.

militia tends more to disorder, than otherwise." In actuality, however, most of the "disorder" during the campaign was a product of anti-Radical agitation, especially in West Tennessee. Most company commanders simply tried to execute their orders and keep the peace. When confrontations occurred, they usually responded with appropriate and reasonable force. Much of the credit for this disciplined behavior rests with General Cooper. His leadership gave the State Guard a more centralized chain of command than had existed prior to his appointment, and his numerous special orders not only directed militia movements but also reiterated the rules of engagement. To be sure, some officers overstepped their authority. Lieutenant Alexander's brief "martial law" in Roane County was certainly an abuse of power. Other officers, however, such as Captain Grisham, exhibited an unexpected human touch in pacifying the opposition. The scope of the State Guard's activities was extensive, but a military despotism it was not. There were no atrocities, at least none for which the militia was responsible. Some ex-Confederates were captured or arrested, but instead of being summarily executed they were usually released after a short incarceration. There was no suppression of the anti-Radical press, which lambasted the militia on virtually every page. There was no interference with the Conservative canvass of the state, in which Etheridge denounced the Brownlow administration at every stop. And there was no official martial law. There were restrictions placed on some activities, such as the sale of liquor, but in most occupied counties life went on as if there was no militia at all. What the State Guard did do was provide protection for Republicans who wanted to meet safely in public and freedmen who wanted to register to vote.[69]

Anti-Radical criticism of the State Guard never abated, but there were several instances where the rhetoric of tyranny lapsed into comic lightheartedness. In May, the *Fayetteville Observer* penned a piece of doggerel titled "Commander-in-Chief, Etc." that mocked Brownlow's employment of force: "He steers the proud old ship of state / And if she sinks, he'll let her—ah / But he will never share her fate, / "Commander-in-Chief, Etcetera." In June, the *Republican Banner* printed a humorous story that portrayed the militiamen as sniveling cowards. As Captain Evans's Company I was moving by rail, the train evidently suffered an accident. According to the *Banner*, as the train screeched to a halt "Brownlow's Bummers" thought they were under attack by Rebels and "screamed like a pack of frightened children or a flock of scared sheep." One private shrieked, "O, my God!" while another begged, "Don't shoot!" As the panic subsided, one demoralized militiaman sobbed, "I thought the rebs'd got me shure!" In July, several Conservative newspapers parodied Col. David M. Nelson's investigation of the Rogersville riot. As the colonel interrogated the "rebel" perpetrators, he discovered that they were actually all officers of the "melish," at which point he promptly bellowed, "Guards! Release these men at once." A final example of State Guard lampooning involved the black militia. The *Union and Dispatch* related the observations of a Nashville "colored man" who shook his head with disapproval at Capt. J. L. Kirk's black troopers: "Dese nigger melishy goin to fool round here tell they gits us all in trouble. They better go back to the corn field whar they belong and then we'll have peace."[70]

Comic stories notwithstanding, the contending sides did despise one another. As General Cooper completed his deployment, the anti-Radicals continued to issue challenges to Radical authority. In the closing weeks of the campaign, the *Union and Dispatch* ran its own version of the Gaut circular that urged "three freeholders" in any county "to qualify themselves . . . and proceed to hold the election and certify the returns to the sheriff." The *Republican Banner* called on "the moral power of the people" to safeguard the ballot box from "Brownlow bullies." To this end it declared that every white man "should consider himself a special policeman authorized to keep the peace." The State Guard now had one final task: to protect the polls and ensure that only "loyal" men cast a ballot. All Tennesseans anxiously awaited the dawn of August 1.[71]

Chapter 5

THE RADICAL ARMY WINS AN ELECTION

MOST TENNESSEANS ANTICIPATED CIVIL DISTURBANCES ON THE DAY OF the election. Radicals were certain that one or more of the many bands of ex-Confederate vigilantes would attack the polling sites, while Conservatives fully expected at least one of the militia companies to fire on the citizenry. No one was more concerned about potential violence than Gen. Joseph A. Cooper. As the commander of nearly nineteen hundred militiamen distributed in more than thirty counties, Cooper bore direct responsibility for ensuring public safety and preserving electoral integrity. He did not shrink from this important duty. In the final week of the campaign, besides completing the deployment of the State Guard, Cooper issued specific election-day instructions to all of his company commanders. He ordered them to work closely with "their Union friends," to position their men in "the best possible advantage to protect the loyal voters," and to "use Every means to preserve the peace."[1]

General Cooper was also worried about the well being of the militiamen themselves, in light of the death of Private Jones and the night attacks against the State Guard in McNairy and Robertson, among other confrontations. In a general order issued the day before the election, Cooper denounced the "armed mobs and outlaws, who . . . persist in keeping the country in a reign of terror by their outrageous conduct." He warned that anyone caught interfering with the State Guard would be "punished to the full extent of the law," and he informed the "disloyal citizens" of those counties occupied by militia that he would hold them "strictly responsible for any violation of this order." Conservatives found the general's last statement particularly offensive. The *Union and Dispatch* derided the general order as a piece of "graceless impudence" and warned that if Cooper ever acted on his threats against "the innocent," then the people of Tennessee would rise up and sweep the militia "out of existence."[2]

Nashville mayor Matt Brown was unimpressed by General Cooper's edicts. Throughout the campaign, Mayor Brown had opposed the Radicals in every way he could, from endorsing the Gaut circular to coauthoring the Conservatives' campaign strategy for Middle Tennessee. He had had run-ins with General Cooper on several occasions, including a sharp exchange on July 2, when the militia general complained to Brown that the Nashville police were culpable in the disruption of Radical meetings in the city. According to Cooper, when someone extinguished the lights during one Radical speech, the police stood by and "winked at the outrage." Brown denied the accusation, just as he denied the authority of Cooper to enforce the law in Nashville. In mid-July, the mayor called on President Johnson to strengthen the federal garrison in Tennessee, seeing that military body as a potential counterforce to the State Guard; it was a view the president also shared. In the final week of the campaign, Brown went a step further and created a "special police" of three hundred men. He then issued a proclamation that mandated how voters were to conduct themselves. This decree stated that the "special police," in conjunction with the federal garrison, was the only legitimate law enforcement body in the city. Alarmed by the mayor's machinations, Governor Brownlow informed Gen. George Thomas that the "special police" was made up mostly of ex-Confederates; he urged Thomas to consult with General Cooper, not the city officials, on matters of peacekeeping.[3]

Brown and Brownlow's competition for the garrison serves as a reminder that the State Guard was not the only instrument of military coercion in Tennessee in 1867. About one thousand U.S. soldiers were stationed in the state at the time of the election and their relationship to the State Guard was often problematic. Reconstruction politics placed these troops in an awkward position. Their commander, Gen. George H. Thomas, privately supported the Radicals and was reluctant to overrule

The Radical Army Wins an Election

Thomas Duncan, 1865. Courtesy of the New York
State Library, Manuscripts and Special Collections.

the Brownlow administration in civil matters. The political campaign of
1867, however, clearly demonstrated that all was not stable in the state.
Thomas had an obligation to prevent open warfare, but because Tennessee was readmitted to the Union in 1866, he lacked the sweeping
powers of the Reconstruction acts, which applied only to the other ten
ex-Confederate states. Wherever possible, Thomas preferred to let the
Tennessee State Guard control the situation, and he advised his officers
that this organization was "among the regularly constituted authorities of
the State." Nevertheless, Thomas could not ignore the many requests
made to his department, by Conservatives and Radicals alike, for military assistance in preserving the peace. From Memphis, a city outside the
realm of the State Guard, Thomas received numerous reports that violence was likely on election day. Fearful of a repetition of the previous

year's horrible race riot in that city, Gen. Ulysses S. Grant ordered Thomas not to "wait for a riot to take place but use the military vigorously to prevent one commencing." Accordingly, in the last week of July, Thomas took personal command in Memphis and delegated riot control in "Nashville and the other larger towns" to his subordinate in the state capital, Gen. Thomas Duncan.[4]

General Duncan's assignment was a thankless task. He had to monitor the election in Nashville yet avoid any hint of "political skullduggery." Furthermore, he had to accommodate both the State Guard and Mayor Brown's "special police," while preventing any armed clashes between these two partisan forces. Adding to Duncan's difficulties were his scattered troop commitments in the counties of Gibson, Obion, Maury, Sumner, and Williamson, the latter three areas simultaneously occupied by some of the controversial black militia units. In most cases, Duncan deferred to General Cooper and the State Guard, but the Franklin riot and the racial tension produced by the black militia compelled Duncan to keep a watchful eye on these three counties. Hoping to improve the awkward command arrangement, General Cooper suggested that Duncan temporarily attach a company of regulars to the State Guard. Duncan, however, thought the reverse would be more appropriate, and two days before the election Cooper agreed to subordinate his lone militia unit in Nashville—Company A, Third Regiment (black)—to General Duncan, much as he had done with his all-black militia forces in Williamson County. To Cooper, a peaceful Radical victory at the polls was more important than a jurisdictional victory over the army. Nashville Conservatives were thankful that the federal troops had not been "prostituted to the service of the Brownlow despotism."[5]

On the eve of the election, General Duncan issued his own orders, which explained election security procedures for Nashville. He instructed the officers of his eclectic command, which evidently came to include the "special police," to station their men at various points throughout the capital and keep them "well in hand." He forbade the troops to go anywhere near the polls unless called on by civil authorities to suppress a confirmed disorder. Finally, he authorized them to arrest any civilian caught carrying a concealed weapon. The *Union and Dispatch* commended Duncan's leadership but criticized his superior, General Thomas, for being a stooge of the Radicals and leaving most of the state "at the mercy of the militia." This newspaper further declared that a fair election was impossible, even though U.S. troops had been

124

ordered to stay away from the polls, because "the militia, of course, will be at the voting places."[6]

Every State Guard officer knew that election-day order and Radical success at the polls depended ultimately on their performance, the federal garrison notwithstanding. For the sake of the democratic process, most militia units actually tried to remain inconspicuous during the hours of voting (9:00 a.m. to 4:00 p.m.), but all were prepared for an emergency. Secretary of State A. J. Fletcher calculated that about 115,000 Tennesseans were registered to vote for the August 1 election. Fewer than 23,000 of them resided in counties containing federal troops. If the militia could not instill confidence among the remainder, especially blacks, and prevent ex-Confederate vigilantes from disrupting the election in Middle and West Tennessee, then it would make no difference if voting in Nashville and Memphis was peaceable, for the Radicals would lose the state. Conscious of the State Guard's critical role, General Cooper reiterated his orders and added that his company commanders were to submit detailed reports on the election in their counties. Having issued this final word, the militia general, "serene and jovial" on the outside, anxiously awaited the election outcome at his Nashville headquarters.[7]

The concentration of more than one thousand militiamen in Middle Tennessee proved a profitable investment on election day, Brownlow and the Radicals won in virtually every county of that region. The election in the Third District, where Radical William B. Stokes and Conservative Eli G. Fleming had fought a nasty campaign, was surprisingly uneventful. The vigilance of Captains Blackburn and Stuart during the campaign accounts for much of the quiet in that section of the state. Having distributed his command through more than ten counties from May to July, Captain Blackburn concentrated in three for the election. He and thirty-six men covered various precincts in DeKalb County, while Lt. William Cravens commanded a thirty-man detachment in Warren and 1st Sgt. John T. Askew protected Cannon (part of the Fourth District) with twenty-five men. The company's official report stated that the "conduct of soldiers and civilians [was] very good." Captain Stuart's Company K, split evenly between Overton and White counties, enjoyed a similarly quiet election day. In the end, the Radicals swept most of the Third District county races, while Stokes trounced Fleming, eight thousand votes to sixteen hundred. In the governor's race, Brownlow polled seventy-nine hundred votes in the Third District against Etheridge's seventeen hundred. Stokes later informed the governor that the Union Leaguers in DeKalb all marched to the polls unmolested and that every black in the district voted the Radical ticket. Fleming claimed bitterly that he lost the election solely because Stokes used the militia as a personal army.[8]

In nearby Rutherford County, Capt. Robert L. Hall enjoyed an equally quiet and successful election day. Arriving in the county only two days before the election, Hall did little to help the Radicals prepare, but he did deploy his men at three important precincts: Murfreesboro, Lavergne, and Sand Spring. In consultation with Registrar F. Sherbrook and Murfreesboro's Conservative mayor Charles Ready, who had deputized fifty men to help keep the peace, Hall agreed to remain in camp and stay away from the polls as long as everything proceeded smoothly. A grateful Mayor Ready courteously provided Captain Hall with election updates throughout the day. County Radicals were evidently satisfied with the arrangement and there is no indication that the militiamen ever left their encampments. In the end, the Radicals won the county, with Brownlow crushing Etheridge, 2,939 votes to 359. Mayor Ready later complimented "the gentlemanly bearing and orderly behavior" of Captain Hall and his Company C. Hall soon returned to Buena Vista (Davidson County) to resume his duty as State Guard reserve with Company A, Third Regiment as an attachment.[9]

Company I in Humphreys also presided over a generally quiet election. Capt. James R. Evans's decision to close all saloons undoubtedly contributed to the calm. The only disturbance was a rock-throwing incident in Waverly between some black voters and white onlookers. Lt. James A. England arrested the troublemakers on both sides and detained them in his camp until the polls closed. The Radicals triumphed, with Brownlow winning 267 votes to Etheridge's 131. Incidentally, the militiamen of this unit participated in the election themselves, in accordance with Section 7 of the Franchise Act of 1867, which authorized company commanders to implement a policy similar to absentee voting. Prior to guarding the polls, thirty-nine militiamen cast ballots for the Radical Horace Maynard, whose Second District included Claiborne County, home of Company I. Evidently, some of the men had forgotten their voting certificates, but Captain Evans permitted them to vote anyway.[10]

For Company F, First Regiment, the election went well, although it was marked by some disappointments. Reporting from Henry County in West Tennessee, Brevet Capt. E. R. Hall stated that everything "passed off quietly" in the three counties occupied by his company, Cheatham, Stewart, and Henry. In Cheatham, the detachment under 1st Sgt. William C. McClanahan never left its camp. Brownlow won that county with 207 votes to Etheridge's 58. In Stewart, Lt. John Roberts posted his men near the Stuart's Station polling site at the request of the registrar. Although no trouble was reported, Brownlow garnered only 252 votes against Etheridge's 631. How the State Guard failed to secure Stewart remains a mystery, especially considering the easy registration of voters and the incident-free occupation during the campaign. As for Henry County, the election there was simply a bust. Due to Registrar J. B. Guthrie's apparent incompetence and former Capt. Shadrack Harris's personal difficulties, no valid registration was ever completed. Governor Brownlow ruled the county's registration null and void, and no official election took place. Inexplicably, nineteen votes for Etheridge were recorded in the final tally.[11]

Capt. John L. Kirk experienced similarly mixed success in Montgomery and Robertson counties. In Clarksville, Kirk and his mostly black detachment worked closely with a "special police" force to ensure a smooth election. When it was over and the Radicals had won, an exultant Kirk declared that he had "Never Seen A Civeler day go off in his Life." Brownlow polled 1,527 votes, Etheridge 588. In Springfield, Lt. David E. Burchfield, whose detachment had come under attack a few days before, stationed his men "a short distance" from the courthouse and afterward reported that "evry thing went off Peaseably more So than I expected." It was not completely peaceable, however: after the polls closed, mounted men rode past his encampment and fired some gunshots. Burchfield claimed his men hit one of the attackers with return fire. Unfortunately for the Radicals, although Brownlow garnered more votes at the Springfield precinct, Etheridge claimed a narrow victory in Robertson, 493 votes to the incumbent's 348. Registrar H. D. Featherston commended Burchfield's performance but regretted having tied down a militia detachment on what proved to be a fruitless task. The registrar realized too late that it was impossible for the Radicals to win the county; there were too many legal Conservative voters.[12]

Unlike many of his counterparts in other counties, Capt. George W. Kirk made a deliberate point of posting guards visibly at the precincts in Franklin. As the polls opened in Winchester, a detachment of militia under Kirk marched through the public square to the courthouse, carrying a large ammunition box. Some militiamen took positions on the second floor of the building, while the remainder stood outside the door to the polls with fixed bayonets. M. C. Whipple, a Republican election clerk, noted that the Conservatives were put "much out of humor" by this martial display. Several ex-Confederates offered a passive challenge by congregating close to the courthouse, but no trouble occurred. Evidently satisfied with the proceedings, the militia departed the scene shortly before noon. Local Conservatives claimed that while he was there, Captain Kirk screened several freedmen as they approached the ballot box to make sure that they deposited Brownlow tickets. One Conservative later stated that "three legal voters" were turned away by militia sentries. Whipple, however, denied that Kirk's men interfered in any way. Etheridge received 313 votes, but Brownlow took the county with 702.[13]

Much to the surprise of many observers, Capt. William O. Rickman maintained a low profile in Marshall County throughout the first of August. With the exception of a fifteen-man patrol sent through the countryside, Rickman and his men remained in camp on the fairgrounds outside Lewisburg, despite some rumors about a threatened riot in the town. Like Captain Hall in Rutherford County, Rickman assigned polling place security to a "special police" force. It consisted of fifteen men under William B. Holden, a Conservative but also a former colonel in the Union army. The only incident of note occurred at the Coney Spring precinct, where some black voters came armed. They agreed to stack their weapons before voting, however, and then departed quietly. Unable to cite any militia transgressions, county Conservatives protested the conduct of the Lewisburg Union League. According to Abner A. Steele, a virulent opponent of "Brownlowism" in the general assembly, white Radicals herded the black Leaguers to the polls like a "drove of sheep." After receiving ballot tickets, colored "red" for Radical, the blacks "voted in a body, like soldiers deliver their fire under orders." Overall, Marshall cast 831 votes for Brownlow and 449 for Etheridge.[14]

Steele was evidently disappointed that the militia kept its distance during the election. Captain Rickman reported that at various times during the day, Steele came out to the encampment of Company H and "tried to get up a conflict." He and some ex-Confederates, who accompanied him, denounced the Radical party and insulted the militiamen as "Horse Thieves and Robbers." Rickman forbade his men to retaliate, but later explained that Steele was precisely the sort of rabble-rouser who made the State Guard necessary.[15]

Rickman's detachment in neighboring Giles County under Lt. John Mankin reported more Radical success at the polls, although a resort to force proved necessary. Mankin commanded forty-five men at Pulaski (including twenty black militiamen received from Company K, Second Regiment, on July 31). At least four Klan dens existed in Giles at that time, but they were passive during the election, just as they had been throughout Mankin's deployment in the county. For most of the morning on August 1, Mankin remained in camp, coming out just once to reprimand an ex-Confederate who had been heckling the militia from afar. Sometime that afternoon, Mankin learned that the sheriff of Giles was disputing Registrar B. J. Sheridan's authority. Because Sheridan was inspecting each ballot, accepting some and throwing out others, the sheriff intervened and halted the voting while he investigated the registrar's actions. Duty-bound to prevent such obstructions, Mankin formed his men and headed for the courthouse, arriving just in time to prevent a rush on the ballot box by several hundred disgruntled voters. Behind a militia cordon, the voting resumed in an orderly manner, but the hour was late and some 200 freedmen had still not voted when the polls closed. Nonetheless, about 950 blacks cast ballots at the Pulaski precinct and Brownlow took the county as a whole with 1,880 votes against Etheridge's 150. A disappointed Edmund Cooper, Conservative candidate for Congress, complained that Sheridan and his fellow registrars permitted many underage blacks to vote. Cooper did, however, compliment Lieutenant Mankin on his firm leadership and "courteous" behavior.[16]

Also in Giles County on August 1 were two squads of black militiamen (besides the detachment under Mankin). Having just subordinated his black militiamen in Davidson and Williamson counties to General Duncan's authority, General Cooper, on July 31, deftly deployed most of these men to areas outside of the army's control. 2nd Lt. John S. Durham, commanding eighteen black militiamen from Company A, Third Regiment, moved by rail to Giles and arrived in Lynnville (north Giles) thirty minutes after the polls opened. A correspondent for the *Republican Banner* reported that the German Durham was "very fearful" of the white populace, muttering "Mein Gott" to himself as he "carefully marched in the rear" of his column en route to the polls. The militia lieutenant's report, however, conveys no such trepidation. Durham stated that after posting his men approximately one hundred yards from the polling place, he quietly watched the election. At one point, a drunk staggered up to the line of voters and tried to make a black man cast his ballot for Etheridge, but the troublemaker was led away by the town constable without the militia having to intervene. When the polls closed at 4:00 p.m., the Lynnville election officials reported that Brownlow had received 219 votes to Etheridge's 17. That evening, as Durham's men awaited rail transportation back to Nashville, they were "entertained in a hospitable manner" by some jubilant Radicals. Lynnville had been easy duty for this black detachment, but Durham closed his report with a statement that may well explain this outcome: "The conduct of the men . . . was highly commendable. Not one of them spoke to a white man."[17]

Similarly, in Prospect (south Giles), a sergeant and ten men from Company G, Second Regiment, arrived just as the election commenced. General Cooper placed this squad at the disposal of Thomas P. Harrison, the election official, but as the militiamen approached the precinct they were "ordered out of town" by Prospect's constable. The militiamen complied and apparently sat idle on the outskirts of town. Later in the day, a procession of armed blacks marched to Prospect, but were forced by civil authorities to turn over their weapons before voting. Many of these blacks asked the militiamen if Capt. James Sumner was with them. Local whites insisted that these blacks were looking for an excuse to cause trouble and if Sumner, who had won infamy among Conservatives for his actions in Williamson County, had been present, "riot and bloodshed" would certainly have ensued.[18]

Two black militia detachments from the Second Regiment were present in Maury County for the election. Lt. George Sumner occupied the county seat of Columbia with about 50 men from Company G, while 1st Sgt. Howard Freeman commanded a 20-man squad from Company K at Spring Hill. Nimrod Porter, an anti-Radical farmer, claimed that there were in actuality some 250 "malisha (blacks) . . . here in the County to intimidate the voters." Porter believed that the presence of this force only excited Maury's blacks and made a riot all the more likely. Although there are no extant reports of the militia detachments' activities, the election in Maury was a great success for the Radicals. As the polls opened in Columbia, white Radicals organized approximately one thousand black voters into a queue and instructed them not to leave the line for any reason. They then moved up and down the line verifying that the blacks had "the ticket they wanted to vote" and making sure that Conservatives did not persuade any to switch their tickets. For three hours the blacks voted while white bystanders "jeered and insulted" them and, in a few instances, tried to break the line. In Spring Hill, the Radicals were similarly successful, though it should be noted that a small contingent of federal troops was on hand in addition to the militia. Overall, Brownlow crushed Etheridge, 2,817 votes to 238. Samuel Arnell, the victorious Radical candidate for Congress in that district, proclaimed the election a "civil revolution. . . . The chattel had become a human creature."[19]

In Williamson County, U.S. troops under Captain Burke provided security at the polls. Capt. James H. Sumner and Lt. Philip Fleming, each with only a fraction of their militia commands on hand, sat in camp outside Franklin, presumably keeping each other company as the election unfolded. Sumner, whose authority had been truncated by General Cooper, opted to make no election report. Fleming merely stated that "everything was quiet." Like some other militia officers, Fleming appears to have conducted an election among his men. Brownlow won the county 1,704 to 574.[20]

Leaving Nashville to the federal garrison, General Cooper distributed most of the black militiamen of Company A, Third Regiment to three other precincts in Davidson County during the morning of August 1. Capt. Michael J. Houston guarded the polls in Antioch with twenty men. Aside from an idle threat by some Rebels who told Houston that they were going to get drunk and "raise a disturbance," all was quiet at that location. 1st Lt. Alexander Gleaves took a squad of twenty men to Goodlettsville. The *Republican Banner* insisted that Gleaves's presence was "contrary to the wishes of the people," although less than a week before, a white Radical named William Scruggs had been murdered there after holding a party meeting in his saloon, attended by blacks. Lastly, Sgt. James M. Pitman proceeded with twenty men to Buena Vista. Prior to his arrival, ex-Confederates had occupied the building designated as a polling place and they now refused to vacate it. The black militia sergeant thereupon announced that he would personally conduct the election under a nearby locust tree. As black voters handed Pitman their ballots, a group of ex-Confederates surrounded the makeshift polling place, waved pistols and shotguns, and shouted that a hundred more Rebels were on the way. Pitman courageously stared down the mob: "I told them I was there to preserve the Peace, and for the protection of the Polls, and I was going to do so." Pitman further warned the whites that he too could get reinforcements. Their threats having no effect, the whites dispersed and Pitman returned to Nashville later that afternoon, turning his ballots over to the adjutant general. Brownlow easily won a majority in Davidson: 5,454 votes to 1,001 for Etheridge.[21]

As the various detachments of Company A arrived back in Nashville, some of the black militiamen began celebrating what they believed would be a decisive Radical victory. One squad roamed the streets "shouting vociferously for Brownlow." Another marched to the home of Conservative T. D. Harris, who had allegedly fired one of his black employees for going to the polls. The angry militiamen "demanded an explanation" for this action but received only a curt order to get off Harris's property. Refusing to leave, the militiamen loitered nearby "cursing, hooting and threatening throughout the night." The *Union and Dispatch* denounced these incidents as "Negro Brownlowism."[22]

The only all-black company not broken into detachments was Capt. Thompson McKinley's Company B, Second Regiment. The situation in Sumner County demanded the presence of his entire command. In the closing days of July, bands of ex-Confederates, presumably under the leadership of "King" Ellis Harper, intensified their intimidation of blacks. According to Radical witnesses, these "bushwhackers and guerrillas threatened that they would waylay and shoot every colored man who should attempt to vote." Moreover, white employers threatened to fire any black employee who went to the polls. The election officials outside of Gallatin also endured "ferocious" harassment. McKinley sent squads through the countryside to "inspire" the freedmen and reassure the Radical leaders, but to no avail. By August 1 every precinct judge and clerk had tendered his resignation rather than risk his life holding an election in which ex-Confederate violence seemed certain.[23]

Only in Gallatin, where McKinley served as voting registrar and political candidate as well as militia captain, did the polls open. But even here, the election encountered difficulties. Conservative mayor William Wright informed McKinley that the State Guard was forbidden to enter the town limits on the day of the election. When McKinley announced his intention to garrison the courthouse with his company and permit his men to vote, Mayor Wright turned to his chief of police, an ex-Confederate named Col. J. J. Turner. Turner armed and deputized virtually every white man he could find and then reputedly vowed to "wipe from the face of the earth the Brownlow militia." Sources differ greatly as to what transpired next. According to McKinley, on August 1 his men established an effective perimeter around the courthouse despite several instances of "very provoking" behavior by local whites. A fanciful anti-Radical post-Reconstruction account, however, describes a near-battle between Turner's men and the black militia. According to this source, as McKinley marched his company toward town in the early morning hours of August 1, Colonel Turner managed to encircle the militia column. Rather than face certain annihilation, McKinley surrendered and his men returned to their camp under guard, while the Conservatives ran the election.[24]

Regardless of whether Turner's feat of arms is a fabrication, McKinley did not maintain peace alone. Before any real battles broke out, Capt. Edwin H. Leib arrived with a company of the U.S. Fifth Cavalry. Simultaneously, hundreds of blacks from other parts of the county arrived to vote, as per an arrangement between the Brownlow administration and the army. Secretary of State A. J. Fletcher instructed McKinley to keep the polls open until every black who so desired had voted. When the day ended, the Radicals had prevailed at the polls, Brownlow garnering 891 votes to Etheridge's 224. McKinley also won his race for the general assembly, 882 to his opponent's 235. About four hundred registered blacks, however, never appeared to vote, having been "disfranchised by the pistol and bowie knife," in the words of the *Daily Press and Times*. Those blacks who did brave the threatened reprisals of the ex-Confederates refused to go home for several days until the tension died down. Although the Radicals were victorious in Sumner, much of the credit for this outcome must go to the U.S. Army.[25]

In Lincoln County, Capt. George E. Grisham had a particularly difficult experience. Initially, he had planned merely to close the saloons, forbid the carrying of weapons, and post his men at discreet distances from the polls. The Conservatives, however, made a last-minute bid to control the election. On July 31, a committee of citizens from Fayetteville approached Grisham and requested that he not allow the blacks to march to the polls in procession. The militia captain replied that there was no law against it, and if legal voters chose to vote en masse, that was their business. That night, the city council passed an ordinance outlawing election-day processions, and the next morning a committee delivered a copy of the statute to Grisham. Unwilling to get into a legal dispute, Grisham agreed to comply with the new law, but stated that he would permit blacks to carry arms to the polls. He had received reports that a band of five hundred to one thousand Rebels was gathering to raid certain precincts and he thought that the blacks should have some means of defense. The Fayetteville committee dismissed the rumored raid and objected to Grisham's decision to let black voters carry arms. In yet another countermove, it suggested that Grisham's Company B share security duty with a "special police" force of twenty-five townsmen. Remarkably unperturbed, Grisham again agreed, but insisted that James Kirkpatrick, a local Radical leader, command the police force. At this point, the negotiations ended and the election commenced.[26]

During the morning parley, some three or four hundred blacks congregated around the militia encampment, no doubt wondering at the delay. Many were armed, but Grisham persuaded them to surrender their weapons until the end of the day. After collecting ballots from his own men, thirty-three of whom voted for Radical candidates back in Washington County, Grisham marched his command to Fayetteville, the throng of blacks following. At the courthouse, Company B fixed bayonets, formed a line in front of the building, and checked the voters, black and white, for weapons. Disgusted by what he considered the illegal presence of militia at the polls, the editor of the *Lincoln County News* unfurled a large flag stenciled "ETHERIDGE." Mayor Robert Farquharson, however, cautioned everyone to cooperate with the militia in the interest of peace. The mayor spent most of the day at his office window, from which he observed a scene of "considerable excitement" and occasional "disorder."[27]

It was well that Grisham took precautions, for ex-Confederates did try to disrupt the voting at a number of precincts. On the advice of Registrar John Carey, Grisham stationed a squad under Cpl. Isaac Love at the polling place in Commoner's district. Some time around noon, an armed group of Rebel horsemen led by Burnell Maleer, "a noted Bushwhacker," arrived, dismounted, and began blocking access to the ballot box. Corporal Love, who apparently had kept his men out of sight, marched rapidly toward the ex-Confederates, who thereupon fled the scene. Similar attempts were thwarted at other locations. Lt. Joseph February received particularly high marks for his work in protecting the voters, although the company's official report offers no details of his actions. Even in Fayetteville, Grisham sensed danger and warned the county sheriff, who had previously threatened the militia captain, that he would defend the courthouse like a fort and make use of the confiscated weapons as a reserve arsenal. In the end, the militia captain reported that everything went well, though he stressed that "bloodshed and riot would have marked the day . . . had not the State troops been present to prevent it." Brownlow received 780 votes in Lincoln against 267 for Etheridge. While Conservatives admitted that Grisham never obstructed any legal voter who sought to deposit a ballot, they insisted that the militia dissuaded many white men from going to the polls at all. Nevertheless, the Conservatives conceded defeat and the "ETHERIDGE" banner was taken down. Captain Grisham applauded the courage of the freedmen and Lincoln's small contingent of white Radicals: "A million cheers for the brave little band of patriots!"[28]

Lt. Nelson McLaughlin, on detached service from Company B in Wilson County, enjoyed comparable success. Though privately worrying over news of illness in his family back in Washington County, McLaughlin resolutely fulfilled his election duties. He stationed his men around the courthouse in Lebanon, "ready to put down a row," but fortunately did not have to resort to force. The election concluded without a single reported instance of harassment or interference. During his deployment, McLaughlin appears to have won the respect of the anti-Radical populace, who described the militia officer as a "most perfect gentlemen." The vote was relatively close: Brownlow got 1,249, Etheridge 788. After the election, McLaughlin thanked the people of Wilson for their civil behavior and expressed his hope for a time "when men shall wear swords no longer in Tennessee."[29]

West Tennessee's election-day experience was considerably more turbulent that Middle Tennessee's. Although the militia performed well, ex-Confederates shut down several precincts and in some instances nearly overwhelmed the State Guard. Given his struggles during the campaign, Capt. John T. Robeson was generally pleased by the election results in his area of operations. While he remained in Union City in Obion County, Robeson ordered Lt. Charles B. Simpson to patrol the countryside from Troy south into Dyer County throughout the day of the election. The voting went smoothly in these two counties, Brownlow winning Obion 272 to 67 and Dyer 316 to 46. In Weakley County, however, Robeson experienced failure. Registrar A. H. Walker, doubtful that the detachment under Lt. James W. Newport of Company G would leave the safety of its encampment outside Dresden, asked Robeson to protect the rural precincts. Robeson complied, sending a squad under Lt. W. G. Fuller. But Fuller arrived too late to prevent Rebel vigilantes from running off more

The Radical Army Wins an Election

than one hundred black voters at one location. Walker claimed that more than 200 Radical votes were lost altogether due to ex-Confederate intimidation. Nevertheless, Brownlow won Weakley, 769 to 282. Lieutenant Newport reported that all was quiet in Dresden.[30]

Capt. Pryor Adkins's experience in Gibson County was the opposite of his lieutenant's in Dresden. The election in Gibson was the closest the State Guard and the ex-Confederates came to pitched battle. Local Radicals reported that about six hundred ex-Confederates had assembled to "drive every Union man out of the county" if the vote went against Etheridge. These Rebels were unafraid of Adkins. His Company G, having "betrayed signs of timidity" to the white community, was ill prepared for any confrontations. Less than a month before, the unit's former captain was relieved for drunkenness. Less than a week before, the company was humiliated by its overreaction to some firecrackers. And less than a day before, Adkins had defused a potential mutiny. Furthermore, with at least nine of his soldiers incapacitated by illness or injury, including one volunteer who had somehow lost an eye, the new militia captain had no more than thirty-five men fit for action. As a result, Adkins probably just wanted to remain in camp and leave election security to the civil authorities in Trenton. Circumstances prevented him from doing so.[31]

On the morning of August 1, a militia detachment under Capt. William C. Holt of Robeson's command arrived unannounced to assist Adkins. Holt's entrance into Trenton, however, may have inflamed passions as much as it sought to subdue them. Carrying a large banner with "W. G. Brownlow" sewn on it, Holt's men marched around the public square before taking a position next to the courthouse. For most of the morning, the election proceeded quietly. Conservatives contented themselves with an anti-Radical rally, where the speakers derided "Brownlowism" or cracked jokes about the militia. By noon, however, trouble had erupted. A number of whites began quarreling with Captain Holt, accusing him of instructing black voters, whom they called "poor deluded dupes," to vote only the Radical ticket. In response, Holt drew his navy revolver, cautioned the whites to tone down their political invective, and then ushered them away from the courthouse. A few minutes later, the whites returned with guns and reinforcements.[32]

As these ominous events transpired, Captain Adkins received an urgent plea from S. Hatchett, the Radical election official, to bring his men immediately to the courthouse. Threats and obscenities filled the air as Adkins and his men approached the public square. The courthouse had become a fortress, bristling with the rifles of Holt's besieged men. On the public square, a large crowd of anti-Radicals surged about, armed "to the teeth." Adkins tried to disperse the crowd, but failed. As his militiamen hastily took refuge in the courthouse, an ex-Confederate named Bill Canby began organizing an assault. Adkins anxiously watched as "Balls of Thread Was Rolled up to anoint With Turpintine to Charge the court house . . . and set it on fire." Canby also allegedly ordered some of his men to head for Adkins's undefended camp and "destroy it." Both militia captains agreed to "pour hell" into the attackers and torch the courthouse themselves if forced to retreat.[33]

At this point, the mayor and other city officials rushed between the antagonists and brokered "an armistice." Holt's "Skullboneans" agreed to leave the town (they eventually went to Weakley County). Adkins remained at the courthouse until the polls closed, although it is not known how many more black voters dared cast their ballot. In the evening, some "reckless youths" fired a few gunshots at Adkins encampment, but no one was hurt. Initial election returns indicated that Etheridge won Gibson County, but the final, official tally gave Brownlow a solid victory, 687 to 277. Company G had demonstrated that it had some mettle after all.[34]

The election in neighboring Madison County was no less desperate for the State Guard. Capt. Judge K. Clingan occupied the Jackson courthouse on July 31 and his Company D "remained under arms" throughout the following day, expecting "a difficulty at any moment." Madison's blacks also feared trouble. At the alleged urging of Clingan, a group of about twenty-five blacks stockpiled guns in a cabin outside Jackson, evidently intending to go to the polls armed. Ex-Confederates caught wind of this "murderous design" and raided the cabin the night before the election, capturing twelve black "insurrectionists" and confiscating their weapons. At dawn bands of ex-Confederates fanned out across the county, apparently as part of a preconceived plan of intimidation. Threatened with loss of employment, loss of life, or both, hundreds of black voters stayed home. Many of those who did go to the polls had their Radical tickets torn from their hands by Rebel "ruffians." Registrar Robert Medlin evidently lost his nerve and left the county before the polls opened. The *Union and Dispatch* claimed that Medlin was traveling by rail spreading an alarm that "colored men were being murdered in Jackson by the wholesale."[35]

Captain Clingan did his best to enforce the laws and protect the voters, but the ex-Confederate challenge was too great. In Jackson, where Clingan personally supervised the election, an estimated 350 to 400 voters, black and white, deposited their ballots without incident. Elsewhere, however, the militia was hard-pressed to protect the polls. At one precinct, a procession of black voters came under fire from "unknown parties." Clingan sent fifteen men under Lt. Robert Armstrong to restore order. The troublemakers fled at the arrival of the militia, but most of the blacks had already fled as well. No sooner had Armstrong departed than Clingan received information of another disturbance. In this instance, however, the report was a ruse; the men Clingan dispatched were "decoyed." Later in the day, another report of an outrage reached Clingan. He rallied out, but was fortuitously warned by some white Radicals that he and his men were heading for an ambush. Clingan later discovered that some Jackson ex-Confederates had even prepared "fireballs, soaked in turpentine" to burn his men out of the courthouse. Tricked and nearly "bushwhacked," Company D failed to provide protection outside Jackson and the Radicals lost the election in Madison. Brownlow garnered 343 votes to Etheridge's 503.[36]

In the aftermath of this defeat for the Radicals, Captain Clingan offered some interesting insights into the state of Reconstruction in West Tennessee. What struck him was the "tyranny . . . of the Conservative Party." Madison County's few white Radicals, he said, "feared to be seen in my presents privately." One episode that stood out in his mind was a conversation about politics that he had with a local Radical. As the two talked, a party of ex-Confederates passed by, at which point Clingan's interlocutor abruptly changed his tune and acted "indignant" toward Governor Brownlow. When the Rebels were gone, the Radical apologized, stating that he acted as he did "in order to preserve the future harmony." The county's blacks were even more afraid of white retribution. According to Clingan, a group of Jackson's "strongest colored radicals," asked by some Rebels which gubernatorial candidate they intended to vote for, declared for Etheridge. When Clingan interrupted the discussion and encouraged these blacks to state the truth, they still refused to endorse Brownlow. "The colored race in this section," Clingan decided, "realize their freedom only to a very limited extent." He was convinced that ex-Confederate terrorism kept hundreds of blacks from the polls. In his view, it would take something more than a single company of State Guard to ensure liberty and justice in Madison County.[37]

McNairy and Lauderdale counties were the only completely peaceful spots in the west. Capt. George Hamilton, whose men had engaged in several skirmishes with ex-Confederate vigilantes in the latter half of July, reported that his men stayed in camp outside Purdy on August 1, ready to aid the registrar if necessary. The election "passed off quietly," however, and Brownlow easily won McNairy 608 to 127. Lt. Joseph M. Alexander also reported a generally quiet election, although he mentioned a few exciting moments. Registrar William McCornice did not oversee the ballot box at the Ripley courthouse but did so at an outlying precinct, with the assistance of six militiamen. Alexander conducted the election in Ripley. Positioning his men around the courthouse, the militia lieutenant took a seat behind the ballot box and screened the voters as they approached. At one point, he noticed that many freedmen had ballots marked "Etheridge." When he asked them if they knew who they were voting for, they replied, "Brownlow." Alexander thereupon took the "Rebel Tickets" from the hands of the illiterate blacks and "gave them the right kind." On another occasion, seventeen freedmen arrived without their voting certificates, but after learning that they were army veterans, Alexander permitted them to deposit their ballots; "they all voted the Radical ticket." White onlookers objected to Alexander's procedures, some claiming that the lieutenant was tearing up Conservative ballots. Irritated by their scrutiny, Alexander snapped at them, warning that he would "wreck the town" and "arrest or kill" anyone who interfered. After this outburst, "things Cooled down." It was well for the Radicals that the vigilant Alexander was on duty in Lauderdale, for Brownlow gained a relatively narrow victory over Etheridge, 296 to 162. For unknown reasons, four of the county's ten precincts did not open on August 1, making the Ripley precinct all the more important.[38]

For the companies of State Guard in East Tennessee, the election was welcome quiet. Capt. Kemp Murphy covered Knox County. Although he had been warned of "an anticipated riot," there was no disturbance of any kind. Brownlow claimed his home county with 2,880 votes to Etheridge's 1,102. Lt. William N. Purdy's unit was split evenly between Monroe and Polk counties. Leaving a sergeant in command at Sweetwater in Monroe, Purdy marched into Benton in Polk County on the morning of August 1, "taking the inhabitants completely by surprise." With the exception of the ranting and profanity of a local Conservative, the election was quiet. Brownlow claimed victories in both counties: in Monroe, 978 to 160; in Polk, 211 to 48. Lieutenant Ellis, on detached assignment from Company I, First Regiment, made no report from Claiborne. Brownlow captured that county easily, 795 to 159. Capt. A. M. Clapp protected the polls in Hawkins County, with most of his men stationed at the Rogersville precinct, site of the July riot. All went well there on election day, Brownlow winning 1,107 to 186, but Clapp noted that some "irksome" Conservative citizens vowed to take revenge when the State Guard left. The militia captain only laughed: "They are so whipped at the ballot box that it will dishearten them. . . . They will not carry out their threats."[39]

Clapp's prophecy proved inaccurate, but for the moment, the Radicals in Tennessee could celebrate a great political triumph. Brownlow polled over 74,000 votes in the state, while Etheridge got about 22,500. In addition, Radicals won all eight congressional races, and the Radical party took control of all but three seats in the legislature. Scholars have rightly noted that black votes contributed substantially to this sizable margin of victory (between thirty-five thousand and forty thousand blacks voted). Black voters made the difference for many Radical candidates in Middle and West Tennessee, where the white votes generally went Conservative. What scholars have overlooked is the critical role of the State Guard in this decisive victory. From the registration process, through the canvass, to the day of the election, thousands of Radical supporters, black and white, enjoyed the protection of the militia. The Radical *Daily Press and Times* declared that "the grand instrumentalities by which we triumphed were, not only *colored suffrage* . . . but also *rebel disfranchisement . . .* and the *loyal militia*," the last making the other two possible. Historian William G. McBride and others have noted that Brownlow would have won reelection without black voters. But would he, and his Radical cohorts for that matter, have won without the State Guard?[40]

Using the vote totals for Brownlow as representative of the Radical vote as a whole, an examination of the election returns indicates that about 33,600 Radical voters (45 percent of the total) came from the thirty-three counties occupied by the State Guard on August 1 (see Appendix C). This figure increases to nearly 39,000 (52 percent) if counties significantly affected by the militia at some point during the campaign are included. These counties include Haywood in the west and Sullivan in the east, both of which witnessed month-long militia occupation, and Bedford, Lawrence, Putnam, Van Buren, and probably

The Radical Army Wins an Election

others in Middle Tennessee, where the militia briefly patrolled or provided security for a specific political event. Although the outcome was disappointing for the Radicals in a few counties, the Brownlow administration was satisfied with the State Guard's overall performance. In the words of the *Knoxville Whig*, it established "the most perfect order" on August 1. In many locations, the militia presided over a quiet election, the Conservative leadership having conceded defeat during the campaign. In others, the militia swiftly intervened when Rebels offered resistance. While Capt. G. W. Kirk in Franklin and Lieutenant Alexander in Lauderdale exhibited excessive arrogance in carrying out their mission, Captains Adkins, Holt, and Clingan deserve high marks for withholding their fire in Gibson and Madison counties. Although it looked for examples of military despotism, the anti-Radical press voiced little substantial criticism of the militia's performance on August 1. It should also be noted that more than ninety-eight hundred Conservative votes were cast in the thirty-three "militia" counties.[41]

In fairness, it must be noted that federal troops also contributed to Radical victory. They certainly helped preserve peace in Memphis and Shelby County, where more than four thousand Radical votes were cast. Moreover, of the 33,600 Radical voters receiving direct militia protection, those in Davidson, Gibson, Maury, Obion, Sumner, and Williamson (11,000 in all) also enjoyed the presence of federal troops. Thus, the State Guard can take full credit for protecting only 22,600 Radical voters on the day of the election. But the army, as an apolitical body, was under strict rules of engagement and was therefore of limited value to the Radical party. Unlike the militia, the army had no authority to enforce voter registration, nor to provide security for the Radical canvass. And it could only respond to crises, not prevent them as many militia captains tried to do through their patrols. To be sure, Capt. Edwin Leib shielded rural blacks from attack as they made their way to the Gallatin precinct, but this was at the specific request of the Brownlow administration. For the most part, the federal detachments stayed in their quarters on August 1. In Davidson County, for example, the troops were confined to the city limits of Nashville under General Duncan, while black militia squads actively defended the polls elsewhere in the county. It is hard to imagine a soldier conducting an election on his own initiative as militia sergeant Pitman did at the Buena Vista precinct. In Maury County, the army detachment never left Spring Hill, whereas most of the county's blacks voted at the

Columbia precinct, where Lt. George Sumner stood watch with fifty black militiamen. The army played an important role, but Radical voters relied far more on the State Guard for protection during the campaign and election of 1867 than on the garrison.[42]

Without the militia as a deterrent, the state's numerous ex-Confederate vigilante bands would undoubtedly have been even more aggressive toward Radical voters. Moreover, the Ku Klux Klan might have emerged as a major instrument of terror a year earlier than it actually did, and Albert Pike's dream of an ex-Confederate "civic guard" might well have become a reality. Would the 33,600 Radical voters located in "militia" counties have cast ballots against such opposition? Would they, and the thousands of others in counties visited by the militia, have even been able to register, let alone vote? As it was, ex-Confederates in the west disrupted voting at several polling sites and spoiled Radical success in Madison, a county occupied by a full company of State Guard. In Tipton and Hardeman counties, where no militia was stationed, ex-Confederates denied an estimated two thousand blacks access to the polls and the Conservatives won. Similarly, Conservatives prevailed in Coffee and Grundy, counties that at most received an occasional militia patrol. According to Radical sources, between eight and fifteen thousand black voters were kept away from the polls in West and Middle Tennessee.[43]

Besides protecting the freedmen, the State Guard also enforced the Franchise Act of 1867. Conservatives tried to circumvent this law via the Gaut circular, and only the vigilance of the State Guard defeated this tactic. In the absence of the militia, Conservatives might have gained control of many precincts and in all likelihood they would have permitted thousands of disfranchised whites to vote. These fraudulent white votes, cast most certainly for Etheridge, coupled with the loss of thousands of black votes for Brownlow would have substantially reduced, if not eradicated, the Radical majority.

A statewide election in 1867 without the State Guard could have resulted in a disaster for the Radicals and the failure of self-Reconstruction in Tennessee. The Conservatives would have made substantial gains in the general assembly, would have acquired as many as four congressional seats, and might have won the gubernatorial race. Even had Brownlow managed to defeat Etheridge, his administration would have ruled with a weaker mandate, and the experiment with black suffrage would have been tarnished. To be sure, Governor Brownlow could have used alternative means to prevent this outcome. He could have arbitrarily tossed out thousands of votes, as he did in 1865, or he could have ruled the entire election null and void. He could also have called on additional federal troops to quell a Rebel opposition that his administration was unable to handle on its own. Any of these actions, however, would have called into question the legitimacy of the Radical government barely a year after the state's readmission to the Union. Congress, which had just put the rest of the former Confederacy under military rule, might well have felt compelled to do likewise to Tennessee. Fortunately for the governor and his party, a homegrown Radical army existed to champion their cause and defend their political hegemony.

In using the State Guard to help win the election of 1867, the Brownlow administration learned two valuable lessons. The first was that black militia units were at least as much a liability as an asset. As commander-in-chief of a newly created "loyal militia," it was perfectly logical for Governor Brownlow to view the enfranchised freedmen as potential recruits. But it was perilous to enlist blacks as sentinels over a profoundly racist white population. White units of Radical militia were bad enough in the anti-Radicals' eyes, but black units were an insufferable outrage, and any clash between black militiamen and white citizens could well trigger a bloody race war. Although General Cooper exercised great care in his deployment of black units, and those units generally acquitted themselves well, Governor Brownlow concluded that the risk of employing them outweighed the benefit. Within a matter of weeks after the election, all companies containing blacks were disbanded, and blacks never again served in the Tennessee State Guard during Reconstruction.

The second lesson that the Brownlow administration learned was that Reconstruction in parts of the state, especially in West Tennessee, was going to require the continued use of military force. Many ex-Confederates had proved alarmingly defiant, and in many locations they were barely subdued. Part of the problem was faulty troop dispositions. While General Cooper did a good job overall in this regard, he could have more efficiently distributed his men to ameliorate the situation in the west. Capt. Robert Hall's company of 110 men was wasted in Rutherford County; a detachment would have sufficed there. Similarly, Lieutenant Burchfield's unit in Robertson could have been better used elsewhere. Furthermore, it is doubtful that three militia companies and a detachment from a fourth were needed to secure East Tennessee. In

Cooper's defense, it should be noted that the governor and the adjutant general had a say in deployment. Brownlow, for instance, insisted that Capt. Kemp Murphy remain in Knoxville. Moreover, Cooper took command of the State Guard while it was still in the process of mobilization. He could sometimes do little more than dispatch companies piecemeal throughout the state as they organized. In any event, an extended period of militia occupation was needed in several counties if the Radical party hoped to establish itself at the local level and if the freedmen there were going to feel safe in exercising their rights as citizens.

Governor Brownlow had hoped to disband the State Guard immediately after the gubernatorial election, but the intransigence of the anti-Radicals compelled him to proceed with caution. As the administration demobilized its Radical army, General Cooper retained some of the best units for continued operations against the ex-Confederates. In August, he shifted the weight of his forces from Middle to West Tennessee. Moreover, he concentrated his companies in the state's principal trouble spots, most notably Madison and Gibson counties. In the weeks ahead, the Tennessee State Guard, albeit reduced in size, would again prove its worth in fighting challenges to Radical Reconstruction.

Chapter 6

Autumn Showdown

Radical victory at the polls gave Reconstruction in Tennessee a new lease on life, but it did not end ex-Confederate lawlessness and the corresponding need for the State Guard. Nevertheless, Governor Brownlow directed General Cooper, soon after the election, to disband all but a few companies of State Guard, beginning with the black units (see Appendix D). Evidently, the governor believed that quiet would return once the election was over. But Tennessee remained a land of turmoil. Unhappy with the results of the election, Rebel vigilantes flouted Radical authority and exacted revenge on black voters in Middle and West Tennessee, and Conservative leaders publicly encouraged the dismissal of black workers who supported the governor. From August to November, the State Guard was engaged in trying to suppress this persistent anti-Radical challenge. Additionally, it was called on in late September to secure once again a Radical political victory during the tense mayoral election in Nashville. All the while, the Brownlow administration demobilized its Radical army.[1]

For General Cooper, maintaining order with an ever-decreasing military force proved a difficult task. Anticipating trouble, he ordered all of his officers to remain at their posts and began regrouping the companies for new assignments. Cooper did not have to wait long for an eruption of renewed anti-Radical hostility. He had no sooner recalled Capt. Robert

Hall's Company C from Rutherford on August 2 than trouble broke out in the county seat of Murfreesboro. It began when Henry McLaughlin, a Conservative newspaperman, got into a fierce argument with Registrar F. Sherbrook over the election returns. In the course of their altercation, McLaughlin assaulted Sherbrook and "gave him a sound thrashing." Some blacks came to the registrar's rescue, but a crowd of whites gathered around to protect McLaughlin. Town police soon arrived and prevented a riot, but Radical leaders nonetheless telegraphed Nashville for help. Before the end of the day, twenty-five militiamen arrived, followed by twenty-five more two days later, all under Lt. Robert G. Miner. Conservatives protested the return of the militia and blamed the "detested" Sherbrook for the commotion. Radical state senator W. Y. Elliott, however, insisted that the situation warranted the presence of an entire company of State Guard. The *Republican Banner* dismissed the senator's concerns, declaring that "there will be no further trouble unless the militia cause it." Trusting Mayor Charles Ready's promise to keep the peace, General Cooper withdrew Lieutenant Miner's detachment to Nashville after about a week's occupation.[2]

As disturbing as the Murfreesboro incident was to General Cooper, the virtual anarchy in the West Tennessee counties of Madison and Gibson was a greater concern. When Col. W. T. Cate of Cooper's staff visited Madison in the first week of August to investigate charges of ex-Confederate interference with the election, he was greeted by "drunken rebels" who hurled curses at him while firing their pistols into the air. Reestablishing law and order in that region became the general's top priority in the immediate aftermath of the election. The first order of business was to replace the ineffectual commands of Capt. J. K. Clingan in Madison and Capt. Pryor Adkins in Gibson with more reliable militia units. Perhaps sensing headquarters' disfavor with his leadership, Adkins promised Cooper that if he could have some more horses he would track down the instigators of the Trenton riot and make "several arrests." Without responding, Cooper withdrew Adkins's Company G and Clingan's Company D to Nashville on August 9 and ordered them to disband. Pvt. Julin Reed of Company G beseeched Governor Brownlow for a commission to raise a fresh company from Scott County, presumably so he could redeem the disgrace of his unit's performance in Gibson. His request was denied.[3]

Rather than beg for a second chance, Captain Clingan dutifully withdrew his company, but his departure from West Tennessee was marred by controversy. Stopping briefly in Trenton en route for Nashville, Clingan allegedly allowed his men to forage without restriction. Apple orchards and cornfields reportedly fell prey to roaming squads of soldiers. A local farmer complained that one group of militiamen dirtied his well, while another claimed that Captain Clingan himself led a party that chased down one of his hogs and killed it. The apparent seriousness of the outrages notwithstanding, General Cooper took no action against Clingan, whose men left Trenton almost as soon as they had arrived.[4]

During the middle weeks of August, the citizens of Gibson and Madison witnessed the arrival of four new companies of State Guard, two for each county. General Cooper placed Capt. John T. Robeson and his company at Trenton in Gibson County with Capt. John L. Kirk's mixed company attached. In Jackson, Madison County, Capt. George W. Kirk took charge and was soon followed by a large contingent of Capt. Joseph H. Blackburn's company from DeKalb. As Blackburn transported his command west, he boasted through the newspapers that "the marauders who infest [Madison County] must be on the alert if they expect to elude the vigilance of the loyal State Guard." Where two mediocre companies had failed, Cooper hoped that four of his best units would succeed.[5]

Cooper briefly considered sending Capt. James H. Sumner's all-black company to Madison County as well. Many Radicals thought a large force of black militia was just what counties like Madison needed and deserved. In denouncing ex-Confederate terrorism in the western section of the state, the *Daily Press and Times* half-jokingly suggested that the Brownlow administration organize into several regiments those "colored men who have been driven off to starve by their rebel employers" and deploy them throughout West Tennessee. "A few days of martial law rigidly enforced," the editor remarked, "would cause a great change." The anti-Radical press replied fiercely to the *Press and Times* editorial. The *Union and Dispatch* regarded the idea of arming thousands of blacks as a frightening indication of "how near we are to the war of races of which so much has been said." Similarly, the *Pulaski Citizen* retorted, "If you really want war in Tennessee, this is the policy that will surely bring it about." Perhaps swayed by such protests, Cooper decided against sending Sumner's unit west and instead disbanded the black captain's company. By the end of August, the only black militiamen on active duty were those in John Kirk's mixed command, stationed in Gibson County.[6]

As Capt. G. W. Kirk set up camp in Jackson, local Radicals deluged him with accounts of Rebel intimidation. "Desperadoes, cut throats and outlaws," reportedly numbering about one thousand, roamed the countryside whipping freedmen, seizing their weapons, and warning white Radicals to leave the county. In one instance, some ex-Confederates allegedly bound and murdered three blacks, and then tossed their corpses into a thicket. Another freedman barely escaped a lynching at the hands of "a pack of demons in the shape of men." Dozens of blacks, many "covered with blood," took refuge near Kirk's encampment, but even there they were harassed by ex-Confederates, who fired their weapons "all night long." With some understatement, Kirk informed General Cooper that "the rebels in this county are behaving very badly." While one Radical believed that "at least five or six hundred men" were needed to suppress the Rebel bands, Kirk was confident that his company's firepower would suffice. In requesting three thousand additional rounds of ammunition from the state quartermaster, Kirk promised to "take good care of it and if necessary make good use of the same."[7]

When Captain Blackburn arrived in Jackson on August 20, bringing the State Guard's strength in the town to about 150 men, the ex-Confederates temporarily halted their activities. Several white residents approached Blackburn and tried to convince him that there had been "no depredations committed" by anyone. As for the three murdered blacks, these residents insisted that the victims had killed each other in a dispute over a card game. Blackburn replied that he intended to conduct a complete investigation of the incident. He then wrote General Cooper that he would have "every thing in perfect peace and harmony" by the end of the month.[8]

In Gibson County, Captain Robeson and Capt. J. L. Kirk encountered more instances of white terrorism. Like blacks in Madison, those in Gibson congregated around the militia encampments and related how they had been beaten and driven from their homes because they had voted for Brownlow. Robeson, who exercised overall command in the county, appears to have stationed Kirk's company in Trenton as a garrison while his unit patrolled the countryside of Gibson and neighboring Dyer County. Vowing to crush ex-Confederate vigilantism even if he had to "brake some ones neck," Robeson made a number of arrests, turning his prisoners over to Dyer's Radical sheriff Tarkington. Moreover, Robeson warned Trenton's whites that he would not leave "Union Men to the mercies of the Rebel mob" (as he believed Captain Adkins and Holt had done) but would instead "burn their Graett and Beautyfull city." Toward the end of August, Robeson reported that Trenton was "rather more quiette than on the day of Election." With characteristic confidence, he added, "Unless they could assinate me You may rest assured that I will ceep all Quiette in Gibson County."[9]

General Cooper decided to retain the State Guard in just one other West Tennessee County—Henry. There, Edwin R. Hall, the new captain of Company F, First Regiment, reported only a few instances of trouble: a man named Trezevant had been distributing anti-Radical literature and local ex-Confederates habitually insulted the militiamen, calling them "Chicken Stealers." With the return of this unit's detachments from Middle Tennessee in mid-August, Hall felt he could keep the peace without incident. By September, the militia captain was more concerned with uniform shortages than Rebel troublemakers. "My men are greatly in need of something to wear," he anxiously reported to the quartermaster, "[and] some of my men are entirely naked." Perhaps the onset of cold weather accounts for this exaggeration, but new clothes did soon arrive. By the middle of September, local Conservatives ceased their criticism and even commented that the militiamen "behaved themselves surprisingly well." Satisfied with his redistribution of forces in the west, General Cooper proceeded to disband Lt. Joseph M. Alexander's command in Lauderdale County and Capt. George Hamilton's in McNairy.[10]

While Cooper focused his attention on West Tennessee, a new wave of lawlessness engulfed Middle Tennessee. On August 5, Capt. George E. Grisham reported that the ex-Confederate guerrilla Burnell Maleer accosted S. H. Taylor, a Lincoln County election official, and demanded at gunpoint the names of "every damned Radical" who had cast a ballot. Taylor talked his way out of the predicament and then fled to the militia encampment, but he pleaded with Grisham not to arrest Maleer for fear of retribution against his home and family. The plight of Lincoln's Radicals only worsened when Grisham's company returned to East Tennessee at the end of August. With the militia gone, Maleer joined forces with ex-Confederate Joe Rodgers of neighboring Franklin County and began what local Radicals dubbed a "reign of terror."[11]

In two lengthy letters to the governor and General Cooper, Simeon Bloom, a white Radical merchant from Lincoln, vividly described the mayhem in his county, which he attributed to the "total depravity of . . . the leading characters of the ex-Confederacy and . . . their deluded followers." According to Bloom, on the night of September 5, a band of ex-Confederates robbed and vandalized the stores of all the "staunch un-conditional union men" in Fayetteville. They also hurled rocks and bricks through the bedroom windows of the new registrar, A. T. Nicks. The following morning, as Bloom and his brother inspected the damage to their store, they discovered that human excrement had been "deposited on the front door step." A few days later, an intoxicated ex-Confederate named Fulgham stormed into Bloom's store and accused the proprietors of using political influence to run him out of business. When Bloom denied the charge, Fulgham drew a knife and then lifted a twenty-pound weight over his head in a threatening manner. Bloom forced the man out with a pistol, but from that point on he and his brother felt compelled to stand guard over their store twenty-four hours a day. Registrar Nicks, reportedly traumatized by his brush with violence, decided to tender his resignation and leave the county. Other county Radicals supposedly feared assassination as well. When Bloom reported these events to the civil authorities, he found them "either powerless or indisposed" to help. Reminding the governor of the risks he and others took in behalf of the Radical party during the campaign, Bloom stated that it would be "shameful" if nothing were done to protect the loyal constituency in Lincoln. "After the avalanche has full head-way," Bloom subsequently warned General Cooper, "it is then too late to stay it in its devastating course." Without explicitly saying so, Bloom was urging the return of the militia.[12]

Lincoln Conservatives tried to downplay the extent of lawlessness in their community. While condemning the spate of vandalism against Radical shopkeepers, they insisted that there were no ex-Confederate vigilante bands in the county. Furthermore, they ridiculed Taylor's story as a "malicious falsehood" circulated by the county's Union League and dismissed most of Bloom's account as "equally destitute of truth." According to the *Fayetteville Observer*, the only "outrage" of note occurred on a certain Friday afternoon when a Union Leaguer was thrown by a "rebellious mule." This newspaper further asserted that Registrar Nicks was still in town and had in fact told Lt. John Mankin, who evidently investigated the alleged Rebel depredations, that the civil authorities had law enforcement well in hand.[13]

The terror in Lincoln soon spread to Giles County, where the militia barely kept in check a growing Ku Klux Klan threat. Passive during the campaign, the Klan came out in full force in the months that followed. During the final week of August, Klansmen began harassing

Radical shopkeepers and one den, led by deputy sheriff Alonzo Peden, targeted the county's Union League for destruction. In response, General Cooper deployed Capt. William O. Rickman's entire company to Pulaski. The night riding continued, however. On August 29, the *Daily Press and Times* reported that a "gang of ruffians" fired a volley of buckshot into the militia encampment outside Pulaski. When Lieutenant Mankin formed a detachment to halt the disturbance, the "ruffians" dispersed but yelled that they "intended to shoot into the camp, or over it, as much as they d—d please." The *Pulaski Citizen* contradicted the Radical version of this incident, claiming that the shooters were "respectable young men" who frequently used "bull-bats" for target practice on the outskirts of town. According to this newspaper, a stray shot, not a deliberate volley, landed in the militia camp. While admitting that the men were probably Klansmen, the *Citizen* stressed that Giles's Klan had "never been known to molest or even speak to any one while out on their mysterious pilgrimages."[14]

Captain Rickman was not convinced of the Klan's reputed harmlessness. On September 8, believing that the Klan intended to attack a black church outside of Pulaski, the militia captain stationed a squad of men around the building. That evening, as the service was ending, the militia squad came under attack and exchanged shots with unidentified assailants. Lieutenant Mankin soon arrived with more men and apparently marched the combined force into the public square, where the militiamen cursed the Rebels and threatened "to burn the town up and demolish the Ku Klux Klan." Two days after this incident, Pulaski mayor William Ballentine demanded that Gen. Thomas Duncan deploy troops to Giles to keep an eye on the militia. Duncan did conduct an investigation into the militia's alleged misconduct, but he found both sides to blame for the county's restlessness. Referring the matter to General Cooper, Duncan declined to send troops. For all practical purposes, Rickman's ninety men were the Brownlow administration's only dependable law enforcers in the southern section of Middle Tennessee.[15]

Elsewhere in Middle Tennessee, Radicals implored General Cooper for continued militia protection. Hickman County Radicals cried that "we are threatened every day, and menaced in every conceivable manner." They requested a squad of militiamen to combat the "rebel element." In Stewart, a county that the Conservatives won, Registrar R. A. Salisbury complained that since the removal of Lt. John Robert's detachment "every man that voted for Brownlow has been threatened." Furthermore, ex-Confederates openly bullied black Union Leaguers and socially ostracized white Radicals. Salisbury vowed to resign if the militia did not return: "I have ten enemies now where I had one before. The men that are making the threats ought to have been hung long ago." Thomas Grundy, a Radical from Williamson County, was similarly displeased by Cooper's removal of militia from his community. Soldiers from the Forty-fifth U.S. Infantry were present, but Grundy believed that only militia could maintain order. After Grundy's request to raise a new company of State Guard was denied, his fears of trouble were evidently realized. Toward the end of August, the *Daily Press and Times* reported that "a ranting crowd of Conservatives" was fomenting unrest in the town of Franklin, site of the July race riot, and that the federal troops were apparently doing nothing to suppress it.[16]

Sumner County, also garrisoned by U.S. troops, became the scene of racial conflict in the latter half of August. There, ex-Confederates targeted the recently disbanded black militiamen of Company B, Second Regiment. Two privates were driven from their homes in Hartsville by armed whites, one by a local physician who bluntly explained that he had "no use for Brownlow's militia" and the other by a group of ex-Confederates who shouted, "There goes a Brownlow negro vote; by God! He can't stay in this town." A third militiaman was fired by his white employer and warned to leave Gallatin or be treated "God d—d rough." In addition to harassing former militiamen, ex-Confederates tried to break up an election in Gallatin for school directors. These incidents were cited in a petition from a group of Sumner Countians calling on General Cooper to reorganize the militia there.[17]

In DeKalb County, the State Guard itself was the target of an ex-Confederate attack. On August 8, white assailants ambushed 1st Sgt. John Askew of Company A, First Regiment, as he left the home of Congressman William B. Stokes. According to the *Daily Press and Times,* Askew's "assassins rushed up and fired several bullets into his body." Initially reported as dead, the militia sergeant eventually recovered from his wounds. The *Fayetteville Observer* joked that Askew had actually been wounded by "squirrel shot" as he attempted to steal watermelons from a local Conservative's farm. Radicals, however, cited "political hatred" for the crime and were shocked by the incident; DeKalb had come to be regarded as a party stronghold. Lt. William L. Hathaway conducted a lengthy, and ultimately futile, manhunt for the perpetrators. Meanwhile Blackburn published a defense of his company's performance in upholding the law during the political campaign. "In no section of the State," he declared, "has there been better order preserved and less personal violence and bloodshed than that which I have had the honor to control, as military commander." When General Cooper transferred Company A to Madison County a week after the shooting, DeKalb Radicals worried that the Rebels might cause more trouble. Blackburn, however, dismissed the attack on Askew as an aberration and believed that Lieutenant Hathaway, as county sheriff, could keep the peace alone. Nevertheless, Cooper stationed Capt. William S. Stuart's Company K in neighboring Warren County.[18]

Blackburn badly underestimated the resolve of DeKalb's ex-Confederates. Anti-Radical terrorism was on the rise, as General Cooper learned through a series of petitions from DeKalb citizens. "No sooner were the militia gone," one petition began, "than a factious spirit began to show itself." This "spirit" was the newly formed Knights of the Golden Circle, one of the more colorfully named dens of the Klan. This organization initiated its activities at the end of August with a parade through the streets of Statesville, a town just across the county line in Wilson. Carrying a Confederate battle flag, the Knights proclaimed their liberation from military rule. Besides treating all Radicals with "insolence," this den reportedly disrupted a biracial church service and a black meeting in Alexandria, both with gunfire, and then murdered "an aged Union man." Insisting that "nothing but force" could quell the Klan in DeKalb and the surrounding counties, the petitioners implored General Cooper to return Captain Blackburn's command, or at least "give us arms, and our brave boys, white and black, will bear and *use them.*" Although Conservative newspapers denounced the petitions as partisan fiction, Blackburn did return with a portion of his command in early September.[19]

Even in East Tennessee, a disturbance dashed the hope for post-election quiet. Capt. A. M. Clapp, who had scoffed at Rebel threats during the election, reported an attack against his unit at Rogersville (Hawkins County). According to the militia captain, on the night of August 23, "a lawless band" surprised some of his men as they slept in the courthouse and drove them out of the building under a hail of rocks. About the same time, a group of ex-Confederates stopped Clapp's servant on the street and insulted him. Unable to catch any of the culprits,

Clapp turned out his entire company and marched it through the streets, "cheering the Gov." all the way.[20]

As incidents of lawlessness and defiance multiplied, General Cooper acted forcefully. On August 26, he issued a bellicose proclamation. Citing "reliable information," he recounted the unrest in Middle and West Tennessee and declared that "forbearance in such cases is no longer a virtue." He would now halt the mustering out of the State Guard, he said, and would continue to occupy "the rebellious localities, until the disloyal citizens, or outlaws, are dealt with for their rebellious and seditious conduct." Moreover, Cooper expanded the jurisdiction of his militia officers, authorizing them to control jail security to ensure that captured offenders would "not be turned out or allowed to escape" by those in sympathy with them. Furthermore, he encouraged all victims of ex-Confederate terrorism to press charges against their attackers. Cooper assured those concerned about rising military expenses that the "disloyal tax-payers will help to bear the burden."[21]

General Cooper's proclamation elicited a fierce anti-Radical rebuttal. The *Union and Dispatch* unleashed an especially vicious editorial barrage of criticism and character assassination. Cooper's circular was "a wordy, bombastic order," this newspaper declared, which smacked of "the imperious command of the tyrant." Ridiculing the general's "reliable information," the *Dispatch* accused him of "greedily" accepting as true the Radical *Press and Times*'s "fancy sketches" of Rebel violence against white Unionists and freedmen. According to the *Dispatch*, there was no significant ex-Confederate intimidation anywhere in the state. The trouble in Madison County, in particular, was dismissed as a vengeful rumor manufactured by Registrar Robert Medlin, whose seat in the Tennessee General Assembly was being contested by the Conservatives. The *Dispatch* suggested that Cooper verify his information before issuing Mexican-style "pronunciamentos."[22]

Other prominent Conservative voices were also raised in protest. Franklin mayor J. B. McEwen addressed a letter to General Cooper denying the recent allegations of misconduct by his constituents. Conceding that a few "idlers" caused some trouble on occasion, the mayor insisted that he could uphold the law without a company of militia. Sumner County whites similarly declared Cooper's allegations of lawlessness "false." Fearing the reactivation of the black militia, the county sent a delegation to Nashville to dissuade the general from deploying any state troops in their county. Cooper, however, made no promises to the delegation.[23]

In some respects, Cooper's circular was a grand bluff. Despite his stated intention to retain most of the State Guard, Cooper disbanded seven companies within a fortnight of his proclamation (see Appendix D). By September 10, more than one thousand militiamen had been mustered out.

Before disbanding, Company I, First Regiment, performed a final service for its state. The unit had recently returned to Tazewell in Claiborne County, and Lt. John Ellis had assumed command following the resignation of Capt. James Evans. On August 30, Sheriff C. D. Willis asked Ellis to assist him in apprehending "a desperate man" named George Campbell. Willis had apparently tried to arrest Campbell, but was chased away at gunpoint. Ellis agreed to help and reinforced the sheriff with a corporal and six men. Willis then returned to the home of Campbell and demanded an immediate surrender. When Campbell foolishly brandished a double-barreled shotgun, the militia squad fired, "killing him instantly." The lack of newspaper coverage suggests that Campbell was a plain felon (though his crime was never stated) and not a political enemy of the Brownlow administration.[24]

With the discharge of most militiamen in August and September, the Radicals incurred their greatest single financial expense in the politics of force—payroll. The paymaster was Maj. E. J. Brooks, a wealthy thirty-one-year-old lawyer and manufacturer from Washington County. In the course of his duties, he disbursed $166,861 in wages to the State Guard, many of the men receiving pay for the first time as they were mustered out. Pay scales were in accordance with U.S. Army regulations: the monthly wages for enlisted men ranged from $16 for privates to $20 for sergeants. The comparable monthly wage for a farm laborer in the late 1860s was between $16 and $18. Unlike a farm worker, however, militiamen also received a one-time subsistence allowance of $12 and were usually reimbursed for legitimate clothing purchases beyond the issue of their basic uniform. After "stoppages" (i.e., fines for losing or damaging equipment or for a disciplinary infraction), a volunteer stood to make a fair sum of money. The men of Company H, First Regiment, for instance, earned an average of nearly $200 each during about eight months of duty. Officers, of course, enjoyed more generous wages. Company commanders earned $70 per month, while their first and second lieutenants earned $50 and $45 respectively. General Cooper appears to have made $300 per month. All officers received a daily subsistence allowance of $1.20, and many had personal servants paid for by the state at the grade of private. Wiley Williams, for instance, a thirty-year-old black shoemaker from Davidson County, tended to Lieutenant Mankin, an officer in the all-white Company H, First Regiment. By the end of their service, some line officers had garnered nearly $1,000.[25]

For many militiamen, payday afforded an opportunity to celebrate, and there was no better place to have fun than Nashville. "The militia recently mustered out are spending money about town quite freely," the *Daily Press and Times* noted with satisfaction, "business under this new impetus is looking up." Anti-Radical newspapers downplayed this supposed economic boon and instead highlighted the rowdy conduct of "Cooper's bummers." According to them, saloons and brothels were the principal beneficiaries of spendthrift militiamen, while the citizenry had to endure the drunken revelry that ensued. Militiamen reportedly roamed the streets shouting at people, picking fights, or "stealing peaches." In one incident, a squad of Captain Blackburn's men rode through the streets, waving revolvers and "inspiring fully as much terror as could be expected." In another, some of Captain Clingan's men snatched the hat off a black minister and ran off laughing. In a third, three men from Company C, First Regiment, barged into a private residence where they harassed two female occupants with lewd flirtations and insults. The timely arrival of the ladies' husbands scared the intruders away. In the wake of such tomfoolery, the *Paris Intelligencer* declared that the capital was "polluted by the filth and obscenities of the dirty melish."[26]

General Cooper was displeased by these incidents. In an effort to dissuade his men from visiting houses of prostitution, most notably those located in a section of the city known as "Smokey Row," he ordered that any soldier contracting "syphilus or Gonorrhea" would have to pay for medical treatment out of his own wages. As for those who got drunk and disturbed the peace, Cooper assisted the city magistrates in bringing them to justice. With the general's approval, Lt. Robert Miner handed over for civil trial the men involved in molesting the two women. These men were jailed on one-thousand-dollar bail. An indeterminate number of other volunteers spent time in the state penitentiary while they waited for their day in court. Most delinquent militiamen, however, faced military tribunals. In one court-martial, Lt. E. R. Brown was drummed out of the service for "habitual drunkenness and utter worthlessness." In another, seven black soldiers, including their lieutenant, H. H. Mitchell (Company G, Second Regiment) received dishonorable discharges for destroying private property. Evidently, on the night of August 14, these men pillaged the farmhouse of Newell Watson, making off with a large number of watermelons. For his part in the crime, Mitchell was publicly reprimanded, dishonorably discharged, and fined twenty-five dollars.[27]

For Pvt. Samuel F. Scott, disbandment brought neither pay nor pleasure, only an unexpected form of punishment: a false accusation of desertion. Described by an associate as "invariably unconditionally loyal," Scott had enthusiastically enlisted in Company G, First Regiment and was apparently one of that troubled unit's better soldiers. While stationed at Trenton, he received word that his wife was sick and near death. Rather than relate his story to Capt. Pryor Adkins, who may have disliked the private, Scott asked 2nd Lt. Alvin Parker for help. Though sympathetic, Parker was unsure of his authority to grant leave. However, 1st Lt. J. M. Alexander, commander of Company F, Second Regiment, happened to be in Trenton at the time and, similarly moved by Scott's plight, told Parker to grant a hardship leave. Evidently, no one informed Adkins of this decision. On July 28, only a few days before the election, Scott left for his home in Morgan County on twenty days' leave. Unfortunately, during his absence Company G was disbanded, and when the unit drew its pay, Scott was incorrectly listed as a deserter, a mistake which the private's benefactor, state senator George W. Keith, claimed was a deliberate "infamy" on the part of Adkins. Ignorant of this "infamy," Scott went to Knoxville and officially mustered out with Capt. Kemp Murphy's company. His application for pay, however, was rejected by Major Brooks, who knew the man only as a deserter. What followed was a legal battle for back pay that lasted nine months. Scott wrote several letters to the paymaster and submitted affidavits from lieutenants Parker and Alexander, as well as Senator Keith. Eventually, Governor Brownlow became involved in behalf of Scott. On May 26, 1868, the State Guard finally paid the private his overdue wages—$69.86.[28]

Although the State Guard continued to disband, General Cooper was still determined to suppress ex-Confederate vigilantism. On September 3, he created a "special command," composed of the eight remaining militia companies, and placed it under the leadership of newly promoted Maj. John T. Robeson (see Appendix D). Officially designated

First Battalion, the streamlined "special command" soon found itself heavily engaged, fighting ex-Confederate bands in some of the most "rebellious" portions of Middle and West Tennessee.[29]

Major Robeson accepted his promotion gratefully, but he made no substantial changes to the Guard's mode of operations. Trusting his captains to fulfill their duties, Robeson continued to hunt down ex-Confederate outlaws in the state's northwest corner, his activities taking him once again into Dyer and Obion counties. Evidently, during the first week of September some Rebels began skulking around the home of the late state senator Almon Case, frightening his widow. When a doctor and a man named Neely, who had been looking after Mrs. Case, came to visit her, a party of Rebels fired on the men with shotguns, badly wounding Neely. Robeson sent a large mounted force under Lt. William Fuller in pursuit, but none of the perpetrators was ever caught. The major was disgusted by the region's pronounced Confederate sympathies. "There is verry few people who wants the civil law enforced if any in these Counties," he wrote. "We will have to hurt Some one before they will behave in West Tenn."[30]

The militia in Madison County fulfilled Robeson's prophecy with bloody results. In the first half of September, Capt. G. W. Kirk was away on sick leave and Captain Blackburn was on emergency duty back in DeKalb. Commanding the militia in Madison were lieutenants William Cravens and Francis M. Kirk, the latter only eighteen years old. Madison's ex-Confederates exploited this apparent absence of seasoned militia leadership to spread their terror. Cravens, who had performed well in independent commands during the recent political campaign, believed that these Rebels were plotting an uprising against the militia. Accordingly, he implemented drastic countermeasures, ordering his men to disarm every ex-Confederate citizen in the county. What followed was a scene reminiscent of Captain Rickman's operations in Franklin County the previous May. Beginning on September 5, militia squads began searching homes and halting people on the streets, confiscating weapons as they were found. In the process, several militiamen abused their authority. In one instance, some privates senselessly killed two mules only to discover that the animals belonged to a local Radical. In another, a squad severely beat a man named Noah Sellers after he allegedly called the militiamen brigands. Outraged whites warned Cravens that if his men persisted in their activities, "they would shoot their d—n welt's out." Unperturbed, the militia lieutenant informed Adjutant General Samuel Hunt that if the ex-Confederates offered armed resistance he would "rally his company and whip out this county." If worst came to worst, he vowed he would "burn every house and kill every man."[31]

Before State Guard headquarters could respond to Cravens's message, the lieutenant's men shot a prominent ex-Confederate, Maj. Thomas H. Hartmus. It seems that on the night of September 10, three militiamen—Cpl. James Evans, Cpl. Isaac Sandlin, and Pvt. Samuel Phelps—confronted Hartmus and demanded his pistol. Hartmus reluctantly complied, muttering something about "usurpation." Evidently incensed by the remark, one of the corporals shot Hartmus in the chest. Conservative sources claimed that the militiamen were drunk and, rather than asking Hartmus for his weapon, they ambushed him and shot him in the stomach. A Radical witness insisted that Hartmus actually instigated the trouble, firing three shots at the militiamen before Corporal Evans gunned him down. Whatever the truth, great excitement ensued. Former Confederate leader J. T. McCutchen hastily organized a posse and went after the militiamen, who after exchanging a few shots with their pursuers ran back to camp, stole some horses, and galloped into the countryside. As a large, armed, and angry white mob approached the militia encampment, Lt. Francis Kirk formed a defensive line and telegraphed Major Robeson that a riot was imminent.[32]

No clash of arms occurred, but the Hartmus controversy had only begun. The following morning, Major Robeson arrived and brought Capt. J. L. Kirk's racially mixed command with him. "Defiantly parading the streets," in the words of one observer, Robeson dispersed the crowd, which had grown to some eight hundred men. After questioning Lieutenants Kirk and Cravens, he sent a detachment after the three fleeing militiamen, who had reportedly left the county by train. In the meantime, Jackson's whites gathered in the public square and cheered as Mayor William Alexander publicly condemned "the lawless acts of the militia." Over the next three days, an eleven-man committee compiled a formal list of protests against the "bloodhounds of Brownlow." Proclaiming that Madison County had been "entirely peaceable and quiet" until the militia arrived, the committee resolved to ask the federal garrison for a temporary contingent of troops. Furthermore, it demanded the immediate relocation of the militia encampment, which was then on the grounds of West Tennessee College. Finally, the committee appointed a three-man delegation to meet with the governor and negotiate the permanent removal of all militia forces from the county.[33]

The Jackson delegation achieved a significant victory over the State Guard. The three members embodied a wide range of political views. W. J. Hurt was one of the few Conservatives to win a seat in the incoming Thirty-fifth General Assembly. Hervey Brown was a moderate Republican who had voted against the militia act the previous February. Thomas C. Muse was a strong Radical who had voted for the act but had come to believe that the State Guard had outlasted its usefulness. Meeting with Governor Brownlow and General Cooper in Knoxville on or about September 16, the delegates argued that the continued presence of the militia in Madison only inflamed passions. Pleading with the executive to remove the militia, the delegates promised that the civil authorities would make a better effort to protect the county's Radicals regardless of race. Brownlow agreed to withdraw the militia as "a fair test of the good intentions" of the people of Madison. General Cooper objected, believing that the militia's removal was a risky "experiment," but he dutifully complied. Over the next several days, Cooper not only withdrew Capt. J. L. Kirk's racially mixed company but officially disbanded it; thus the last of the black militiamen were gone. The other companies soon left for new assignments. At the end of the month, W. P. Bond, a Radical circuit court judge in West Tennessee, reported that justice was being served in Madison County and that he had sentenced several ex-Confederate criminals without fear of reprisal. The *Press and Times,* however, observed these developments with disapproval. Commenting on Hartmus's speedy recovery from his wound, this newspaper ruefully noted that "poor Senator Case and our other murdered loyalists do not recover so quickly."[34]

As the Brownlow administration resolved the problem of law enforcement in Madison County, a new, more serious, crisis erupted in Nashville. The city's municipal election, scheduled for September 28, became the occasion for an exciting political showdown. The previous month, Radicals had bickered over whom to run for mayor. One faction nominated Augustus E. Alden while another selected Abram Myers. Alden had ably served the party as registrar for Davidson County, but he was a carpetbagger from Minnesota, disliked by many native Radicals. Myers enjoyed black support, but he lacked the governor's endorsement. Delighted by the Radical rift, Conservatives backed H. S. Scovel, a respectable though uninspiring Republican moderate who also had the support of a third Radical faction, one sponsored by the *Daily Press and Times*. Myers's accidental death on September 7 simplified the choices but polarized the electorate. As most Radicals united behind Alden, Conservatives abruptly declared their intention to conduct the election in accordance with the city charter, which stipulated that only white males could vote and that the civil authorities, not registrars appointed by the governor, controlled the election machinery. In effect, the Conservatives were arguing that their city government operated like a state-chartered bank or railroad, and that therefore the state franchise act, with its much despised provision for black suffrage, did not apply to a municipal election. City Radicals were quick to call on the governor for help.[35]

Brownlow took decisive measures to defeat this Conservative challenge. First, he appointed B. J. Sheridan, a party stalwart, as the new county registrar. Then, on September 18, he proclaimed that "the franchise law is a part and parcel of the constitution, has been sustained by the supreme court of Tennessee, and all elections held in violation of said law are null and void, and of no effect whatever." When incumbent mayor W. Matt Brown threw his powerful support to the Conservative position, and then announced his candidacy for reelection, Brownlow prepared for civil war. On September 22, he ordered General Cooper to concentrate "immediately all the troops, Infantry and Cavalry," in the Nashville precincts. Anticipating such a command, Cooper had already set his militia companies in motion. In less than six days, the entire First Battalion, Tennessee State Guard, was in Nashville. As this force arrived, the militia general admonished the Conservatives "to desist from any attempt to hold any election in violation of the Franchise Law."[36]

Rightly believing that General Cooper intended to enforce Brownlow's decree "at the point of the bayonet," Conservatives denounced the "high-swelling and blood-portending" actions of the administration. Mayor Brown was especially vehement. On September 24, he proclaimed that the election would take place as required by the city charter, adding that "we shall hardly be deterred from the performance of that duty by any force of mere militia with which our good and quiet citizens are threatened." He furthermore augmented the city police force by three hundred men. Hoping for peace, however, Brown encouraged the Radicals to hold their own election under the franchise act. Thus, the mayor was recommending that the city hold a dual election and then "let the courts, the only proper arbiters, decide in the end."

Seeking federal support, Brown wrote President Andrew Johnson, explained his position, and urged the president to use U.S. troops against Brownlow's "standing army" should the latter attempt "the seizure by armed force of our City." Though sympathetic to the Conservative position, Johnson left the matter to the appropriate military leaders.[37]

The garrison in Nashville watched these developments closely. As the tension mounted, the army officers debated their proper course of action. Gen. Thomas Duncan believed that Mayor Brown's position was "the correct one" and suggested that federal troops provide security for both elections. "For those who hold their election illegally," he stated, "it will only be an innocent amusement." Gen. George Thomas disagreed with his subordinate. For him, two competing elections guaranteed violence. Accepting Brownlow's "construction of the law," Thomas instructed Duncan to recognize only the governor's authority and to aid the State Guard in enforcing the franchise act. As a result of Mayor Brown's communication with President Johnson, however, Gen. Ulysses S. Grant overruled Thomas and imposed new constraints on the federal troops in Nashville. Grant stated that "the military cannot set up to be judge as to which set of election judges have the right to control, but must confine their action to putting down hostile mobs." These instructions seemed to vindicate the position of Mayor Brown, who was "exceedingly pleased," for it appeared that two elections would be held after all.[38]

The Brownlow administration was indifferent to Grant's decision. Determined to thwart the mayor's political maneuvers, branded a "Little Rebellion" by the *Whig* and outright treason by General Cooper, the administration steadily strengthened its military power in the city. On September 25, the State Guard took possession of the city armory to prevent its "seizure by Rebels." On the twenty-sixth, General Cooper ordered three recently discharged militia officers, McKinley, Houston, and Fleming, to reorganize their black companies for use as a reserve force. Finally, on the twenty-seventh, Governor Brownlow proclaimed that "an insurrection exists in the City of Nashville." He then called on the garrison to render assistance in suppressing it. While the governor awaited a reply from General Thomas, Maj. John T. Robeson sent militia detachments into the city's ten voting districts, instructing his officers to bivouac at the polling places and to permit only those election officials appointed by Registrar Sheridan to operate the polls. Flaunting the power of the State Guard, Captain Rickman paraded his company through the streets with "his Band playing and Colors flying."[39]

This militant posturing convinced General Thomas that the army could not remain neutral during the election. Warning that "a collision is inevitable," he asked General Grant for clarification of the rules of engagement. Thomas claimed that if the militia and city police came to blows, the army would have to choose sides or prevent both elections altogether. But to enforce a dual election, he added, would "be a practical decision against State authority and against the franchise law." Clearly, Thomas favored the Radicals, but Grant repeatedly ordered him not to take sides, stating that his duty was simply to "prevent conflict" and "preserve peace." After exchanging telegrams with his superior for three days, however, Thomas received orders that resolved his dilemma. At 9:00 p.m. on September 26, Grant significantly modified his instructions to Thomas. "The military cannot be made use of to defeat the executive of a State," Grant averred. "You are not to prevent the legal State force from the execution of its orders." Thomas could now in good conscience uphold actions taken by the Tennessee State Guard. The next morning, as Brownlow was declaring a state of insurrection, the general visited Mayor Matt Brown and bluntly informed him that the army would "sustain the governor in case of collision."[40]

Mayor Brown and the city council were crestfallen at the sudden turn of events. Brown denounced Thomas's decision as a "signal and deplorable mistake," but under pressure from several councilmen he agreed to concede the contest to Brownlow. Alderman John Coltart alone urged the council to continue its resistance and hold an election under the city charter "at all hazards, no matter what may be the consequences." No one seconded his motion, however. General Thomas had reinforced the garrison with over one thousand men, bringing U.S. troop strength in Nashville to fourteen hundred. This force, combined with the six hundred militiamen of the State Guard, left the city police heavily outnumbered. On the afternoon of September 27, Brown notified the public of the council's decision and then withdrew from the race. Blaming Thomas for "forcibly preventing a peaceable election," the mayor insisted that enforcing the franchise act in Nashville was "clearly illegal." In a bitter letter to President Johnson, Brown cried that the city was in "a state of organized anarchy never parallelled."[41]

In accordance with an agreement between generals Cooper and Thomas, the State Guard relinquished control of the polls to the federal garrison shortly after the election began. The militiamen returned to their bivouacs and the army presided over a generally quiet election.

Registrar Sheridan reportedly combed the streets ensuring that every black man in the city voted the Radical ticket, while Captain Blackburn allegedly scoured the "cellars and attics" in search of surreptitious charter voting. "Martial law reigned as completely as it did during the battle of Nashville," observed the *Republican Banner*. To this newspaper, the election was little more than "military dictation" from the "unmilitary" Thomas. To other anti-Radicals, the election was a "disgusting farce" enacted by "Satan's twin brother"—Governor Brownlow. Desperate to prevent the impending Radical triumph, Mayor Brown made a final plea to General Thomas on the afternoon of September 28, asking permission to hold an election under the charter, "late as it is," or to hold one at a subsequent date. "If you, general, desire to see equal justice," the mayor chided, "you will see that we are permitted to hold such an election without the interference from the State militia." Thomas politely refused the mayor's request, reiterating that a peaceful election under the charter was impossible. In the end, A. E. Alden became mayor in a landslide over Scovel, 2,423 votes to 258, and Radicals took control of the city council. Governor Brownlow telegraphed State Guard headquarters to express his "entire approval" of Cooper's leadership and the militia's performance during the crisis. The politics of force had prevailed once again, but, in the words of General Thomas, "how narrowly [Tennessee] escaped from a condition of War."[42]

The drama of the Nashville election did not end with the closing of the polls. With federal troops departing as quickly as they had arrived, the lame-duck Mayor Brown endeavored to secure an injunction against Registrar Sheridan's certification of the election returns. On the morning of October 2, after Radical chancellor Horace Harrison dismissed the injunction, the mayor's friends on the city council warned him that the State Guard planned to "make a 'clean shuckling' of the old administration" if he remained defiant. Brown remained defiant. When Mayor-elect Alden arrived at city hall to assume his duties, Brown barred his entrance. "I believe you to be illegally elected," he declared, "and therefore cannot surrender you the office." Alden immediately reported this to Governor Brownlow, who instructed General Cooper to use "whatever force is necessary . . . to overcome any illegal resistance." Accordingly, Cooper ordered Captain Blackburn to effect the transfer of municipal power.[43]

Blackburn's mission was a success, although the anti-Radical press depicted his confrontation with Brown as a piece of burlesque. At 5:00

p.m. on October 2, Blackburn and Lieutenant Hathaway arrived outside city hall with about forty mounted men. At the approach of a large crowd of black and white onlookers, the militia formed a line of battle, the "ignorant young tow-heads" presenting a "horrid front." Blackburn, accompanied by Hathaway and five enlisted men, then entered the building and, after supposedly getting lost on the third floor, found the mayor in conversation with several other Conservative politicians. According to one Conservative witness, the militiamen "sported shockingly bad hats." As Brown feigned surprise at the arrival of this inelegant armed party, Blackburn ordered him to turn over the mayoral books and keys. When Brown asked the militia captain if he intended to use force, Blackburn, who reportedly "trembled with excitement," replied that he had orders to "take possession" of the office. Brown then demanded to see written authorization, which Blackburn produced after some hesitation. As the mayor slowly read the orders, his fellow Conservatives growled protests at the militiamen, who "manifested considerable uneasiness." Evidently satisfied with the authenticity of Blackburn's orders, Brown departed the building and addressed the multitudes in pompous style: "I have surrendered my office, but I want you to understand that I yield only to the bayonet." The whites in the crowd cheered wildly at their mayor's audacious exit, while the "shabby" detachment of militiamen countered with a "hideous 'yi, yi.'" Leaving a squad behind to protect Mayor Alden, who apparently had been waiting outside, Blackburn and his "critter company" sauntered off toward the courthouse, where they spent the night. "Thus ended the Brownlow-Alden *coup d' etat.*"[44]

The Nashville election is an instructive example of Brownlow's force politics in action. The *Banner* howled that the whole episode was a case of "*might* overruling *right*." Radical "might" was unmistakable, but Conservative "right" was a matter of debate. Radicals denied that the use of militia constituted military usurpation. Rather, the governor had employed justifiable force against a "pestiferous rebel Mayor" who, incidentally, had never taken any oath of allegiance. Moreover, Radicals insisted that the Brownlow administration was not motivated by partisan politics, citing Adjutant General Samuel Hunt's vote for Scovel as compelling proof. In any case, Brownlow could not have permitted such an unprecedented event as a dual election, however reasonable the idea may have seemed to people like Mayor Brown, without subverting the franchise act and losing credibility. When Brown and his allies pressed the issue, the State Guard stymied their efforts. To be sure, the federal garrison played a critical role, but its involvement mostly prevented a street battle, one in which the more numerous and better led, trained, and equipped militia would have surely routed the city police and arrested the "charter party" officials. Arguably, the aggressive use of militia risked civil violence, but without its presence, the Conservative scheme would likely have been carried to fruition. The army certainly would not have stopped it, for without a potential clash between militia and city police to give it a pretext for stepping in, the U.S. soldiers would have stayed in their barracks on September 28. Consequently, a dual election would have taken place in spite of Brownlow's decrees. Whether the Conservatives retained control of the city, or merely held the Radicals at bay temporarily while the courts sorted out the confusion, anti-Radicalism would have gained immeasurable political capital.[45]

All things considered, the State Guard performed commendably in the Nashville controversy, as it had during the state election. General Cooper and his officers appreciated the gravity of the situation and exercised tight discipline over their enlisted men throughout the crisis. There were no serious disturbances, violent or otherwise. Captain Blackburn's conduct during the Brown standoff is a good example of the State Guard's professional-like behavior. The militia captain had authority to physically oust the mayor, yet he responded to Brown's obstinacy with politeness and restraint.

While acknowledging the State Guard's able performance, the officers of the federal garrison were not overly impressed by its military bearing. In the aftermath of the election, Company C, First Regiment was camped outside the army base in Nashville, the Ash Barracks, the men sharing a water hole with the U.S. soldiers. The army officers soon came to detest what they considered a "laxity of discipline" on the part of this unit. "I noticed the Privates," Lt. Robert P. Wilson complained on one occasion, "attending to the call of nature in full view of the houses and public highways." Lt. Scott Payne reported another disgraceful encounter. Returning to camp one night, he discovered a militiaman lying on the side of the road "in a beastly state of intoxication." He regarded the inebriate "a disgusting object to behold." Other officers considered the militia an outright danger. According to Lt. F. W. Foote, a group of militiamen accosted one his men near the water hole in an attempt to steal his "pantaloons." When the soldier resisted, his attackers splashed water in his face, splattered his uniform with mud, and broke his water pitcher. Other federal soldiers received similar treatment, one almost having his hat stolen. A final indignity proved nearly fatal. Riding past the militia encampment one evening, a cavalry sergeant was fired on by a party of militiamen, the shot passing "within less than four feet of his head."[46]

After placing a guard around the water hole, General Duncan demanded that General Cooper exercise greater control over his men. Never one to take misconduct lightly, Cooper ordered Capt. Robert L. Hall to head an investigation of the army's charges and ensure "that Such Cases do not Occur again." Hall asked Duncan for affidavits, but he refused to speak directly with any of the general's lieutenants, perhaps resenting their aspersions against his leadership. In some respects, the antics of his men were typical of the sort of pranks played amongst rival services. In the end, Hall merely confined a few suspects to the workhouse and declared the matter closed. In the meantime, Nashville authorities appear to have put an end to Company C's practice of relieving itself in public. On October 7, the city police arrested four militiamen for "indecent exposure."[47]

Culminating the State Guard's string of shameful incidents was one that could be termed the Mollie Brown affair. On the night of October 6, Lt. William G. Fuller received a pass and, with a large sum of cash in pocket, went into town for "a little fun in the jungles." More precisely, the lieutenant made a visit to Smokey Row. While there, he drank heavily and enjoyed the affections of pretty Mollie Brown, an orphan girl turned prostitute. At some point during the night, he produced a roll of bills worth $220, but gave his companion a mere 50 cents with which he expected her to go and buy him a beer. Brown, however, apparently waited for the lieutenant to pass out and then took the whole purse. After sobering up, an enraged Fuller tracked Brown down and demanded at gunpoint the return of his money. When she brashly refused, he dragged the girl into court on the charge of theft. Before the lieutenant could make his case, however, General Cooper ordered Fuller dishonorably discharged for drunkenness and conduct unbecoming an officer. Anti-Radical newspapers had a good laugh over the whole affair. Fuller later apologized profusely for his misdeeds and, on Major Robeson's recommendation (Fuller had been a capable officer in the field), the sentence was eventually commuted to honorable discharge. Nevertheless, Fuller's fate, like that of Captain Chambers and lieutenants

Brown and Mitchell before him, demonstrates that wayward officers received little mercy in the State Guard.[48]

In his addresses to the incoming Thirty-fifth General Assembly on October 9 and 10, Governor Brownlow made no reference to the Nashville election nor to his militia's misadventures afterward. Rather, he exulted that the Radicals' now seemingly uncontested political control would enable the party to transform Tennessee into "the Harbinger of the New South." Among his many proposals, Brownlow urged the assembly to allocate funds for public education and internal improvements, recommended an extension of civil liberties to the freedmen, and unveiled a plan to attract white immigrants to the state. In order to pay for these new programs and enhance the state's image abroad, however, the standing army would have to go. Brownlow acknowledged the State Guard's crucial contribution to Radical victory, but he was "anxious to rid the State of this item of expense." Listening with pride and satisfaction to their executive's words were three former militia captains, Representative Thompson McKinley, Principal Clerk of the House George E. Grisham, and Doorkeeper James H. Sumner. McKinley played an important role in this "New South" agenda, sponsoring the "Common Carriers" bill, which granted blacks equal access to public transportation, and supporting the "Omnibus" bill, which initiated extravagant railroad construction.[49]

Confident that the anti-Radical threat was now pretty much contained, Brownlow proceeded to reduce the size and scope of militia activities. On October 11, General Cooper turned operational command over to Major Robeson, while most of the militia staff officers resigned their commissions. At about the same time, Adjutant General Sam Hunt resigned and was replaced by Daniel T. Boynton. By October 15, the State Guard consisted of only four companies. Major Robeson decided to deploy these units to the state's familiar trouble spots. Captain Rickman returned to Pulaski, while the remaining three companies headed to West Tennessee.[50]

Rickman did not stay in Pulaski for long. In mid-October, he inaugurated an ambitious plan to "make the Rebels strate" throughout southern Middle Tennessee. While Lt. John J. Mankin occupied Lewisburg in Marshall County with twenty-three men, Rickman marched the main body sixty-one miles to Tullahoma in Franklin County, where his career as a militia officer had begun six months before. Once there, he sent his mounted section on an extensive fifteen-day sweep through Franklin, Lincoln, and Giles counties. In the end, the mission proved more a cat-and-mouse game than a decisive blow at ex-Confederate vigilantism. The Klan eluded his grasp, and his men grew weary of the seemingly interminable patrols. When Rebels torched a portion of his unit's winter quarters, Rickman fumed that Franklin remained "one of the most Rebellious places in Middle Tenn." Nevertheless, his mere presence appears to have kept much of the region's chronic lawlessness in check. Rickman eventually lost his passion for the State Guard, however. At the end of October, he wrote that he needed to move his family to East Tennessee, "where thay can see Loyal People." He then departed on what turned out to be permanent leave. In one of his last communications with headquarters, the veteran militia captain proudly declared, "I am a soldier." Lieutenant Mankin assumed command of Company B some time in November.[51]

Militia law enforcement in West Tennessee was as frustrating as in Middle. After establishing his headquarters at Trenton with one company under Capt. William Holt, Major Robeson stationed Capt. Robert Hall in Union City and Capt. E. R. Hall in Jackson—the ex-Confederates in Madison County having apparently failed their "fair test" agreement of the previous month. A company of federal troops, also stationed at Union City, helped keep Obion County relatively quiet, but Robeson declared that the social and political climate in the rest of the section was "worse than in 61." On October 14, an estimated one hundred mounted Rebels welcomed his return to Gibson County with a wild dash through the streets of Trenton aimed at raiding the militia commissariat. Robeson's exact countermeasures are unknown, but he appears to have withdrawn his company from Union City and used it to reinforce his positions in Jackson and Trenton. In any event, he informed the governor that the county's Rebels "are only kept down by Fear." Besides trying to suppress ex-Confederate vigilantes, Robeson sought to rectify the dismal Radical voting record in Henry County, which failed to hold a valid election in August. To this end, the major went to Paris in November and supervised Registrar James Guthrie's registration of the county's loyal voters.[52]

Left behind in Trenton during Robeson's many excursions was Capt. William C. Holt. For much of the deployment, he had served under Robeson as the "junior" captain of Company E, First Regiment, but with Robeson's promotion to major at the beginning of September,

Holt assumed full command in his own right. Unfortunately, most of the men in the company were Robeson volunteers and they (including Lieutenant Fuller prior to his discharge) disliked Holt, thinking him incompetent. Further complicating the growing disharmony within the unit was the appointment of Lt. Moses Kinman, a Holt supporter, to replace the popular Fuller. Divided loyalties inevitably undermined unit cohesion and, throughout the autumn, men deserted Company E in a slow but steady stream. Those who remained got into trouble. Sometime in October, a group of militiamen reportedly killed the livestock of a local farmer, producing a needless, albeit minor, controversy for the Brownlow administration.[53]

Major Robeson was appalled by these developments and by the decline of his old company, formerly one of the best in the State Guard. On October 14, with General Cooper's blessing, he relieved Holt of command. Holt, however, had political friends who used their influence to get him reinstated two weeks later. Resigned to having to work with Holt, Robeson ordered the company into winter quarters, while he attended to matters elsewhere in West Tennessee. With the exception of an occasional desertion, the men of Company E appear to have sat quietly in camp for the duration of their service.[54]

Company E's experience reveals that, like every military organization, the Tennessee State Guard suffered its share of desertion. Nearly forty men deserted Company E, mostly during Holt's tenure, although that total was not indicative of the militia at large. Over the course of the entire deployment, about 155 militiamen deserted, barely 8 percent of the mobilized force. Moreover, with the exception of Holt and Captain Clingan (who lost twenty-six men to desertion while stationed in Madison County), desertion never prevented State Guard officers from carrying out their mission. Eighty-eight militiamen deserted while on duty in the west, a ratio of nearly one man in five. The *Republican Banner* attributed this to delinquent payroll, but the hostile ex-Confederate climate unquestionably contributed. The desertion rate in Middle Tennessee was substantially lower: sixty-four men altogether (about one in twenty). In East Tennessee, the rates were negligible: only three men deserted in that part of the state. Significantly, very few black militiamen deserted. The four all-black units experienced just one desertion among them. The mixed companies reported seventeen, but there is no indication of these men's race. Regardless of whether they were white or black,

Captain Grisham probably spoke for all militia commanders when he referred to the ten men who deserted from his unit as "worthless individuals." Some officers spent a great deal of energy hunting down such men. Captain Clingan, for example, pursued Pvt. Francis M. Jack all the way to Bradley County, his unit's muster point. While being transported back to Nashville by rail, however, Jack leaped from the train and disappeared.[55]

Rounding out the State Guard's activities for the year, Capt. E. R. Hall maintained an uneasy peace in Madison County. The white citizens there were displeased by what they considered the unethical practices of their new registrar, Galen E. Green. Apparently, as a purveyor of beef to the State Guard, Green had been exaggerating ex-Confederate lawlessness so as to retain the presence of the militia, his principal customer, while using his profits to buy black political support. Ignoring this alleged profiteering, Captain Hall agreed with Green that vigilantes dominated the countryside. Throughout November, he searched in vain for a "gang of highwaymen" who had reportedly robbed a number of black homes. He had hoped for help from the civil authorities, but he found the white leadership uncooperative and the citizenry hostile. In Jackson, the militiamen endured daily verbal abuse—"Damned Cowardly Brownlow Sons of b—s" was a frequent insult—and occasionally found their lives in danger. In one instance, three ex-Confederates ambushed a lone militia sentry and tried to steal his rifle before being scared off by the timely arrival of the relief guard. In another, the company supply wagon was intercepted and delayed by a group of Rebels toting double-barreled shotguns. Hall ordered his men to shoot anyone who willfully interfered with their duties, but Sheriff George C. Perkins persuaded the militia captain to retract this command lest the county experience a repetition of the Hartmus shooting.[56]

Nonetheless, Jackson once again became the scene of a near-riot. It happened on the night of November 23. Evidently, one of Hall's men was courting a local girl, and during one of their meetings, the town constable arrested the militiaman for allegedly disturbing the peace. A black witness inexplicably cheered the arrest and cursed the soldier for being "one of Brownlow's melish." After his release later that evening, the humiliated soldier headed back to town, "swearing that he would kill the negro" who had mocked him. Some of his companions grabbed their rifles and followed him. When the militiamen entered the public square, several surprised and apprehensive townspeople opened fire, some of the shots ironically coming from the law office of Hervey Brown, one the delegates who had earlier negotiated the removal of the militia from Madison County. After discharging a volley of their own, the militiamen fell back to camp, where Captain Hall now had the entire company on full alert. Learning that a large group of whites was assembling "for the purpose of *charging* my *Camp*," Hall personally conducted a two-hour patrol through the streets to head off trouble. The following day, Hall courageously attended a town meeting where angry whites protested the presence of his militia company. One citizen reportedly recommended that the mayor bar the militia from the town limits and that the police shoot violators on sight. Hall insisted that ex-Confederate agitators were to blame for the shooting affray and for the general "ill feeling" toward his men. Reiterating his commitment to law enforcement, he demanded that the townspeople assist him in this task. He doubted, however, that a change of heart would be forthcoming. In closing a lengthy report to General Cooper, he stated that "if Rebels in this county want a fight with me or the Militia they can have it."[57]

The ex-Confederates may have displayed such fighting spirit in Madison and elsewhere because they knew that Captain Hall and the rest of the militia would soon be mustered out. Following the governor's address in October, the general assembly produced legislation that would eventually prompt the governor to complete his demobilization of the State Guard. On October 15, Stephen J. Matthews of Blount County introduced Senate Bill 16, "to Reduce Military Expenses," which called for extensive cuts in the militia's budget. On November 22, the Matthews's bill passed the Senate with little opposition, seventeen to two. In the house, several Radicals from Middle and West Tennessee resisted the bill's passage but ultimately lost their fight forty-eight to eighteen. All but one of the no votes in the house came from legislators whose counties had received militia protection at some point during the year. On December 13, Brownlow signed into law An Act to Reduce the Military Expenses of the State. This new law in no way repealed the militia act, but through its elimination of important staff positions, its restrictions on officer pay, and its strict limits on quartermaster purchases, it would clearly reduce the State Guard's effectiveness. In keeping with the law's spirit, the adjutant general disbanded two more militia companies, including that of Capt. E. R. Hall.[58]

Legislative concerns over cost were well founded. As of October 1, the Radical army had cost the taxpayers $194,595, an expense that ranked second only to payment on the state debt, and one that amounted to 11 percent of all treasury disbursals for the fiscal year. Before it was over, the price tag for the deployment of 1867 would reach $329,127, split almost evenly between pay and supplies. Given the large sums involved, rumors of malfeasance invariably touched the Quartermaster Department and Paymaster Department. Throughout the autumn of 1867, H. H. Thomas steadily fell behind in his payments to various militia contractors. Furthermore, Paymaster Brooks was accused of having "absconded from the State" with $7,000. It took Brooks months to clear his name, but in the meantime, the assembly ordered an audit of all the adjutant general's financial records. An investigative committee discovered that much of the paperwork in the quartermaster and paymaster offices was in disarray and asked Thomas for a "detailed statement" of all militia expenses and shortfalls. Unwilling or unable to explain his department's disorganization, Thomas resigned before the year was out. Rather than sort through the morass of vouchers, receipts, invoices, bills of lading, payrolls, and account books, the committee recommended that a specialist take charge. Accordingly, on February 3, 1868, the general assembly passed the so-called Boone Act, whereby Thomas's assistant Albert E. Boone assumed control of both the quartermaster and paymaster departments at the rank of colonel. His mission was to "examine and perfect" the ledger of the State Guard "so as to render said accounts with the State, complete and intelligible."[59]

It took Boone several months, but by the summer of 1868 he had accounted for every penny spent on the militia. In doing so, he removed all claims against the state by unpaid militiamen by either paying them off or dismissing their case. Additionally, he settled all accounts with the railroad companies and various suppliers. In keeping with a legislative resolution calling on the federal government to pay for the State Guard, Boone then sent a bill for over $300,000 to the Tennessee delegation in Congress. Having provided the State Guard with its munitions free of charge, however, not to mention hundreds of U.S. troops to uphold the laws, Congress ignored this presumptuous request. Although the Tennessee government had to pay for its standing army in the end, the general assembly was pleased both by the thoroughness of Boone's accounting and by "his integrity, his morals, and especially his business qualifications." In an era that became known, in part, for its financial corruption, Boone's responsible bookkeeping stands as a refreshing example of fiscal probity.[60]

Rectitude in the adjutant general's office notwithstanding, many Radicals watched the dismantling of their partisan army with growing concern. Major Robeson was particularly disturbed. To him, disbanding the militia in the face of an armed and dangerous foe only invited more lawlessness. Governor Brownlow sympathized with his field commander but could only hope that "the factious elements would quiet down" once the State Guard was gone. State Supreme Court Justice Sam Milligan doubted whether the anti-Radicals could be so easily placated. In a letter to President Johnson, Milligan predicted that the Rebels' intractable political bitterness and racial hostility would lead to a "collision of arms, unless prevented by a standing army."[61]

Unfortunately for men like Robeson and Milligan, Tennessee's Radical army was virtually nonexistent as 1867 came to an end. On January 13, 1868, Adjutant General Daniel Boynton suspended all militia operations and placed the remaining two companies on indefinite furlough. Just a week before, Klansmen in Giles County had attacked a black store in Pulaski, killing one freedman and wounding several others. Whether this would have occurred had militia been present can never be known, but what is known is that after the militia left, the Klan in Giles greatly increased its acts of terrorism. By the time the militia act was officially repealed on February 1, the Klan throughout Tennessee had inaugurated an unprecedented campaign of violent counter-Reconstruction. Whereas 1867 had been a year of success and optimism for the Radical Party, 1868 would be a year of doubt and fear.[62]

Chapter 7

THE YEAR OF THE PAPER MILITIA

THE BROWNLOW ADMINISTRATION AND THE TENNESSEE GENERAL Assembly soon regretted disbanding the State Guard. Although this organization had not eliminated the ex-Confederate threat to Reconstruction, it had at least kept the numerous vigilante groups at bay and thereby given black and white Radicals in Middle and West Tennessee a fighting chance. With the demobilization of the militia in February 1868, however, Rebel paramilitarism intensified, with the infamous Ku Klux Klan taking the lead. Within a matter of days after the last company of State Guard mustered out, Radical leaders began calling for its reactivation. The democratic process, however, does not always respond to a crisis with celerity. Months would pass before the general assembly empowered the governor with new laws and a new militia force with which to combat the Klan. Throughout the proceedings, legislators argued over the nature of force politics and the necessity of a standing army. All the while, Ku Kluxism ran amok.

The Ku Klux Klan emerged as a major challenge to Reconstruction throughout the South in 1868. Historian Allen Trelease has pointed out that the Klan was a decentralized organization, one whose activities varied from state to state and county to county. "Klan" was really a generic term used to identify a legion of ex-Confederate vigilante bands. Tennessee alone endured the lawlessness of such Klan-like outfits as the Pale

Faces (Maury County), and the Red Caps (Humphreys County), in addition to the original Ku Klux Klan of Giles County. Whatever their name, these seemingly ubiquitous dens shared a common goal—the reassertion of white supremacy and the defeat of Reconstruction. In Tennessee, if the outright overthrow of the Brownlow administration was impractical, the destruction of Radicalism at the grass-roots level was not. Using the national election on November 3, 1868, as a rallying point, the Klan in Middle and West Tennessee unleashed a campaign of racial and political terrorism. Historian Thomas Alexander has described this campaign as a "psychological war," one in which the Klan relied more on fear than on violence to achieve its ends. In fact, however, the organization perpetrated a great deal of violence. Many Klansmen not only wanted to frighten blacks and Radicals, they wanted to kill them.[1]

In February, Samuel Arnell, one of Tennessee's Radical Congressmen, notified Governor Brownlow that "letter after letter is pouring in upon me . . . in regard to the Ku Klux Klans." Arnell was not exaggerating. The story of the Klan's terrorism in Tennessee in 1868 is well documented. Voluminous investigative reports by state authorities and by U.S. authorities, including the Freedmen's Bureau, reveal a widespread and deadly Klan menace. Between January and August 1868, the Klan committed literally hundreds of acts of violence in at least thirty Middle and West Tennessee counties. The particulars become mind-numbing in their repetitiveness. The Klan whipped, beat, threatened, shot, and lynched black and white Radicals. The Klan burned schools, robbed homes, and disrupted church services. And the Klan attacked the Radical party, crippling it in many counties.[2]

This political damage was the Klan's most significant contribution to counter-Reconstruction. Where Rebel vigilantes had failed in 1867, the Klan vowed to succeed. Commissioners of registration continued to be principal targets. "I am in danger," exclaimed Registrar Robert Wiley from Marshall before resigning out of fear. "The Ku Klux are all through the county." Registrar James F. Koger of Overton County was not as fortunate as Wiley. In June, Klansmen murdered him. Rather than suffer a similar fate, the registrar in Fayette County succumbed to Klan threats and added known ex-Confederates to his voting roster. Union Leagues also felt the wrath of the Klan. By May, night riding in Giles, Maury, and Williamson had effectively eradicated the leagues in those counties. Klansmen later tortured and killed S. A. Bierfield, a white Radical, and one of his black friends when the two men tried to revitalize their party in Williamson. Other political leaders also fell victim to Klan assaults. In a near-reprise of Senator Almon Case's assassination the previous year, Klansmen dragged the geriatric state senator William Wyatt from his home in Lincoln County in early April and beat him into unconsciousness. Wyatt had recently voted to reactivate the State Guard. One Freedmen's Bureau agent asserted that a fair and peaceful election in November was unlikely in much of Middle Tennessee as long as the Klan rode unpunished.[3]

Klan strength is difficult to determine. Sometime leader Nathan B. Forrest claimed that there were 40,000 Klansmen in Tennessee (and 550,000 throughout the South). These figures are probably inflated, even if they include organizations other than the official Ku Klux Klan, but the Klan's size was nevertheless impressive. An estimated 300 Klansmen operated in Murfreesboro (with 1,000 in Rutherford County at large), 400 in Pulaski (Giles County), and 500 in Columbia (Maury County). In Obion County, sixty Klansmen stalked the countryside under the leadership of Martin Vowell, an ex-Confederate whom militia major John Robeson had briefly incarcerated in 1867. On July 4, Klan dens staged militant parades in several Middle Tennessee counties. One in Bedford reached a climax when some fifty Klansmen accosted two local Radicals and whipped them through the streets of Shelbyville. Watching helplessly was John J. Mankin, a former officer in the State Guard. Less than five months before, he had commanded a full company of the now disbanded militia.[4]

As Klan terrorism spread, the general assembly scrambled to counter it. Hoping to avoid the financial and political burden that recreating the State Guard would entail, Radical legislators first tried to strengthen county law enforcement by increasing the power of the sheriffs. On February 1, An Act to Amend an Act for the Protection of Sheriffs passed into law. The original law had authorized sheriffs to create County Guards to combat lawlessness. Taking into account the ex-Confederate animus in many counties, the new law permitted (presumably loyal) sheriffs to recruit as posse members any citizen of the state. Moreover, it allowed them to pursue criminals to any part of the state. Furthermore, if civil authorities in counties wracked by lawlessness failed to create County Guards, the governor was authorized to intervene and appoint a new sheriff.[5]

The legislation was motivated in part by Sheriff James W. Tarkington's tribulations in Dyer County. Tarkington had worked closely with Maj. John Robeson in 1867 and was probably the only Radical law enforcer in West Tennessee at the beginning of 1868. In early January, he and his deputized son clashed with ex-Confederate guerrilla leader William Duncan on the streets of Dyersburg. Tarkington wounded Duncan and another Rebel in apprehending him, but was himself wounded, while his son was killed. Several days later, twenty "desperadoes" broke Duncan out of jail, and the outlaw took refuge in Madison County. Tarkington asked Governor Brownlow for one hundred militiamen to help him enforce the law, warning that the county would fall to the anti-Radicals in the November election without them. No militia was forthcoming, although former State Guard lieutenant William Fuller joined Tarkington's County Guards. The general assembly did award the sheriff a portion of Duncan's bounty—$333.33. The sum was poor compensation for a dead son.[6]

In practice, the amended sheriffs act was no more effective than the old law. Fear of Klan retribution made effective law enforcement impossible in many counties. Klansmen in Rutherford cowed the Radical sheriff with a midnight whipping. In Marshall, the Brownlow administration could find no sheriff willing to arrest any member of the Klan. Even the efforts of a few aggressive sheriffs proved unsatisfactory. When the sheriff of Fentress County openly joined a Rebel gang, the governor appointed Claiborne Beaty, a veteran of wartime Union guerrilla operations, to uphold the law, but Beaty became bogged down in a fruitless year-long struggle with a number of Rebel vigilante groups. In Sumner County, former State Guard lieutenant I. N. Phillips took charge and recruited eighty discharged black militiamen for his posse, "Phillips Militia." This force helped the Radical party prevail in the March county elections, but when Conservative authorities arrested Phillips for an alleged murder, army captain Edwin Leib had to step in to restore order. In Wayne County, Sheriff Elijah Thurman successfully employed his County Guards in protecting black ironworkers from a Klan attack in August, but it took the arbitration of a Freedmen's Bureau agent to broker an uneasy, and temporary, peace. James Tarkington eventually stepped down as Dyer's sheriff, claiming that he could never suppress the ex-Confederates without military force.[7]

Many Radical leaders soon came to believe that the sheriffs act was insufficient and that the State Guard was needed again. On February 27,

178

a majority in the house, led by Jesse E. McNair of Gibson County, voted to repeal the Act to Reduce the Military Expenses, the law that had precipitated the final disbandment of the militia. The repeal effort never made it to the senate floor, but the two houses did present Governor Brownlow with a resolution calling on the executive to dispatch militia to the state's troubled regions in order to provide security for the county elections in March. Brownlow must have been nonplussed by the assembly's request. At the time, there were no active militia units in the state, and with the essential repeal of the 1867 militia act, the governor could not reactivate the State Guard without a new law. Instead of deploying militia, Brownlow urged the loyal citizens of Middle and West Tennessee to keep lists of Klan perpetrators for future prosecution and defend themselves as best they could within the limits of the law.[8]

Militia advocates regrouped and in the first week of March introduced a bill to reorganize the State Guard. On March 16, the assembly enacted a second militia act by solid majorities in both houses. The new law was notable both for its swift passage and for its fatal limitations. The first sections were a facsimile of the previous law. Most of the other sections, however, imposed parsimonious spending constraints. Although he signed the bill, Brownlow was dissatisfied with it. The 1867 militia act was designed to protect an election and preempt any anti-Radical challenges. In order to overcome the full-blown Klan conspiracy of 1868, Brownlow believed he needed something more potent. The new law granted him no special powers, such as the authority to declare martial law, and its financial constraints and limitations on staff personnel made equipping and supplying the militia volunteers difficult. While anti-Radical newspapers ignored the new militia act, the *Knoxville Whig* derisively called it "an abortion." Brownlow never took action under its provisions.[9]

For every Radical who desired a reactivated militia, there seemed to be one who insisted on alternatives. Besides passing new sheriff and militia acts, legislators at the end of February urged the governor to call on the garrison for help. Specifically, they wanted U.S. troops to occupy selected counties during local elections on March 7. Evidently, Gen. George H. Thomas provided a few squads of soldiers for election duty and Radicals won most of the county offices (only in Marshall did the Klan appreciably interfere with voting), but the troops were withdrawn immediately afterward. Klan reprisals followed this latest Radical political success and Governor Brownlow found himself calling on the army again. On April 10, he requested General Thomas to station fifty men in Maury County, the scene of a recent spate of vicious Klan lynchings. "Matters have been growing worse than ever since the State militia were disbanded," Brownlow told the general. Thomas again agreed to provide troops for the occasion, but he balked when Brownlow asked for six more county deployments in May and June. The general wanted to help crush the Klan, but he refused to let his men be used as troubleshooters to be rushed from one part of the state to the next. Reminding Brownlow that Tennessee was in full exercise of its civil functions, he encouraged the governor to use the recent sheriff and militia legislation "vigorously." He personally thought a reactivated State Guard would be especially suitable to the task of fighting the Klan.[10]

As Klan atrocities multiplied in the spring and summer, Brownlow chafed at his inability to fight back. Even some anti-Radicals began to protest Klan terrorism. Ex-Confederates in Carroll County joined their Radical neighbors in publicly condemning the Klan. Nimrod Porter of Maury County also fumed when Klansmen began harassing his black servant. "Things must be stopt some way," he declared. But he worried about the governor's reaction to the terrorism: "I greatly dread the consequences I fear the result." After Samuel Arnell reported his narrow escape from a Klan lynch mob on June 14, Brownlow took the drastic action Porter dreaded. On July 6, he ordered a special session of the legislature to meet later in the month.[11]

Governor Brownlow's address on July 28 to the reconvened legislature was one of the most forceful and provocative of his gubernatorial career. Chastising the members for repealing the militia act (he ignored that body's reenactment in March), he proclaimed that the state was in the death grip of the Ku Klux Klan. According to him, the Klan's objectives were manifold: "the overthrow of the existing State Government, the abolition of colored suffrage, the immediate enfranchisement . . . of every rebel who fought to destroy the Government, and a wiping from the statute books of all the [Radicals'] wholesome and patriotic laws." After explaining the deficiencies of local law enforcement and the reluctance of the federal garrison to take decisive action, Brownlow requested a militia law that would enable him to suppress the Klan, regardless of the cost. Moreover, he "emphatically" recommended that Klansmen be "declared outlaws by special legislation, and punished with death wherever found." Lastly, he admonished the legislators that if they equivocated in this matter, the executive branch would hold them responsible for every citizen "butchered in cold blood."[12]

Anticipating the governor's hard-line tactics, anti-Radicals voiced strong protest against the "extraordinary" legislative session. The *Republican Banner* printed excerpts from numerous county newspapers denouncing the "miserable radical oligarchy." These newspapers spoke of "Brownlow's hell" and the administration's "negro and penitentiary militia." They claimed that the Union Leagues were arming and drilling for battle and warned that anti-Radical men "would think no more of killing . . . niggers than they would of killing snakes." Fearing that Brownlow's conduct was leading to civil war, Conservatives bombarded President Andrew Johnson with pleas to intervene with the army. A. O. P. Nicholson of Maury County was particularly concerned. He regarded the governor's actions as "a declaration of war" that would result in a "bloody collision." In his diary, Nimrod Porter may have best summed up the anti-Radical attitude: "Brownlow is mad."[13]

As the general assembly digested the governor's message, individuals from all political camps promoted universal suffrage as a solution to the impending showdown. Conservative John C. Gaut urged the assembly to consider a statewide referendum on the franchise question. The Assembly took no action on this suggestion. John M. Lea, a moderate Republican, implored Governor Brownlow to lift the franchise restrictions for the sake of republican liberty and the "Anglo-Saxon" race. "Ku Klux organizations would be compelled to disband," he reasoned, for with a restored right to vote "the excuse for vindictiveness would have ceased." Stating that Reconstruction and its inherent divisiveness had to end sooner or later, Lea challenged Brownlow to exhibit magnanimity. Playing on these overtures, more than a dozen former Confederate generals, all alleged leaders in the Klan, including N. B. Forrest, also petitioned the state government to remove all political disabilities from the white majority as a means of ending the crisis. Without explicitly mentioning the Klan, they insisted that its actions were a justifiable response to continued Radical proscription. Finally, the generals intimated that suppression of the Klan ultimately lay in their hands. "As inducement and reason to your honorable body not to organize [the State Guard], we pledge ourselves to maintain the order and peace of the State with whatever influence we possess." Brownlow respected Lea for his sincerity but considered him naïve. The governor regarded the generals' petition as a veiled threat by "unreconstructed Ku Klux rebels" and spurned their proposal.[14]

The "extraordinary" session of the Thirty-fifth General Assembly was an important event in Tennessee's Reconstruction. As the extra session got underway, the senate assumed responsibility for drawing up the legislation that made Ku Kluxism a crime. The house formulated the appropriate militia enforcement act, one that authorized the governor to mobilize a State Guard and declare martial law. In the meantime, a joint committee commenced an extensive investigation into Klan outrages. Although all but three of the approximately ninety attending members were Radicals, it soon became apparent that the legislature was not in agreement over precisely how to suppress the Klan. The debates and votes reveal a surprising amount of dissension, particularly over the use of force. In many respects, the eventual enactment of Brownlow's requested countermeasures in 1868 was more difficult than the passage of the militia act in 1867.[15]

A number of house legislators exhibited reservations about recreating the State Guard. On August 7, William Bosson of Rutherford County pushed through a resolution calling on the military committee to scrap the militia bill in favor of a renewed effort to gain the services of the garrison. On August 10, William F. Prosser of Davidson County endorsed Judge Lea's idea and urged the assembly to consider lifting the franchise restrictions as a means of pacifying the ex-Confederate opposition. Prosser stressed that disfranchisement "was never intended to be permanent" and that indefinite proscription only fueled anti-Radical propaganda. All the while, opponents of the militia bill read petitions from their home counties protesting the reactivation of the State Guard.[16]

As the session went on, Tennessee's congressional Radicals and other party spokesmen demanded that the assembly act. Horace Maynard, speaking at a Republican convention held in Nashville on August 12–13, called the legislature a "sham government" and rebuked the members for their apparent indecisiveness. Samuel Arnell questioned the members' "manhood." Roderick R. Butler was less accusatory, but in a letter to the governor he too urged strong action. The Nashville convention formally recommended the passage of "an efficient military bill" with as little delay as possible. For legislators worried about the cost of remobilizing the militia, the convention resolved that counties dominated by the Klan should pay it. Impressed by the convention's sense of urgency, state legislator D. G. Thornburgh of Jefferson County called for the incorporation of the convention's recommendations into the existing militia bill, followed by its immediate passage.[17]

Despite the party's exhortations, legislators spent the last weeks of August wrangling over not only the wording but also the necessity of the force bills. In the house on August 25, Martin T. Ryder of Shelby County and Newton Hacker of Washington County entered into an especially mean-spirited debate over the militia bill. Ryder objected to any new militia legislation, insisting that the March law "was equal in every respect to the emergency, if properly enforced." When Hacker denounced these remarks as anti-Radical subterfuge, an offended Ryder retorted that he had "only presented to the House its own child." Hacker rejoined that "the signs of the times were not as black and portentous then as they are now." The next day, fifty-one Radicals passed the militia bill over the strenuous protests of seventeen members. In addition to reiterating Ryder's arguments, the opponents claimed that a State Guard capable of defeating the Klan would cost more than one million dollars and, therefore, would be "suicidal to the credit of the State." Moreover, they believed that foisting such an exorbitant expenditure on the counties was a terrible injustice. Finally, they objected to the bill's provision for martial law. Elihu S. Williams of Smith County feared that invoking martial law would make the Conservatives' charges of despotism a reality. Duly noting their colleagues' protest, the majority applauded the militia bill's transmission to the senate.[18]

While the senate examined the militia bill, anti-Radical observers raised their voices in renewed outcry against it. President Johnson received more letters begging him to intercede. One writer wailed that once the militia bill was passed "all the viscious and evil Disposed Negroes in Tenn . . . will be mustered in, with a sprinkle of white men." At a public rally in Nashville, such familiar Conservative leaders as A. S. Colyar, Matt Brown, and John Gaut hurled condemnations at the Radical legislators. Although they had exhausted their worst insults the year before, the speakers still decried the militia bill as a "monstrous" and "infamous" measure that would make Brownlow a king. The *Republican Banner* compared the extra session of the general assembly to "the horrors of the Holy Inquisition." More disturbing to the state government than the Conservatives' predictable denunciations, however, were Nathan B. Forrest's increasingly bellicose comments. After the governor snubbed the ex-Confederate generals' petition, Forrest went on the stump calling on disfranchised whites to resist "Brownlowism" to the utmost. In a widely reprinted newspaper interview on August 28, he defended the Klan as "a protective political military organization," one he would gladly "cooperate with," although he claimed he was not a member. When asked his opinion of the pending militia bill, Forrest replied that "if the militia are

Nathan B. Forrest, 1863–64. From Miller's
Photographic History of the Civil War.

called out, we cannot but look upon it as a declaration of war." Claiming
that the Klan consisted of forty thousand law-abiding Tennesseans, he
was confident it could withstand any attacks from the State Guard. "We
will resist to the last," he warned. "Not a radical will be left alive."[19]

Forrest's statements alarmed many Radical leaders. The usually
intrepid *Daily Press and Times* expressed doubts about a reactivated State
Guard's chances of suppressing the numerically superior Klan. Similarly
affected, A. V. S. Lindsley of Davidson County and several other Radicals
in the senate delayed passage of the militia bill, and proposed that a special delegation entreat President Johnson to bring the full force of the U.S.
Army down on the Klan. This latest alternative to an "efficient military
bill" provoked another round of heated debates in both houses. Senate
hard-liners such as William J. Smith of Hardeman County, who had
lobbied for a permanent militia force since 1865, refused to be intimidated
by anti-Radical rhetoric and insisted on mobilizing the State Guard.

Berry Lyle of Montgomery County spoke for the moderates when he argued that remobilizing the militia "would be arming one neighbor against another," necessitating federal intervention in the end. In the house, Newton Hacker spearheaded a strong effort to derail the proposed conference with the president. "This Legislature presents a most humiliating spectacle to the world," he declared, "when it at this late day turns aside from the real objects for which it was assembled, and commences to fritter away our precious time and the peoples' money in a worse than fruitless appeal to Andrew Johnson. . . . *He is an enemy to our State government.*" A majority in both houses, however, supported the idea of seeking federal aid in addition to passing a militia bill. On September 1, a formal resolution creating the proposed special delegation passed both chambers.[20]

As the special delegation headed to Washington D.C., Samuel Arnell expressed his displeasure over the assembly's failure to enact a militia law. "Have our friends in that body," he privately asked Governor Brownlow, "not even the courage of self-defense & only the blindness of bats?" Arnell had no sooner posed the question than a turning point occurred in the legislature. On September 2, the joint committee on Klan activities submitted its report. Presenting more than eighty affidavits as evidence, the committee declared that the Ku Klux Klan was a real organization that, "by a system of anti-lawry and terrorism," had subjugated the Radical party and the freedmen in many parts of Middle and West Tennessee and jeopardized Radical success at the polls in November. The committee further asserted that Klansmen had committed an average of one murder a day over the preceding six months. Accordingly, it recommended the speedy creation of a militia force to be used at the governor's discretion.[21]

Shocked by the magnitude of Klan terror, the general assembly accelerated both the anti-Klan bill and the militia bill. On September 7, after weeks of revising the anti-Klan bill, the senate passed it, fifteen to seven. Three days later, the house approved the bill with minimal discussion, forty-six to twenty-one. Officially titled An Act to Preserve the Public Peace, the new law defined a Klansman as a person who associated with "any secret organization . . . that shall prowl through the country or towns of this State, by day or by night, disguised or otherwise, for the purpose of disturbing the peace." The minimum punishment upon conviction was a fine of five hundred dollars and five years in the state penitentiary. Significantly, the death penalty was not attached as Governor Brownlow had hoped, although anyone found guilty would be "rendered infamous," (i.e., permanently deprived of such political liberties as the right to vote and hold public office). The law further stipulated that anyone willfully interfering with an election or intimidating voters would suffer the same fate as a convicted Klansman.[22]

The militia bill underwent a crucial last-minute change before it too was passed. A number of senators insisted that the governor's power to declare martial law be constrained. They amended the bill so that imposing martial law in a county required the consent of the district's circuit judge and attorney general, the county's senator and representatives, and at least ten "unconditional" Union men from the county in question. On September 9, the senate passed the amended militia bill, fourteen to seven. The house initially balked at the change, arguing that it emasculated the threat of martial law. After a joint meeting on the evening of the tenth, however, the house consented and the bill finally passed. Officially titled An Act to Enforce the Laws of the State, the new militia law (the third during Reconstruction) authorized the governor to reorganize the Tennessee State Guard along the same lines as the 1867 act. It granted the executive certain discretionary funds to carry out his mission and empowered him to declare martial law under specific conditions. And it required that those counties occupied by the militia pay for any deployment of troops. The *Republican Banner* denigrated the new laws as "a most cumbrous mass of legal absurdities," but they theoretically granted Brownlow everything he needed to wipe out the Klan.[23]

Although strong majorities ultimately supported both the anti-Klan and militia bills, and both passed in a relatively short period of time (forty-five days), the proceedings clearly demonstrated a profound concern over the politics of force. An analysis of voting reveals some significant patterns. Legislators from Middle and West Tennessee, knowing that counties in their sections would bear the physical and financial brunt of martial law and a reactivated State Guard, were particularly disturbed by the militia bill. The three Conservative members of the house predictably voted against it, but so did twelve Radicals from Middle Tennessee and two from West. Notable among the Radical dissenters were Jacob Brown of Franklin County, William Bosson of Rutherford County, and Jesse McNair of Gibson County, men who had benefited politically from militia occupation in 1867. In the all-Radical senate, the opposition was more pronounced. Five of the chamber's twenty-two members in attendance, all from Middle and West Tennessee, steadfastly resisted both bills. Samuel Arnell referred to these men as "timid servants," but they did persuade the assembly to renew its efforts to gain the assistance of the U.S. Army, and they were influential in placing constraints on the governor's power to declare martial law.[24]

Shortly after the extra session adjourned, Governor Brownlow acted. In a proclamation of September 16, he condemned the Ku Klux Klan and called for the organization of loyal militia companies. Ordering the Klan to disband voluntarily and submit to the laws before he actually fielded his Radical army, Brownlow warned its leaders that he would not hesitate "to put down armed marauders by force." Cognizant of Tennesseans' fears of race war, he stressed that he would "first call into the field only white troops, holding the colored companies, when organized, as a reserved corps." Acknowledging the misgivings of many legislators about employing a militia, he further stated that if the federal garrison agreed to furnish a sufficient force to maintain order during the November election, he would not call the State Guard into service at all.[25]

On this last point, the Brownlow administration soon received favorable news. On September 11–12, as the general assembly was completing the passage of the force bills, the state's special delegation met with President Johnson. Three Radicals made up the delegation: state senator William H. Wisener of Bedford County and house members James H. Agee of Campbell County and Thomas A. Hamilton of Shelby County. All three had supported the militia bill, but each hoped the president would provide U.S. troops in lieu of a State Guard. After describing the Klan's violent activities and its intent to overthrow the state government, the delegates explained their preference for U.S. troops. A clash between the Klan and the State Guard, they argued, would be bloody (although they believed that the Brownlow administration would prevail in such a struggle), whereas U.S. troops could suppress the Klan and protect the ballot box with minimal bloodshed. Several anti-Radicals from Tennessee warned the president not to believe the special delegation's depictions of Klan atrocities. Dreading the partisan law enforcement of the State Guard, however, they privately recommended that he provide troops for the time being to keep the peace. Whether or not moved by such advice, Johnson was certainly appalled by the Klan's alleged depredations. At the end of the meeting he promised to sustain Tennessee's civil authorities with federal troops. As a result, the State Guard would remain a force on paper only.[26]

The day after his militia proclamation, Governor Brownlow received word from General Thomas that the federal garrison, including a fresh regiment made available by the War Department, was at the state's disposal. Brownlow immediately took advantage of this military windfall by asking Thomas to station one company in each of eleven Middle and nine West Tennessee counties. He stressed that Giles, Lincoln, Marshall, Maury, Fayette, Gibson, and Obion were the most lawless counties of the twenty. In a peculiar statement, he added that "the presence of federal troops in each county named will quiet things, whereas the presence of State militia would exasperate them." At the beginning of September, the army's strength in Tennessee was only 370 soldiers. By October 1, it had grown to about 2,000. It was a force equal in size to the State Guard of 1867 yet concentrated in fewer locations. Three companies occupied Maury County alone. Nimrod Porter, one of that county's strongest anti-Radicals, claimed that he could see army tents wherever he looked. He further grumbled that the "yankeys" foraged through his orchards without permission.[27]

The presence of federal troops seemed to guarantee a peaceful election. Klan night riding lessened in October, although many dens, fearing gubernatorial reprisals, had already curtailed their violence at the end of August. Tennessee Radicals supported the Republican presidential candidate Ulysses S. Grant, whose campaign slogan was "Let Us Have Peace." They expected an easy victory. Conservatives, hoping to capture a few congressional seats, aligned themselves with the national Democratic party and endorsed its presidential candidate, Horatio Seymour. Furthermore, they formed Democratic political clubs throughout the state. The Conservatives' attitude toward the Klan had always been mixed. On the one hand, they rejoiced over its effectiveness in weakening the Radical party apparatus in many counties. On the other, they deprecated its tactics when the extralegal violence prompted Governor Brownlow to call the emergency session of the general assembly. Relieved that the governor had opted to use U.S. troops instead of militia, Conservatives were nevertheless disappointed that the state had been placed under de facto military rule. Such were the "fruits of the mighty K.K.K.," remarked one Conservative sarcastically.[28]

As the election soon demonstrated, the federal garrison was a poor substitute for the State Guard when it came to protecting the polls, not to mention the Radical canvass and the registration of black voters.

Unlike the militia deployment of 1867, the U.S. Army detachments in 1868 generally remained in camp and made no effort to enforce the anti-Klan law. One army captain in Marshall County, citing his strict rules of engagement, ignored a white Radical's plea for help in apprehending Klansmen who had just murdered a black tenant farmer. Whereas militia officers were committed to the Radical cause, many army officers were indifferent or, in a few cases, even in sympathy with the Conservatives. A more serious shortcoming with General Thomas's occupation in 1868 was that all of his units were infantry and could not, therefore, effectively pursue Klan outlaws had they chosen to. When infantry replaced the vigilant Capt. Edwin Leib's cavalry command in Sumner County in late September, the so-called Harper gang resumed its terrorist activities with impunity. Other Klan vigilantes were also quick to realize the army's limitations as a law enforcer. Dispensing with their now illegal hoods and robes, Klansmen continued to intimidate blacks and voting registrars. On October 19, Brownlow was compelled to void the registration in Lincoln County after his commissioner confessed that he had certified Rebels under duress. Eventually, the Klan returned to its violent methods as well. Just before the election, Klan raiders in Middle and West Tennessee swept through several counties, whipping some blacks and shooting others, in a final effort to dissuade Radicals from voting. There is no indication that the army did anything to stop these crimes.[29]

Grant carried the state of Tennessee on November 3, but the election returns reflect a dramatic drop in the Radical vote. The army ensured that the day of the election itself was quiet, but the political damage to the Radical party was already done. Whereas Brownlow received 74,437 votes in August 1867, fifteen months later Grant garnered only 56,606, a difference of 17,831. As scholars have noted, virtually the entire difference is accounted for by counties terrorized by the Klan. Despite the presence of some twenty companies of federal troops, thousands of blacks stayed away from the polls out of fear.[30]

A key factor in this reversal of Radical fortunes, one overlooked by scholars, is the absence of the Tennessee State Guard. A comparison of the 1867 and 1868 returns from the twenty-eight counties in Middle and West Tennessee that received militia protection in 1867 illustrates the vital role that the State Guard played in Radical political success (see Appendix E). Whereas Conservatives eked out victories in four

The Year of the Paper Militia

"militia" counties in 1867, they captured thirteen in 1868, including seven that were occupied by federal troops. The outcome in Middle Tennessee is particularly striking. In Lincoln County, anti-Radicals seized control of the precincts and conducted an election in violation of the franchise act. The army officer in charge considered declaring martial law, but ultimately opted just to prevent rioting. The vote in that county was Conservatives 558, Radicals 4. In Franklin County, the sheriff persuaded an army officer to send a squad into one of the few functioning precincts, but the detachment remained for only fifteen minutes. With ex-Confederates chanting, "Shoot the damned Radicals," the election there was a sham. In several other counties, especially Giles, the Radicals were simply overwhelmed. They nearly lost in Maury, despite the presence of three infantry companies, and in Rutherford, where a self-appointed white police force in Murfreesboro turned many prospective black voters away.[31]

In West Tennessee, the decline in Radical strength was less pronounced but no less discouraging. Here, too, the federal detachments offered mostly symbolic protection. In Dyer and Obion, counties that militia major John T. Robeson had painstakingly secured for the Radicals in 1867, black turnout dropped by more than 65 percent. The polls in Gibson County never even opened thanks to preelection Klan terrorism. It does appear, however, that the army helped the Radicals win a narrow victory in the restless county of Madison.[32]

Deprived of the State Guard's partisan security, the Radical party lost over 12,500 votes, mostly from blacks, in the "militia" counties alone. Conversely, the Conservative tally in these counties increased by over 4,000. Admittedly, these may have been legally cast, but Freedmen's Bureau agent George E. Judd reported that anti-Radicals in Rutherford County unabashedly stuffed some of the ballot boxes. As they had hoped, Conservatives gained nominal majorities in two congressional districts. Governor Brownlow, however, refused to recognize the legitimacy of those results and, in a reprise of his arbitrary vote tossing of 1865, he nullified the returns from selected counties overrun by the Klan and declared the Radical candidates victorious.[33]

A year without the State Guard had been a painful time for many Tennessee Radicals. The legislature's initial decree disbanding this standing army and Brownlow's later decision to rely solely on federal troops instead of militia placed Reconstruction at the mercy of the Ku Klux Klan for most of 1868. In an address to the legislature a week after the election, Brownlow applauded the overall Radical victory. Commenting on his use of force, the governor explained that by employing the army "no expense to the State has been incurred." Nevertheless, the price in freedmen's blood and the disruption of party organization at the local level made the 1868 election a Pyrrhic victory for the Radicals. Through its campaign of terrorism, the Klan destroyed most of the Union Leagues outside of East Tennessee and, ironically, prompted renewed efforts to repeal the franchise acts, the legal linchpin of Radical power. Even Brownlow began suggesting a conditional removal of political disabilities.[34]

Ku Kluxism did not end with the November election but continued unpunished as the federal troops returned to their barracks and the militia remained merely a force on paper. Within a matter of weeks, however, this seemingly incessant Klan defiance turned Brownlow's joy into wrath. In the spring of 1869, Tennessee's Radical army would stage a powerful return.

Chapter 8

THE STATE GUARD VERSUS THE KLAN

ON FEBRUARY 10, 1869, GOVERNOR BROWNLOW TENDERED HIS resignation and prepared to take his seat in the U.S. Senate, to which the Tennessee General Assembly had elected him more than fifteen months earlier. On February 25, DeWitt C. Senter, the speaker of the state senate and a dedicated Radical, was sworn in as governor. This transition of power came at a critical time during Tennessee's Reconstruction. The Klan had recently resumed its violent activities and the state government was determined to destroy this ex-Confederate challenge once and for all. Three weeks prior to announcing his resignation, Brownlow mobilized the militia, and five days before handing the gubernatorial reins to Senter, he declared martial law in nine counties. It was the final action of one of Tennessee's most controversial governors. The stage seemed set for an exciting and decisive showdown between the Radical State Guard and the Rebel Ku Klux Klan.[1]

Radicals were disappointed by the U.S. Army's failure to stop Klan terrorism. After the presidential election, the *Daily Press and Times* vented its frustration: "Let the damnable Kukluxers be shot down and exterminated if there is no other way of putting an end to the outrages of this wicked conclave." By January 1869, Klan violence had again reached alarming proportions. Radical newspapers reported increased Ku Kluxism in the counties of Coffee, Davidson, Fentress, Gibson, Giles, Overton,

Maury, Lawrence, and Sumner. Overton was especially overrun. Some two hundred Klansmen openly stalked the streets of Livingston, the county seat, disarming the freedmen and defying Radical authority. The U.S. internal revenue collector fled the town after some of these vigilantes raided his home. State legislator Rufus Dowdy of neighboring Fentress County barely evaded an apparent kidnapping attempt as he traveled through Overton. The situation in many of these counties seemed to warrant martial law and the deployment of militia. But with the exception of Overton, no county met the stringent martial law prerequisites of the recent militia act. The general assembly's concern over an executive abuse of power had paralyzed the state's response to terrorism.[2]

Radical Tennesseans found encouragement in Arkansas's concomitant experience with the Klan. In November 1868, Republican governor Powell Clayton declared martial law in more than a dozen counties, and over the next four months he fought the Klan with a biracial militia force of two thousand men. Moreover, he employed a number of undercover agents, some of whom successfully infiltrated the Klan and obtained lists of members and den locations. Despite the outcry against his ruthless tactics, Clayton attained satisfactory results. His militia killed several Klansmen, captured many more, and essentially broke the organization's back. Governor Brownlow was no less vigorous than Clayton, and he had already used his own militia effectively in 1867. There seemed to be no reason why he could not also defeat the Klan in Tennessee, provided he was given a free hand to do so.[3]

In December, legislators in both houses of the general assembly presented an amendment to the militia act that would enhance the governor's ability to declare martial law. A key supporter in the senate was the usually moderate William Wisener. He considered the army's withdrawal in November an egregious breach of President Johnson's promise to help suppress Klan outlaws and believed that martial law was the only way that the state could "swing up these assassins." In the house, William W. Murray of Carroll County acknowledged the seriousness of martial law but passionately defended its necessity. He tried to overcome his colleagues' fears of a Brownlow dictatorship by reminding them that the "sanguinary Kuklux" was the state's main concern. A few legislators moved to table the amendment and some even tried to repeal the force acts of the previous September, but a majority of Radicals were willing to risk military despotism in order to crush the Klan. With the

The State Guard versus the Klan

house voting in favor fifty-five to nine and the senate seventeen to five, the "martial law" bill passed into law on January 16, 1869. John Bowles of Klan-oppressed Overton County reportedly whooped for joy at the outcome, his cry described as a cross between "the bray of an Andalusian jack" and "the howl of a laughing hyena." Decrying martial law as "no law," the anti-Radical press branded the new decree the "crowning iniquity" of Radicalism.[4]

The *Republican Banner* rightly predicted that Governor Brownlow would soon unleash his "dogs of war" on the Klan. On January 20, the governor issued a formal call for loyal militia volunteers. "Outrages have been long borne," he said, "but the executive is not to be cajoled or terrified." He closed his brief proclamation with a promise to make Middle and West Tennessee "as orderly and quiet" as East Tennessee. Brownlow refrained from declaring martial law for the time being, but he appointed Gen. Joseph A. Cooper to command once again the reactivated State Guard and ordered all companies to assemble in Nashville as soon as they organized.[5]

Contrary to the assertions of some historians, the Brownlow administration had little difficulty finding recruits for its second mobilization of the State Guard. James Patton and Thomas Alexander erroneously state that the governor's call for volunteers in September 1868 "got inadequate response" and that Brownlow was "forced to rely" on the army. In actuality, while he gladly left election-day law enforcement to the federal garrison, Brownlow unofficially assembled a militia force on paper, one that could rapidly mobilize if needed. Several days prior to the governor's militia proclamation of January 1869, Adjutant General Daniel Boynton activated a portion of this force. Moreover, he commissioned Sheriff Claiborne Beaty of Fentress County a captain in the State Guard, authorized him to recruit more men, and renamed his County Guards the "Special County Police Force" for Overton, thereby providing immediate relief to that beleaguered part of the state. Newer companies also began to form. One future captain, Edwin E. Winters, a twenty-nine-year-old carpetbagger from Michigan, opened a recruiting office in Nashville the day after the militia proclamation. Hanging a large poster printed with the popular wartime cry "Rally 'round the Flag," he enrolled about forty whites from Davidson County, some of whom were born in such northern states as New York, Pennsylvania, and Massachusetts, and such countries as Ireland and Canada. His first lieutenant, P. A. Tillet, recruited several more volunteers from East Tennessee. On February 11, the adjutant general mustered in Winters's polyglot command of eighty-eight men (average age, 23.6 years), with eighteen-year-old Patrick S. Cromwell of Nashville receiving the second lieutenancy.[6]

After accepting his reappointment as commander-in-chief of the State Guard, General Cooper assumed complete control over the militia buildup. His first general order indicated that he reserved the right to approve or reject commissions. Concerned as always with discipline and professionalism, Cooper declared that he would accept only loyal men of "good moral character." On January 26, he formed his general staff, which included his nineteen-year-old son, John Cooper, and Larken B. Gamble, the general's efficient aide-de-camp during the 1867 deployment. Maj. Albert S. Bayless, a fifty-four-year-old farmer from Washington County, served as the quartermaster. He had Civil War experience as a staff officer in the Ninth Tennessee Cavalry (Union).[7]

Besides experience and leadership ability, Cooper brought a strong command presence to the capital. Through a series of interviews with Nashville newspapers, he thoughtfully kept the public apprised of military issues. To alleviate anti-Radical fears of race war, Cooper announced that "no colored soldiers" would be mustered in; the militia would comprise only whites, mostly from East Tennessee. He cautioned, however, that if the Klan continued to resist, he would not hesitate to form black militia units and place them in the field. Regarding the prospect of martial law, Cooper promised that the administration would not make that decision until the State Guard was ready for action. Until then, he urged local authorities to demonstrate a willingness to fight the Klan. When the editor of the *Republican Banner* denounced the militia buildup as "stupid" and accused the administration of trying to outshine Arkansas's Governor Clayton, Cooper politely replied that he would maintain firm control over his men. The general then shrewdly invited the *Banner* to denounce the Klan, but the editor "modestly" responded that his newspaper had no real influence among the state's ex-Confederates. For the most part, Cooper's statements were in keeping with Brownlow's policies, but in response to a question regarding the fate of captured Klansmen, the general declared flatly that the guilty "*would be hung.*"[8]

Perhaps discomfited by General Cooper's last comment, the *Banner* on January 23 shocked its readers with a false report of martial law.

The State Guard versus the Klan

Warning that it was to be declared "in a day or two," the newspaper listed what it believed were twenty-five targeted counties, eleven in West Tennessee and fourteen in Middle. Furthermore, the *Banner* claimed that some two thousand militiamen were already equipped, with more on the way. Before the Brownlow administration could repudiate these falsehoods, frantic petitions from over half of the named counties poured into the executive office. Some expressed indignation, insisting that occupation by "Cooper's legions" was unnecessary because no Klan existed in their counties, while others included resolutions promising to make a stronger effort to suppress the Klan using local resources.[9]

Several counties, not content with written protests, sent delegations to Nashville to plead their case directly. General Cooper met with many of these delegates, but he was unimpressed by their asseverations. He upbraided the Madison delegates when they stated that they thought they could keep the peace on their own: "It is remarkably strange that you gentlemen have so recently discovered your ability to enforce the laws." Speaking in behalf of the Brownlow administration, the general similarly dismissed the arguments of other delegates. "We have had enough preambles and resolutions," he told the delegation from Rutherford. "We want action." He warned all of his visitors that if they did not help the state government "knock the Kuklux in the head," they could expect martial law. Dismayed by the delegations' rough treatment, the anti-Radical *Memphis Appeal* howled, "We are in the hands of the Philistines."[10]

The martial law scare coupled with Cooper's stern admonitions seems to have had a salutary effect in a few instances. Prominent anti-Radicals such as Arthur S. Colyar of Franklin County and Abner A. Steele of Marshall began publicly condemning Ku Kluxism. Radicals in Lincoln County reported a bipartisan effort to suppress the Klan. There, on January 29, the constable of Fayetteville arrested a Klansman and confined him to jail for a week. At about the same time in Maury County, the commander of a small army detachment in Columbia, at the request of the civil authorities, agreed to help guard two recently apprehended Klansmen while they awaited trial. The most significant reaction to the Brownlow administration's hard-line approach, however, was Nathan B. Forrest's so-called disbandment order to the Klan at the end of January. Frustrated by the Klan's wanton violence and poor discipline, and likely fearful of a Clayton-style militia campaign against the organization,

Forrest secretly ordered every den in Tennessee to curtail its activities, destroy its regalia, and go underground temporarily. For probably the only time in his life, the fearsome cavalry raider was backing out of a fight.[11]

Although many Klan dens appear to have obeyed their Grand Wizard's orders, the State Guard, ignorant of this development, continued to mobilize. The personnel records for this mobilization are incomplete and less detailed than those of 1867, but it appears that between January 28 and February 18, nineteen companies, totaling approximately sixteen hundred white soldiers, mustered into service and encamped on the outskirts of Nashville (see Appendix F). What had taken the adjutant general over four months to do in 1867 took less than one month in 1869.[12]

Many familiar faces returned to organize and lead this resurrected Radical army. One of them, William L. Hathaway, quickly raised a company of eighty-six horsemen from DeKalb County. He secured the services of John B. Taylor, age thirty-five, as his first lieutenant. William F. Cravens returned to serve again as second lieutenant. Hathaway further helped raise a second company of seventy-eight men, also from DeKalb. Levi N. Woodsides, a twenty-nine-year-old miller from Liberty, commanded this unit. His lieutenants were McAdoo D. Vanetta, a thirty-eight-year-old farmer worth nine thousand dollars, and John B. Turner, a former private in the 1867 Guard. All the militia officers from DeKalb had served in Joseph H. Blackburn's Union command during the Civil War.[13]

Also returning for duty were Judge K. Clingan and William N. Purdy. Among Clingan's ninety-seven volunteers from Bradley County were William L. Hicks, a twenty-eight-year-old farmer, serving as first lieutenant, and Powell H. Low, a twenty-four-year-old laborer and former bugler in the Fourth Tennessee Cavalry (Union). Significantly, only a few of the recruits from Bradley were veterans of the 1867 campaign. Moreover, Clingan's new company was rather young; the men averaged 19.7 years of age. His unhappy experience in West Tennessee in 1867 perhaps dissuaded many of his original volunteers from joining a second time. Purdy's sixty-man company from Monroe may have included many of his former soldiers. As in 1867, Purdy appears to have had no lieutenants.[14]

George W. Kirk, another veteran of the 1867 State Guard, supervised the formation of two companies from Greene County. His own consisted of about eighty men including his former second lieutenant, Henry C. Sanders, who now served as first lieutenant, and twenty-four-year-old Caswell T. Tipton, a small farmer and wartime first sergeant, now as the second lieutenant. Little is known about the second and much smaller company from Greene. 1st Lt. Joseph A. Moore and 2nd Lt. Jackson Grant commanded its forty-one men. Moore had been an officer in the "paper militia" that Adjutant General Boynton activated earlier in January.[15]

One of Kirk's former militia sergeants, twenty-two-year-old Henry M. Cutshaw, served as first lieutenant in a large company from neighboring Washington County. Henry C. Yates, age twenty-one, commanded this unit's 101 men, some of whom came from George E. Grisham's 1867 command. The average age of the men was 20.4 years. Henry A. Cox, a twenty-four-year-old subsistence farmer, was elected to the second lieutenancy. Both lieutenants had Civil War experience, but Yates did not. Interestingly, six of the company's enlisted men were members of the large Shelton clan across the state line in Madison County, North Carolina. Confederate troops massacred thirteen civilians there in 1863. Three of the victims were Sheltons. The family may have seen the Tennessee State Guard as a means of revenge.[16]

Michael Roberts, the twenty-six-year-old former first sergeant from Kemp Murphy's 1867 command, helped organize another company from Washington and served as its second lieutenant. Alexander R. P. Toncray, age twenty-six, commanded this company of ninety-two men, some of whom came from Carter County. Robert A. Smith, age twenty-eight, was elected first lieutenant. All three officers were Civil War veterans, Toncray having served as a captain in the Tenth Tennessee Cavalry (Union).[17]

Robert L. Hall of Knox began reorganizing his old Company C, First Regiment, at the end of January, but shortly before departing for Nashville he resigned his commission for unstated reasons. Two of his old noncommissioned officers, Joseph O. Manson and Noah N. West, stepped in to complete the task, enrolling enough additional men for a second company. The twenty-three-year-old Manson commanded the larger of the two, a unit of 104 men, and gained the services of newly elected 1st Lt. J. D. Steele and 2nd Lt. Morgan C. Hackworth, age twenty-seven, a former sergeant in the First Tennessee Infantry (Union). The twenty-seven-year-old West became the second lieutenant in the other company (seventy-four men) serving under Capt. John Haynes, a former company commander in the Ninth Tennessee Cavalry (Union), and twenty-year-old 1st Lt. W. C. Chandler, a farm laborer and Civil War veteran. Chandler did not last long. On February 22, he was dishonorably discharged for drunkenness.[18]

From Union County came ninety-five men under George W. Browning, a twenty-seven-year-old farmer. The average age of the enlisted men was 20.5 years. Daniel F. Smith, a private in the 1867 Guard, had originally been asked by the adjutant general to command this unit, but he opted to serve as second lieutenant instead. The twenty-six-year-old Smith brought a strong Unionist background to his position. He was one of the bridge burners of 1861 and had used his home as a secret meeting place for Unionist guerrillas until his capture in 1862. Released after a few months in captivity, he returned to the fight. After the war, he worked as a farm laborer. The company's first lieutenant was forty-one-year-old Jacob Sharp, a middling farmer from Maynardville who had requested a commission in 1867 but for unknown reasons did not receive one. All three officers had served during the Civil War in the same company of the First Tennessee Infantry (Union).[19]

John W. Roberts, a second lieutenant of Shadrack Harris's 1867 command, moved up to first lieutenant in 1869. He served under thirty-four-year-old Capt. Jefferson C. French and over twenty-seven-year-old 2nd Lt. James R. French in a command consisting of seventy men from Jefferson County. The two Frenches were not related. Lieutenant French was a farm laborer from Flat Gap who brought some wartime noncommissioned officer experience to his new post. Captain French was a well-to-do cotton factor from Nashville, worth nearly $30,000. Although he apparently did not serve in the war, he was a good Radical, serving as Jefferson County's registrar in 1867. He further demonstrated his political credentials in a rather peculiar way. In a cryptic letter to Andrew Johnson written shortly before he joined the State Guard, French asked the president "not to leave the Government without its constitutional provisions." He also stated that "the union men of the north and south will enforce this measure. Liberty or monarchy." Friends of the president informed him that French was "very drunk" when he wrote this letter.[20]

Several units had no direct links with the 1867 State Guard. Among these fresh Radical warriors was a company of ninety-seven men from Blount County. James P. Edmondson, a veteran of the Ninety-eighth

Illinois Mounted Infantry, commanded. His first lieutenant, Samuel A. Cowan, age twenty-six, was a survivor of the tragic *Sultana* explosion. Cowan had applied for a commission in 1867, but like Jacob Sharp had not received it. Twenty-year-old Nathan H. Greer, a farm laborer, served as the unit's second lieutenant. Edmondson and Cowan were members of the Maryville Union League, an organization that dominated politics in Blount County for much of the Reconstruction period. Although no muster roll for this company exists, it is likely that several of its volunteers were also members of this league.[21]

Sevier County contributed as many as eighty-seven men to the militia buildup. Samuel M. Hammer, a twenty-one-year-old salesman, commanded these volunteers. His father was state legislator Jonathan M. Hammer, a strong supporter of the anti-Klan and militia acts. In raising his company, Hammer was reunited with his wartime comrade Lemuel Bogart, age twenty-three. As teenagers during the Civil War the two had served in the same artillery battery (and probably worked the same gun). Bogart, a farm laborer, was elected first lieutenant, while Andrew J. Harris, a wartime cavalry sergeant, became second lieutenant.[22]

The largest company mustered into service, a unit of 120 men, came from Carter County. Christopher C. Wilcox, a saddler in his mid-forties from Elizabethton, commanded these mountain boys. Wilcox was one of the most experienced officers in the State Guard. He had fought throughout the Civil War in the Thirteenth Tennessee Cavalry (Union), mostly as a company commander, and finished the conflict with the rank of major. His most exciting action occurred in September 1864, when he led the raiding party that killed the famous Confederate cavalry leader John Hunt Morgan in Greeneville, Tennessee, and effectively destroyed his forces. Wilcox's two militia lieutenants were Daniel Rowe, a wartime lieutenant, and thirty-three-year-old Jacob Hendrickson, a well-to-do farmer and former captain in the Eighth Tennessee Cavalry (Union). Hendrickson and Wilcox were two of Carter's delegates to the Greeneville Convention in 1861.[23]

A. N. Roach organized a company of eighty-six men from McMinn County. Little more is known about this unit besides the names of the two lieutenants: J. Smith Riggs and John T. Rider, the latter a twenty-seven-year-old Civil War veteran. E. H. Gurney raised a company of seventy-nine men from Anderson and Roane counties. This unit's lieutenants, Alfred N. Ragle and Thomas T. Wilson, brought with them

Christopher C. Wilcox, 1864. From Scot and
Angel's *History of the Thirteenth Regiment.*

experience as officers in the First Tennessee Infantry (Union). Ragle had
participated in an extensive antiguerrilla operation in Middle Tennessee
during the final months of 1864.[24]

The last company to muster came from Carroll County, the only
militia unit from West Tennessee. 1st Lt. John L. Murray was its sole
officer. With the arrival of Murray and his forty volunteers in Nashville
on February 18, General Cooper declared the mobilization of the Tennessee State Guard complete, although other companies were still trying to form.[25]

The 1869 Guard was different in some respects from its 1867 counterpart. Fifteen of the nineteen companies came from East Tennessee,
compared to twelve out of twenty-one in 1867. Moreover, five companies were raised in counties not represented in the 1867 mobilization.

The most significant difference, however, was that the State Guard of 1869 was all white, whereas about five hundred blacks had served in 1867. Many 1867 volunteers declined to serve in 1869, but the large number of white troops who did enlist suggests that Radicalism was not lacking in strength. Of the fifty-five men serving as company officers in 1869, only fourteen were veterans of the 1867 deployment. The military and socioeconomic background of the officer corps in 1869 is, however, remarkably similar to that of the 1867 Guard. Forty-one of the 1869 militia officers were Civil War veterans, sixteen as officers (the respective figures for 1867 are forty-four and sixteen). The average age in 1869 was 27.1 years, virtually the same as in 1867. Additionally, 1870 census data on twenty-six company officers reveals that they, like their 1867 brethren, were mostly married farmers with children whose property value averaged about thirty-two hundred dollars (three thousand dollars in 1867). Although many of the names were new, there was little measurable difference between the officer corps of the two Guards. The militia leaders of 1869 possessed the same vigor, maturity, and dedication that marked the officers of 1867.

As the companies began arriving in Nashville in early February, General Cooper took steps to get the men into fighting trim. With Capt. J. P. Edmondson acting as the training officer, Cooper ordered all companies to conduct a minimum of four hours of drill each day. Evidently, some of the training included techniques in border patrol for, as Cooper explained to some journalists, he hoped to prevent Klansmen from neighboring states from crossing over and helping the Tennessee Klan. In addition to training, Cooper instructed his officers to study and read aloud selections from the U.S. Army's Articles of War and to maintain strict accountability of their men. When a few militiamen caused some disturbances in downtown Nashville, Cooper confined all of his soldiers to their camps and forbade the consumption of alcohol, except for a ration of beer. On the afternoon of February 18, Cooper inspected the troops as part of a grand review and appears to have judged them ready for action.[26]

At this point, General Cooper established a tighter chain of command over the State Guard than had existed in 1867. The regimental structure of the first militia deployment was more a formality than a working reality; the twenty-one companies typically operated as separate, quasi-autonomous units scattered all over the state. Given the strength and ubiquity of the Ku Klux Klan in 1869, however, such

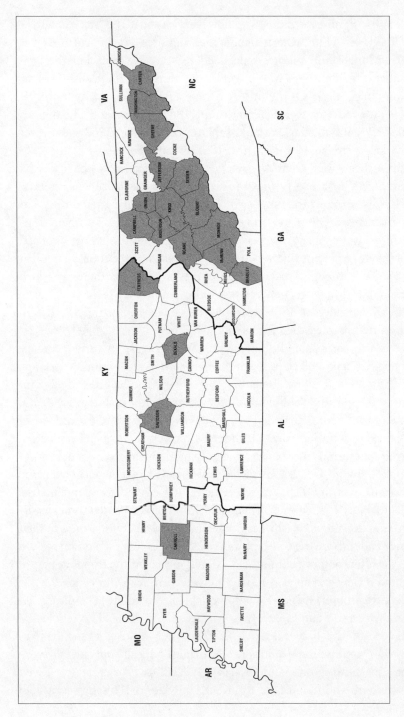

Tennessee State Guard muster points in 1869.

dispositions risked destruction in detail. Thus, Cooper restored the integrity of the traditional regiment, enabling multiple companies to fight in concert under the direction of a field-grade officer. Shortly after his grand inspection, he appointed Larken B. Gamble lieutenant colonel of the First Regiment, with Maj. Judge K. Clingan as the executive. William L. Hathaway subsequently became commander of the Second Regiment, with Maj. George W. Kirk as the executive (see Appendix F). The four handpicked men were all seasoned militia officers who understood the nuances of Reconstruction's politics of force.[27]

The regimental structure greatly enhanced logistical efficiency. Each company appointed a supply officer who worked directly with a regimental quartermaster who in turn reported to Maj. Albert Bayless. Although the quartermaster records for 1869 are less detailed than those of 1867, Bayless appears to have closely monitored the State Guard's supply needs; there were few shortages and fewer complaints during the deployment. The quartermaster department also supervised a smooth distribution of firearms. The state had apparently retained possession of its army ordnance after the 1867 deployment and constructed a proper armory in the interim. As the volunteer companies rendezvoused in Nashville, a team of gunsmiths inspected and cleaned over 1,500 rifles prior to distribution. Throughout the deployment, Bayless maintained a reserve arsenal of 480 rifles and sixty-six thousand rounds of ammunition.[28]

As the Radical army completed its organization, many legislators in the general assembly renewed their objections to its existence. Klan activity had declined over the preceding weeks and these legislators saw no reason for continuing the militia mobilization. In the state senate, Hiram Patterson of Smith County, a consistent opponent of the use of force, recommended that no more than four companies of militia be activated. In the house, a majority resolved to stop the creation of a standing army altogether. I. A. Taylor of Carter County argued that, due to the "crippled condition" of the state treasury, the militia would "greatly add to our indebtedness." On February 10, a resolution directing Governor Brownlow to disband the entire State Guard passed, thirty-five to twenty-three. Among the majority were fifteen members who barely three weeks earlier had voted for the martial law amendment. Although the hawkish William J. Smith buried both the house resolution and Patterson's proposal in his senate military committee, anti-Radicals delighted over what they believed was the general assembly's waning enthusiasm for "Brownlowism." "Strip them of the Militia," one Conservative said of the governor's supporters, "& their power is gone."[29]

Far from being stripped of his Radical army, Governor Brownlow at last began his war against the Klan. On February 20, he declared martial law in nine counties: Gibson, Haywood, and Madison in West Tennessee and Giles, Jackson, Lawrence, Marshall, Maury, and Overton in Middle. He further ordered General Cooper to deploy the State Guard "at once, and continue them in service until we have unmistakable evidence of the purpose of all parties to keep the peace." At least one scholar has rightly questioned the inclusion of Lawrence and Jackson in the martial law edict. These counties had no significant history of lawlessness. State legislator W. P. H. Turner of Lawrence County, whom the anti-Radical press incorrectly identified as a Radical, was "greatly astonished" that his "law abiding" county had been placed under martial law, without his consent no less. The omission of such Klan strongholds as Dyer, Franklin, Lincoln, Obion, and Rutherford counties from the governor's decree is equally surprising. Anti-Radicals in Lincoln County quietly counted their blessings. The *Fayetteville Observer* made little mention of the militia deployment after its county was spared the governor's wrath. Whatever the rationale behind the selections, the *Republican Banner* denounced the martial law proclamation as "a last desperate move" by the much-hated "Brownlow regime."[30]

As Brownlow issued his declaration of martial law, the body of a Cincinnati detective named Seymour Barmore washed up on the bank of the Duck River in Maury County. Several months before, Brownlow had hired Barmore to infiltrate the Klan in Giles County and essentially do for his administration what Governor Clayton's agents did in Arkansas: obtain hard evidence of Ku Kluxism. Evidently, Barmore did acquire some useful information, for General Cooper intimated to some of the protesting county delegates that he had the names of several Klansmen. In any event, the nightriders of Giles and Maury discovered the spy amongst them and, on January 11, a group of them dragged Barmore from a Nashville-bound train and summarily executed him in a nearby forest. The recovery of the detective's body six weeks later helped rally lukewarm Radicals against the Klan. State legislator John M. Cordell of Scott County, an erstwhile opponent of the militia, helped push through a resolution calling on General Cooper "to bring to justice the perpetrators of this most cruel, wicked and atrocious murder."

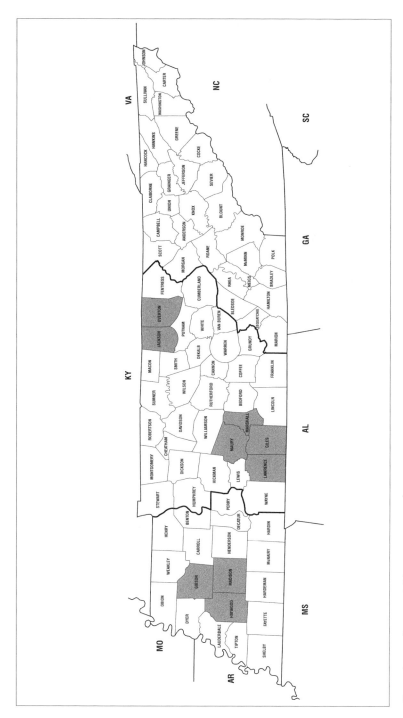

Counties under martial law in 1869.

Barmore's death added a timely sense of urgency to Brownlow's martial law proclamation.[31]

On February 23, five companies of State Guard under Lieutenant Colonel Gamble marched into Giles County. Using Pulaski as his headquarters, Gamble established a "military district" consisting of Giles and the adjacent counties of Lawrence, Marshall, and Maury (see Appendix G). After closing the civil courts, he urged the citizens to assist him in "ferreting out those disturbers of the Public Peace that they may be dealt with as they deserve." Simultaneously, Gamble dispatched militia units throughout his zone of control with orders to arrest any suspected Klansman, or at least those whose names were on a secret list provided by General Cooper. Maury resident Nimrod Porter decried this "terrible state of affairs" and feared that the militia would show no quarter.[32]

Gamble's entrance was impressive, but his raids netted few Rebel vigilantes. Although the militia apprehended some Klansmen in Giles County, many suspects evaded capture by fleeing across the state line into Alabama. Among these fugitives was Frank McCord, the editor of the *Pulaski Citizen,* an anti-Radical newspaper that appears to have shutdown temporarily during the militia dragnet. Most Klansmen, however, simply went into hiding as per Forrest's instructions. In Maury, a county described by one historian as "a loyal province of the Invisible Empire," the militia forces could find no one to arrest and soon returned to their base camp around Pulaski. Far from suffering the horrors of martial law, several Maury Conservatives actually embarked on a pleasant deer hunt during this period, an excursion that took them into militia-occupied Lawrence County as well.[33]

While producing meager results, the flurry of militia activity spawned a number of spectacular rumors. The *Union and American* reported that Gamble had ordered the summary execution of four of his captives. This newspaper also claimed that the militia was holding "forty prominent citizens" as hostages to ensure Klan quiescence. Whether or not he believed these stories, one Freedmen's Bureau agent in Columbia in Maury County considered the situation "deplorable." He recommended to his commander that the army reopen the Bureau courts in those areas affected by martial law.[34]

Before Lieutenant Colonel Gamble could undertake further anti-Klan operations, DeWitt Senter became governor and implemented a significant change in policy. Although Senter was less extreme politically

DeWitt C. Senter, 1869–70. Courtesy of Special Collections Library, University of Tennessee, Knoxville.

than Brownlow (he opposed black suffrage, for example), he regarded the Klan with the same contempt as his predecessor. As a state senator, he had voted for the expanded gubernatorial power that he now possessed. Furthermore, in his inaugural address of February 25, Senter stressed his commitment to law and order. Expecting the worst from the new governor, the *Union and American* warned Senter to rescind martial law or face a revolution. This newspaper's fears were unfounded, for where Brownlow had been authoritarian, Senter proved to be conciliatory. On February 27, Senter modified the martial decree by reopening the civil courts and ordering General Cooper and his subordinates to cooperate with local law enforcement much as the State Guard had done in 1867. A relieved *Republican Banner* proclaimed the governor's decision "welcome news," although Gamble waited at least three days before complying with this abrupt directive.[35]

A number of factors account for Senter's relaxation of martial law. In the senate, moderate Radicals had reintroduced the house resolution calling for the State Guard to disband. On February 26, the motion narrowly failed ten to eight, but the vote reflected the legislature's growing opposition to a standing army and martial law. As Senter watched this development in the general assembly, he was deluged by a fresh round of petitions protesting the militia deployment. The magistrates and sheriffs of Giles, Lawrence, and Marshall insisted that their counties were quiet and that they could suppress the Klan, if it ever showed itself again, without the militia. Finally, shortly after his inauguration, Senter had an interesting conversation with Judge James O. Shackleford of the state Supreme Court. In the presence of General Cooper, Shackleford informed the governor that the judiciary had strong misgivings about martial law in a time of peace and urged him to consider restoring civil authority as soon as possible, lest the executive branch forfeit its popular support.[36]

The "modification" to martial law did not end the militia deployment. Radical hard-liners worried that a complete suspension of military operations would encourage renewed Rebel vigilantism. Dismissing the county petitions as disingenuous indignation, Senator Joshua B. Frierson of Maury County cautioned that if the militia was disbanded, the anti-Radicals would "chuckle in their sleeves, and the Ku Klux Klan [would] rise up again." Senter shared his former colleague's concerns and, during the first week of March, he clarified his new policy. The State Guard would remain on active duty until the county authorities produced "practical evidence" of their intentions to uphold the laws. Moreover, wherever sheriffs and constables were remiss in their duties, militia officers would be permitted to intervene. In short, like Brownlow before him, Senter wanted to see some Klan outlaws arrested, prosecuted, and convicted.[37]

With Senter's approval, General Cooper continued to deploy the State Guard. Moving much of his command by steamboat, Lieutenant Colonel Hathaway led seven companies into Livingston in Overton County on March 5 and established another military district, one that covered Jackson and Overton counties (see Appendix G). Like Gamble, however, Hathaway discovered that the Klan's wave of terror had largely subsided. Jackson was so quiet that troops were never stationed there.

Hathaway did conduct mounted patrols through Overton, which captured one Klansman, but these were mostly mop-up operations. For six weeks prior to the militia's arrival, Sheriff Claiborne Beaty's special county police force had effectively suppressed the Klan. A former Unionist guerrilla from that part of the state, Beaty knew the country well and, despite a shortage of ammunition, aggressively rooted out a number of Klan dens. Rather than make arrests, however, he was content to drive these bands into Kentucky. As a result, the rather large militia command, after its arrival, either simply guarded the state border or stayed in camp.[38]

Lieutenant Colonel Hathaway apparently chafed at the lack of excitement in Overton County. In the latter part of March, he led an expedition into neighboring Putnam, a county beyond the limits of martial law, on the pretext of pursuing fugitive Klansmen. This foray, which accomplished little, culminated in a dramatic show of force in the town of Cookeville. Witnesses claimed that Hathaway "boastingly and defiantly perambulated the streets with drawn pistols, bursting caps at quiet and peaceable citizens, demanding perfect obedience to his commands." Evidently, he also made a few arrests in violation of the modified martial law decree. When he returned to Overton, he received a direct order to begin cooperating with justices of the peace in upholding the law. Hathaway also found the citizens in that part of the state eager for his men to leave.[39]

At the end of March, Radical delegates from Overton visited the governor in Nashville to negotiate the removal of the militia from their county. Thanking the governor for his efforts in fighting the Klan, they contended that the crisis had passed and that there was nothing further for the militia to do. Not only were the troops eating everything in the vicinity of Livingston, the delegates complained, but they were also succumbing to a measles epidemic that had recently struck the militia encampment. While complimentary of Hathaway's overall performance, the Cookeville incident notwithstanding, they recommended that the force of 600 militiamen be reduced to fifty. General Cooper thought the full occupation should continue until some examples had been made "to terrify evil doers." Governor Senter, however, accepted the sincerity of the delegation and promised to withdraw some of the companies, beginning with Sheriff Beaty's special police force.[40]

If the State Guard deployment in Middle Tennessee seemed anticlimactic, militia activities in West Tennessee produced a few instances of drama. Between March 2 and 5, Maj. Judge K. Clingan and five companies headed for Humboldt in Gibson County, where they established a military district over Gibson, Haywood, and Madison counties (see Appendix G). For Clingan, the deployment was a return to his 1867 area of operations. Madison whites protested this latest militia occupation, claiming that the Klan had been nothing more than a "will-o-the-wisp" and had long since disappeared. West Tennessee Radicals, however, were delighted by the militia's presence, particularly Humboldt's school superintendent W. H. Stilwell, who had earlier boasted that "two weeks of real working mounted militia would conquer" the Klan. Another Radical, J. C. Reaves of nearby Weakley, even requested that the State Guard extend its jurisdiction to include his county. According to him, the Klan was still active, albeit discreetly, around the county seat of Dresden.[41]

Major Clingan soon found that some Klan dens were willing to fight. On March 10, in response to reported Klan outrages against the black community in western Haywood, he sent a detachment of twenty men under Lt. Powell Low to investigate. Low spent most of his time patrolling the vicinity of Woodville, but perhaps suspecting that Klansmen were using neighboring Lauderdale County as a safe haven, he crossed the boundary and began searching farmhouses for Rebel outlaws. When the owner of one farm accused the militiamen of trespassing, he claimed they fired on him. This incident contributed to a growing resentment among local whites. Returning that evening to Woodville, Low bivouacked under arms—wisely so, as it turned out, for at 9:00 p.m. "an organization of outlaws" attacked the militia unit. One anti-Radical newspaper contended that about a dozen "bold determined men" carried out the attack, while another claimed that the assailants were merely "small boys." Low, however, estimated that the force consisted of as many as one hundred mounted Klansmen. In any event, after standing his ground for four hours, the lieutenant commenced a slow retreat to Brownsville, exchanging sporadic fire with the Rebels until about 10:00 a.m. the following day. Despite the apparent intensity of the skirmish, Low reported only one casualty among his men. Klan casualties are unknown.[42]

With the willing assistance of Haywood sheriff S. S. Sherman, Major Clingan soon launched a counter-attack. On March 21, he led a force of 150 men back to Woodville. Ordering Capt. William Hicks to seal off the roads with strong pickets, Clingan rushed into the town with 30 mounted men, hoping to catch any Klansmen by surprise. In a house-by-house search conducted under a cold rain, the militiamen apprehended one of the men believed to have been involved in the shoot-out with Low. Three other suspects managed to escape with the help of the townspeople. Disappointed by the results, Clingan halted all business in Woodville and assembled the town's leading citizens for a meeting. Castigating them for their complicity in the region's lawlessness, the major demanded that they disclose the Klan's hiding places. This proved fruitless. Realizing that his listeners were either in league with the Klan or afraid of reprisals should they cooperate with him, Clingan handed his lone prisoner over to Sheriff Sherman and returned to Humboldt on March 24.[43]

Clingan's punitive raid may not have captured many Klansmen, but it did subdue Haywood's defiant ex-Confederates. According to the *Daily Press and Times,* many of the county's Klan outlaws fled to Arkansas, where Governor Clayton had recently ended his militia campaign. Whereas Captain Hicks had asserted that a "reign of terror" existed in Haywood County before the Woodville occupation, Lt. Smith Riggs described a "quiet condition" in its aftermath. Riggs even believed that the improved situation would permit the governor to disband many of the militia companies.[44]

Having brought order to his military district in March, Major Clingan incited a needless controversy in April. In the early part of the month, he posted an order under the heading "Department of Forky Deer," referring to the nearby northern and southern tributaries of the Forked Deer River. When Mr. A. Richardson, a former Confederate captain, crossed out the "y" in Forky and penciled in "ed," Clingan had him arrested and charged with "mutilation of general orders." A militia tribunal meted out a harsh and unusual punishment. Richardson was tied to a telegraph pole by his thumbs, where he languished for more than four hours, during which time the occupants of several passing trains gawked at the spectacle.[45]

Gibson whites condemned Clingan's extralegal punishment. Describing the militia major as a "wooden-headed jackanapes," the *Republican Banner* reminded its readers that martial law had been modified to prevent such outrages. This newspaper joined a chorus of demands calling for an immediate removal of all the militia from West Tennessee. After his release, Richardson levied a $100,000 civil lawsuit against Clingan. Later in the month, however, he apparently had an altercation with two militiamen and received a bullet in his thigh. The *Banner* described the incident as an assassination attempt. Richardson recovered from his wound, but he also appears to have dropped the lawsuit.[46]

Richardson's ordeal was only the latest on a growing list of civilian grievances against the State Guard during the spring of 1869. With no Klan to fight, some of the militiamen in Giles County began preying on the very people they came to protect. On the evening of March 1, a Private Adams raped a twelve-year-old black girl on the outskirts of Pulaski. Discovering what had happened, the girl's father and some other black men chased Adams into the woods and severely beat him. Summoned to investigate the incident, Capt. E. E. Winters interrogated the blacks and the injured Adams, who was recovering in the home of a black widow. Shocked by what he learned, Winters reportedly stated that the militia private should be shot for his heinous crime. Similarly, after hearing the story, Lieutenant Colonel Gamble vowed that he would "have no mercy on the miscreant." Misinterpreting these officers' indignation as a license to exact revenge, a group of freedmen dragged Adams from his bed the next morning and killed him. Interestingly, the State Guard took no action against the black community.[47]

The rape precipitated a vociferous round of protests against the militia occupation. Giles County blacks asked Governor Senter to remove his soldiers. Although they complimented the officers of the State Guard, they professed little faith in the enlisted men. Anti-Radicals in the county went further in their remonstrance. Complaining that militia deserters roamed the countryside causing trouble, nearly six hundred whites from virtually every district in the county signed petitions denouncing the State Guard and calling for its removal. Additionally, county leaders staged a formal protest in Pulaski on March 7, one attended by thousands of citizens of both races. According to the *Republican Banner,* the participants condemned the militia "with one voice as if [they] were praying." Invited to speak, General Cooper came down from Nashville and defended the overall conduct of his men. He reminded his listeners of the lawlessness of the Klan and drew cheers from the freedmen when he reassured them that the militia was still their friend, the isolated rape notwithstanding. In contrast to Cooper's measured words, Captain Winters, who was providing security for the event, reportedly excoriated a nearby crowd with an "inflammatory and incendiary" speech. Disparaging the organizers of the protest as a "G—d d—d set of rebels," he warned the blacks that if the militia left Giles, "the Ku Klux would be as numerous as ever." When the county sheriff asked Winters to calm down, the militia captain shouted back that his unit was going to stay in the county until "Hell froze over."[48]

Despite his subordinate's harangue, Lieutenant Colonel Gamble took seriously the peoples' dissatisfaction with his command. In addition to the single case of rape, which was the militia's worst offense, a number of militiamen, often under the influence of liquor despite Gamble's standing order against the purchase or consumption of "any intoxicating beverage," committed several acts of theft against the civilian population and, in one instance, recklessly fired at a wagon driver. Although some of the allegations against his men were proved false, Gamble meted out harsh punishment to the guilty. In March, he convened no less than eight courts-martial. For various misdeeds, six noncommissioned officers were reduced to the ranks, their insignia stripped off in the presence of the men. For desertion and chicken stealing, two privates (on separate occasions) had one side of their heads shorn and placards bearing the inscription "Deserter" hung around their necks. After suffering this indignity, the two men were "dishonorably drummed out of camp and the service . . . to the tune of the Rogues march." When civil authorities in Pulaski tried to indict one militia sergeant for a "malicious shooting," Captain Winters intervened and demanded that the soldier face a military tribunal. The magistrates complied, knowing that the defendant would receive justice.[49]

Gamble's swift punishment of wayward militiamen not only restored discipline within his military district but also improved relations with the white populace. Anti-Radical newspapers commended his leadership. Toward the end of March, the *Pulaski Citizen* stated that everything was "serene" in Giles County. Although Gamble periodically reminded the citizenry that "this Kuklux business must be broken up," the absence of any real vigilantism compelled him to restrict most of his men to camp. Civil authorities in Maury thanked the militia commander for not stationing troops in their county; a detachment of U.S. troops helped keep the peace there. As April arrived, Gamble's main concern, like that of his colleagues in the other two military districts, was not the Klan, but measles and pneumonia.[50]

Like the Civil War armies before it, the State Guard's greatest nemesis was disease. With hundreds of men camped in close quarters at each military district, it did not take long for measles and other maladies

The State Guard versus the Klan

to run through the ranks. At the end of March, about 110 militiamen in Pulaski (24 percent of the force stationed there) were bedridden with measles or pneumonia; in Humboldt, the sick numbered 125 (30 percent), some of whom later succumbed to an outbreak of spotted fever; in Livingston, at least 38 men (7 percent) became ill. Fortunately, fatalities among the militia were low, but the measles epidemic still afflicted one in five men at the three military districts combined. Dr. J. W. Thornburgh, the chief surgeon of the State Guard, and his assistants established well-provisioned field hospitals, but their powders, pills, oils, and ointments brought little relief. What did help was a sanitation directive that required the militiamen to strike tents and air their blankets every other day, replace straw bedding weekly, police the grounds for litter and refuse, and improve personal hygiene. Toward the end of April, the measles crisis had passed and the *Daily Press and Times* described the recovering militiamen as "vigorous and hearty."[51]

Governor Senter was less sanguine. The futility of the militia campaign was becoming more and more obvious to him. The Klan had refused to come out and fight, and most citizens were reluctant to hand over known Klansmen to the State Guard. Consequently, there was little to do in the way of legitimate law enforcement for the hundreds of militiamen stationed in the three military districts. The *Daily Press and Times*, on more than one occasion, credited the militia with restoring order in the state, but while the call for volunteers undoubtedly contributed to the cessation of Klan activities, the actual deployment of troops accomplished little. Highlighting the futility of the deployment was an event that occurred on March 25. In response to a supposed Klan shooting in Wilson (a county not under martial law), General Cooper dispatched a portion of his two-company reserve to arrest the perpetrators. They turned out to be blacks. Anti-Radicals had a good laugh: the *Union and American* sarcastically referred to the culprits as the "negro Ku-klux." The men were soon released, but the episode demonstrated that the real Klan crisis had passed.[52]

Beginning on March 26, the Senter administration commenced a large-scale reduction of militia forces. The numerous bipartisan and biracial petitions had persuaded the governor that the Klan was more or less neutralized, despite the lack of arrests. As he issued preliminary orders to disband, General Cooper praised his men for their "good behavior their Soldierly appearance and good conduct" in preserving the peace. He withdrew to the capital all but two companies in each military district. Left behind were his most dependable commanders and units: in Humboldt were Major Clingan with Captains Hicks and Hammer; in Livingston, Major Kirk with Captains French, Sanders, and Woodsides; and in Pulaski, Captains Winters and Manson. Within a fortnight, more than one thousand militiamen, under the temporary command of Lt. Col. L. B. Gamble, had gathered in "Camp Cooper" on the north side of Nashville.[53]

Discipline in Camp Cooper proved an unexpected challenge to the officers of the State Guard. Most of the men were anxious to receive their final pay and discharge and they were in no mood for Lieutenant Colonel Gamble's strict campground policies. Instead of relaxing, the men spent endless hours cleaning their gear and weapons prior to turn-in. Furthermore, until the companies were formally mustered out, Gamble placed Nashville off limits, warning his men that anyone found outside the encampment, unless on official business, would be punished as a deserter. Nonetheless, many volunteers still slipped away to the big city only to face a court-martial after they had sobered up. Evidently fatigued by the tedious daily regimen, Pvt. Thomas Barrett (Company E, First Regiment) staged a one-man rebellion against the State Guard. On the morning of April 8, he flatly refused to participate in a dress parade. When his company commander, John Haynes, ordered Barrett to fall out, the private took a swing at the captain. A court-martial penalized Barrett one month of pay and assigned him ten days of extra duty. Captain Haynes also appears to have briefly tied the insubordinate private up by his thumbs.[54]

Demobilization also produced a few more confrontations between civilians and the militia. These incidents, however, grew out of frustration more than a desire to overawe or intimidate. On April 11 in Nashville, William L. Hathaway, a colonel without a regiment, had a run-in with a citizen named Frank Tealey. As the two men waited for a streetcar, Tealey claimed Hathaway "swaggered toward him" and demanded to know whether he was "for or against Brownlow"; when Tealey said he was against the former governor, Hathaway and some accompanying militiamen surrounded the man and began kicking him. According to Hathaway, Tealey instigated the whole difficulty by insulting the State Guard "in a very offensive tone"; with his honor besmirched, Hathaway accosted the man and knocked him into a gutter.

The State Guard versus the Klan

Hathaway was arrested for assault and battery and paid a fine. The anti-Radical press claimed that the militia colonel then went on a drinking binge until his discharge.[55]

Captain Winters had a similarly disgraceful experience in Pulaski. On April 19, while searching for a deserter, Winters passed by the tin shop of J. M. McKenzie, where he heard a "peculiar whistle." Thinking some sort of trick was being played on him, he burst into the store and demanded to know what "d—d-s—n-of-a-b—h" had whistled at him. According to Winters, the shopkeeper fled at his entrance. According to McKenzie, he chased the militia captain away with a shotgun. Winters later returned to the tin shop, accompanied by one of his lieutenants and the county sheriff, to exact an apology for the whistle. As the three men approached, a large crowd gathered outside the store. To Winters they seemed "the most villainous looking men I ever set my eyes on," and he braced for a riot. But at that point, McKenzie came out and offered a humorous explanation for the whole affair. Evidently, while constructing a new mousetrap, he had caught his fingers in the jaw and let out a whistle of pain, not defiance. Winters accepted the story as an apology and, after admonishing the crowd to behave, he left. A week later, Winters's company was withdrawn to Nashville, leaving only Capt. J. O. Manson's unit in the Pulaski military district. As he departed, Winters reportedly gave three cheers for the militia and "three groans for the d—d rebel hole, Pulaski."[56]

Many Radicals in Middle and West Tennessee were distressed by the demobilization of the State Guard. Almost from the moment he began withdrawing units from the field, Governor Senter began receiving reports of renewed Ku Kluxism and requests for militia protection. One alarmed Radical from Maury opined that "to disband the militia is to disband the Radical party in this county." To counter the effect of the anti-Radical rallies in March, Radicals from Giles County held their own meeting on April 8 calling on the governor to maintain the militia occupation. "A withdrawal of the militia," explained one resolution, "would result in a fresh and increased outburst of lawlessness and violence." Radical state senator William A. Garner of Lawrence County attended the meeting and added that the presence of militia was imperative "until every Kuklux . . . had been ferreted out and punished to the fullest extent of the law." Far from wanting the State Guard to leave, other Radicals from southern Middle Tennessee actually requested additional militia companies for duty in Lincoln and Marshall, counties where Rebel vigilantism was allegedly on the rise.[57]

The State Guard versus the Klan

Signs of renascent Ku Kluxism also appeared in the Livingston military district. Around the beginning of May, a dozen Klansmen from Overton entered the county seat on horseback. Capt. J. C. French attempted to arrest them, but the men evaded capture by dashing off into the countryside. Fearing the return of Klan terrorism, one Radical from Overton privately expressed the hope that the governor would allow Sheriff Beaty to return to help quell various "renewed difficulties" with law enforcement.[58]

Whatever crimes the ex-Confederates were committing in Middle Tennessee in April and May, the Klan itself appears to have had little to do with them. At a second party meeting in Pulaski in early May, when only one militia company remained, many Radicals displayed increasing indifference toward the continued presence of the militia. When A. B. Charpie, a carpetbagger from Indiana, asked the delegates for personal testimonies against the Klan he received "no response." Shortly after this meeting, "unknown parties" fired a few shots in the vicinity of the militia camp and then vanished. Although some Radicals blamed the Klan, the *Pulaski Citizen* dismissed the incident as a hoax, an opinion shared by Captain Manson, the new commander of the military district.[59]

West Tennessee was a different story, however. On May 15, Major Clingan reported from Gibson that the "Kuklux have been raging in this county within last three weeks." During that time, "masked men" assaulted freedmen in Gibson on at least seven occasions. School superintendent Stilwell privately railed against what he considered Governor Senter's "useless" approach to fighting the Klan. "Oh, if we could have given the Rebels the lesson here that Gov. Clayton gave them in Arkansas," he mused, "all would soon be well." The situation in Haywood was just as discouraging. That county was in a "very feverish & excited Condition," according to local Radicals. They warned the governor that "it would not be safe to withdraw the Militia."[60]

Interpreting the governor's "modified" martial law as broadly as he could, Major Clingan tried to neutralize the Klan menace. At the beginning of May, he established strict curfews over Humboldt and Trenton and increased his patrols. He probably implemented the same policy in Brownsville in Haywood County and Jackson in Madison County, where he had deployed detachments from Captain Hicks's company. At one point, he managed to arrest a suspected Klansman accused of brutally beating a freedman, but a civil magistrate released the defendant despite the strong evidence against him. Mocked by local Rebels as the "hero of

Forky Deer" and exasperated by his inability to suppress the Klan with the dwindling force at his disposal, Clingan recommended that Senter reimpose the full weight of martial law and reinforce his command. "Our troops will never amount to anything," the major lamented, "unless those parties commiting depredations have come to fear them."[61]

Radicals beyond the Humboldt military district shared Clingan's frustration. State legislator James O. K. Reeves of Fayette implored Governor Senter to declare martial law in his county and deploy a company of militia at once. According to him, ex-Confederate intimidation made registration for the state election in August impossible. Apparently expecting the governor to employ the State Guard as Brownlow had during the campaign of 1867, Reeves warned Senter that more than two thousand Radical votes were in jeopardy. From Henry County, Senter received a private letter describing a horrifying instance of Klan terrorism. Sometime in April or May, four Klansmen entered the home of Virgil Bingham, a black tenant farmer, and accused him of having poisoned his landlord's horses. Ignoring his pleas of innocence, the intruders first whipped Bingham's wife and then hung him up by a rope, three times, in an effort to extract a confession. Bingham stoically endured this torment and the Klansmen eventually left, warning the freedman to tell no one of his experience. In light of such atrocities, Major Clingan probably spoke for most Radicals in West Tennessee, particularly blacks, when he told Governor Senter that "these people want protection and will support the man who they think will do it."[62]

The manifest resurgence in Rebel lawlessness did not affect disbandment. Having withdrawn the bulk of the State Guard to Nashville, Governor Senter proceeded to order all but five companies to muster out. The process began on May 6 and ended on May 14, with some of the companies from East Tennessee receiving their final pay in Knoxville. This left in the field only Captains Hicks and Hammer at Humboldt, Captain Manson at Pulaski, Captain French at Livingston, and Captain Edmondson in Nashville. Furthermore, on May 17, Senter relieved General Cooper and all field grade officers of duty. He then appointed Frank Hyberger the new adjutant general. After barely three months of active service, during which time many units saw no action, Tennessee's Radical army was essentially gone.[63]

Although the militia campaign was winding down, the impact of its financial cost was just beginning. In April, Maj. Albert Bayless calculated that at least $63,000 would be needed to pay the fourteen companies sta-

The State Guard versus the Klan

tioned at Camp Cooper, not to mention the five units still in the field. Comptroller George W. Blackburn, however, alarmed the governor by telling him that there were virtually no funds available for such a large disbursal. Only after hastily arranging loans of $50,000 from a bank in New York and $55,000 from the First National Bank in Nashville could the Senter administration discharge its Radical army with pay. Overall, the total cost of the 1869 deployment amounted to $225,851, much of it paid for by loans.[64]

As it had been in 1867, anti-Radical criticism of these expenditures was fierce throughout the militia campaign. Before any units had even organized, the *Union and American* wailed that "the credit of the state is to suffer from the mad folly of our Radical rulers." Several newspapers cynically claimed that the militia call-up, combined with martial law, was part of a corrupt bargain between the Brownlow administration and certain New York financiers to bankrupt anti-Radical businesses and property holders. As proof of the conspiracy, they cited a dramatic decline in the value of state bonds. Referring to the State Guard as an "elephant" that devoured more than sixty thousand dollars per month out of the treasury, the *Republican Banner* declared that the state economy might never recover. Angry Radical taxpayers from East Tennessee demanded that their leaders enforce the clause in the militia act stipulating that counties placed under martial law foot the bill. Such a policy, however potent it may have sounded at the time it was enacted, proved unworkable. The civil authorities from the three counties comprising the Humboldt military district, for instance, banded together to resist the "militia tax." Branding it "tyrannical legislation," they vowed never to pay it. And they never did. Only Fentress County was ever compelled to pay the direct cost of anti-Klan law enforcement. On May 17, 1869, in a case dating back to the previous year, Judge L. C. Houk ordered the chairman of the county court to pay the cost of organizing and maintaining Sheriff Beaty's special police force. Significantly, Houk grounded his decision in the sheriff act, not the militia act. It is unclear whether Fentress had to pay for Beaty's activities in neighboring Overton County as well.[65]

Political considerations, as well as financial, may also have contributed to Senter's decision to disband the State Guard in the face of continued, albeit sporadic, Klan activity. Since his inauguration, he had sought to build a following among moderate Radicals and Conservatives, groups that opposed both disfranchisement and a standing army. In seeking his party's nomination for the upcoming gubernatorial election (scheduled for August 5), however, Senter discovered that many staunch Radicals, including several militia officers, did not like his politics. During a chaotic party convention in Nashville on May 20–21, Senter found himself competing with Radical hard-liner William B. Stokes for the nomination. Among Stokes's delegates were a number of militia officers, most notably William L. Hathaway. As the two factions disrupted the proceedings with insults and threats, Hathaway denounced many of Senter's supporters as Rebels and friends of N. B. Forrest. To be sure, Hathaway did not speak for all militia officers—General Cooper, in fact, later joined the Senter camp—but his attitude must have disturbed the governor. In the end, the Radical party split, and Senter and Stokes both canvassed the state as candidates for governor. (Rather than nominate a candidate of their own, Conservatives opted to back Senter.) The deep divisions within the Radical party and the uncertain loyalty of some militia officers probably made disbandment seem imperative to Senter lest the State Guard be used against him.[66]

Shortly after the convention, on May 22, General Cooper dutifully stepped down (for the second time) as commander of the State Guard. This act was a quiet, though significant, moment in Tennessee's Reconstruction. While historians generally focus on the autocratic style of Governor Brownlow, some unfairly comparing him to the seventeenth century English tyrant Oliver Cromwell, virtually all of them overlook the true sword of Radicalism, Joseph A. Cooper. It was Cooper, not Brownlow, who most resembled the infamous Lord Protector, at least at first glance. Cooper was an accomplished military man who, as leader of the State Guard, Tennessee's equivalent of Cromwell's New Model Army, was in the best position to seize or abuse power had he so chosen. In early 1869, especially, such opportunity presented itself. At that time, Cooper commanded a partisan militia force, whose officers he had essentially handpicked and whose enlisted men, like himself, largely came from East Tennessee. More importantly, Cooper commanded this standing army during a time of crisis, martial law, and gubernatorial transfer of power. As it had in 1867, the anti-Radical press saw the potential for a military dictatorship. At one point, the *Union and American* contended that Cooper was "running the machine," while Governor Senter stood timidly in the background. But while Cooper did display a degree of ruthlessness in his campaign against the Klan, he never superseded the governor's authority. Radicals praised the general's integrity, and even many anti-Radicals came to respect him. After Cooper seriously injured himself in a fall on April 3, the *Union and American* actually wished him a speedy recovery. While Governor Brownlow's actions were in some cases indefensible, General Cooper's were almost uniformly admirable. Rather than let the State Guard become an instrument of oppression and persecution, or a weapon in intraparty politics, he ensured that it operated as a responsible defender of both the Reconstruction process and the civil rights of the freedmen. In later years, Cooper's friends likened him to the ancient military leader, Cincinnatus, who served the Roman Republic with honor before returning to his farm or, in Cooper's case, to a new position as U.S. internal revenue collector for Knox County.[67]

The remnant of the Radical army outlasted its general by only a few weeks. At the end of May, it performed a final, limited service: security for a statewide judicial election. Throughout his tenure, Governor Brownlow had appointed judges to the state Supreme Court and a number of circuit courts, rather than permit them to be elected as the constitution stipulated. In keeping with his more moderate approach, Governor Senter, at the behest of the legislature, scheduled a special judicial election for May 27 for all three Supreme Court seats and selected circuit court positions. Much to the chagrin of the Conservatives, Senter also ordered the commissioners of registration to enforce the franchise act. The special election posed a problem for those counties still under martial law, albeit "modified." Captain Hammer informed the governor that, under the circumstances, he did not think that the Humboldt military district should participate in the election. Senter, however, evidently authorized Hammer to permit an election and, although there are no details of the militia's exact dispositions, the event passed off quietly. Radical candidates won all three seats on the Supreme Court.[68]

In contrast to Humboldt, and just about everywhere else for that matter, the judicial election in Clarksville in Montgomery County for circuit court officers nearly degenerated into a bloodbath. Montgomery was the only county in the Tenth Circuit (which also included Cheatham, Dickson, Robertson, and Stewart) where Radical candidates William A. Peffer and Jay Buck received a majority for the respective offices of circuit judge and attorney general. Anti-Radical fraud and intimidation apparently accounted for the Conservative success in the other counties, and only the vigorous enforcement of the franchise act by Registrar H. W. Bunker enabled the Radical candidates to win in Montgomery. Conservatives claimed that hundreds of Kentucky blacks illegally participated in the election. Nevertheless, Radicals were still hard pressed to win the county. According to Peffer, ex-Confederates subjected the Radicals, especially whites, to "all manner of insult and indignity, Scorn, contempt, and threats." At one polling place in Clarksville, an angry citizen obstructed a column of blacks and slapped their white leader as they marched toward the ballot box. Elsewhere, blacks and whites were seen carrying weapons at they went to the polls. Fearing a riot, Jay Buck telegraphed Senter for help: "Union men here are liable to be killed before night. Send troops. . . . Don't fail." The governor complied, but immediate relief was not forthcoming; a train collision with a cow blocked the rail line until the following day.[69]

On the morning of May 29, Capt. James P. Edmondson arrived at Clarksville with a company of about ninety militiamen. Although the election had passed off without violence, the town was still unsettled. Rebels stalked the streets vowing that the "d—d Yankees and niggers" would not vote in the upcoming August election, and rumors abounded that blacks were planning to burn the town. Speaking for the Radicals, Peffer confided to Senter that "our lives are now only secure because of the presence of troops." Preferring to let the citizens cool off, Captain Edmondson bivouacked his men on the grounds of the courthouse. The *Clarksville Weekly* described them as "very quiet and respectful in their demeanor." The excitement soon abated, however, and Clarksville returned to its daily routine. Sometime in early June, the company of militia returned to Nashville.[70]

By the summer of 1869, if not sooner, the State Guard had become politically superfluous. More and more Radicals were ready for a return to normalcy. On May 29, the state Supreme Court ruled unconstitutional Brownlow's practice of invalidating county voter registrations. This decision effectively restored the suffrage to at least thirty thousand Conservative Unionists. On June 5, Governor Senter began publicly repudiating disfranchisement and announced his intention to work with the next legislature to remove all remaining political disabilities. In doing so, he gained the support of virtually all Conservatives and ex-Confederates, who collectively began calling themselves Democrats. Throughout the summer the governor replaced old Brownlow registrars with commissioners who basically enrolled any native male of the requisite age. With its commander-in-chief now seeking Democratic votes, the State Guard obviously would have no role in the August election. On June 18, the adjutant general abolished the Pulaski military district. Grateful whites from Giles County promised the governor their votes and their help in making Tennessee "the garden spot of the New World." On June 21, the military districts at Humboldt and Livingston were also abolished.[71]

Once again, a large contingent of militiamen, impatiently awaiting their discharge, occupied Camp Cooper. Captain Edmondson, the new commandant, was less rigid than Colonel Gamble, but he still wanted to disband with order and dignity. To this end, he established a "ring guard" around the camp to prevent enlisted men from sneaking off to town. The enlisted men, however, found other forms of carousal. On July 6, volunteers from several companies milled around the camp spring. Some of the men were apparently inebriated and looking for trouble, for as Pvt. Samuel T. Cox of Company D, Second Regiment, arrived to collect water for his unit, Pvt. Wilson Jarmon of Company I, First Regiment, sidled up to him and insulted Cox's water containers as "S— Potts." Thinking Jarmon was joking, Cox shot back some profanity of his own. At that point Jarmon tackled Cox and began kicking him. Excited militiamen from both companies rushed to the scene; some tried to stop the fight, but most encouraged the melee with shouts and laughter. Pvt. John Brown, a self-appointed champion for Company D, broke through the crowd, grasped two large rocks, and challenged Jarmon to a one-on-one bout. Jarmon gamely accepted, but only after Brown agreed to fight hand-to-hand. With a corporal acting as an impromptu referee, the two men wrestled for a few minutes before a patrol squad intervened. Even then the two pugilists refused to quit, Brown hurling one his rocks at Jarmon, and only the arrival of a pistol-waving Lt. Powell Low ended the row. At bayonet point, Brown and Jarmon were taken to the guardhouse, where for two hours they were hung up by their thumbs.[72]

A second controversial incident occurred later that day. Displeased by what he considered the unfair treatment of one of his men, Captain Manson of Company I released Private Jarmon over the objections of Captain Hicks, the officer of the day. On Captain Edmondson's orders, Hicks and Low arrested Manson for "a breach of discipline." A lengthy court of inquiry ensued, during which numerous witnesses described the events of July 6 in rather graphic but often conflicting detail. In the end, Captain Edmondson restored Manson to his command and attributed the entire disturbance to company rivalry. As the units began mustering out the following week, a group of U.S. soldiers from the nearby federal garrison picked a fight with some of the militiamen, exchanging a few gunshots before officers from both sides regained control.[73]

Such were the final, inglorious acts of the Tennessee State Guard. By the end of July, every militiaman with the exception of a few staff personnel had been discharged. For the Radicals, the politics of force was finally over.

The militia deployment of 1869 was a disappointment. What had started out as a bold showdown with the Ku Klux Klan had sputtered into a desultory peacekeeping mission, in which the force employed was out of proportion to the danger. Nevertheless, the State Guard's overall contribution in neutralizing the Klan cannot by denied. During the period of mobilization and during the actual deployment, the Klan was conspicuously quiet. Ironically, this inactivity undermined the rationale for martial law and deprived the State Guard of its reason for being. Rather than receiving laurels for destroying Klan dens and bringing nightriders to justice, the militia endured constant criticism for its occasional abuses of authority and its general disruption of daily life. Even many Radicals realized that the militia campaign was an excessive and expensive use of force, one that contributed to intraparty dissension. Given the outcome, the Klan's avoidance of any head-on confrontations with the State Guard must be judged a masterful course of action. An unqualified militia triumph over the Klan, or even a few bloody engagements, could well have held the Radical party together in the summer of 1869.

Instead, the Radical party disintegrated. Disenchanted by their governor's alliance with the Democrats, several militia officers campaigned against him in the statewide election. While running for seats in the general assembly, former majors Clingan and Kirk canvassed East Tennessee in behalf of Stokes. At one party rally, Kirk bellowed, "I oppose Universal Suffrage and spurn the idea of enfranchising a class of men known . . . as the Ku Klux Klan." Some veterans of the 1867 State Guard also fought hard for a Stokes victory. George E. Grisham first tried to buy the *Daily Press and Times* in order to use it against Senter and then tried to start a new, pro-Stokes newspaper in Nashville, but both efforts failed due to insufficient funds. Meanwhile, James H. Sumner, the maligned black militia captain, ran for the legislature from Davidson County under the Stokes banner. In the end, the militia candidates lost their races, as did Stokes, while Democrats gained strong majorities in the assembly. Infuriated by the outcome, William L. Hathaway shot a Senter supporter in DeKalb County during a post-election altercation. Having chased Rebel vigilantes for more than three years, the former militia colonel now

The State Guard versus the Klan

found himself on the run as a fugitive. The defeated Stokes howled that the election was a sham and charged the Conservatives with fraud. Moreover, he inexplicably accused Senter of threatening to use the militia against him. Senter, of course, had already disbanded the militia. Nevertheless, Stokes's accusation, coupled with the political animosity of many militia officers toward the incumbent, suggests that Tennessee Radicals came close to taking the path of their brethren in Arkansas and Louisiana, where the militia became a combatant in the vicious intraparty power struggles that wracked those states in the early 1870s.[74]

Regardless of what the militia might have become in the hands of politically desperate men, Governor Senter could have used a few companies of State Guard in the aftermath of the election. To the surprise and outrage of all Radicals, the Klan resumed its terrorist activities. Not content with regaining their political rights, Klansmen viewed the demise of Radicalism as an invitation to reestablish racial order. From Dyer, Weakley, Rutherford and Sumner counties, among others, came new reports of Klan outrages against the freedmen and the powerlessness of the civil authorities to prevent them. Adjutant General Hyberger assured Thompson McKinley of Sumner that "active measures will at once be instituted to put down such lawlessness." If he was being honest, then Hyberger's promise could only have meant a reactivation of the State Guard.[75]

There would be no third appearance of the Radical army, however. Democrats in the general assembly repealed both the anti-Klan legislation of 1868 and the militia act, including its amended provisions for martial law. In their stead, they passed an ineffectual law that delegated punishment of the Klan to the county authorities. Rather than veto these measures, Senter tried to reason with his erstwhile political allies. In a special message delivered before the assembly on February 2, 1870, the governor affirmed the existence of a "formidable" outlaw "*organization*" and the need for a force adequate to suppress it. Senter weakened his address, however, with deferential phraseology that reduced the request to a plea. When the legislature ignored him, he took his case to the federal government. Several Tennessee Radicals in Congress, including Senator Brownlow, had already preceded him. Alarmed by the rapid decline of their party's fortunes, the Tennessee delegation had been lobbying for months to have their state subjected to military Reconstruction. But President Grant considered preposterous the idea of imposing the

Reconstruction acts on Tennessee. He did augment the state's federal garrison to 430 soldiers, however, although he did not change the army's essentially passive mission.[76]

While the Radicals fought futile rearguard actions, the Democrats steadily achieved counter-Reconstruction in 1870. At a constitutional convention held in January 1870, attended by only a few Radical delegates, Democrats introduced revisions designed to consolidate and perpetuate their hold on power. The most significant change—permitting a state poll tax—maintained the legal fiction of black suffrage, but would effectively disfranchise most freedmen. Mindful of the key role the State Guard played during Reconstruction, the new constitution also placed great limitations on the governor's power to employ force. Mobilization of the militia was restricted to times of "rebellion or invasion," while martial law was forbidden entirely. On January 26, the convention passed the new constitution, fifty-six to eighteen. Joseph H. Blackburn, a delegate from DeKalb County and a former militia officer, voted with the minority. On March 26, the voters ratified the constitution and then prepared for the gubernatorial election, rescheduled for November of even-numbered years, in accordance with the new Constitution. Winning that election handily, John C. Brown, a former Confederate general and a one-time leader of the Ku Klux Klan, became Tennessee's governor in 1871. Democrats took six of the eight congressional seats as well. Little more than a year after Senter abandoned the politics of force, the Radical party was relegated to the mountains of East Tennessee and the Democrats put an end to Reconstruction. Foreseeing this outcome, Nimrod Porter recorded his delight: "Fare well to all Radicals. May you only be known by history in the Future, Amen."[77]

Conclusion

THE SUCCESS OF COUNTER-RECONSTRUCTION DEMORALIZED MANY veterans of the Tennessee State Guard and the many citizens who had come to depend on them for protection. Former commander George E. Grisham lamented that with the Democrats in power, "we are henceforth the serfs—menial slaves of our enemies." Speaking from the Radical stronghold of East Tennessee, Grisham was certainly exaggerating his party's plight, but his statement aptly described the situation in West Tennessee. With hundreds of Klan nightriders still terrorizing that section well into 1870, W. H. Stilwell, a white Radical from Gibson County, remarked bitterly that the Union's supposed victory over the Confederacy five years earlier was "the most gigantic falsehood of the age."[1]

Perhaps sharing this sentiment, several militia officers left Tennessee in search of other law enforcement activities. In 1870, George W. Kirk went to North Carolina and took command of the militia forces fighting the Klan in that former Confederate state. In less spectacular fashion, Judge K. Clingan became a U.S. marshal and went to the Oklahoma Territory, where he subsequently settled down and adopted three Cherokee orphans. James H. Sumner became a sheriff in Mississippi, mistakenly believing that blacks had a better chance of gaining equality in a Deep South state. Even Joseph A. Cooper eventually left the land that he had so ably defended. In 1880, he moved to Kansas. At a ceremony honoring the old general in 1895, guest speakers praised Cooper's many military exploits. There was no mention of his service in the State Guard, however, for it had been inglorious and seemingly fruitless.[2]

This silence is unwarranted, for the State Guard performed remarkably well given the trying circumstances under which it operated. As Radical warriors, Tennessee militiamen were some of the most active agents of Reconstruction in the state. With regard to politics, the State Guard proved an invaluable tool for the Radical party. It did not disfranchise the ex-Confederate majority, but it did enforce this controversial measure. In doing so, the militia preserved the integrity of the electoral process for the state's loyal voters and thereby ensured Radical control over the government. No other organization protected the ballot box as effectively, neither county sheriffs, who lacked the strength if not the will, nor the federal garrison, which usually lacked the jurisdiction. With regard to racial policies, the State Guard did not grant civil and political liberty to the freedmen, but it did its best to make sure that blacks were able to exercise their new rights and privileges. In doing so, the militia helped empower a race that often hesitated to assert itself without the guaranteed backing of the state. To be sure, most white militiamen shared the racism prevalent in America, and they probably viewed black suffrage as a political expedient, but while on duty they courageously defended the freedmen, often at their own peril. Several white militia officers, especially Captain Clingan, displayed genuine compassion for the former slaves, while those who commanded the mixed companies generally treated their black volunteers as equals of their white counterparts.

In addition to promoting Radicalism, the State Guard waged an effective police campaign against the numerous anti-Radical challenges to Reconstruction. In 1867, despite some abuses of power, it successfully shielded the state election from Rebel vigilantism and Conservative interference, and then later foiled what could be described as an anti-Radical *putsch* during the Nashville mayoral election. Gen. William P. Carlin, head of the Freedmen's Bureau in Tennessee, offered a succinct and fitting assessment of this first militia deployment: "The *State Militia* has probably had a good influence in keeping the lawless under subjection and assisting in the enforcement of Civil law though in many instances their conduct has been such as not to insure them the respect of the people [i.e., anti-Radical whites]."[3]

In 1869, the reactivation of the State Guard, coupled with the imposition of martial law, halted Klan terrorism in Middle and West Tennessee. Operating out of three strong military districts, the State Guard maintained the peace for several months. Most scholars have discounted the importance of this second deployment because it lacked decisiveness; there was no significant combat between the militia and the Klan. When looking for examples of successful anti-Klan operations, historians usually cite Governor Powell Clayton's 1868 campaign in Arkansas. Charles J. Rector, for instance, contends that the "Militia War" in Arkansas "may well have been the most successful counter-terrorism campaign waged by a southern state during Reconstruction." Otto H. Olsen asserts that Clayton's policies "constituted the only successful resistance to the Klan that occurred anywhere in the Reconstruction South." Rector's statement has merit, but timing had much to do with the different outcomes in Arkansas and Tennessee. After watching their brethren in Arkansas get thrashed, Tennessee Klansmen adopted a strategy of evasion toward the State Guard. In other words, the Tennessee Klan opted not to fight, but instead to hide from a superior military force that would likely have defeated it in open battle. Nonetheless, as a counterterrorist organization, the State Guard still achieved a qualified success, for while it was deployed the Klan stayed inactive. In this sense, Olsen's statement is well off the mark. Where the Arkansas militia won by feat of arms, the Tennessee State Guard won by forfeit.[4]

The State Guard's effectiveness against the Klan evidently impressed William Holden, North Carolina's Republican governor. In 1870, he invited George W. Kirk to organize and lead a militia force against the Klan in the Tar Heel State. At the head of six hundred troops, many of them Tennessee volunteers, Kirk swept through the violent counties of Alamance and Caswell, arrested one hundred suspects, and briefly suppressed the Klan during the summer. Had his new benefactor, Governor Holden, not been impeached and removed from office by a legislature controlled by Democrats, Kirk might have achieved the lasting success that eluded the State Guard in Tennessee.[5]

Its significant accomplishments notwithstanding, the State Guard ultimately failed to sustain Reconstruction in Tennessee. It may have repelled ex-Confederate vigilantes in 1867 and briefly dispersed the Klan in 1869, but it never entirely eliminated these paramilitary threats, which gradually inflicted fatal wounds on the Radical party in many parts of the state. Tennessee Radicals may have agreed that a certain amount of force was necessary to protect the loyal citizenry and make the process of Reconstruction work, but they vacillated in their commitment to a standing army. Regardless of their "radicalism," most Radicals disliked repressive policies. Consequently, the supreme challenge for governors Brownlow and Senter was deciding when to apply force, to what degree, and for how long. Where the near totality of the Civil War rarely brought into question the use of military power, the quasi-peace of Reconstruction made the politics of force an endlessly problematic and frustrating issue.

Financial considerations further complicated the implementation of force. Fielding the Radical army was an expensive undertaking for the Brownlow and Senter administrations. In all, the Radicals poured almost

$555,000 into the politics of force, which amounted to more than 10 percent of the $5 million state debt left behind by the Radicals. When viewed in comparative context, however, these expenditures are hardly out of line. Republican governors in Arkansas spent about $530,000 on their militia forces, most of it during Governor Clayton's imposition of martial law in 1868. In South Carolina, where the militia was all black and sporadically used, the cost was $375,000. In Louisiana, the militia cost $100,000, a figure that does not include the large New Orleans Metropolitan Police. George Kirk's short campaign against the Klan in North Carolina cost the taxpayers of that state nearly $75,000. Although the Tennessee State Guard proved the most expensive militia force used by any Reconstruction administration, virtually all southern Republican governments were breaking open their war chests to combat the ex-Confederate threat.[6]

The overt militancy of counter-Reconstruction demanded a forceful response regardless of the cost. While Appomattox marks the traditional end of the Civil War and President Johnson's 1866 decrees mark its official end, a civil war raged on in Tennessee (as it did throughout much of the former Confederacy). Anti-Radical politicians steadfastly rejected the legitimacy of the Radical government, while Rebel vigilantes in West and Middle Tennessee made a mockery of peace. Radicals had to suppress these subversive activities or lose all credibility as the governing authorities. Any action requiring force, however, had to be well thought out. *Violence in America,* an extensive study of organized violence and state response, lists several supposedly universal factors essential for effective control of a lawless populace. The state must have a justifiable reason for resorting to force. The force must be applied consistently so as to preempt violence, not simply react to it, and the force must be proportionate to the threat so as to minimize the inevitable repression of civil liberty. Finally, the instrument of force must be constituted of determined yet conscientious leaders and a rank and file that is "well-trained, highly disciplined, and loyal."[7]

Tennessee's Reconstruction administration met some of these criteria, but fell short on others. The violent activities of ex-Confederates vigilantes, Klan or otherwise, clearly warranted a resort to force. And the officers and men of the State Guard were certainly up to the task, although "highly disciplined" would be an overstatement. Unfortunately, the executive branch adopted an erratic course of law enforcement. From

1865 to 1866, Governor Brownlow tried to rely on the U.S. Army or local sheriffs to maintain order. The results were unsatisfactory; anti-Radical lawlessness only increased. In 1867, Brownlow at last mobilized a powerful militia and deployed it to great effect during the various state and municipal elections. In 1868, however, he and the Tennessee General Assembly unwisely disbanded the militia in the face of growing Ku Kluxism, and then later temporized over whether to reorganize it, let alone employ it. When Brownlow finally unleashed the State Guard again in 1869, its operations verged on overkill; the Klan had already gone underground. Under Governor Senter, the militia was further handicapped by a vague policy of "modified" martial law and then disbanded altogether. The following year, after Democrats had gained control of the legislature, Senter tried in vain to reorganize the militia for use against a renascent Klan. Throughout, the Radicals' use of force was plagued by paradox. Whenever they employed it, the situation soon no longer seemed to require it; whenever they withdrew it, the situation quickly seemed to demand its return. Brownlow and Senter were often able to contain anti-Radical violence, but they never prevented its recurrence. In short, the Rebels' paramilitary defiance outlasted the Radicals' commitment to armed suppression.

This outcome was not inevitable. Had Brownlow and Senter used the militia differently, Reconstruction may have lasted well into the 1870s, thereby giving their party time to complete its work. In hindsight, the Radicals might have done better had they created a small, but permanent, militia force and deployed it throughout the Reconstruction period, or at least from 1867 onward. Texas Republicans under Governor Edmund Davis achieved remarkable success using a small but highly mobile state police against the Klan. Between 1870 and 1873, this biracial force of two hundred mounted troopers arrested approximately seven thousand perpetrators—an incredible figure. In the more populous Tennessee, such a strike force might have comprised five full companies, equipped with a complete mounted section, and commanded by the most capable and dedicated officers. (General Cooper seems to have recognized the potential of a few elite militia companies when he created the short-lived "special command" in late 1867.) With one unit stationed in Nashville as a ready reserve, the other four could have rotated through the most lawless counties of Middle and West Tennessee, staying in a given area for no more than a month at a time, circumstances permitting, so as not to overburden the citizenry. Five hundred militiamen judiciously employed would have probably been large enough to keep Rebel vigilantes in check yet small enough to assuage concerns about military despotism.[8]

Had the Brownlow administration retained even a portion of the State Guard in 1868, much of the Klan's terror might have been forestalled, thereby rendering unnecessary the belated and awkward deployment of 1869 with its controversial declaration of martial law. A small, standing militia may also have been more economical than the two large mobilizations that actually took place. Based on payroll and quartermaster data, the yearly cost of fielding a State Guard of five companies would have been approximately $230,000. Whereas the actual militia forces cost $555,000 over roughly fifteen months of active service (both deployments combined), the hypothetical militia force would have cost $460,000 for twenty-four months of service.[9]

While this ideal scenario offers an explanation for how the Radicals might have stayed in power, it does not indicate when the politics of force would have ended. At some point, the Radicals had to declare their party sufficiently entrenched and the freedmen adequately prepared for normal relations to at last resume. To be sure, many Radicals believed that political proscription of ex-Confederates had to continue indefinitely, but it is hard to imagine anyone tolerating a standing army for however long that meant. Still, given the success of counter-Reconstruction in 1870, the Radicals should have tried using force for a little longer than they actually did.[10]

Conjecture about what the State Guard might have accomplished should not, however, overshadow what it did accomplish. As a military organization, it brought order to those parts of the state mired in political and racial strife. As a partisan body, it enabled the Radical party to exercise authority out of proportion to its numbers, while also bringing encouragement to the thousands of freedmen who were participating in American democracy for the first time. As an instrument of coercion, it represented a model for how a standing army should conduct itself. Despite anti-Radical propaganda depicting military despotism, the officers and men of the State Guard generally displayed laudable professional-like behavior and rarely infringed on the liberties of law-abiding citizens. Reconstruction in Tennessee may continue to receive unfavorable judgments, and the Radicals do deserve some historical censure, but the performance of the State Guard should be accorded respect.

Appendix A

Tennessee State Guard, 1867

Unit[a]	Commander	Personnel	Muster county and date
A/1	Joseph H. Blackburn	96	DeKalb (Middle), 1 April
B/1	George E. Grisham	115	Washington (East), 1 May
C/1	Robert L. Hall	110	Knox (East), 31 May
D/1	Judge K. Clingan	93	Bradley (East), 11 May
E/1	John T. Robeson	111[b]	Carroll (West), 8 May
F/1	Shadrick T. Harris	113	Jefferson (East), 1 June
G/1	Silas L. Chambers	83	Anderson (East), 10 June
H/1	William O. Rickman	94	Franklin/Bedford (Middle), 1 May
I/1	James R. Evans	101	Grainger (East), 3 June
K/1	William S. Stuart	87	Putnam (Middle), 1 June

First Regiment = 1,003 men

Unit[a]	Commander	Personnel	Muster county and date
A/2	George W. Kirk	86	Greene (East), 6 June
B/2	Thompson McKinley	102	Sumner (Middle), 10 June
C/2	John L. Kirk	130[c]	Greene (East), 6 June
D/2	Kemp Murphy	73	Knox (East), 19 July
E/2	George Hamilton	64	McNairy (West), 18 June
F/2	Joseph M. Alexander	55	Roane (East), 6 July
G/2	James H. Sumner	114	Davidson (Middle), 27 June
H/2	A. M. Clapp	44[d]	Jefferson (East), 26 July
I/2	William N. Purdy	51	Monroe (East), 22 July
K/2	Philip J. Flemming	61	Williamson (Middle), 29 July

Second Regiment = 780 men

Unit[a]	Commander	Personnel	Muster county and date
A/3	Michael J. Houston	92	Davidson (Middle), 30 July

Total = 1,875 men

Note: Companies in **bold** contained black militiamen.

[a]Denotes Company/Regiment

[b]Reflects the merger of Robeson's 77 men with William C. Holt's 34 men.

[c]Includes 61 men recruited from Montgomery County on July 23–27.

[d]Clapp's muster roll is incomplete and illegible in places.

Appendix B

State Guard Dispositions as of August 1, 1867

Unit	County location with approximate troop strength[a]
A/1	DeKalb (Blackburn + 35), Warren (Cravens + 30), Cannon (25)
B/1	Lincoln (Grisham + 70), Wilson (McLaughlin + 40)
C/1	Rutherford (R. Hall + 110)
D/1	Madison (Clingan + 75)
E/1	Obion (Robeson), Dyer (Simpson), Weakley (Fuller), Gibson (Holt + 30)
F/1	Henry (E. Hall + 55), Stewart (Roberts + 20), Cheatham (30)
G/1	Gibson (Adkins + 45), Weakley (Newport + 40)
H/1	Marshall (Rickman + 65), Giles (Mankin + 25)
I/1	Humphreys (Evans + 60), Claiborne (Ellis + 40)
K/1	White (Stuart + 45), Overton (40)
A/2	Franklin (G. Kirk + 85), possibly some in Bedford
B/2	Sumner (McKinley + 100)
C/2	Montgomery (J. Kirk + 100), Robertson (Burchfield + 30)
D/2	Knox (Murphy + 70)
E/2	McNairy (Hamilton + 60)
F/2	Lauderdale (Alexander + 50)
G/2	Williamson (J. Sumner + 45), Maury (G. Sumner + 55), Giles (10)
H/2	Hawkins (Clapp), possibly some in Sullivan
I/2	Polk (Purdy + 25), Monroe (25),
K/2	Williamson (Fleming + 20), Giles (20 attached to H/1), Maury (20)
A/3	Davidson (Houston + 70), Giles (Durham + 20)
	Total counties with State Guard on day of the election = 33

[a]The "+" indicates the number of troops under the mentioned officer.

Appendix C

1867 Gubernatorial Election Returns from Militia Counties

Middle Tennessee

County	Radical vote	Conservative vote	
Cannon	430	157	
Cheatham	207	58	
DeKalb	864	182	
Davidson	5,454	1,001	Federal troops present
Franklin	702	313	
Giles	1,880	152	
Humphreys	267	131	
Lincoln	780	267	
Marshall	831	449	
Maury	2,817	238	Federal troops present
Montgomery	1,527	588	
Overton	411	17	
Robertson	348	493	
Rutherford	2,939	359	
Stewart	252	631	
Sumner	891	224	Federal troops present
Warren	415	158	
White	356	28	
Wilson	1,249	788	
Williamson	1,704	574	Federal troops present
	24,324	6,808	

West Tennessee

County	Radical vote	Conservative vote	
Dyer	316	46	
Gibson	687	277	Federal troops present
Henry	0	19	
Lauderdale	296	162	
Madison	343	503	
McNairy	608	127	
Obion	272	67	Federal troops present
Weakley	769	282	
	3,291	**1,483**	

East Tennessee

County	Radical vote	Conservative vote
Claiborne	795	159
Hawkins	1,107	186
Knox	2,880	1,022
Monroe	978	160
Polk	211	48
	5,176	**1,416**

Total	33,586	9,866
Tennessee total	74,437	22,486

Note: Counties in **bold** highlight a Conservative majority.
Vote source: Hopkins and Lyons, *Tennessee Votes*.

Appendix D

Demobilization Chronology of the State Guard

Unit	Last commander	Disbandment date	Days active
A/3	Houston	August 14, 1867	15
K/2	Fleming	August 15, 1857	17
B/2	McKinley	August 16, 1867	67
G/2	Sumner	August 19, 1867	53
G/1	Adkins	August 20, 1867	71
F/2	Alexander	August 21, 1867	46
B/1	Grisham	September 4, 1867	127
D/2	Murphy	September 4, 1867	47
H/2	Clapp	September 4, 1867	40
I/2	Purdy	September 4, 1867	44
E/2	Hamilton	September 5, 1867	79
K/1	Stuart	September 7, 1867	99
I/1	Ellis	September 10, 1867	99
D/1	Clingan	September 20, 1867	132
C/2	J. L. Kirk	September 21, 1867	107
A/1	Blackburn	October 1, 1867[a]	183–97
A/2	G. W. Kirk	October 12, 1867	128
C/1	R. L. Hall	December 7, 1867	191
F/1	E. R. Hall	December 7, 1867	190
H/1	Mankin	February 11, 1868	286
E/1	Holt	February 11, 1868	279

Sources: General Order Nos. 8–11, 16, 18–28, 30, 33, Reel 9, Vol. 27, TAGO; Special Order Nos. 86, 97, 164, 179, 200–201, Reel 9, Vol. 33, TAGO.

Note: Units in **bold** contain black militiamen.

[a]Mounted section retained until October 14.

Special Command (First Battalion—September 3, 1867)

Major John T. Robeson
A/1, B/1 (formerly H/1), C/1, D/1, E/1, F/1, A/2, C/2

Appendix E

1868 Presidential Returns from Former Militia Counties

Middle Tennessee

County	Radical vote	(Loss from 1867)	Con./Dem. vote	(Gain from 1867)	
Cannon	311	(-119)	177	(+20)	
Cheatham	73	(-134)	80	(+22)	
DeKalb	626	(-238)	262	(+80)	
Davidson	4,518	(-936)	1,450	(+449)	Federal troops present
Franklin	82	(-620)	118	(-195)	Federal troops present
Giles	561	(-1,319)	611	(+459)	Federal troops present
Humphreys	102	(-165)	119	(-12)	
Lincoln	4	(-776)	558	(+291)	Federal troops present
Marshall	166	(-665)	856	(+407)	Federal troops present
Maury	1,910	(-907)	1,011	(+773)	Federal troops present
Montgomery	1,034	(-493)	684	(+96)	Federal troops present
Overton	299	(-112)	25	(+8)	
Robertson	212	(-236)	406	(-87)	Federal troops present
Rutherford	956	(-1,983)	842	(+483)	Federal troops present
Stewart	120	(-132)	830	(+199)	
Sumner	465	(-426)	378	(+154)	Federal troops present
Warren	342	(-73)	166	(+8)	
White	165	(-191)	37	(+9)	

Middle Tennessee (cont.)

County	Radical vote	(Loss from 1867)	Con./Dem. vote	(Gain from 1867)
Wilson	850	(-399)	1,218	(+430)
Williamson	561	(-1,143)	835	(+261)
	13,357	**(-10,967)**	**10,663**	**(+3,855)**

West Tennessee

County	Radical vote	(Loss from 1867)	Con./Dem. vote	(Gain from 1867)	
Dyer	118	(-198)	346	(+300)	Federal troops present
Gibson	0	(-687)	0	(-277)	Federal troops present
Henry	168	(+168)	148	(+129)	
Lauderdale	67	(-229)	453	(+291)	
Madison	289	(-54)	267	(-236)	Federal troops present
McNairy	520	(-88)	75	(-52)	
Obion	85	(-187)	139	(+72)	Federal troops present
Weakley	506	(-263)	226	(-56)	
	1,753	**(-1,538)**	**1,654**	**(+171)**	

	Radical vote	(Loss from)	Con./Dem. vote	(Gain from)
Total	**15,110**	**(12,505)**	**12,317**	**(+4,026)**
Tennessee total	**56,606**	**(-17,831)**	**26,151**	**(+3,675)**

Notes: Federal Troops occupied six other counties in 1868: Bedford, Fayette, **Hardeman**, Shelby, **Tipton**, and Wayne. The Radicals lost votes in Bedford, Fayette, and Wayne while gaining in the others. Conservatives gained in all six. The combined Radical loss for these counties was only 184 votes, but the combined Conservative gain was 1,088.

Counties in **bold** highlight a Conservative/Democratic majority.

Vote source: Hopkins and Lyons, *Tennessee Votes*.

Appendix F

Tennessee State Guard, 1869

Unit	Commander	Personnel	Muster county
A/1	James P. Edmondson	97	Blount (East)
B/1	William L. Hicks	98	Bradley (East)
C/1	Edwin E. Winters	88	Davidson (Middle)
D/1	George W. Browning	97	Union (East)
E/1	John Haynes	74	Knox (East)
F/1	Edwin H. Gurney	79	Anderson/Roane (East)
G/1	Alexander R. Toncray	92	Carter/Washington (East)
H/1	Samuel M. Hammer	87	Sevier (East)
I/1	Joseph O. Manson	104	Knox/Campbell (East)
K/1	A. N. Roach	86	McMinn (East)

First Regiment: 902 men (Lt. Col. Larken B. Gamble, Maj. Judge K. Clingan)

Unit	Commander	Personnel	Muster county
A/2	John B. Taylor	86	DeKalb (Middle)
B/2	Levi N. Woodsides	78	DeKalb (Middle)
C/2	Henry C. Sanders	84[a]	Greene (East)
D/2	Jefferson C. French	70	Jefferson (East)
E/2	Joseph A. Moore	41	Greene (East)
F/2	Henry C. Yates	101	Washington (East)
G/2	Christopher C. Wilcox	120	Carter (East)
H/2	John L. Murray	40	Carroll (West)
I/2	William N. Purdy	60	Monroe (East)

Second Regiment: 680 men (Lt. Col. William L. Hathaway, Maj. George W. Kirk)

Fentress County Guards

Unit	Commander	Personnel	Muster county
—	Claiborne Beaty[b]	81	Fentress (Middle)

Total=1,582 (1,663 including Beaty's men)

^aNo precise information on personnel strength for this company could be found. The above figure is a supposition based on General Order No. 1, which stipulated that a captaincy was contingent on raising a company of at least eighty-four men. Because this requirement was obviously not enforced, it is impossible to know even the minimum number of men who may have served in this company.

^bBeaty was sheriff of the Fentress County Guards. During the militia campaign, he received a special commission in the State Guard and an augmentation in manpower.

Appendix G

State Guard Dispositions as of March 5, 1869

Counties under Martial Law

Gibson, Haywood, and Madison, with Militia headquarters at Humboldt (Gibson)

Giles, Lawrence, Marshall, and Maury, with Militia headquarters at Pulaski (Giles)

Jackson and Overton, with Militia headquarters at Livingston (Overton)

Humboldt (420 men)	Pulaski (467 men)	Livingston (601 men)	Nashville (160 men)
Major Clingan	Lt. Col. Gamble	Lt. Col. Hathaway/ Major Kirk	General Cooper
B/1 (Hicks)	A/1 (Edmondson)	A/2 (Taylor)	G/2 (Wilcox)
E/1 (Haynes)	C/1 (Winters)	B/2 (Woodside)	H/2 (Murray)
G/1 (Toncray)	D/1 (Browning)	C/2 (Sanders)	
H/1 (Hammer)	F/1 (Gurney)	D/2 (French)	
K/1 (Roach)	I/1 (Manson)	E/2 (Moore)	
		F/2 (Yates)	
		I/2 (Purdy)	
		Sheriff Beaty	

Notes

INTRODUCTION

1. George C. Rable, *But There Was No Peace: The Role of Violence in the Politics of Reconstruction* (Athens: Univ. of Georgia Press, 1984), 15; Michael Les Benedict, *The Fruits of Victory: Alternatives in Restoring the Union, 1865–1877* (Philadelphia: Lippincott, 1975), 21, 98–99. Benedict contends that the "grasp of war" concept greatly influenced the thinking of many Republicans throughout the nation.
2. Verton M. Queener, "A Decade of East Tennessee Republicanism, 1867–1876," East Tennessee Historical Society *Publications* 14 (1942): 59; James Alex Baggett, *The Scalawags: Southern Dissenters in the Civil War and Reconstruction* (Baton Rouge: Louisiana State Univ. Press, 2003), 2–3, 125–26.
3. For some critics of force, see James E. Sefton, *The United States Army and Reconstruction, 1865–1877* (Baton Rouge: Louisiana State Univ. Press, 1967), 207–10; and Rable, *But There Was No Peace*, 189–91. For some advocates of force, see Michael Perman, *Reunion Without Compromise: The South and Reconstruction, 1865–1868* (Cambridge: Cambridge Univ. Press, 1973), 3–12, 346; and Allen W. Trelease, *White Terror: The Ku Klux Klan Conspiracy and Southern Reconstruction* (Baton Rouge: Louisiana State Univ. Press, 1971), xxix–xxxix. Without taking sides on the matter, Hugh Davis Graham and Ted Robert Gurr make the provocative statement that "the North won the Civil War, but in its very triumph created hostilities that contributed to one of the greatest and most successful waves of vigilante violence in [U.S.] history." Graham and Gurr, *Violence in America: Historical and Comparative Perspectives* (Washington, D.C.: GPO, 1969), 636.
4. David W. Crofts, "Reconstruction in Tennessee: An Assessment for Thaddeus Stevens," West Tennessee Historical Society *Papers* 43 (1989): 27.

5. James Welch Patton, *Unionism and Reconstruction in Tennessee, 1860–1869* (Chapel Hill: Univ. of North Carolina Press, 1934), 83–123; E. Merton Coulter, *William G. Brownlow, Fighting Parson of the Southern Highlands* (Chapel Hill: Univ. of North Carolina Press, 1937), 262–374; Thomas B. Alexander, *Political Reconstruction in Tennessee* (Nashville: Vanderbilt Univ. Press, 1950), 163–75.

6. U.S. Congress, both houses, *Ku Klux Conspiracy, Report of the Joint Select Committee into the Condition of Affairs in the Late Insurrectionary States,* 13 vols. (Washington, D.C.: GPO, 1872), 1:454, 458; Ira P. Jones, "Reconstruction in Tennessee," in *Why the Solid South? Or Reconstruction and Its Results,* ed. Hilary A. Herbert (Baltimore: R. H. Woodward, 1890), 191–98.

7. Patton, *Unionism and Reconstruction,* 176–77, 235; Coulter, *Brownlow,* 332.

8. Alexander, *Political Reconstruction,* 149–50, 167.

9. Robert H. White, Stephen V. Ash, and Wayne C. Moore, eds., *Messages of the Governors of Tennessee,* 11 vols. to date (Nashville: Tennessee Historical Commission, 1952–), 5:552–53; Sefton, *United States Army and Reconstruction,* 236.

10. Otis A. Singletary, *Negro Militia and Reconstruction* (New York: McGraw-Hill, 1957), 4, 13, 145. For an excellent state study on law enforcement during Reconstruction see Ann Patton Baenziger, "The Texas State Police During Reconstruction: A Reexamination," *Southwestern Historical Quarterly* 72 (1969): 470–91.

11. Trelease, *White Terror,* 9, 18, 182. While deferring to Trelease's findings, Eric Foner credits the State Guard with a "drastic curtailment" of Klan activities in the early months of 1869. See Eric Foner, *Reconstruction: America's Unfinished Revolution, 1863–1877* (New York: Harper & Row, 1988), 439–40.

12. John Hope Franklin, *Reconstruction After the Civil War* (Chicago: Univ. of Chicago Press, 1961), 121, 161–62.

Chapter 1

1. Charles L. Lufkin, "A Forgotten Controversy: The Assassination of Senator Almon Case of Tennessee," *West Tennessee Historical Society Papers* 39 (1985): 37–50; Tennessee General Assembly, *Public Acts of Tennessee,* 34th General Assembly, 2nd adjourned sess. (Nashville, 1867), Resolution No. 68.

2. Tennessee General Assembly, *Public Acts of Tennessee,* 34th General Assembly, 2nd adjourned sess. (1867), Resolution No. 58; Samuel Mayes Arnell, "The Southern Unionist," unpublished manuscript, Special Collections, Univ. of Tennessee, Knoxville, n.d., 313; White, Ash, and Moore, *Messages* 5:550–51.

3. Patton, *Unionism and Reconstruction,* 3–25; Paul H. Bergeron, Stephen V. Ash, and Jeanette Keith, *Tennesseans and Their History* (Knoxville: Univ. of Tennessee Press, 1999), 132–39.

4. David Madden, "Unionist Resistance to Confederate Occupation: The Bridge Burners of East Tennessee," East Tennessee Historical Society *Publications* 52–53 (1980–81): 22–39; Bergeron, Ash, and Keith, *Tennesseans and Their History,* 139–57; James M. McPherson, *What They Fought For, 1861–1865* (Baton Rouge: Louisiana State Univ. Press, 1994), 38; *Report of the Adjutant General of the State of Tennessee of the Military Forces in the State, from 1861–1866* (Nashville, 1866); Stephen V. Ash, *Middle Tennessee Society Transformed, 1860–1870: War and Peace in the Upper South* (Baton Rouge: Louisiana State Univ. Press, 1988), 84–106, 143–74; Noel C. Fisher, *War at Every Door: Partisan Politics and Guerrilla Violence in East Tennessee, 1860–1869* (Chapel Hill: Univ. of North Carolina Press, 1997).

5. Verton M. Queener, "The Origins of the Republican Party in East Tennessee," East Tennessee Historical Society *Publications* 13 (1941): 77–84; Baggett, *Scalawags,* 125–26; Alexander, *Political Reconstruction,* 18–32; Coulter, *Brownlow,* 235–93.

6. White, Ash, and Moore, *Messages* 5:456; Arnell, "Southern Unionist," 272–74; Alexander, *Political Reconstruction,* 87, 104–5; Jones, "Reconstruction in Tennessee," 182–83.

7. Queener, "Origin of the Republican Party," 86–87; White, Ash, and Moore, *Messages* 5:488–500.

8. White, Ash, and Moore, *Messages* 5:443.

9. White, Ash, and Moore, *Messages* 5:445, 462, 546–48; Bobby L. Lovett, "Memphis Riots: White Reactions to Blacks in Memphis, May 1865–July 1866," *Tennessee Historical Quarterly* 38 (1979): 9–33; Alexander, *Political Reconstruction,* 99–10, 123–24.

10. Alexander, *Political Reconstruction,* 88–89, 127–29; *Ku Klux Conspiracy* 1:455–56. Several times in July 1865, Etheridge declared Brownlow's governorship a tyranny, urged Tennesseans to disregard the franchise laws, and countenanced violence against blacks.

11. Thomas B. Alexander, "Political Reconstruction in Tennessee, 1865–1870," in *Radicalism, Racism, and Party Realignment: The Border*

States During Reconstruction, ed. Richard O. Curry (Baltimore: John Hopkins Press, 1969), 59–61; LeRoy P. Graf, Ralph W. Haskins, and Paul H. Bergeron, eds., *The Papers of Andrew Johnson,* 16 vols. (Knoxville: Univ. of Tennessee Press, 1967–2000), 10:512–14; Horace Maynard to Governor Brownlow, May 26, 1866, Box 1, Folder 9, W. G. Brownlow Papers, MS 1940, Special Collections, Univ. of Tennessee, Knoxville (hereafter cited as Brownlow Papers); Governor Brownlow to W. E. Kelley, Mar. 8, 1866, E. E. Patton Papers, Calvin M. McClung Historical Collection, East Tennessee History Center, Knoxville (hereafter cited as Patton Papers).

12. Eugene G. Feistman, "Radical Disfranchisement and the Restoration of Tennessee, 1865–1866," *Tennessee Historical Quarterly* 12 (1953): 145–47; Brooks D. Simpson, *Let Us Have Peace: Ulysses S. Grant and the Politics of War and Reconstruction, 1861–1868* (Chapel Hill: Univ. of North Carolina Press, 1991), 140; William J. Ulrich, "The Northern Military Mind in Regard to Reconstruction, 1865–1872: The Attitudes of Ten Leading Union Generals" (Ph.D. diss., Ohio State Univ., 1959), 233–35; Tennessee General Assembly, *Public Acts of Tennessee,* 34th General Assembly, extra sess. (1866), chaps. 2–3; Alexander, *Political Reconstruction,* 110–11.

13. Governor Brownlow to W. D. Kelley, Mar. 8, 1866, Patton Papers; Robert Ramsey to Governor Brownlow, Mar. 5, 1866, Box 1, Folder 9, Brownlow Papers; Feistman, "Radical Disfranchisement," 148; U.S. Congress, *House Executive Documents, Report of the Secretary of War,* 40th Cong., 2nd sess. (Washington, D.C.: GPO, 1867), 182–83.

14. Alexander, *Political Reconstruction,* 177–79; Trelease, *White Terror,* 8–10. An army investigation into the Klan, conducted in the fall of 1866, concluded that there was no evidence of any "military organizations" in the state, but the officer in charge does not seem to have looked much beyond the environs of Nashville. Graf, Haskins, and Bergeron, *Papers of Andrew Johnson* 11:344–45; Simpson, *Let Us Have Peace,* 153.

15. J. Noah to Governor Brownlow, Aug. 20, 1866, Patton Papers; J. Noah to Governor Brownlow, Aug. 24, 1866, Reel 1, Box 1, Folder 8, William G. Brownlow, Papers of the Governors, GP 21, Tennessee State Library and Archives, Nashville (hereafter cited as Governor Brownlow Papers); Congress, *House Executive Documents, Report of the Secretary of War* (1867), 183.

16. Arnell, "Southern Unionist," 289; *Nashville Daily Press and Times,* Sept. 16, Nov. 9, 1866.

17. Congress, *House Executive Documents, Report of the Secretary of War* (1867), 183, 199–202; Paul D. Phillips, "A History of the Freedmen's Bureau in Tennessee" (Ph.D. diss., Vanderbilt Univ., 1964), 275–76.

18. White, Ash, and Moore, *Messages* 5:527; Sefton, *United States Army and Reconstruction,* 261.

19. Petition to Leonidas C. Houk, Aug. 8, 1866, Houk Papers, Calvin M. McClung Historical Collection, East Tennessee History Center, Knoxville (hereafter cited as Houk Papers); Coulter, *Brownlow,* 318–19; *Nashville Daily Press and Times,* Oct. 9, 1866; Forrest Conklin, "Wiping Out 'Andy' Johnson's Moccasin Tracks: The Canvass of Northern States by Southern Radicals, 1866," *Tennessee Historical Quarterly* 52 (1993): 125–27.

20. White, Ash, and Moore, *Messages* 5:534–35.

21. White, Ash, and Moore, *Messages* 5:555. "Iron-glove regime" is a typical example of White's negative attitude toward the Brownlow administration.

22. James W. Patton, *Unionism and Reconstruction,* 86, 93; White, Ash, and Moore, *Messages* 5:413–14; Tennessee General Assembly, *Senate Journal,* 34th General Assembly, 1st sess. (1865), 54, 58, 61; *Nashville Daily Press and Times,* Apr. 25, 26, May 6, 1865.

23. Tennessee General Assembly, *House Journal,* 34th General Assembly, 1st sess. (1865), 36, 80, 104, 132, 176–77, 186, 194, 230, 260; Robert M. McBride and Dan M. Robison, *Biographical Directory of the Tennessee General Assembly,* 6 vols. to date (Nashville: Tennessee Historical Commission, 1975–), 2:844–45; William Jay Smith, "Autobiographical Sketch (1823–1913)," Special Collections, Univ. of Tennessee, Knoxville; Janet B. Hewett, ed., *The Roster of Union Soldiers, 1861–1865,* 21 vols. (Wilmington, Del.: Broadfeet, 1997–2000), 20:561; Tennessee General Assembly, *Senate Journal,* 34th General Assembly, 1st sess. (1865), 165, 180, 185; Alexander, *Political Reconstruction,* 24.

24. Graf, Haskin, and Bergeron, *Papers of Andrew Johnson* 8:99, 440; Sefton, *United States Army and Reconstruction,* 261; Ulrich, "Northern Military Mind," 212–13; Tennessee General Assembly, *Public Acts of Tennessee,* 34th General Assembly, 1st sess. (1865), Resolution No. 39 and chap. 24.

25. Graf, Haskins, and Bergeron, *Papers of Andrew Johnson* 9:367; Sefton, *United States Army and Reconstruction,* 261; Coulter, *Brownlow,* 331.

26. Tennessee General Assembly, *Public Acts of Tennessee,* 34th General Assembly, 2nd adjourned sess. (1867), chap. 35; Tennessee General Assembly, *Public Acts of Tennessee,* 34th General Assembly, extra sess.

(1866), chap. 2; Alexander, "Political Reconstruction in Tennessee," 55; Lucile Deaderick, ed., *Heart of the Valley: A History of Knoxville, Tennessee* (Knoxville: East Tennessee Historical Society, 1976), 95; Charles Stuart McGehee, "Wake of the Flood: A Southern City in the Civil War, Chattanooga, 1838–1873" (Ph.D. diss., Univ. of Virginia, 1985), 169–71; Walter J. Fraser Jr., "Lucien Bonaparte Eaton: Politics and the Memphis *Post*," West Tennessee Historical Society *Papers* 20 (1966): 20–45; Stanley F. Rose, "Nashville and Its Leadership Elite" (Master's thesis, Univ. of Virginia, 1965), 36; *Nashville Daily Press and Times,* Sept. 29, 1866; White, Ash, and Moore, *Messages* 5:516; Patton, *Unionism and Reconstruction,* 228–29, 232.

27. Graf, Haskins, and Bergeron, *Papers of Andrew Johnson* 11:234, 288, 362.
28. Tennessee General Assembly, *House Journal,* 34th General Assembly, 2nd adjourned sess. (1867), 37, 85, 177; *Nashville Daily Press and Times,* Dec. 21, 1866, Jan. 24, Feb. 1, 1867; *Fayetteville Observer,* Feb. 14, 1867.
29. *Nashville Union and Dispatch,* Jan. 27, 1867; Tennessee General Assembly, *House Journal,* 34th General Assembly, 2nd adjourned sess. (1867), 192–93.
30. *Nashville Daily Press and Times,* Jan. 19, 26, Feb. 1, 1867; *Nashville Union and Dispatch,* Jan. 27, Feb. 2, 17, 1867; *Knoxville Whig,* Jan. 30, Feb. 27, 1867.
31. Tennessee General Assembly, *House Journal,* 34th General Assembly, 2nd adjourned sess. (1867), 233, 257, 263–65; *Nashville Union and Dispatch,* Feb. 17, 1867.
32. Tennessee General Assembly, *Senate Journal,* 34th General Assembly, 2nd adjourned sess. (1867), 280, 284, 301–9; *Nashville Union and Dispatch,* Feb. 17, 1867.
33. Tennessee General Assembly, *House Journal,* 34th General Assembly, 2nd adjourned sess. (1867), 294–96, 300–301; Tennessee General Assembly, *Senate Journal,* 34th General Assembly, 2nd adjourned sess. (1867), 327; *Nashville Daily Press and Times,* Feb. 20, 1867.
34. Tennessee General Assembly, *Public Acts of Tennessee,* 34th General Assembly, 2nd adjourned sess. (1867), chap. 24.
35. White, Ash, and Moore, *Messages* 5:499.

Chapter 2

1. *Knoxville Whig,* Mar. 6, 1867; White, Ash, and Moore, *Messages* 5:559–60.
2. White, Ash, and Moore, *Messages* 5:553–55. In a private letter to a concerned Conservative, Brownlow vaguely explained that the militia would deploy only to the "most rebellious counties." Brownlow to S. L. Warren, Mar. 16, 1867, Reel 2, Box 3, Folder 1, Governor Brownlow Papers.
3. Alexander, *Political Reconstruction,* 142–46; Susie Lee Owens, "The Union League of America: Political Activities in Tennessee, the Carolinas, and Virginia, 1865–1870" (Ph.D. diss., New York Univ., 1943), 40–81; Phillips, "History of the Freedmen's Bureau," 272; Arnell, "Southern Unionist," 285.
4. *Fayetteville Observer,* Feb. 21, Mar. 7, 1867; *Knoxville Whig,* Mar. 27, 1867; *Nashville Union and Dispatch,* Feb. 24, 1867; *Pulaski Citizen,* Feb. 22, 1867.
5. Coulter, *Brownlow,* 332–33; *Nashville Daily Press and Times,* Feb. 25, 1867; Tennessee General Assembly, *Public Acts of Tennessee,* 34th General Assembly, 2nd adjourned sess. (1867), Resolution No. 91; Graf, Haskins, and Bergeron, *Papers of Andrew Johnson* 12:81; *Nashville Union and Dispatch,* Mar. 1, 1867; Governor Brownlow to George H. Thomas, Mar. 1, 1867, Reel 2, Box 3, Folder 1, Governor Brownlow Papers; *The American Annual Cyclopedia and Register of Important Events* (New York, 1867), 705.
6. General Order No. 1, Mar. 6, 1867, Tennessee Adjutant General's Office, Papers, Reel 8, Vol. 26, RG 21, Tennessee State Library and Archives, Nashville (hereafter cited as TAGO).
7. Newton T. Beal to Governor Brownlow, Mar. 30, 1867, Reel 1, Box 2, Folder 1; John T. Rushing to Governor Brownlow, May 24, 1867, Reel 1, Box 2, Folder 2; Russ B. Davis to Governor Brownlow, Feb. 22, 1867, Reel 1, Box 2, Folder 1; C. Underwood to Governor Brownlow, Mar. 29, 1867, Reel 1, Box 2, Folder 2; Robert Galbraith to Governor Brownlow, Mar. 4, 1867, Reel 1, Box 2, Folder 1, all in Governor Brownlow Papers; John Enoch to H. H. Thomas, June 24, 1867, Reel 2, Box 10, Folder 5, TAGO; William Bunker to Governor Brownlow, June 8, 1867, Reel 1, Box 2, Folder 1, Governor Brownlow Papers.

8. All requests for commissions are contained in either the Tennessee Adjutant General files or the Governor Brownlow Papers. Samuel S. Couch to James Hale, Feb. 2, 1867, Reel 2, Box 10, Folder 5, TAGO; Coulter, *Brownlow*, 267; James P. Brownlow to W. O. White, Mar. 8, 1867, Reel 10, Vol. 45, TAGO (this letter is an example of the form letters Adjutant General Brownlow sent to all commissioned officers). During the Civil War, James P. Brownlow earned the brevet rank of brigadier general as commander of the First Tennessee Cavalry (Union). *Report of the Adjutant General*, 13, 301.

9. James H. Watson to adjutant general's office, May 27, 1867, Reel 2, Box 11, Folder 3; W. O. White to Samuel Hunt, Apr. 3, 1867, Reel 2, Box 11, Folder 3; James M. Dickerson to James P. Brownlow, May 23, 1867, Reel 2, Box 10, Folder 5, all in TAGO; *Nashville Union and Dispatch*, June 9, 1867; George E. Grisham to H. H. Thomas, June 27, 1867, Reel 2, Box 10, Folder 3, TAGO. The fluctuating company letter designations have also created some headaches for the researcher. For example, the TAGO folder labeled "Company A, 1st Regiment" contains early muster rolls for three different companies, the final Company A, and two which were subsequently reclassified. Fortunately, this confusion occurs in only a few instances.

10. Madden, "Unionist Resistance to Confederate Occupation," 28–35; Thomas B. Alexander, *Thomas A. R. Nelson of East Tennessee* (Nashville: Tennessee Historical Commission, 1956), 18, 112–13; *Index to the Compiled Service Records of Volunteer Union Soldiers Who Served in Organizations from the State of Tennessee*, National Archives and Records Services, Washington D.C. 1962, Reel 11, (hereafter cited as CSR Index); *Report of the Adjutant General*, ix.

11. Coulter, *Brownlow*, 289, 345; Commission for A. E. Boone, Apr. 25, 1867, Reel 5, Box 25, Folder 7; Frank Travis to H. H. Thomas, Apr. 23, 1867, Reel 2, Box 11, Folder 3; General Order No. 1, Mar. 6, 1867, Reel 8, Vol. 26; Expenditures of Account of the Quartermaster Department, Tennessee State Guard, March 1867–July 1868, Reel 4, Box 22, Folder 7, all in TAGO; H. H. Thomas to Joseph H. Blackburn, Mar. 27, 1867, Reel 2, Box 3, Folder 1, Governor Brownlow Papers. A list of some of the quartermaster's field agents is included in Reel 4, Box 22, Folder 5, TAGO.

12. Governor Brownlow to W. E. Alcorn, Apr. 20, 1867, Reel 2, Box 3, Folder 1, Governor Brownlow Papers; William C. Davis, *Rebels and Yankees: The Fighting Men of the Civil War* (New York: Gallery Books, 1989), 132; Itemized Costs for a Standard Issue Militia Uniform

(1867–1869), Reel 13, Vols. 75, 76, 82; Capts. R. L. Hall, G. W. Kirk, and G. E. Grisham to H. H. Thomas, June 10, 20, 22, 1867, Reel 2, Box 10, Folder 3; Capt. J. L. Kirk to General Cooper, June 22, 1867, Reel 2, Box 10, Folder 3, all in TAGO.

13. Tennessee General Assembly, *House Journal*, 34th General Assembly, 1st adjourned sess. (1866), 535; Governor Brownlow to E. M. Stanton, Feb. 26, 1867, Reel 2, Box 3, Folder 1; H. H. Thomas to Benjamin Franklin, Feb. 27, 1867, Reel 2, Box 3, Folder 1, both in Governor Brownlow Papers; Samuel L. Warner to Governor Brownlow, Mar. 11, 1867, Box 1, Folder 10, Brownlow Papers; *Nashville Daily Press and Times*, Mar. 20, Apr. 4, 1867; Bill of Lading, Apr. 10, 1867, Reel 2, Box 10, Folder 3; Thomas Duncan to James P. Brownlow, Apr. 24, 1867, Reel 2, Box 10, Folder 5, both in TAGO.

14. *Nashville Republican Banner*, Apr. 30, May 3, 1867; Davis, *Rebels and Yankees*, 54–58; Equipment Turn-in Report, Company F, 1st Regiment, Dec. 31, 1867, Reel 4, Box 23, Folder 2; James P. Brownlow to Capt. Thompson McKinley, June 7, 1867, and Samuel Hunt to Lt. Philip Fleming, July 30, 1867, Reel 2, Box 9, Folder 5; Shipping Invoice, May 30, 1867, Reel 2, Box 10, Folder 3, all in TAGO.

15. *Bristol News*, Mar. 7, 1867; *Nashville Union and Dispatch*, Mar. 17, May 10, 1867; *Pulaski Citizen*, Mar. 8, 1867; *Nashville Republican Banner*, May 4, 24, 1867; W. A. Tucker to Governor Brownlow, Mar. 9, 1867, Reel 1, Box 2, Folder 1, Governor Brownlow Papers.

16. General Order No. 2, June 7, 1867, Reel 8, Vol. 26; Jebukiah Anderson to James P. Brownlow, May 10, 1867, Reel 2, Box 10, Folder 4; Robert L. Raulston to James P. Brownlow, June 15, 1867, Reel 2, Box 11, Folder 2, all in TAGO.

17. Muster Roll for Company A, 1st Tennessee State Guard, 1867, Reel 4, Box 22, Folder 1, TAGO; Reel 1, CSR Index; Hewett, *Roster of Union Soldiers* 20:405; *Report of the Adjutant General*, iii, 223; *The Goodspeed Histories of Cannon, Coffee, DeKalb, Warren and White Counties* (McMinnville, Tenn.: Ben Lomand Press, 1972), 953; War Department, *War of the Rebellion: A Compilation of the Official Records of the Union and Confederate Armies* (hereafter cited as *OR*), 70 vols. (Washington, D.C.: GPO, 1880–1901), ser. 1, 23 (1): 17, 155–58, 202, 23 (2): 834, 32 (1): 55, 162, 494, 45 (1): 415, 45 (2): 433, 49 (1): 891–92, 49 (2): 460, 904, 911; Will T. Hale, *History of DeKalb County, Tennessee* (1915; reprint, McMinnville, Tenn.: Ben Lomand Press, 1969), 222; Thomas G. Webb, *DeKalb County* (Memphis: Memphis State Univ. Press, 1986), 31, 39–40; Graf, Haskins, and Bergeron, *Papers of Andrew Johnson* 8:155.

18. *OR*, ser. 2, 8:726–29.
19. *Goodspeed Histories*, 953; *Nashville Daily Press and Times*, Feb. 4, 1867; Joseph Blackburn to H. H. Thomas, May 4, 1867, Reel 2, Box 10, Folder 4, TAGO; Muster Roll for Company A, 1st Tennessee State Guard, TAGO; Reels 4 and 6, CSR Index; Hewett, *Roster of Union Soldiers* 20:432, 470; *Report of the Adjutant General*, vi, 230–31; *OR*, ser. 1, 23 (1): 209–10; Webb, *DeKalb County*, 33; Bureau of the Census, Schedules of Population for Tennessee, 1870 (DeKalb County) (hereafter cited as Census of Tennessee, 1870, followed by county), provides information on thirty-seven of the company's personnel.
20. Muster Roll for Company H, 1st Tennessee State Guard, Reel 5, Box 23, Folder 4, TAGO; Reel 13, CSR Index; Hewett, *Roster of Union Soldiers* 20:544; *Report of the Adjutant General*, x, 430; *OR*, ser. 1, 49 (2): 543, 608; House, *Sheafe v. Tillman*, 41st Cong., 2nd sess., H. Misc. Doc. 53, 265; *Nashville Union and Dispatch*, Mar. 30, 1867.
21. William O. Rickman to James P. Brownlow, Mar. 27, Apr. 2, 25, May 1, 1867, Reel 2, Box 11, Folder 2, TAGO; Joseph Ramsey to Governor Brownlow, Mar. 23, 1867, Governor Brownlow Papers; Muster Roll for Company H, 1st Tennessee State Guard, TAGO.
22. William O. Rickman to James P. Brownlow, May 13, June 3, 1867, Reel 2, Box 11, Folder 2, TAGO; Census of Tennessee, 1870 (Bedford County), 400; G. W. Farnum to Samuel Hunt, May 8, 1867, Reel 2, Box 10, Folder 4; G. W. Farnum to James P. Brownlow, June 13, 1867, Reel 2, Box 11, Folder 1, both in TAGO; House, *Sheafe v. Tillman*, 264; Census of Tennessee, 1870 (Franklin County), 141/125; Muster Roll for Company H, 1st Tennessee State Guard, TAGO.
23. Putnam County Petition to Governor Brownlow, Mar. 13, 1867, Reel 1, Box 2, Folder 2, Governor Brownlow Papers; Reel 14, CSR Index; Hewett, *Roster of Union Soldiers* 20:566; *Report of the Adjutant General*, 234; William S. Stuart to James P. Brownlow, Mar. 29, 1867, Reel 2, Box 11, Folder 3, TAGO; William S. Stuart to Governor Brownlow, Apr. 1, 1867, Reel 1, Box 2, Folder 2, Governor Brownlow Papers; James P. Brownlow to William S. Stuart, Apr. 6, 1867, Reel 10, Vol. 45, TAGO; White County Petition to Governor Brownlow, Apr. 22, 1867, Box 1, Folder 10, Brownlow Papers.
24. Muster Roll for Company K, 1st Tennessee State Guard, Reel 5, Box 24, Folders 1 and 2; William S. Stuart to James P. Brownlow, May 8, 1867, Reel 2, Box 11, Folder 3, both in TAGO; William S. Stuart to Governor Brownlow, June 26, 1867, Reel 1, Box 2, Folder 2, Governor Brownlow Papers; Smith County Petition to Joseph A. Cooper, July 28, 1867, Reel 2, Box 11, Folder 2; William B. Stokes to Joseph A. Cooper,

Aug. 10, 1867, Reel 2, Box 11, Folder 3, both in TAGO; Reel 12, CSR Index; Hewett, *Roster of Union Soldiers* 20:532; *Report of the Adjutant General,* 190, 418.

25. Phillips, "History of the Freedmen's Bureau," 272; William G. McBride, "Blacks and the Race Issue in Tennessee Politics, 1865–1876" (Ph.D. diss., Vanderbilt Univ., 1989), 214.

26. *Nashville Union and Dispatch,* Apr. 3, 19, 1867; Muster Roll for Company E, 1st Tennessee State Guard, Reel 4, Box 23, Folder 1, TAGO; Reels, 5, 13 and 14, CSR Index; Hewett, *Roster of Union Soldiers* 20:454, 546, 557; *Report of the Adjutant General,* 233, 481, 486A. H. Walker to Governor Brownlow, Apr. 15, 1867, Box 1, Folder 10, Brownlow Papers; *Harper's Weekly,* Feb. 23, 1867; Thomas Hopper to adjutant general's office, May 20, 1867, Reel 2, Box 11, Folder 1; John T. Robeson to James P. Brownlow, Mar. 21, 1867, Reel 2, Box 11, Folder 3, both in TAGO; Census of Tennessee, 1870 (Weakley County), 108, 194.

27. Census of Tennessee, 1870 (Gibson County), 472; Muster Roll supplement to Company E, 1st Tennessee State Guard, Reel 4, Box 23, Folder 1, TAGO; Reels 7 and 8, CSR Index; Hewett, *Roster of Union Soldiers* 20:478, 493; *Report of the Adjutant General,* 474, 483; Lufkin, "Forgotten Controversy," 43–44; C. Underwood to Governor Brownlow, Apr. 15, 1867, Reel 1, Box 2, Folder 2; Obion County Petition to Governor Brownlow, Apr. 13, 1867, Reel 2, Box 4, Folder 7, both in Governor Brownlow Papers..

28. Muster Roll of Company E, 1st Tennessee State Guard, Reel 4, Box 23, Folder 1; General Order No. 16, Sept. 3, 1867, Reel 9, Vol. 27; John T. Robeson to Joseph A. Cooper, Sept. 11, 1867, Reel 2, Box 11, Folder 3, all in TAGO.

29. Muster Roll for Company E, 2nd Tennessee State Guard, Reel 5, Box 24, Folder 7, TAGO; Census of Tennessee, 1870 (Hardin County), 346 (Humphreys County), 16, and (McNairy County), 244; R. M. Thompson and Fielding Hurst to Governor Brownlow, Mar. 21, 1867, Reel 1, Box 2, Folder 2, Governor Brownlow Papers; Reels 6 and 13, CSR Index; Hewett, *Roster of Union Soldiers* 20:466, 540.

30. Muster Roll for Company D, 1st Tennessee State Guard, Reel 4, Box 22, Folder 4, TAGO; Reel 3, CSR Index; Hewett, *Roster of Union Soldiers* 20:426; *OR,* ser. 1, 10 (1): 70, 23 (2): 582, 31 (3): 144, 52 (1): 49; *Report of the Adjutant General,* 111, 675.

31. Bureau of the Census, Schedules of Population for Tennessee, 1860 (Bradley County), 144 (hereafter cited as Census of Tennessee, 1860, followed by county), and Census of Tennessee, 1860 (Bradley County),

332; Myra Inman, *A Diary of the Civil War in East Tennessee,* ed. William R. Snell (Macon, Ga.: Mercer Univ. Press, 2000), 117, 244; McBride and Robison, *Biographical Directory* 2:167–68; Tennessee General Assembly, *House Journal,* 34th General Assembly, 1st adjourned sess. (1866), 494, 548–49, extra sess., 24–25, 39, 49–50, 2nd adjourned sess. (1867), 101, 213, 242–43.

32. Muster Roll for Company D, 1st Tennessee State Guard, Reel 4, Box 22, Folder 4, TAGO; *Knoxville Whig,* Mar. 20, 1867; J. K. Clingan to Adjutant General, May 4, 1867, Reel 2, Box 10, Folder 5, TAGO; Reels 1 and 8, CSR Index; Hewett, *Roster of Union Soldiers* 20:397, 491; *Report of the Adjutant General,* 104, 397. Otis A. Singletary wrongly assumes that there were black volunteers in Clingan's company. See Singletary, *Negro Militia and Reconstruction,* 47.

33. *Knoxville Whig,* Sept. 25, 1867; Muster Roll for Company D, 1st Tennessee State Guard, Reel 4, Box 22, Folder 4, TAGO.

34. *Knoxville Whig,* May 15, 1867; Governor Brownlow to Joseph A. Cooper, June 22, 1867, Reel 2, Box 10, Folder 4, TAGO; Graf, Haskins, and Bergeron, *Papers of Andrew Johnson* 12:254; Governor Brownlow to Samuel Hunt, May 31, 1867, Reel 2, Box 10, Folder 4; Muster Roll for Company C, 1st Tennessee State Guard, Reel 4, Box 22, Folder 3, both in TAGO; *Nashville Daily Press and Times,* July 20, 1867; Reel 15, CSR Index; Hewett, *Roster of Union Soldiers* 20:580; *Nashville Union and Dispatch,* July 20, 1867.

35. Reel 6, CSR Index; Hewett, *Roster of Union Soldiers* 20:469; *OR,* ser. 2, 6:416, 998, 7:16, 23, 1175, 1229, 1263–64, 8:6, 71, 159, 208, 225, 230, 307, 364; *Knoxville Whig,* May 24, 1865.

36. *OR,* ser. 2, 8:6; *Knoxville Whig,* May 24, 1865; Fisher, *War at Every Door,* 157; Muster Roll for Company F, 1st Tennessee State Guard, Reel 4, Box 23, Folder 2, TAGO; *OR,* ser. 2, 45 (2): 592; Hewett, *Roster of Union Soldiers* 2:64, 17:450, 20:546; Census of Tennessee, 1870 (Jefferson County), 316; Reel 13, CSR Index; *Report of the Adjutant General,* 122.

37. Muster Roll for Company F, 1st Tennessee State Guard, Reel 4, Box 23, Folder 2, TAGO; *Nashville Union and Dispatch,* May 15, 1867.

38. Reel 5, CSR Index; Hewett, *Roster of Union Soldiers* 20:447; *Report of the Adjutant General,* 414; Census of Tennessee, 1870 (Claiborne County), 303; James R. Evans to James P. Brownlow, Mar. 27, Apr. 3, 10, 1867, Reel 2, Box 10, Folder 5, TAGO; James R. Evans to James P. Brownlow, May 14, 1867, Folder 471, Patton Papers; Allen P. Tate to James P. Brownlow, Apr. 27, 1867, Reel 2, Box 11, Folder 3, TAGO.

39. Muster Roll for Company I, 1st Tennessee State Guard, Reel 5, Box 23, Folder 5; James R. Evans to James P. Brownlow, May 15, 1867, Reel 2, Box 10, Folder 5, both in TAGO; Graf, Haskins, and Bergeron, *Papers of Andrew Johnson* 12:311; Reel 5, CSR Index; Hewett, *Roster of Union Soldiers* 20:445–46; *Report of the Adjutant General*, 70; Census of Tennessee, 1870 (Claiborne County), 291.

40. Census of Tennessee, 1870 (Scott County), 245, 252; Reels 3, 11, and 12, CSR Index; Hewett, *Roster of Union Soldiers* 20:423, 525, 529; *Report of the Adjutant General*, 48, 93; Muster Roll for Company G, 1st Tennessee State Guard, Reel 5, Box 23, Folder 3, TAGO; *Nashville Union and Dispatch*, May 5, 1867; Silas L. Chambers to H. H. Thomas, May 15, 1867, Reel 2, Box 10, Folder 5, TAGO; Reels 11 and 12, CSR Index; Census of Tennessee, 1870 (Union County), 234; "Alpha" to editor of *Cincinnati Gazette*, May 27, 1867, Houk Papers; Graf, Haskins, and Bergeron, *Papers of Andrew Johnson* 12:342.

41. Reel 8, CSR Index; Hewett, *Roster of Union Soldiers* 20:494; Fisher, *War at Every Door*, 68, 87; *OR*, ser. 2, 32 (2): 386, 39 (1): 232–34, 52 (1): 517.

42. *OR*, ser. 2, 39 (1), 235–37, 45 (1), 810, 45 (2): 608, 49 (1): 325, 337–39, 550, 49 (2): 446–47, 509, 556, 622, 738.

43. *Knoxville Whig*, Mar. 27, 1867; Governor Brownlow to Joseph S. Fowler, Mar. 23, 1867, Reel 2, Box 3, Folder 1, Governor Brownlow Papers; Muster Roll for Company A, 2nd Tennessee State Guard, Reel 5, Box 24, Folder 3, TAGO; Reel 13, CSR Index; Hewett, *Roster of Union Soldiers* 20:551; *Report of the Adjutant General*, 236; *Jonesboro Union Flag*, Apr. 19, 1867, quoted in *Nashville Union and Dispatch*, Apr. 21, 1867.

44. Fisher, *War at Every Door*, 188; Petition of Joseph M. Alexander to the Commissioner of Claims, 1873, Southern Claims Commission, Case File No. 19833; Joseph M. Alexander to James P. Brownlow, June 22, 1867, Reel 2, Box 10, Folder 4; Joseph M. Alexander to Joseph A. Cooper, June 30, 1867, Reel 2, Box 10, Folder 4; Muster Roll for Company F, 2nd Tennessee State Guard, Reel 5, Box 25, Folder 1, all in TAGO. In his petition to the Federal government, Alexander claimed that the U.S. Army confiscated his horse (valued at two hundred dollars) and four hundred pounds of tobacco from his store (valued at four hundred dollars). His claim was "disallowed" for lack of corroborating evidence.

45. Oliver P. Temple, *East Tennessee and the Civil War* (Cincinnati: R. Clarke, 1899), 572; Reels 1, 6, and 11, CSR Index; Hewett, *Roster of Union*

Soldiers 20:397, 460, 522; *Report of the Adjutant General,* 620, 628; Muster Roll for Company D, 2nd Tennessee State Guard, Reel 5, Box 24, Folder 6, TAGO; Census of Tennessee, 1870 (Johnson County), 38.

46. Muster Roll for Company I, 2nd Tennessee State Guard, Reel 5, Box 25, Folder 4, TAGO; Reel 12, CSR Index; Hewett, *Roster of Union Soldiers* 20:539; *Report of the Adjutant General,* 100; Muster Roll for Company H, 2nd Tennessee State Guard, Reel 5, Box 25, Folder 3, TAGO; Census of Tennessee, 1870 (Knox County), 118.

47. Coulter, *Brownlow,* 290, 333; N. C. Davis to Governor Brownlow, May 18, 1867, Reel 1, Box 2, Folder 1, Governor Brownlow Papers; Caleb Gain to Samuel Hunt, Mar. 29, 1867, Reel 2, Box 11, Folder 1, TAGO; Joseph T. Wilson, *The Black Phalanx* (1890; reprint, New York: Arno Press, 1968), 142; Joseph T. Glatthaar, *Forged in Battle: The Civil War Alliance of Black Soldiers and White Officers* (New York: Free Press, 1990), 256–61; Stephen V. Ash, "Postwar Recovery: Montgomery County, 1865–1870," *Tennessee Historical Quarterly* 36 (1977): 212; Graf, Haskins, and Bergeron, *Papers of Andrew Johnson* 9:48–49; Ulrich, "Northern Military Mind," 220–21.

48. Reel 6, CSR Index; Hewett, *Roster of Union Soldiers* 20:463; *OR,* ser. 1, 39 (1): 846; Census of Tennessee, 1870 (Washington County), 330; Watauga Association of Genealogists, *History of Washington County, Tennessee* (Jonesboro, Tenn., Walsworth Press, 1988), 92, 105; *Jonesboro Union Flag,* Oct. 6, 1865; George E. Grisham and seven others to L. C. Houk, Sept. 22, 1866, Houk Papers; Steve Humphrey, *That D—d Brownlow . . .* (Boone, N.C.: Appalachian Consortium Press, 1978), 320; *Nashville Daily Press and Times,* Oct. 24, 1866, Mar. 1, 1867.

49. George E. Grisham to James P. Brownlow, Mar. 20, 1867, Reel 2, Box 11, Folder 1, TAGO; *Jonesboro Union Flag,* Apr. 5, 1867; *Nashville Union and Dispatch,* Apr. 21, 1867.

50. George E. Grisham to Governor Brownlow, Apr. 13, 1867, Reel 1, Box 2, Folder 1, Governor Brownlow Papers; *Nashville Daily Press and Times,* Apr. 19, 1867; Muster Roll for Company B, 1st Tennessee State Guard, Reel 4, Box 22, Folder 2, TAGO; Reels 5 and 10, CSR Index; Hewett, *Roster of Union Soldiers* 20:448, 513; *Report of the Adjutant General,* 81, 92, 95, 520; Census of Tennessee, 1870 (Washington County), 212.

51. *Jonesboro Union Flag,* Apr. 5, 1867; *Nashville Daily Press and Times,* Apr. 19, 1867; *Nashville Union and Dispatch,* May 7, 1867; *Knoxville Whig,* May 8, 1867.

52. Samuel Hunt to John L. Kirk, June 8, 1867, Reel 2, Box 9, Folder 5, TAGO; Reel 8, CSR Index; Muster Roll for Company C, 2nd Tennessee State Guard, Reel 5, Box 24, Folder 5, TAGO.

53. James P. Brownlow to Thompson McKinley, Mar. 25, 1867, Reel 10, Vol. 45, TAGO; Walter T. Durham, *Rebellion Revisited: A History of Sumner County, Tennessee from 1861 to 1870* (Gallatin, Tenn.: Sumner County Museum Association, 1982), 283–84, 296, 300, 308; *Nashville Union and Dispatch,* July 28, 1867; *Memphis Daily Appeal,* June 14, 1867; *Nashville Daily Press and Times,* Sept. 18, 1866; Thompson McKinley to Governor Brownlow, Oct. 22, 1866, Reel 1, Box 1, Folder 8, Governor Brownlow Papers; *Knoxville Whig,* Apr. 24, 1867; Graf, Haskins, and Bergeron, *Papers of Andrew Johnson* 9:49–51, 12:75. Patton, in *Unionism and Reconstruction,* 176, describes McKinley's unit as "one of the most notorious of the Negro companies."

54. Cummings to Governor Brownlow, Mar. 13, 1867, Box 1, Folder 10, Brownlow Papers; H. H. Thomas to M. Cummings, Mar. 15, 1867, Reel 2, Box 3, Folder 1, Governor Brownlow Papers; Muster Roll for Company B, 2nd Tennessee State Guard, Reel 5, Box 24, Folder 4, TAGO; Peter Maslowski, *Treason Must Be Made Odious: Military Occupation and Wartime Reconstruction in Nashville, 1862–1865* (Millwood, N.Y.: KTO Press, 1978), 108.

55. Nelson Turner to Joseph A. Cooper, July 4, 1867, Reel 2, Box 11, Folder 3, TAGO; *Nashville Union and Dispatch,* July 28, 1867; Durham, *Rebellion Revisited,* 271–72, 275, 300; *Nashville Republican Banner,* May 3, 1867.

56. Bobby L. Lovett, *The African-American History of Nashville Tennessee, 1780–1930* (Fayetteville: Univ. of Arkansas Press, 1999), 209; Rose, "Nashville and Its Leadership Elite," 68; *Pulaski Citizen,* Mar. 29, 1867; *Nashville Union and Dispatch,* Mar. 28, 1867; *Memphis Daily Appeal,* June 11, 1867.

57. *Nashville Union and Dispatch,* Mar. 28, 1867; Muster Roll for Company G, 2nd Tennessee State Guard, Reel 5, Box 25, Folder 2, TAGO; Hewett, *Roster of Union Soldiers* 5:138, 405. The size of this company was soon reduced by one when Pvt. Pleasant Terry accidentally shot and killed his comrade, Pvt. Tony Cato, during a barroom brawl. *Nashville Republican Banner,* June 30, 1867.

58. *Memphis Daily Appeal,* July 16, 1867; *Nashville Union and Dispatch,* July 9, 1867; *Nashville Daily Press and Times,* July 10, 1867.

59. Muster Roll for Company K, 2nd Tennessee State Guard, Reel 5, Box 25, Folder 5, TAGO; *Nashville Union and Dispatch,* Aug. 16, 1867; Muster Roll for Company A, 3rd Tennessee State Guard, Reel 5, Box

25, Folder 6, TAGO; Hewett, *Roster of Union Soldiers* 4:389; Wilson, *Black Phalanx,* 468; Bobby L. Lovett, "The Negro's Civil War in Tennessee, 1861–1865," *Journal of Negro History* 61 (1976): 47–48; *Nashville Daily Press and Times,* July 31, 1867; *Nashville Republican Banner,* Aug. 3, 1867.

60. Coulter, *Brownlow,* 333, 338–39; Trelease, *White Terror,* 24; Patton, *Unionism and Reconstruction,* 176; White, Ash, and Moore, *Messages* 5:570; Alexander, *Political Reconstruction,* 149; Singletary, *Negro Militia and Reconstruction,* 15.

61. Singletary, *Negro Militia and Reconstruction,* 22–25; Eric Hoffer, *The True Believer: Thoughts on the Nature of Mass Movements* (New York: Harper & Row, 1951), 39–47, 99.

62. General Order No. 2, June 7, 1867, Reel 8, Vol. 26, TAGO; Census of Tennessee, 1870 (Knox County), 224; Temple, *East Tennessee and the Civil War,* 572; Oliver P. Temple, *Notable Men of Tennessee, from 1833 to 1875: Their Times and Their Contemporaries* (New York: Cosmopolitan, 1912), 102–4; Reel 3, CSR Index; Hewett, *Roster of Union Soldiers* 20:430; *Report of the Adjutant General,* 13; William H. Powell, *List of Officers of the Army of the United States from 1779 to 1900* (Detroit: Gale Research, 1967), 782; *A Survivor of Two Wars: Biographical Sketch of General Joseph A. Cooper* (Knoxville, J. H. Bean and Co., 1895), 3, 7–13.

63. Temple, *Notable Men of Tennessee,* 101, 106–8; *Survivor of Two Wars,* 6, 8–11, 17–18.

64. *Nashville Daily Press and Times,* Nov. 16, Dec. 7, 1866; Graf, Haskins, and Bergeron, *Papers of Andrew Johnson* 10:176–77, 11:147–48, 381–82.

65. Graf, Haskins, and Bergeron, *Papers of Andrew Johnson* 8:471, 553, 12:265; Joseph A. Cooper to L. C. Houk, Apr. 28, 1867, Houk Papers; Temple, *Notable Men of Tennessee,* 101; *Knoxville Whig,* July 17, 1867.

66. *Nashville Daily Press and Times,* June 8, 1867; *Knoxville Whig,* July 17, 1867; *Nashville Republican Banner,* June 9, 1867.

67. Circular No. 1, June 19, 1867, Reel 9, Vol. 27; Order No. 2, July 10, 1867, Reel 9, Vol. 27, both in TAGO; Governor Brownlow to General Cooper, July 18, 1867, Reel 1, Box, 1, Folder 1, Governor Brownlow Papers; Special Order No. 23, July 22, 1867, Reel 9, Vol. 33, TAGO.

68. Special Order No. 7, July 1, 1867, Reel 9, Vol. 33; Governor Brownlow to H. H. Thomas, June 5, 1867, Reel 2, Box 10, Folder 3; Captain Grisham to A. E. Boone, July 27, 1867, Reel 2, Box 10, Folder 3, all in TAGO; H. H. Thomas to Captains Rickman and Blackburn, Apr. 26, May 23, 1867, Reel 2, Box 3, Folder 1, Governor Brownlow Papers; J. K. Woodard to H. H. Thomas, June 6, 1867, Reel 2, Box 10, Folder 3,

TAGO; H. H. Thomas to Captains Grisham, Hall, Rickman, and Robeson, Apr. 23–26, 1867, Reel 2, Box 3, Folder 1, Governor Brownlow Papers. Despite Cooper's instructions, at least one officer remained obtuse. In requesting rations for thirty days, Capt. A. M. Clapp told the overworked A. E. Boone to "be so kind as to attend to it immediately," adding that "if the requisition is not correct, you will please correct it." Captain Clapp to A. E. Boone, Aug. 15, 1867, Reel 2, Box 10, Folder 3, TAGO.

69. General Order No. 3, July 10, 1867, Reel 8, Vol. 26; Joseph A. Cooper to adjutant general, July 26, 1867, Reel 10, Vol. 46, TAGO. Possibly unhappy with the joint Robeson-Holt command in West Tennessee, General Cooper sometimes referred to Captain Holt's portion of the unit as Company B, Third Regiment. Nevertheless, Holt remained under Robeson's authority throughout the campaign. Special Order No. 120, Sept. 2, 1867, Reel 9, Vol. 33, TAGO.

CHAPTER 3

1. *Nashville Union and Dispatch,* Mar. 21, 1867; White, Ash, and Moore, *Messages* 5:561.
2. White, Ash, and Moore, *Messages* 5:562; Lonnie E. Maness, "Henry Emerson Etheridge and the Gubernatorial Election of 1867: A Study in Futility," West Tennessee Historical Society *Papers* 47 (1993): 41–42; Alexander, *Political Reconstruction,* 142.
3. Lonnie E. Maness, "Emerson Etheridge and the Union," *Tennessee Historical Quarterly* 48 (1989): 97–105; Maness, "Henry Emerson Etheridge," 43; *Nashville Republican Banner,* May 26, 1867; Patton, *Unionism and Reconstruction,* 136.
4. Maness, "Henry Emerson Etheridge," 43–45; White, Ash, and Moore, *Messages* 5:565–66; Coulter, *Brownlow,* 336.
5. *Knoxville Whig,* May 8, 1867; *American Annual Cyclopedia* (1867), 707.
6. *Fayetteville Observer,* May 9, 1867; *Paris Intelligencer,* May 11, 1867; Graf, Haskins, and Bergeron, *Papers of Andrew Johnson* 12:254, 263–64.
7. *Knoxville Whig,* May 22, 1867; General Order No. 1, Mar. 6, 1867, Reel 8, Vol. 26; Capt. Clingan to James P. Brownlow, May 25, 1867, Reel 2, Box 10, Folder 5, both in TAGO. Perhaps motivated by Clingan's request, the state legislature printed four thousand copies of Hardee's training manual. *Nashville Daily Press and Times,* June 17, 1867.

8. H. Walker to Governor Brownlow, Apr. 15, 1867, and E. Cooper to Governor Brownlow, May 27, 1867, Box 1, Folder 10, Brownlow Papers; J. P. Ledbetter to L. C. Houk, Apr. 29, 1867, Houk Papers; Horace H. Thomas to Russell A. Salisbury, Apr. 8, 1867, H. H. Thomas to James Cockerell, May 6, 1867, and H. H. Thomas to William Coward, May 6, 1867, Reel 2, Box 3, Folder 1, Governor Brownlow Papers.

9. White, Ash, and Moore, *Messages* 5:534–35, 553–55; General Order No. 2, June 7, 1867, Reel 8, Vol. 26, TAGO; *Knoxville Whig*, May 8, 1867; Philip M. Hamer, *Tennessee: A History, 1673–1932*, 4 vols. (New York: American Historical Society, 1933), 2:619–20; Alexander, *Political Reconstruction*, 150; Jones, "Reconstruction in Tennessee," 196; *Nashville Republican Banner*, May 11, 1867.

10. Fisher, *War at Every Door*, 189; J. W. Brown to Governor Brownlow, May 21, 1867, Reel 1, Box 2, Folder 1, Governor Brownlow Papers; Arthur Cyrus Hill, "The History of the Black People of Franklin County, Tennessee" (Master's thesis, Univ. of Minnesota, 1982), 112–16.

11. Congress, *House Executive Documents, Report of the Secretary of War* (1867), 226.

12. *Fayetteville Observer*, May 23, 1867; Captain Rickman to James P. Brownlow, May 28, 1867, Reel 2, Box 11, Folder 2, TAGO; Congress, *House Executive Documents, Report of the Secretary of War* (1867), 227.

13. Congress, *House Executive Documents, Report of the Secretary of War* (1867), 227; Captain Rickman to James P. Brownlow, May 31, 1867, Reel 2, Box 11, Folder 2, TAGO; Samuel Hunt to Governor Brownlow, June 3, 1867, Box 1, Folder 10, Brownlow Papers.

14. Congress, *House Executive Documents, Report of the Secretary of War* (1867), 225, 227–28; *Nashville Republican Banner*, June 5, 1867; Samuel Hunt to Governor Brownlow, June 3, 1867, Box 1, Folder 10, Brownlow Papers.

15. *Nashville Republican Banner*, May 26, 1867; Samuel Hunt to Governor Brownlow, June 3, 1867, Box 1, Folder 10, Brownlow Papers; Congress, *House Executive Documents, Report of the Secretary of War* (1867), 228–29; Captain Rickman to James P. Brownlow, May 29, 1867, Reel 2, Box 11, Folder 2, TAGO.

16. Congress, *House Executive Documents, Report of the Secretary of War* (1867), 228–29; Samuel Hunt to Governor Brownlow, June 3, 1867, Box 1 Folder 10, Brownlow Papers; Captain Rickman to James P. Brownlow, May 29, 1867, Reel 2, Box 11, Folder 2, TAGO.

17. Congress, *House Executive Documents, Report of the Secretary of War* (1867), 225–26; *Nashville Union and Dispatch*, May 31, 1867; Graf, Haskins, and Bergeron, *Papers of Andrew Johnson* 12:299–301.

18. *Nashville Republican Banner,* May 26, 30, 31, June 2, 4, 5, 6, 8, 25, July 9, 1867.

19. *Pulaski Citizen,* June 7, 1867; *Nashville Daily Press and Times,* June 1, 3, 1867; *Knoxville Whig,* June 5, 1867; Captain Rickman to James P. Brownlow, May 31, 1867, Reel 2, Box 11, Folder 2, TAGO.

20. *Nashville Union and Dispatch,* June 7, 1867; Samuel Hunt to Governor Brownlow, June 3, 1867, Box 1, Folder 10, Brownlow Papers; Congress, *House Executive Documents, Report of the Secretary of War* (1867), 225–30; Captain Rickman to Samuel Hunt, June 4, 1867, Reel 2, Box 1, Folder 2, TAGO; Graf, Haskins, and Bergeron, *Papers of Andrew Johnson* 12:315–17.

21. Captain Rickman to James P. Brownlow, May 31, June 3, 12, 1867, Reel 2, Box 11, Folder 2; Muster Roll for Company H, 1st Regiment, Reel 5, Box 23, Folder 4, both in TAGO. Rickman later tried to appoint Cpl. Joseph B. Clark to the still-vacant second lieutenancy, but headquarters never granted Clark a commission. Captain Rickman to General Cooper July 9, 1867, Reel 2, Box 11, Folder 2, both in TAGO.

22. *Knoxville Whig,* June 5, 1867; *Nashville Union and Dispatch,* June 7, 12, 1867; *Nashville Republican Banner,* June 5, 18, 25, 1867; H. H. Thomas to Governor Brownlow, June 7, 1867, Box 1 Folder 10, Brownlow Papers. William Crane, a local sutler for the militia, had done a brisk business with Captain Rickman and was sad to see his unit leave. He tried in vain to get Franklin's citizenry to sign a petition asking Rickman to stay. *Nashville Republican Banner,* June 21, 25, 1867.

23. Webb, *DeKalb County,* 40–42, 119; Fisher, *War at Every Door,* 189; J. T. Thompson to Governor Brownlow, Apr. 13, 1867, Reel 1, Box 2, Folder 2; James T. Exum to Governor Brownlow, Apr. 13, 1867, Reel 1, Box 2, Folder 1, both in Governor Brownlow Papers; Captain Blackburn to H. H. Thomas, May 4, 1867, Reel 2, Box 10, Folder 4, TAGO.

24. Muster Roll for Company A, 1st Regiment, Reel 4, Box 22, Folder 1, TAGO; *Nashville Republican Banner,* May 12, June 7, 11, 1867; William Baker to Governor Brownlow, June 6, 1867, Patton Papers; Warren County petition to Governor Brownlow, June 8, 1867, Box 1, Folder 10, Brownlow Papers; William Baker to Governor Brownlow, June 18, 28, 1867, Reel 1, Box 2, Folder 1, Governor Brownlow Papers; Special Order No. 1, June 21, 1867, Reel 9, Vol. 33, TAGO.

25. *Nashville Republican Banner,* May 12, June 2, 18, 1867; Monroe Seals, *History of White County, Tennessee* (Spartanburg, S.C., 1974), 74, 77.

26. Webb, *DeKalb County,* 37–39; Alexander, *Political Reconstruction,* 152; *Harper's Weekly,* Feb. 23, 1867; Mary Jean DeLozier, "The Civil War

and Its Aftermath in Putnam County," *Tennessee Historical Quarterly* 38 (1979): 456; *Nashville Republican Banner,* May 31, June 25, 1867; *Nashville Daily Press and Times,* June 24, 1867.

27. Fisher, *War at Every Door,* 189; *Nashville Union and Dispatch,* May 17, 21, 1867; *Nashville Daily Press and Times,* June 1, 1867; Phillips, "History of the Freedmen's Bureau," 299–300; *Nashville Republican Banner,* May 12, 1867.

28. *Nashville Republican Banner,* May 21, 28, 1867; *Nashville Union and Dispatch,* June 14, 1867; *Nashville Daily Press and Times,* June 1, 1867.

29. Captain Clingan to James P. Brownlow, May 25, 1867, Reel 2, Box 10, Folder 5, TAGO; *Nashville Union and Dispatch,* May 31, 1867; *Nashville Daily Press and Times,* June 1, 1867.

30. *Nashville Union and Dispatch,* May 31, June 1, 1867; Muster Roll for Company D, 1st Regiment, Reel 4, Box 22, Folder 4, TAGO; Jones, "Reconstruction in Tennessee," 197.

31. *Nashville Union and Dispatch,* May 31, June 1, 1867.

32. McBride, "Blacks and the Race Issue," 214–15; Captain Clingan to Samuel Hunt, June 14, 1867, Reel 2, Box 10, Folder 5, TAGO; *Pulaski Citizen,* May 31, 1867; *Nashville Daily Press and Times,* July 18, 1867.

33. L. Kelley to Governor Brownlow, June 12, 1867, Reel 1, Box 2, Folder 1, Governor Brownlow Papers; Mrs. S. Fry to James P. Brownlow, June 25, 1867, Reel 2, Box 11, Folder 1, TAGO; *Cleveland Banner,* June 13, 1867; Captain Clingan to A. E. Boone, June 25, 1867, Reel 2, Box 10, Folder 3, TAGO.

34. *Nashville Republican Banner,* June 16, 1867; Captain Clingan to James P. Brownlow, June 17, 1867, Reel 2, Box 10, Folder 5; Special Order NA June 19, 1867, Reel 9, Vol. 33, TAGO.

35. Fisher, *War at Every Door,* 189–90; Mingo Scott, *The Negro in Tennessee Politics and Governmental Affairs, 1865–1965: "The Hundred Years Study"* (Nashville: Rich Print, 1965), 18; *Nashville Union and Dispatch,* June 4, 1867; Captain Robeson to Samuel Hunt, June 16, 1867, Reel 2, Box 11, Folder 3, TAGO.

36. Captain Robeson to Samuel Hunt, June 16, 18, 22, 1867, Reel 2, Box 11, Folder 3, TAGO; Graf, Haskins, and Bergeron, *Papers of Andrew Johnson* 12:373; Captain Robeson to Governor Brownlow, June 22, 1867, Reel 1, Box 2, Folder 2, Governor Brownlow Papers; Captain Robeson to Frank Hyberger, June 23, 1867, Reel 2, Box 11, Folder 3, TAGO.

37. Captain Robeson to Samuel Hunt, June 16, 22, 1867, Reel 2, Box 11, Folder 3, TAGO; Captain Robeson to Governor Brownlow, June 22, 1867, Reel 1, Box 2, Folder 2, Governor Brownlow Papers; Morning

Report for Company E, 1st Regiment, June 21, 1867, Reel 4, Box 23, Folder 1, TAGO.

38. Captain Robeson to Samuel Hunt, June 16, 22, 1867, Reel 2, Box 11, Folder 3; Captain Robeson to Governor Brownlow, June 22, 1867, Reel 2, Box 11, Folder 3, both in TAGO.

39. *Nashville Daily Press and Times,* Apr. 19, 1867; *Nashville Union and Dispatch,* Apr. 16, July 3, 1867; Fisher, *War at Every Door,* 188; Hamer, *Tennessee* 2:626.

40. *Nashville Republican Banner,* May 22, 1867.

41. *Nashville Union and Dispatch,* June 5, July 3, 1867; *Pulaski Citizen,* June 14, 1867; *Clarksville Chronicle,* June 14, 1867; Jones, "Reconstruction in Tennessee," 197.

42. Graf, Haskins, and Bergeron, *Papers of Andrew Johnson* 12:314; *Pulaski Citizen,* June 14, 1867; *Knoxville Whig,* July 3, 1867.

43. *Nashville Union and Dispatch,* July 9, 31, 1867.

44. Fisher, *War at Every Door,* 188; *Knoxville Whig,* June 12, 1867; A. W. Howard to Governor Brownlow, June 4, 1867, Box 1, Folder 10, Brownlow Papers.

45. *Knoxville Whig,* June 12, 1867; Graf, Haskins, and Bergeron, *Papers of Andrew Johnson* 12:308–12; Congress, *House Executive Documents, Report of the Secretary of War* (1867), 230–31.

46. Graf, Haskins, and Bergeron, *Papers of Andrew Johnson* 12:309–12.

47. Congress, *House Executive Documents, Report of the Secretary of War* (1867), 231–32; *Nashville Daily Press and Times,* July 31, 1867.

48. *Knoxville Whig,* June 12, 26, 1867.

49. David M. Nelson to Lieutenant Ellis, June 3, 1867, and Lieutenant Ellis to H. H. Thomas, July 10, 27, 1867, Reel 2, Box 10, Folder 3; Quartermaster Expenditures, April 1867–February 1868, Reel 4, Box 22, Folder 5, both in TAGO; Tennessee General Assembly, *House Journal,* 35th General Assembly, extra sess. (1868), 26. Numerous ration invoices from Totten and other grocers to most of the militia companies can be found in Reel 2, Box 10, Folder 3, TAGO.

50. Jones, "Reconstruction in Tennessee," 196; Patton, *Unionism and Reconstruction,* 177–78; Hamer, *Tennessee* 2:626; Alexander, *Political Reconstruction,* 151–52; Maness, "Henry Emerson Etheridge," 47–48; A. W. Howard to Governor Brownlow, June 4, 1867, Box 1, Folder 10, Brownlow Papers; *Knoxville Whig,* June 12, 1867. Captain Grisham took a brief leave of absence from his command in Sullivan to participate in a Radical counter-rally during Etheridge's stop in Jonesboro on June 5. *Nashville Daily Press and Times,* June 12, 1867.

51. *Nashville Republican Banner,* June 9, 1867; *Nashville Daily Press and Times,* June 10, 22, 1867; *Knoxville Whig,* June 19, July 3, 1867.
52. Hamer, *Tennessee* 2:620.

CHAPTER 4

1. Special Orders Nos. 1–44, June 21–July 31, 1867, Reel 9, Vol. 33, TAGO; *Nashville Republican Banner,* June 9, 27, 28, 1867; Graf, Haskins, and Bergeron, *Papers of Andrew Johnson* 12:343. Joining "Generalissimo" Cooper was Samuel Hunt, who replaced his cousin James P. Brownlow as adjutant general in July. Brownlow resigned to accept a commission in the U.S. Army and a duty assignment in California. Tennessee Secretary of State, *Tennessee Blue Book, 1999–2000* (Nashville, 2000), 488; Coulter, *Brownlow,* 267, 324.
2. White, Ash, and Moore, *Messages* 5:568; *American Annual Cyclopedia* (1867), 707.
3. White, Ash, and Moore, *Messages* 5:568–70.
4. *American Annual Cyclopedia* (1867), 708; *Nashville Republican Banner,* July 6, 1867; Graf, Haskins, and Bergeron, *Papers of Andrew Johnson* 12:369; *Nashville Union and Dispatch,* July 4, 1867. In his interview, Johnson also described the Radical government in Tennessee as "the worst despotism he had ever heard of."
5. *American Annual Cyclopedia* (1867), 708; *Nashville Daily Press and Times,* July 8, 1867; *Knoxville Whig,* July 3, 1867; *Nashville Republican Banner,* July 21, 1867.
6. *Memphis Daily Appeal,* June 12, 1867; Arnell, "Southern Unionist," 314–15; *Knoxville Whig,* July 3, 1867; Brian Steel Wills, *A Battle from the Start: The Life of Nathan Bedford Forrest* (New York: HarperCollins, 1992), 335–36; Trelease, *White Terror,* 14–23; Alexander, *Political Reconstruction,* 179–81.
7. Hamer, *Tennessee* 2:627–28; McBride, "Blacks and Race Issue," 215–16; Phillips, "History of the Freedmen's Bureau," 300–301.
8. *Nashville Daily Press and Times,* June 24, July 10, 1867; Owens, "Union League of America," 66–68. New York Leaguers reportedly made a "munificent contribution" to the Radical party of Tennessee.
9. *Memphis Daily Appeal,* June 14, 1867; *McMinnville Enterprise,* June 29, July 6, 1867; Lewis L. Faulkner to General Cooper, July 6, 1867, Reel 2, Box 11, Folder 1; William Baker to General Cooper, July 10, 1867, Reel 2, Box 10, Folder 4, both in TAGO.

10. James P. Brownlow to General Cooper, June 28, 1867, Reel 2, Box 10, Folder 4; Special Order No. 16, July 12, 1867, Reel 9, Vol. 33, both in TAGO; *McMinnville Enterprise*, July 6, 20, 1867; William Baker to General Cooper, July 10, 1867, Reel 2, Box 10, Folder 4, TAGO.
11. Captain Stuart to General Cooper, July 3, 1867 (two letters), Reel 2, Box 11, Folder 3, TAGO. Stuart's rage may have been further exacerbated by "a very severe spell of Cramp Colic," a stomach ailment which evidently made moving around quite painful. Captain Stuart to H. H. Thomas, June 15, 1867, Reel 2, Box 10, Folder 3, TAGO.
12. Captain Stuart to General Cooper, July 16, 18, 1867, Reel 2, Box 11, Folder 3, TAGO; *Nashville Union and Dispatch*, July 23, 28, 1867.
13. *Nashville Daily Press and Times*, June 26, 1867; Special Order No. 15, July 9, 1867, TAGO, Reel 9, Vol. 33; Marsha Young Darrah, "Political Career of Col. William B. Stokes of Tennessee" (Master's thesis, Tennessee Technological Univ., 1968), 148–49. The militia detachment in Overton may have accompanied Stokes during his stump of the region. Darrah states that when Stokes arrived in the county, "he was met by a contingent of former Union soldiers on horseback."
14. *Nashville Daily Press and Times*, July 22, 26, 1867; House, *Sheafe v. Tillman*, 188–89; *Nashville Union and Dispatch*, July 12, 1867; *McMinnville Enterprise*, July 20, 1867; *Pulaski Citizen*, July 26, 1867; *Nashville Republican Banner*, July 18, 1867.
15. *Nashville Republican Banner*, July 18, 20, 24, 1867; *Nashville Daily Press and Times*, July 18, 1867.
16. Captain Rickman to Samuel Hunt, June 25, 1867, Reel 2, Box 11, Folder 2; Morning Report of Company H, 1st Tennessee State Guards, June 30, 1867, Reel 5, Box 23, Folder 4, both in TAGO; *Nashville Union and Dispatch*, June 28, 1867; Fisher, *War at Every Door*, 189. On June 12, Governor Brownlow invalidated Giles's registration of voters due to "frauds and irregularities." *Pulaski Citizen*, June 14, 1867. While seeking a commission in the State Guard, Registrar Wiley assembled a number of militia recruits from Marshall County. Until Rickman arrived in Lewisburg, Wiley's volunteers appear to have served in an extralegal capacity. Robert Wiley to H. H. Thomas, June 1, 1867, Reel 2, Box 10, Folder 3, TAGO.
17. *Nashville Union and Dispatch*, June 28, 1867; Special Order No. 11, July 3, 1867, Reel 9, Vol. 33; Captain Rickman to Samuel Hunt, June 25, 1867, Reel 2, Box 11, Folder 2, both in TAGO; *Nashville Daily Press and Times*, July 6, Aug. 5, 1867; Captain Rickman to Lt. L. B. Gamble, Aug. 2, 1867, Reel 1, Box 8, Folder 6, TAGO.

18. *Nashville Republican Banner,* June 25, 1867; *Nashville Daily Press and Times,* July 6, 1867; Muster Roll for Company A, 2nd Tennessee State Guard (1867), Reel 5, Box 24, Folder 3; Special Order No. 2, June 21, 1867, Reel 9, Vol. 33, both in TAGO.

19. Jacob W. Brown to Governor Brownlow, July 2, 1867, Patton Papers; *Nashville Daily Press and Times,* July 8, 1867; *Memphis Daily Appeal,* Aug. 1, 1867.

20. *Nashville Union and Dispatch,* July 7, 10, 1867; *Nashville Daily Press and Times,* July 9, 10, 1867; *Pulaski Citizen,* July 12, 1867; Muster Roll for Company A, 2nd Tennessee State Guard (1867), Reel 5, Box 24, Folder 3, TAGO.

21. *Nashville Union and Dispatch,* July 7, 10, 1867; *Knoxville Whig,* July 10, 1867; *Nashville Republican Banner,* July 9, 14, 24, 1867; Taz. W. Newman to General Cooper, Nov. 25, 1867, Reel 2, Box 11, Folder 2; Special Order No. 14, July 9, 1867, Reel 9, Vol. 33; General Order No. 15, Aug. 28, 1867, Reel 9, Vol. 27, all in TAGO.

22. Capt. G. Kirk to H. H. Thomas and A. E. Boone, July 17, 21, 1867, Reel 2, Box 10, Folder 3; Captain Grisham to General Cooper, July 21, 1867, Reel 2, Box 11, Folder 1, both in TAGO; House, *Sheafe v. Tillman,* 101; A. M. Shook to A. S. Colyar, Nov. 21, 1905, Arthur S. Colyar Papers, Southern Historical Collection, Univ. of North Carolina, Chapel Hill; Jacob W. Brown to General Cooper, July 12, 1867, Reel 2, Box 10, Folder 4, TAGO.

23. Special Orders Nos. 5, 6 (June 28, 1867), and 17 (July 13, 1867), Reel 9, Vol. 33; Captain Evans to General Cooper, July 1, 16, 1867, Reel 2, Box 10, Folder 5, both in TAGO; Fisher, *War at Every Door,* 189; William Welch to Governor Brownlow, July 14, 1867, Box 1, Folder 10, Brownlow Papers. Lieutenant Ellis remained in Claiborne County throughout the campaign.

24. *Nashville Daily Press and Times,* July 1, 1867; *Nashville Union and Dispatch,* July 2, 1867; *Nashville Republican Banner,* June 29, July 2, 1867.

25. Special Order Nos. 9–10, July 3, 1867, Reel 9, Vol. 33, TAGO; Congress, *House Executive Documents, Report of the Secretary of War* (1867), 197–98; Lieutenant Roberts to General Cooper, July 4, 1867, Reel 2, Box 11, Folder 3, TAGO. Originally, Roberts was assigned to go to Cheatham and Hall to Stewart, but Cooper reversed their destinations at the last minute.

26. Fisher, *War at Every Door,* 188; Cheatham County Petition to Governor Brownlow, June 3, 1867, Reel 2, Box 4, Folder 7, Governor Brownlow Papers.

27. *Nashville Daily Press and Times,* July 3, 1867; *Nashville Union and Dispatch,* July 4, 1867; *Nashville Republican Banner,* July 5, 1867.

28. *Nashville Republican Banner,* July 5, 8, 12, 28, Aug. 3, 1867; *Nashville Daily Press and Times,* July 11, 1867; *Clarksville Weekly Chronicle,* July 12, 1867; *Nashville Union and Dispatch,* July 4, 1867.

29. *Nashville Republican Banner,* June 15, 16, 18, 1867; *Memphis Daily Appeal,* June 19, 1867.

30. Durham, *Rebellion Revisited,* 302; *Nashville Union and Dispatch,* June 30, 1867.

31. Special Order No. 7, July 1, 1867, Reel 9, Vol. 33, TAGO; Durham, *Rebellion Revisited,* 300, 302; *Nashville Republican Banner,* July 14, 1867.

32. *Nashville Republican Banner,* June 30, July 14, 18, 1867; Muster Roll for Company B, 2nd Tennessee State Guard (1867), Reel 5, Box 24, Folder 4, TAGO; George B. Guild, "Reconstruction Times in Sumner County," *American Historical Magazine* 8 (1903): 363.

33. *Nashville Daily Press and Times,* July 10, 12, 1867; Samuel Hunt to General Thomas Duncan, July 7, 1867, Reel 2, Box 3, Folder 1, Governor Brownlow Papers; Lt. Merritt Barber to Samuel Hunt, July 9, 1867, Reel 2; Box 10, Folder 4; Special Order No. 13, July 8, 1867, Reel 9, Vol. 33, both in TAGO.

34. *Nashville Republican Banner,* July 9, 17, 1867; *Nashville Daily Press and Banner,* July 12, 15, 1867; *Nashville Union and Dispatch,* July 10, 1867. On Apr. 12, 1864, Confederate cavalry raiders under Nathan B. Forrest captured Fort Pillow (Lauderdale County, Tennessee) and reportedly massacred black soldiers who attempted to surrender. See Glatthaar, *Forged in Battle,* 156–57; Wills, *Battle from the Start,* 179–96.

35. *Nashville Union and Dispatch,* July 10, 11, 1867; *Nashville Daily Press and Times,* July 11, 1867. In an apparent misread of the sources, James W. Patton incorrectly contends that Company G "stood threateningly by" during Etheridge's speech. Captain Sumner was probably under General Cooper's direct command on the day of the Conservative rally. The general had come down from Nashville that morning to coordinate the activities of the militia and the Federal troops. Patton, *Unionism and Reconstruction,* 177; *Nashville Republican Banner,* July 11, 1867.

36. *Nashville Union and Dispatch,* July 10, 11, 16, 18, 28, 1867; *Nashville Republican Banner,* July 17, 23, 1867.

37. *Nashville Daily Press and Times,* July 11, 17, Aug. 1, 1867; Special Orders Nos. 25, 34, and 36, July 22, 29, 30, 1867, Reel 9, Vol. 33; W. T. Allmond to General Thomas Duncan, July 29, 1867, Reel 2, Box 10, Folder 5, both in TAGO; *Nashville Union and Dispatch,* July 11, 31, 1867; *Nashville*

Republican Banner, July 11, 31, Aug. 1, 1867; Capt. D. M. Burke to Adjutant General of Tennessee, July 30, 1867, Reel 10, Vol. 46, TAGO. Maury County authorities originally requested military assistance from the Federal garrison, but General Duncan referred the matter to General Cooper, who dispatched Lieutenant Sumner.

38. Captain Sumner to A. E. Boone, July 29, 1867, Reel 2, Box 10, Folder 3, TAGO.

39. Governor Brownlow to General Cooper, July 11, 1867, Reel 1, Box 1, Folder 1, Governor Brownlow Papers; *Nashville Daily Press and Times,* July 15, 24, 1867.

40. *Nashville Daily Press and Times,* July 20, 1867; *Knoxville Whig,* July 24, 1867; Captain Hall to H. H. Thomas, June 13, 1867, Reel 2, Box 10, Folder 3, TAGO; *Nashville Union and Dispatch,* July 20, 1867; *Nashville Republican Banner,* July 20, 1867.

41. L. Waters to General Cooper, July 2, 1867, Reel 2, Box 11, Folder 3, TAGO; *Nashville Republican Banner,* July 28, 1867.

42. John Carey to Governor Brownlow, July 8, 1867, Reel 1, Box 2, Folder 1, Governor Brownlow Papers; *Fayetteville Observer,* July 11, 1867; *Nashville Republican Banner,* July 21, 1867.

43. Captain Grisham to General Cooper, July 26, 1867, Reel 2, Box 11, Folder 1, TAGO; *Jonesboro Union Flag,* Aug. 16, 1867; *Fayetteville Observer,* Aug. 1, 1867.

44. *Jonesboro Union Flag,* Aug. 16, 1867; Captain Grisham to General Cooper, July 31, 1867, Reel 2, Box 11, Folder 1, TAGO.

45. Special Order No. 27, July 24, 1867, Reel 9, Vol. 33, TAGO; Fisher, *War at Every Door,* 189; *Nashville Daily Press and Times,* July 19, 24, 1867; *Nashville Republican Banner,* July 25, 1867; John L. Roberts to General Cooper, July 27, 1867, Reel 2, Box 11, Folder 3; Muster Roll for Company C, 2nd Tennessee State Guard (1867), Reel 5, Box 24, Folder 5, both in TAGO. Kirk's new recruits may not have been full-fledged militiamen. General Cooper referred to them as a "Citizen Company." Special Order No. 138, July 26, 1867, Reel 9, Vol. 33, TAGO.

46. Special Order No. 28, July 24, 1867, Reel 9, Vol. 33; H. D. Featherston to General Cooper, July 26, 1867, Reel 2, Box 11, Folder 1; Lieutenant Burchfield to General Cooper, July 30, 1867, Reel 2, Box 10, Folder 4, all in TAGO; *Nashville Daily Press and Times,* Aug. 1, 1867; *Nashville Union and Dispatch,* Aug. 2, 1867.

47. *Nashville Daily Press and Times,* June 27, July 18, 1867; Special Order No. 3, June 21, 1867, Reel 9, Vol. 33, TAGO; *Nashville Republican Banner,* June 26, 1867; *Fayetteville Observer,* July 11, 1867.

48. Special Order No. 4, June 25, 1867, and No. 12, July 8, 1867, Reel 9, Vol. 33; Captain Chambers to General Cooper, June 28, 1867, Reel 2, Box 10, Folder 5; Lt. L. B. Gamble to General Cooper, July 14, 1867, Reel 2, Box 11, Folder 1, all in TAGO; *Knoxville Whig,* Dec. 12, 1866; *Nashville Daily Press and Times,* July 15, 1867; General Order No. 3, July 17, 1867, Reel 9, Vol. 27, TAGO; Captain Chambers to Governor Brownlow, July 16, 1867, Reel 1, Box 2, Folder 1, Governor Brownlow Papers; *Nashville Republican Banner,* July 10, 1867. Through the intercession of numerous friends, Chambers eventually received an honorable discharge. John M. Cordell to General Cooper, Nov. 11, 1867, Reel 2, Box 10, Folder 5; Scott County Petition to General Cooper, Nov. 15, 1867, Reel 2, Box 11, Folder 2; General Order No. 35, Jan. 14, 1868, Reel 9, Vol. 27, all in TAGO.

49. Special Order Nos. 12 and 39, July 8, 31,1867, Reel 9, Vol. 33, TAGO; Reel 1, CSR Index; Hewett, *Roster of Union Soldiers* 20:394; Census of Tennessee, 1870 (Scott County), 255; *Memphis Daily Appeal,* July 16, 1867; *Nashville Republican Banner,* Aug. 1, 1867; *Nashville Union and Dispatch,* July 31, 1867; James H. McNeilly, "Reconstruction in Tennessee," *Confederate Veteran Magazine* 28 (1920): 342; Captain Adkins to General Cooper, July 31, 1867, Reel 2, Box 10, Folder 4, TAGO.

50. Captain Robeson to Horace H. Thomas, July 12, 1867, Reel 2, Box 10, Folder 3; Captain Robeson to Samuel Hunt, July 12, 15, 1867, Reel 2, Box 11, Folder 3, both in TAGO.

51. Captain Robeson to Samuel Hunt, July 27, 1867, Reel 2, Box 11, Folder 1, TAGO. The anti-Radical sentiment in Lauderdale was likely intensified by a mid-July address by Nathan B. Forrest during a Conservative rally at Fort Pillow, site of the Civil War massacre. *Knoxville Whig,* July 17, 1867.

52. Special Order NA, June 19, 1867, Reel 9, Vol. 33, TAGO; Fisher, *War at Every Door,* 190; Emma Inman Williams, *Historic Madison: The Story of Jackson and Madison County Tennessee, from the Prehistoric Moundbuilders to 1917* (Jackson, Tenn.: Madison County Historical Society, 1946), 190–93; *Memphis Daily Appeal,* July 11, 1867.

53. Williams, *Historic Madison,* 193–94; Captain Clingan to General Cooper, July 11, 15, 1867, Reel 2, Box 10, Folder 5; Captain Clingan to General Cooper, June 24, and A. E. Boone, June 25, 1867, Reel 2, Box 10, Folder 3; Wing E. Ramsey to Adjutant General of Tennessee, July 18, 1867, Reel 10, Vol. 46; Muster Roll for Company D, 1st Tennessee State Guard (1867), Reel 4, Box 22, Folder 4, all in TAGO.

54. Captain Clingan to General Cooper, July 11, 1867, Reel 2, Box 10, Folder 5, TAGO; *Nashville Daily Press and Times,* July 11, 1867.

55. Captain Clingan to General Cooper, July 11, 15, 1867, Reel 2, Box 10, Folder 5, TAGO.

56. Special Order Nos. 8 and 48, July 3, Aug. 2, 1867, Reel 9, Vol. 33; Boyd Cheatham (Edgefield & Kentucky) to General Cooper, July 3, 1867, Reel 2, Box 10, Folder 5, both in TAGO; Fisher, *War at Every Door,* 189; *Nashville Daily Press and Times,* July 3, 9, 1867; *Memphis Daily Appeal,* July 23, 1867; *Paris Intelligencer,* July 6, 1867; *Nashville Republican Banner,* July 9, 1867.

57. Captain Hamilton to H. H. Thomas, July 2, 1867, Reel 2, Box 10, Folder 3, TAGO; Fisher, *War at Every Door,* 189; *Nashville Daily Press and Times,* July 20, 1867; *Memphis Daily Appeal,* July 25, 1867.

58. *Nashville Daily Press and Times,* July 31, 1867; *Nashville Republican Banner,* July 31, 1867.

59. *Nashville Daily Press and Times,* July 31, 1867; *Nashville Republican Banner,* July 31, 1867; Muster Roll for Company E, 2nd Tennessee State Guard (1867), Reel 5, Box 24, Folder 7, TAGO; Congress, *House Executive Documents, Report of the Secretary of War* (1867), 189.

60. Muster Rolls for Company A, H, I, 1st Regiment, B, 2nd Regiment, Tennessee State Guard (1867), Reel 4, Box 22, Folder 1, Reel 5, Box 23, Folders 4, 5, Box 24, Folder 4; Captain Grisham to General Cooper, July 21, 1867, Reel 2, Box 11, Folder 1; General Order No. 34, Dec. 7, 1867, Reel 9, Vol. 27, all in TAGO.

61. *Nashville Daily Press and Times,* July 26, 1867; Fisher, *War at Every Door,* 188; *Nashville Union and Dispatch,* July 23, 1867.

62. *Nashville Daily Press and Times,* July 26, 1867; *Knoxville Whig,* July 24, 1867; *Nashville Union and Dispatch,* July 23, 1867.

63. *Athens Republican,* July 26, 1867; Special Order No. 26, July 23, 1867, Reel 9, Vol. 33, TAGO; *Nashville Union and Dispatch,* July 25, 1867.

64. Lieutenant Brown to General Cooper, July 25, 1867, Reel 2, Box 10, Folder 4, TAGO; McBride, "Blacks and the Race Issue," 215; Lieutenant Alexander to General Cooper, July 31, 1867, Reel 2, Box 10, Folder 4, TAGO.

65. Boyd M. Cheatham to H. H. Thomas, June 18, 1867, Reel 2, Box 10, Folder 3, TAGO; H. H. Thomas to Joseph Hoxie, Aug. 8, 1867, Reel 2, Box 3, Folder 1; H. H. Thomas to President of Mobile & Ohio Railroad, July 7, 1867, Reel 2, Box 3, Folder 1, both in Governor Brownlow Papers; Sam B. Jones to H. H. Thomas, June 27, July 2, 1867, Reel 2, Box 10, Folder 3; Boyd M. Cheatham to General Cooper, July 3, 1867, Reel 2, Box 10, Folder 5; J. L. Williams to J. M. Houston,

Sept. 23, 1867, Reel 13, Vol. 82, all in TAGO; Tennessee General
Assembly, *House Journal,* 35th General Assembly, extra sess. (1868), 26.
For a map of the principal rail lines in Tennessee during this period, see
Bergeron, Ash, and Keith, *Tennesseans and Their History,* 115.

66. Governor Brownlow to General Cooper, July 25, 1867, Reel 1, Box 1,
Folder 1, Governor Brownlow Papers; *Knoxville Whig,* July 30, 1867;
Nashville Union and Dispatch, July 31, 1867; *Nashville Republican
Banner,* July 26, 27, Aug. 1, 1867; *Nashville Daily Press and Times,*
Aug. 2, 1867; Special Order No. 33, July 29, 1867, Reel 9, Vol. 33,
TAGO; Fisher, *War at Every Door,* 188.

67. Special Order Nos. 37 and 40–42, July 30, 31, 1867, Reel 9, Vol. 33,
TAGO; W. Y. Elliott to Governor Brownlow, July 15, 1867, Patton
Papers; W. Bosson and W. Y. Elliott to General Cooper, July 26, 1867,
Reel 2, Box 10, Folder 4, TAGO; *Nashville Republican Banner,* Aug. 1,
1867.

68. House, *Sheafe v. Tillman,* 101; Lt. L. B. Gamble to General Cooper,
Sept. 6, 1867, Reel 1, Box 8, Folder 6; Lieutenant Cravens to General
Cooper, Sept. 7, 1867, Reel 1, Box 8, Folder 6, TAGO; *Nashville Daily
Press and Times,* July 27, Aug. 9, 1867; *Knoxville Whig,* Aug. 7, 1867;
Special Orders Book, 1867, Reel 9. Vol. 33, TAGO.

69. Graf, Haskins, and Bergeron, *Papers of Andrew Johnson* 12:434.

70. *Fayetteville Observer,* May 9, 1867; *Nashville Republican Banner,* June 30,
Aug. 1, 1867; *Nashville Union and Dispatch,* July 25, Aug. 1, 1867.

71. *Nashville Union and Dispatch,* July 1867; *Nashville Republican Banner,*
July 20, 1867.

CHAPTER 5

1. Circular No. 2, July 25, 1867, Reel 9, Vol. 27, TAGO.

2. General Order No. 4, July 31, 1867, Reel 9, Vol. 27, TAGO; *Nashville
Union and Dispatch,* Aug. 2, 1867.

3. *Nashville Union and Dispatch,* July 3, 31, 1867; *Nashville Daily Press and
Times,* July 26, Aug. 1, 1867; Graf, Haskins, and Bergeron, *Papers of
Andrew Johnson* 12:410; Gideaon Welles, *Diary of Gideon Welles,
Secretary of the Navy under Lincoln and Johnson,* John T. Morse, jr. ed. 3
vols. (Boston: Houghton Mifflin, 1911), 3:140; Congress, *House
Executive Documents, Report of the Secretary of War* (1867), 235–37;
Governor Brownlow to George H. Thomas, July 20, 1867, Reel 2, Box
3, Folder 1, Governor Brownlow Papers. The Metropolitan Police was

only partially organized in the summer of 1867, and the Radicals were still fighting the legal injunction against it.

4. Sefton, *United States Army and Reconstruction*, 261; *American Annual Cyclopedia* (1867), 708; *Nashville Daily Press and Times*, July 26, 1867; Congress, *House Executive Documents, Report of the Secretary of War* (1867), 184, 232–35; John Y. Simon, ed., *The Papers of Ulysses S. Grant*, 24 vols. to date (Carbondale: Southern Illinois Univ. Press, 1967–), 17:236–38. Thomas was under no illusions about the anti-Radicals' attitude toward the army. He knew that they disliked him and regarded the Federal garrison as merely a lesser evil than the militia. Prior to the State Guard's mobilization, his regulars endured frequent criticism in the press, and on one occasion his men were involved in a ridiculous rock-throwing incident with white Nashvillians. Thomas's public acknowledgment of the lawfulness of the State Guard prompted the *Union and Dispatch* to insult the general as a man who was "not as sharp as we [took] him to be" (see *Nashville Daily Press and Times*, Mar. 18, 1867; *Pulaski Citizen*, Apr. 12, 1867; and *Nashville Union and Dispatch*, Jan. 2, May 30, 31, 1867).

5. Sefton, *United States Army and Reconstruction*, 184; Congress, *House Executive Documents, Report of the Secretary of War* (1867), 182–84, 460–61; General Cooper to Post Commander, Nashville, July 29, 1867, Reel 2, Box 10, Folder 5, TAGO; *Nashville Daily Press and Times*, July 26, 30, 1867; *Nashville Union and Dispatch*, July 20, 1867. A detachment of Federal troops had been at Spring Hill (Maury County) since the beginning of July and General Duncan notified the residents that it would remain there "until after the election." *Nashville Republican Banner*, July 10, 1867.

6. *Nashville Daily Press and Times*, July 31, 1867; *Nashville Union and Dispatch*, Aug. 2, 1867.

7. *Nashville Daily Press and Times*, July 25, Aug. 2, 1867; Circular NA, July 31, 1867, Reel 9, Vol. 27, TAGO.

8. Lieutenant Cravens to Headquarters, Tennessee State Guard, Sept. 7, 1867, Reel 1, Box 8, Folder 6, TAGO; Darrah, "Political Career of W. B. Stokes," 149, 282; McBride, "Blacks and the Race Issue," 219; W. B. Stokes to Governor Brownlow, Aug. 12, 1867, Patton Papers.

9. Report of Company C, 1st Regiment, Sept. 5, 1867, Reel 1, Box 8, Folder 6, TAGO; House, *Sheafe v. Tillman*, 113–15, 193, 199, 203; Anne H. Hopkins and William Lyons, *Tennessee Votes: 1799–1976* (Knoxville: Univ. of Tennessee Press, 1978), 48; General Order No. 6, Aug. 3, 1867, Reel 9, Vol. 27, TAGO.

10. Report of Company I, 1st Regiment, Sept. 5, 1867, Reel 1, Box 8, Folder 6; Lieutenant England to General Cooper, Aug. 4, 1867, Reel 2, Box 10, Folder 5, both in TAGO; Hopkins and Lyons, *Tennessee Votes*, 48; Tennessee General Assembly, *Public Acts of Tennessee*, 34th General Assembly, 2nd adjourned sess. (1867), chap. 26, sec. 7; *Nashville Daily Press and Times*, Aug. 3, 1867; Captain Evans to Headquarters, Tennessee State Guard, July 22, 1867, Reel 2, Box 10, Folder 5, TAGO.

11. Report of Company F, 1st Regiment, Sept. 5, 1867, Reel 1, Box 8, Folder 6; Capt. E. R. Hall to Lt. L. B. Gamble, Aug. 17, 1867, Reel 2, Box 11, Folder 1, both in TAGO; Hopkins and Lyons, *Tennessee Votes*, 48.

12. Report of Company C, 2nd Regiment, Sept. 5, 1867, Reel 1, Box 8, Folder 6; Lieutenant Burchfield to General Cooper, Aug. 2, 1867, Reel 2, Box 10, Folder 4, both in TAGO; *Nashville Union and Dispatch*, Aug. 3, 1867; Hopkins and Lyons, *Tennessee Votes*, 48; H. D. Featherston to General Cooper, Aug. 2, 1867, Reel 2, Box 11, Folder 1, TAGO.

13. House, *Sheafe v. Tillman*, 83–85, 138–39; Hopkins and Lyons, *Tennessee Votes*, 48.

14. Report of Company H, 1st Regiment, Sept. 5, 1867, Reel 1, Box 8, Folder 6; Captain Rickman to Lt. L. B. Gamble, Aug. 2, 1867, Reel 1, Box 8, Folder 6; Captain Rickman to Lt. L. B. Gamble, Aug. 7, 1867, Reel 2, Box 11, Folder 2, all in TAGO; House, *Sheafe v. Tillman*, 38, 46–48, 50, 61, 65–66, 69; Hopkins and Lyons, *Tennessee Votes*, 48.

15. Report of Company H, 1st Regiment, Sept. 5, 1867, Reel 1, Box 8, Folder 6; Captain Rickman to Lt. L. B. Gamble, Aug. 2, 1867, Reel 1, Box 8, Folder 6; Captain Rickman to Lt. L. B. Gamble, Aug. 7, 1867, Reel 2, Box 11, Folder 2, all in TAGO. Rickman offered this additional comment on Steele: "He will soon Kill *him* Self and So I would reckamen that *He* go to *his* Grave un noticed."

16. Special Order No. 44, July 31, 1867, Reel 9, Vol. 33, TAGO; Trelease, *White Terror*, 23–24; Report of Company H, 1st Regiment, Sept. 5, 1867, Reel 1, Box 8, Folder 6; Captain Rickman to Lieutenant Gamble, Aug. 7, 1867, Reel 2, Box 11, Folder 2, both in TAGO; House, *Sheafe v. Tillman*, 90–91, 101–2, 264–66; *Pulaski Citizen*, Aug. 2, 1867; Hopkins and Lyons, *Tennessee Votes*, 48.

17. *Nashville Republican Banner*, Aug. 3, 1867; Lieutenant Durham to Captain Houston, Aug. 2, 1867, Reel 2, Box 10, Folder 5, TAGO; *Nashville Daily Press and Times*, Aug. 5, 1867; Report of Company A, 3rd Regiment, Sept. 5, 1867, Reel 1, Box 8, Folder 6, TAGO.

18. Special Order No. 38, July 31, 1867, Reel 9, Vol. 33, TAGO; *Pulaski Citizen*, Aug. 2, 1867; *Nashville Republican Banner*, Aug. 3, 1867.

19. Special Orders Nos. 34 and 43, July 29, 31, 1867, Reel 9, Vol. 33, TAGO; entries for July 30 and Aug. 1, 1867, Nimrod Porter Diary, Nimrod Porter Papers, MSS 1094, Southern Historical Collection, Univ. of North Carolina, Chapel Hill (hereafter cited as Porter Diary); Arnell, "Southern Unionist," 316–19; *Nashville Republican Banner,* Aug. 3, 1867; Hopkins and Lyons, *Tennessee Votes,* 48.

20. Report of Company K, 2nd Regiment, Sept. 5, 1867, Reel 1, Box 8, Folder 6, TAGO; Governor Brownlow to Lieutenant Fleming, July 21, 1867, Reel 1, Box 2, Folder 11, Governor Brownlow Papers; Hopkins and Lyons, *Tennessee Votes,* 48.

21. Special Order Nos. 40–42, July 31, 1867, Reel 9, Vol. 33; Report of Company A, 3rd Regiment, Sept. 5, 1867, Reel 1, Box 8, Folder 6, both in TAGO; *Nashville Republican Banner,* Aug. 2, 1867; *Knoxville Whig,* July 30, 1867; Sgt. J. M. Pitman to Captain Houston, Aug. 3, 1867, Reel 2, Box 11, Folder 2, TAGO; Hopkins and Lyons, *Tennessee Votes,* 48.

22. *Nashville Republican Banner,* Aug. 2, 1867; *Nashville Union and Dispatch,* Aug. 3, 1867.

23. *Nashville Daily Press and Times,* Aug. 2, 3, 1867; Durham, *Rebellion Revisited,* 303; Report of Company B, 2nd Regiment, Sept. 5, 1867, Reel 1, Box 8, Folder 6, TAGO.

24. Report of Company B, 2nd Regiment, Sept. 5, 1867, Reel 1, Box 8, Folder 6, TAGO; Guild, "Reconstruction Times in Sumner County," 362–64.

25. *Nashville Daily Press and Times,* Aug. 2, 3, 1867; Congress, *House Executive Documents, Report of the Secretary of War* (1867), 460–61; Hopkins and Lyons, *Tennessee Votes,* 48.

26. Report of Company B, 1st Regiment, Sept. 5, 1867, Reel 1, Box 8, Folder 6, Captain Grisham to General Cooper, Aug. 5, 1867, Reel 2, Box 11, Folder 1, both in TAGO; *Knoxville Whig,* Aug. 7, 1867.

27. Report of Company B, 1st Regiment, Sept. 5, 1867, Reel 1, Box 8, Folder 6, TAGO; *Knoxville Whig,* Aug. 7, 1867; *Nashville Daily Press and Times,* Aug. 5, 1867; House, *Sheafe v. Tillman,* 26, 34; Alexander, *Political Reconstruction,* 154–55.

28. Report of Company B, 1st Regiment, Sept. 5, 1867, Reel 1, Box 8, Folder 6; Captain Grisham to General Cooper, Aug. 5, 1867, Reel 2, Box 11, Folder 1, both in TAGO; Hopkins and Lyons, *Tennessee Votes,* 48; House, *Sheafe v. Tillman,* 27, 174; Alexander, *Political Reconstruction,* 155; Captain Grisham to Samuel Hunt, Aug. 2, 1867, Reel 2, Box 11, Folder 1, TAGO.

29. *Jonesboro Union Flag,* Aug. 16, Sept. 6, 1867; *Memphis Daily Appeal,* Aug. 1, 1867; Hopkins and Lyons, *Tennessee Votes,* 48. McLaughlin resigned his commission a week after the election in order to go home and care for his family. Captain Grisham lamented the loss of this "valuable and honest officer." Special Order No. 65, Aug. 9, 1867, Reel 9, Vol. 33; Captain Grisham to General Cooper, Aug. 6, 1867, Reel 2, Box 11, Folder 1, both in TAGO.

30. Captain Robeson to General Cooper, Aug. 13, 1867, Reel 2, Box 11, Folder 2; Report of Company E, 1st Regiment, Sept. 5, 1867, Reel 1, Box 8, Folder 6, both in TAGO; A. H. Walker to Governor Brownlow, Aug. 2, 1867, Reel 1, Box 2, Folder 2, Governor Brownlow Papers; Hopkins and Lyons, *Tennessee Votes,* 48; Report of Company G, 1st Regiment, Sept. 5, 1867, Reel 1, Box 8, Folder 6, TAGO.

31. *Nashville Daily Press and Times,* Aug. 9, 1867; *Nashville Union and Dispatch,* Aug. 11, 1867; Captain Adkins to General Cooper, Aug. 2, 1867, Reel 2, Box 11, Folder 3, TAGO. See chapter 4 for details on this militia unit's internal difficulties. Also adding to Adkins's worries was the Conservative gubernatorial canvass, which concluded its tour of the state with a grand rally in Humboldt (Gibson County) on July 31. There, Emerson Etheridge urged his followers to ostracize socially all the Radicals in the county, including their children. Owens, "Union League of America," 71.

32. Report of Company G, 1st Regiment, Sept. 5, 1867, Reel 1, Box 8, Folder 6; Captain Adkins to General Cooper, Aug. 1867, Reel 2, Box 10, Folder 4, both in TAGO; *Nashville Union and Dispatch,* Aug. 6, 11, 1867; McNeilly, "Reconstruction in Tennessee," 342. General Cooper certainly doubted Adkins's ability to keep the peace in Gibson County, but it is not clear whether he or Captain Robeson authorized Holt to go to Trenton on August 1. Holt may have acted on his own.

33. Report of Company G, 1st Regiment, Sept. 5, 1867, Reel 1, Box 8, Folder 6; Captain Adkins to General Cooper, Aug. 1867, Reel 2, Box 10, Folder 4, both in TAGO; *Nashville Union and Dispatch,* Aug. 6, 11, 1867.

34. *Nashville Union and Dispatch,* Aug. 11, 1867; Captain Adkins to General Cooper, Aug. 1867, Reel 2, Box 10, Folder 4, TAGO; Hopkins and Lyons, *Tennessee Votes,* 48; McNeilly, "Reconstruction in Tennessee," 340. The term "skullbonean" undoubtedly refers to the nearby town of Skullbone, a Unionist stronghold during the Civil War, but the *Union and Dispatch* is likely using the term sarcastically, equating the militia with piracy.

35. Report of Company D, 1st Regiment, Sept. 5, 1867, Reel 1, Box 8, Folder 6, TAGO; *Nashville Union and Dispatch,* Aug. 6, 1867; *Nashville Daily Press and Times,* Aug. 9, 1867.

36. Report of Company D, 1st Regiment, Sept. 5, 1867, Reel 1, Box 8, Folder 6, TAGO; *Nashville Daily Press and Times,* Aug. 9, 12, 1867; Hopkins and Lyons, *Tennessee Votes,* 48.

37. Report of Company D, 1st Regiment, Sept. 5, 1867, Reel 1, Box 8, Folder 6, TAGO.

38. Captain Hamilton to Lt. L. B. Gamble, Aug. 6, 1867; Reports of Companies E and F, 2nd Regiment, Sept. 5, 1867, Reel 1, Box 8, Folder 6, both in TAGO; Hopkins and Lyons, *Tennessee Votes,* 48; Lieutenant Alexander to General Cooper, Aug. 3, 11, 1867, Reel 2, Box 10, Folder 4, TAGO; *Nashville Daily Press and Times,* Aug. 8, 1867.

39. Reports of Companies D, H, and I, 2nd Regiment, Sept. 5, 1867, Reel 1, Box 8, Folder 6, TAGO; Hopkins and Lyons, *Tennessee Votes,* 48; Captain Clapp to General Cooper, Aug. 6, 1867, Reel 2, Box 10, Folder 5, TAGO.

40. Bergeron, Ash, and Keith, *Tennesseans and Their History,* 166; Alexander, *Political Reconstruction,* 156–60; McBride, "Blacks and the Race Issue," 218–23; *Nashville Daily Press and Times,* Aug. 10, 1867. Precise election figures vary slightly from source to source; this study relies mostly on Hopkins and Lyons, *Tennessee Votes.*

41. *Knoxville Whig,* Aug. 21, 1867; *Nashville Daily Press and Times,* Aug. 5, 1867.

42. In his brief commentary on the event, historian Brooks Simpson makes no mention of the State Guard and simply credits the U.S. Army for ensuring a peaceful election. Simpson, *Let Us Have Peace,* 188.

43. Hopkins and Lyons, *Tennessee Votes,* 48; Alexander, *Political Reconstruction,* 161–62; *Nashville Daily Press and Times,* Aug. 3, 5, 1867; Hamer, *Tennessee* 2:629.

Chapter 6

1. White, Ash, and Moore, *Messages* 5:586; *Nashville Daily Press and Times,* Aug. 13, 16, 1867; Owens, "Union League of America," 171–72; *Fayetteville Observer,* Aug. 15, 1867.

2. *Nashville Daily Press and Times,* Aug. 3, 1867; *Nashville Republican Banner,* Aug. 3, 1867; *Nashville Union and Dispatch,* Aug. 3, 1867; Special Order Nos. 46, 50, and 75, Aug. 2, 4, 10, 1867, Reel 9, Vol. 33;

W. Y. Elliott to General Cooper, Aug. 5, 1867, Reel 2, Box 10, Folder 5, both in TAGO.

3. *Nashville Daily Press and Times*, Aug. 9, 1867; Special Order Nos. 70–71, Aug. 9, 1867, Reel 9, Vol. 33; Captain Adkins to General Cooper, Aug. 9, 1867, Reel 2, Box 10, Folder 4, both in TAGO; Julin Reed to Governor Brownlow, Aug. 10, 1867, Reel 1, Box 2, Folder 2, Governor Brownlow Papers.

4. Richeson and N. N. Northrup to General Cooper, Aug. 10, 1867, Reel 2, Box 11, Folder 2, TAGO.

5. Special Order Nos. 54–56 (Aug. 6, 1867), 67 (Aug. 9, 1867), and 89 (Aug. 15, 1867), Reel 9, Vol. 33, TAGO; *Nashville Daily Press and Times*, Aug. 12, 16, 1867.

6. Special Order Nos. 57 and 68, Aug. 6, 9, 1867, Reel 9, Vol. 33, TAGO; *Nashville Daily Press and Times*, Aug. 7, 1867; *Nashville Union and Dispatch*, Aug. 8, 1867; *Pulaski Citizen*, Aug. 9, 1867.

7. *Nashville Daily Press and Times*, Aug. 20, 27, 1867.

8. Captain Blackburn to General Cooper, Aug. 21, 1867, Reel 2, Box 10, Folder 4, TAGO.

9. Captain Robeson to General Cooper, Aug. 26, 1867, Reel 2, Box 11, Folder 3; Captain Robeson to Lt. L. B. Gamble, Aug. 27, 30, 1867, Reel 2, Box 11, Folder 3, TAGO.

10. Capt. E. R. Hall to Lt. L. B. Gamble, Aug. 17, 1867, Reel 2, Box 11, Folder 1; Capt. E. R. Hall to A. E. Boone, Sept. 2, 6, 1867, Reel 2, Box 10, Folder 3, both in TAGO; *Nashville Daily Press and Times*, Sept. 17, 1867; Special Order Nos. 63 and 72, Aug. 9, 1867, Reel 9, Vol. 33, TAGO.

11. Captain Grisham to General Cooper, Aug. 5, 1867, Reel 2, Box 11, Folder 1; Special Order No. 108, Aug. 28, 1867, Reel 9, Vol. 33, both in TAGO; *Nashville Daily Press and Times*, Aug. 30, 1867.

12. Simeon Bloom to Governor Brownlow, Sept. 6, 1867, and Bloom to General Cooper, Sept. 11, 1867, Reel 2, Box 10, Folder 4, TAGO.

13. *Fayetteville Observer*, Aug. 29, Sept. 26, Oct. 3, 1867.

14. *Nashville Daily Press and Times*, Aug. 30, Sept. 4, 1867; Trelease, *White Terror*, 25; Special Order No. 101, Aug. 21, 1867, Reel 9, Vol. 33, TAGO; *Pulaski Citizen*, Sept. 6, 1867.

15. *Pulaski Citizen*, Sept. 13, 20, 27, 1867; *Nashville Daily Press and Times*, Sept. 12, 13, 1867.

16. *Nashville Daily Press and Times*, Aug. 27, Sept. 13, 1867; R. A. Salisbury to General Cooper, Aug. 13, 1867, Reel 2, Box 11, Folder 3; Thomas Grundy to General Cooper, Aug. 4, 1867, Reel 2, Box 11, Folder 1, both in TAGO.

17. *Nashville Daily Press and Times* Aug. 29, 1867.

18. *Nashville Daily Press and Times,* Aug. 13, 16, 30, 1867; *Fayetteville Observer,* Aug. 29, 1867; Special Order No. 62, Aug. 9, 1867, Reel 9, Vol. 33, TAGO.

19. DeKalb County petition to General Cooper, Sept. 8, 1867, Reel 2, Box 10, Folder 4, TAGO; *Nashville Daily Press and Times,* Aug. 30, Sept. 10, 16, 1867; *Nashville Republican Banner,* Sept. 17, 1867; *Nashville Union and Dispatch,* Sept. 17, 1867; Special Order No. 115, Aug. 31, 1867, Reel 9, Vol. 33, TAGO.

20. Captain Clapp to General Cooper, Aug. 24, 1867, Reel 2, Box 10, Folder 5, TAGO.

21. Tennessee State Guard Circular, Aug. 26, 1867, Reel 9, Vol. 27, TAGO. The Freedmen's Bureau corroborated many of General Cooper's findings. In addition to numerous instances of economic proscription, it reported over 150 cases of violence by whites against blacks in Middle and West Tennessee between June 1 and October 1. Congress, *House Executive Documents, Report of the Secretary of War* (1867), 688. Captain Clingan, whose Company D had been slated for disbandment, marched his command into the town of Franklin as Cooper's circular went to press. Special Order No. 106, Aug. 24, 1867, Reel 9, Vol. 33, TAGO.

22. *Nashville Union and Dispatch,* Aug. 27, 28, 29, 31, Sept. 7, 1867.

23. *Nashville Republican Banner,* Aug. 31, 1867; *Nashville Daily Press and Times,* Sept. 5, 6, 1867; Durham, *Rebellion Revisited,* 304.

24. Special Order No. 100, Aug. 21, 1867, Reel 9, Vol. 33; Lieutenant Ellis to General Cooper, Aug. 30, 1867, Reel 2, Box 10, Folder 5; C. D. Willis to General Cooper, Sept. 2, 1867, Reel 2, Box 11, Folder 3; James R. Evans to General Cooper, Sept. 2, 1867, Reel 2, Box 10, Folder 5, all in TAGO. Evans resigned in order to attend to his duties as chancery court clerk of Claiborne County. Captain Evans to State Guard Headquarters, July 22, 1867, Reel 2, Box 10, Folder 5, TAGO.

25. Census of Tennessee, 1870 (Washington County), 230, and (Davidson County), 3/262; E. J. Brooks to Samuel Hunt, July 24, 1867, Reel 2, Box 10, Folder 4; Special Order No. 162, Oct. 4, 1867, Reel 9, Vol. 33, both in TAGO; Tennessee General Assembly, *House Journal,* 35th General Assembly, extra sess. (1868), 26; General Order No. 1, Mar. 6, 1867, Reel 8, Vol. 26; Payroll vouchers for 1867–68, Reel 4, Box 22, Folder 8, both in TAGO; Alrutheus A. Taylor, *The Negro in Tennessee, 1865–1880* (Washington, D.C.: Associated Publishers, 1941), 124; Payroll for Company H, 1st Regiment, Reel 5, Box 23, Folder 5, TAGO. Wiley Williams is listed on Mankin's Payroll Voucher No. 20.

26. *Nashville Daily Press and Times,* Aug. 21, Sept. 7, 1867; *Nashville Republican Banner,* Aug. 9, 17, 18, 20, 23, Sept. 6, 1867; *Nashville Union and Dispatch,* Aug. 17, Sept. 7, 1867; *Paris Intelligencer,* Aug. 31, 1867.

27. General Order Nos. 7, 12, and 13, Aug. 9, 21, 24, 1867, Reel 9, Vol. 27; Lt. Joseph Grace to James S. Hull, Aug. 27, Sept. 7, 30, Oct. 1, 1867, Reel 2, Box 11, Folder 1, both in TAGO; *Nashville Union and Dispatch,* Sept. 7, 8, 1867; *Nashville Daily Press and Times,* Sept. 7, 1867. Smokey Row's notoriety first emerged during the Civil War, when the city was under Federal occupation. To the chagrin of many commanding officers, thousands of soldiers visited the place and, more often than not, contracted venereal disease as a consequence. See Maslowski, *Treason Must Be Made Odious,* 129–31.

28. Furlough for Private Samuel F. Scott, July 28, 1867, Lieutenant Alexander to Samuel Scott, Dec. 9, 1867, George W. Keith to Governor Brownlow, Apr. 6, 1868, Governor Brownlow to Albert E. Boone, Apr. 8, 1868, Samuel Scott to A. E. Boone, Apr. 8, 30, 1868, A. E. Boone to Samuel Scott, May 26, 1868, Reel 4, Folder 8, Box 22; Lieutenant Parker to General Cooper, Nov. 7, 1867, Reel 2, Box 11, Folder 2, both in TAGO.

29. General Order No. 16, Sept. 3, 1867, Reel 9, Vol. 27, TAGO; *Nashville Daily Press and Times,* Sept. 4, 1867.

30. Major Robeson to Samuel Hunt and General Cooper, Sept. 6, 1867 (two letters), Reel 2, Box 11, Folder 3; Major Robeson to Capt. A. E. Boone, Sept. 5, 1978, Reel 2, Box 10, Folder 3; Major Robeson to Lt. L. B. Gamble, Sept. 9, 1867, Reel 2, Box 11, Folder 3, all in TAGO; *Nashville Daily Press and Times,* Sept. 13, 1867.

31. Special Order No. 107, Aug. 28, 1867, Reel 9, Vol. 33; Major Robeson to General Cooper, Sept. 12, 1867, Reel 2, Box 11, Folder 3; Lieutenant Cravens to Samuel Hunt, Sept. 7, 1867, Reel 2, Box 11, Folder 1, all in TAGO; *Nashville Republican Banner,* Sept. 14, 17, 1867; Williams, *Historic Madison,* 194. On August 28, Captain Kirk became ill with fever and jaundice and was placed on indefinite bed rest. Dr. W. W. Drake to General Cooper, Sept. 3, 1867, Reel 2, Box 10, Folder 4, TAGO.

32. Major Robeson to General Cooper, Sept. 12, 1867, Reel 2, Box 11, Folder 3, TAGO; *Nashville Republican Banner,* Sept. 14, 17, 1867; *Nashville Union and Dispatch,* Sept. 17, 1867; Captain Blackburn to Samuel Hunt, Sept. 19, 1867, Reel 2, Box 10, Folder 4, TAGO; Williams, *Historic Madison,* 194; *Nashville Daily Press and Times,* Sept. 18, 1867.

33. Major Robeson to General Cooper, Sept. 12, 1867, Reel 2, Box 11, Folder 3, TAGO; *Nashville Union and Dispatch,* Sept. 17, 18, 1867; *Nashville Republican Banner,* Sept. 17, 1867; Williams, *Historic Madison,* 194, 279, 530; *Nashville Daily Press and Times,* Sept. 18, 1867.

34. *Nashville Republican Banner,* Sept. 17, 1867; McBride and Robison, *Biographical Directory* 1:85, 2:446–47, 653; Tennessee General Assembly, *House Journal,* 34th General Assembly, 2nd adjourned sess. (1867), 301; Tennessee General Assembly, *Senate Journal,* 34th General Assembly, 2nd adjourned sess. (1867), 327; *Nashville Daily Press and Times,* Sept. 19, 26, 1867; *Knoxville Whig,* Sept. 25, 1867; *Nashville Union and Dispatch,* Sept. 19, 1867; Special Order No. 128, Sept. 17, 1867, Reel 9, Vol. 33, TAGO; W. P. Bond to Governor Brownlow, Oct. 1, 1867, Reel 1, Box 2, Folder 1, Governor Brownlow Papers.

35. Patton, *Unionism and Reconstruction,* 229–30; Robert M. McBride, "Northern, Military, Corrupt, and Transitory: Augustus E. Alden, Nashville's Carpetbagger Mayor," *Tennessee Historical Quarterly* 37 (1978): 63–65; McBride, "Blacks and the Race Issue," 262–65; Gary L. Kornell, "Reconstruction in Nashville, 1867–1869," *Tennessee Historical Quarterly* 30 (1971): 278; Nashville Petition to Governor Brownlow, Sept. 14, 1866, Patton Papers.

36. Patton, *Unionism and Reconstruction,* 230; Congress, *House Executive Documents, Report of the Secretary of War* (1867), 186; McBride, "Blacks and the Race Issue," 264; *Nashville Union and Dispatch,* Sept. 21, 1867; Governor Brownlow to General Cooper, Sept. 22, 1867, Reel 1, Box 1, Folder 1, Governor Brownlow Papers; Special Order Nos. 133 (Sept. 21, 1867) and 136 (Sept. 25, 1867), Reel 9, Vol. 33, TAGO; State Guard Proclamation, Sept. 23, 1867, Reel 1, Box 1, Folder 1, Governor Brownlow Papers; *Nashville Daily Press and Times,* Sept. 20, 25, 1867. Brownlow's position was supported by the Radical state supreme court, which in its decision in *Ridley v. Sherbrook* (Mar. 21, 1867) upheld the constitutionality of the Franchise Act. See Patton, *Unionism and Reconstruction,* 120–23.

37. *Nashville Republican Banner,* Sept. 24, 1867; *Nashville Union and Dispatch,* Sept. 25, 27, 1867; Kornell, "Reconstruction in Nashville," 281; Congress, *House Executive Documents, Report of the Secretary of War* (1867), 186; Graf, Haskins, and Bergeron, *Papers of Andrew Johnson* 13:99–101.

38. Congress, *House Executive Documents, Report of the Secretary of War* (1867), 184–85, 187–88; *Nashville Daily Press and Times,* Sept. 1867; Simons, *Papers of Ulysses S. Grant* 17:362.

39. *Knoxville Whig*, Sept. 25, 1867; *Nashville Union and Dispatch*, Sept. 27, 29, 1867; Governor Brownlow to General Cooper, Sept. 25, 1867, Reel 1, Box 1, Folder 1, Governor Brownlow Papers; Special Order Nos. 139 and 144–46 (Sept. 26, 1867), 147 and 149 (Sept. 27, 1867), Reel 9, Vol. 33, TAGO; Governor's Proclamation, Sept. 27, 1867, Reel 1, Box 2, Folder 11, Governor Brownlow Papers. The black militia companies were never actually reactivated, the crisis having passed before their officers could reassemble the volunteers.

40. Congress, *House Executive Documents, Report of the Secretary of War* (1867), 189–91; Sefton, *United States Army and Reconstruction*, 229–30; *Nashville Daily Press and Times*, Sept. 28, 1867; Welles, *Diary of Gideon Welles* 3:211–12.

41. Congress, *House Executive Documents, Report of the Secretary of War* (1867), 191–92; *Nashville Republican Banner*, Sept. 28, 1867; *Nashville Union and Dispatch*, Sept. 28, 1867; *Nashville Daily Press and Times*, Sept. 28, 1867; Graf, Haskins, and Bergeron, *Papers of Andrew Johnson* 13:116. Johnson shared Brown's disgust with the actions of Grant and Thomas, but the president learned of the Army's deployment too late to countermand its orders. Simpson, *Let Us Have Peace*, 201–2.

42. Congress, *House Executive Documents, Report of the Secretary of War* (1867), 193–97; *Nashville Daily Press and Times*, Sept. 28, 1867; Special Order No. 152, Sept. 28, 1867, Reel 9, Vol. 33, TAGO; Kornell, "Reconstruction in Nashville," 280; Patton, *Unionism and Reconstruction*, 231; *Nashville Republican Banner*, Sept. 29, 1867; *Nashville Union and Dispatch*, Sept. 29, 1867; Rose, "Nashville and Its Leadership Elite," 39; Governor Brownlow to General Cooper, Sept. 29, 1867, Reel 1, Box 1, Folder 1, Governor Brownlow Papers; Simons, *Papers of Ulysses S. Grant* 17:362.

43. Patton, *Unionism and Reconstruction*, 231; *Nashville Union and Dispatch*, Oct. 3, 1867; *Nashville Republican Banner*, Oct. 2, 3, 1867; Certification Statement of B. J. Sheridan, Oct. 1, 1867, Box 1, Folder 1, Samuel Arnell Papers, MS 823, Special Collections, Univ. of Tennessee, Knoxville; Governor Brownlow to General Cooper, Oct. 2, 1867, Reel 1, Box 1, Folder 1, Governor Brownlow Papers; General Cooper to Captain Blackburn, Oct. 2, 1867, Reel 9, Vol. 33, TAGO.

44. *Nashville Republican Banner*, Oct. 3, 1867; *Nashville Union and Dispatch*, Oct. 3, 1867; *Knoxville Whig*, Oct. 9, 1867; Kornell, "Reconstruction in Nashville," 279–81. With Brown's final capitulation, Mayor Alden secured the revocation of the longstanding injunction against the Metropolitan Police. By the end of October, the Alden administration enjoyed the protection of a Radical police force consisting of fifty men

under Commissioner Henry Stone. *Nashville Republican Banner,* Oct. 4, 1867; *Nashville Daily Press and Times,* Oct. 4, 1867; Henry Stone to Governor Brownlow, Oct. 31, 1867, Reel 1, Box 2, Folder 2, Governor Brownlow Papers.

45. *Nashville Republican Banner,* Oct. 2, 1867; *Nashville Daily Press and Times,* Sept. 30, Oct. 4, 1867. James Sefton points out that the Nashville election was the U.S. Army's "baptism of fire in the art of preventing election disorders in a state over which it had no civil jurisdiction." Sefton, *United States Army and Reconstruction,* 229.

46. Lt. Robert P. Wilson to General Duncan, Oct. 2, 1867, Reel 2, Box 11, Folder 3; Lt. Scott Payne to General Duncan, Oct. 2, 1867, Reel 2, Box 11, Folder 2; Lt. F. W. Foote to General Duncan, Oct. 3, 1867, Reel 2, Box 11, Folder 1; General Duncan to General Cooper, Oct. 3, 7, 1867, Reel 2, Box 10, Folder 5, all in TAGO.

47. General Duncan to Headquarters, Tennessee State Guard, Oct. 4, 1867, Reel 2, Box 11, Folder 1; General Cooper to Capt. R. L. Hall, Oct. 4, 1867, Reel 2, Box 10, Folder 5; Capt. R. L. Hall to General Duncan, Oct. 4, 1867, Reel 2, Box 11, Folder 1; General Duncan to General Cooper, Oct. 7, 1867, Reel 2, Box 10, Folder 5; James Everett to General Cooper, Oct. 13, 1867, Reel 2, Box 10, Folder 5, all in TAGO; *Nashville Union and Dispatch,* Oct. 8, 1867.

48. *Nashville Republican Banner,* Oct. 8, 1867; *Nashville Union and Dispatch,* Oct. 8, 1867; *Nashville Daily Press and Times,* Oct. 8, 1867; General Order Nos. 31 (Oct. 8, 1867) and 35 (Jan. 14, 1868), Reel 9, Vol. 27; Lieutenant Fuller to General Cooper, Nov. 11, 1867, and Company E, 1st Regiment Petition to General Cooper, Nov. 11, 1867, Reel 2, Box 11, Folder 1, both in TAGO.

49. White, Ash, and Moore, *Messages* 5:571–91; *Fayetteville Observer,* Oct. 17, 1867; Lovett, *African American History of Nashville,* 209; McBride, "Blacks and the Race Issue," 245.

50. General Order No. 32, Oct. 11, 1867, Reel 9, Vol. 27; Lt. L. B. Gamble to General Cooper, Oct. 11, 1867, Reel 2, Box 11, Folder 1, both in TAGO; *Tennessee Blue Book,* 488; *Nashville Daily Press and Times,* Oct. 8, 10, 1867; *Nashville Union and Dispatch,* Oct. 9, 1867; Special Orders Nos. 166–68, 171, and 175–76, Oct. 8–10, 1867, Reel 9, Vol. 33, TAGO. Shortly after stepping aside, Cooper accepted a nomination for the U.S. Senate, but when the Tennessee General Assembly voted on October 22, only six Radicals endorsed him. His name was withdrawn after the first ballot. Governor Brownlow won the office on the third ballot with sixty-three votes to runner-up William B. Stokes's thirty-

nine. The senate position would not actually come open, however, until 1869. White, Ash, and Moore, *Messages* 5:592–94.

51. Captain Rickman to General Cooper, Oct. 24, 1867 (two letters), and to Daniel T. Boynton, Oct. 28, 1867, Reel 2, Box 11, Folder 2; Morning Report for Company B, 1st Battalion, Tennessee State Guard, Oct. 31, 1867, Reel 4, Box 22, Folder 2, both in TAGO. In addition to the Klan, supply shortages arose to vex Captain Rickman. In a testy communication with the quartermaster, he queried, "Where is my Bacon? I must have some." At the end of October, his unit received part of an eight-thousand-pound distribution of bacon. Captain Rickman to A. E. Boone, Oct. 14, 1867, Reel 2, Box 10, Folder 4; Boone to the Adjutant General of Tennessee, Oct. 18, 1867, Reel 10, Vol. 46, both in TAGO.

52. Major Robeson to Daniel T. Boynton, Oct. 15, 1867, Reel 2, Box 11, Folder 3, TAGO; Major Robeson to Governor Brownlow, Oct. 18, 1867, Reel 1, Box 2, Folder 2, Governor Brownlow Papers; *Nashville Daily Press and Times,* Oct. 31, Nov. 8, 1867; Henry County Petition to Governor Brownlow, Nov. 20, 1867, Box 1, Folder 10, Brownlow Papers.

53. Major Robeson to General Cooper, Sept. 11, 1867, Reel 2, Box 11, Folder 3; Muster Roll for Company E, 1st Regiment (1867), Reel 4, Box 23, Folder 1; General Cooper to Major Robeson, Nov. 6, 1867, Reel 9, Vol. 27, all in TAGO.

54. Special Order Nos. 180 and 192 (Oct. 14, 30, 1867), Reel 9, Vol. 33; Isaac J. Roach and John Norman to General Cooper, Oct. 23, 1867, Reel 2, Box 11, Folder 3; Major Robeson to General Cooper, Nov. 26, 1867, Reel 2, Box 11, Folder 3, all in TAGO.

55. General Order No. 14, Aug. 27, 1867, Reel 9, Vol. 27; Muster Rolls for the Tennessee State Guard, Reels 4–5, Boxes 22–25, both in TAGO; *Nashville Republican Banner,* Sept. 17, 1867; Captain Grisham to James P. Brownlow, July 12, 1867, Reel 2, Box 11, Folder 1; Captain Clingan to Samuel Hunt, Aug. 28, 1867, and Clingan to General Cooper, Sept. 11, 1867, Reel 2, Box 10, Folder 5, both in TAGO; *Nashville Daily Press and Times,* Aug. 29, 1867.

56. Alvin Allen to Governor Brownlow, Nov. 6, 1867, Box 1, Folder 10, Brownlow Papers; *Nashville Union and Dispatch,* Nov. 26, 1867; Capt. E. R. Hall to General Cooper, Nov. 24, 1867, Reel 2, Box 11, Folder 1, TAGO.

57. Capt. E. R. Hall to General Cooper, Nov. 24, 1867, Reel 2, Box 11, Folder 1, TAGO.

58. McBride and Robison, *Biographical Directory* 2:611; Tennessee General Assembly, *Senate Journal,* 35th General Assembly, 1st sess. (1868), 47,

147–48; Tennessee General Assembly, *Senate Journal,* 35th General Assembly, 1st sess. (1868), appendix, Comptroller's Report, 100–102; Tennessee General Assembly, *House Journal,* 35th General Assembly, 1st sess. (1868), 337–38; Tennessee General Assembly, *Public Acts of Tennessee,* 35th Assembly, 1st sess. (1868), chap. 21; Special Order No. 200, Dec. 7, 1867, Reel 9, Vol. 33, TAGO. For unknown reasons, Thompson McKinley abstained from voting on Senate Bill 16.

59. Tennessee General Assembly, *Senate Journal,* 35th General Assembly, 1st sess. (1868), Appendix, Comptroller's Report, 100; Tennessee General Assembly, *Senate Journal,* 36th General Assembly, 1st sess. (1869), Appendix, Comptroller's Report, 73; Snapp Thomas to H. H. Thomas, July 22, 1867, Thornburgh and Hoskins to G. W. Blackburn, Aug. 24, 1867, M. J. Childress to H. H. Thomas, Sept. 9, 1867, Thornburgh and Hoskins to D. G. Thornburgh, Sept. 11, 1867, Reel 2, Box 10, Folder 3, TAGO; *Knoxville Whig,* Feb. 19, Mar. 4, 11, 1868; Tennessee General Assembly, *Public Acts of Tennessee,* 35th General Assembly, 1st sess. (1868), Resolution Nos. 18, 73, 97, and 102, chap. 39.

60. Tennessee General Assembly, *House Journal,* 35th General Assembly, extra sess. (1868), 25–27; Tennessee General Assembly, *Public Acts of Tennessee,* 35th General Assembly, 1st sess. (1868), Resolution No. 78; A. E. Boone to all ten Congressional Representatives and Senators from Tennessee, June 6, 1868, Reel 2, Box 9, Folder 5, TAGO; General Assembly to Governor Brownlow, Sept. 3, 1868, Patton Papers.

61. Major Robeson to General Cooper, Dec. 1, 1867, Reel 2, Box 11, Folder 3, TAGO; Arnell, "Southern Unionist," 329; Graf, Haskins, and Bergeron, *Papers of Andrew Johnson* 13:321, 446.

62. Special Order No. 201, Jan. 13, 1868, Reel 9, Vol. 33, TAGO; Trelease, *White Terror,* 32–33; Tennessee General Assembly, *Public Acts of Tennessee,* 35th General Assembly, 1st sess. (1868), chap. 33, sec. 10. On February 11, Boynton mustered out the last two companies of militia.

CHAPTER 7

1. Trelease, *White Terror,* xv–xlvii; Alexander, *Political Reconstruction,* 177.
2. Samuel Arnell to Governor Brownlow, Feb. 4, 1868, Patton Papers; Tennessee General Assembly, *Joint Military Committee Report on the Ku Klux Klan, Senate Journal,* 35th General Assembly, extra sess. (1868), 131–68 (also printed in the *House Journal,* 35th General Assembly,

185–223); House, *Sheafe v. Tillman,* 1–315; U.S. Congress, *House Executive Documents, Report of the Secretary of War,* 40th Cong., 3rd sess. (1868), 143–87; see also the reports of Freedmen's Bureau agents in Middle and West Tennessee for 1868 under the headings "Records Relating to Outrages" (Reel 34) and "Narrative Reports of Operations and Conditions" (Reels 16, 18) in Bureau of Refugees, Freedmen, and Abandoned Lands (1865–1869), Records of the Assistant Commissioner for the State of Tennessee, RG 105, NA (hereafter cited as BRFAL); McBride, "Blacks and the Race Issue," 391.

3. Robert Wiley to Governor Brownlow, Feb. 14, 1868, Box 1, Folder 11; Fayette County Petition to Governor Brownlow, Feb. 24, 1868, Box 1, Folder 11, both in Brownlow Papers; Phillips, "History of the Freedmen's Bureau," 302–3, 318; Congress, *House Executive Documents, Report of the Secretary of War* (1868), 172, 178–82; Arnell, "Southern Unionist," 338; Tennessee General Assembly, *Senate Journal,* 35th General Assembly, extra sess. (1868), 140–41.

4. Wills, *Battle from the Start,* 351; Trelease, *White Terror,* 34–35, 45; Phillips, "History of the Freedmen's Bureau," 305, 312; Congress, *House Executive Documents, Report of the Secretary of War* (1868), 166; Oliver Otis Howard, *Autobiography of Oliver Otis Howard, Major General United States Army,* 2 vols. (New York: Baker & Taylor, 1908), 2:378–79; House, *Sheafe v. Tillman,* 264–67.

5. Tennessee General Assembly, *Public Acts of Tennessee,* 35th General Assembly, 1st sess. (1868), chap. 33.

6. J.W. Tarkington to Governor Brownlow, Jan. 8, 1868, Reel 1, Box 2, Folder 3, Governor Brownlow Papers; *Nashville Daily Press and Times,* Jan. 31, Mar, 11, 1868; Tennessee General Assembly, *Public Acts of Tennessee,* 35th General Assembly, 1st sess. (1868), Resolution Nos. 103 and 107.

7. Trelease, *White Terror,* 35; Arnell, "Southern Unionist," 335–36; Rufus Dowdy to Governor Brownlow, July 9, 1868 (two letters), Reel 1, Box 2, Folder 3, Governor Brownlow Papers; Durham, *Rebellion Revisited,* 312–15; Congress, *House Executive Documents, Report of the Secretary of War* (1868), 182–85; Alexander, *Political Reconstruction,* 185–86; Bergeron, Graf, and Haskins, *Papers of Andrew Johnson* 14: 512–14; *Nashville Daily Press and Times,* Mar. 18, 1868. John Pitts, a resident of Wayne County at the time, incorrectly identifies Thurman's County Guards as "a company of Brownlow militia." The Tennessee State Guard was never stationed in Wayne County. John Pitts, *Personal and Professional Reminiscences of an Old Lawyer* (Kingsport, Tenn.: Southern Publishers, 1930), 123.

8. Tennessee General Assembly, *House Journal,* 35th General Assembly, 1st sess. (1868), 654–55; Tennessee General Assembly, *Public Acts of Tennessee,* 35th General Assembly, 1st sess. (1868), Resolution No. 189; Phillips, "History of the Freedmen's Bureau," 316; *Nashville Daily Press and Times,* Mar. 5, 1868.

9. Tennessee General Assembly, *Public Acts of Tennessee,* 35th General Assembly, 1st sess. (1868), chap. 70; *Knoxville Whig,* Mar. 11, 1868.

10. Tennessee General Assembly, *House Journal,* 35th General Assembly, 1st sess. (1868), 593–94; *Nashville Daily Press and Times,* Mar. 10–12, 1868; Congress, *House Executive Documents, Report of the Secretary of War* (1868), 13–14; White, Ash, and Moore, *Messages* 5:611–12. General Thomas may also have felt ill equipped to fight the Klan effectively. With the exception of Capt. Edwin Leib's company in Sumner County, the Federal garrison had no cavalry. General Duncan facetiously described his force in Nashville as the "wooden-leg corps." Graf, Haskins, and Bergeron, *Papers of Andrew Johnson* 14:403–4.

11. Graf, Haskins, and Bergeron, *Papers of Andrew Johnson* 14:369–70; Porter Diary, Apr. 23, May 3, June 1, 1868; Kathleen R. Zebley, "Samuel Mayes Arnell and Reconstruction in Tennessee," *Tennessee Historical Quarterly* 53 (1994): 254; White, Ash, and Moore, *Messages* 5:608–9.

12. White, Ash, and Moore, *Messages* 5:609–14.

13. *Nashville Republican Banner,* July 19, 1868; Graf, Haskins, and Bergeron, *Papers of Andrew Johnson* 14:419–20, 461–62, 484, 487; Porter Diary, July 29, 1868.

14. Tennessee General Assembly, *House Journal,* 35th General Assembly, extra sess. (1868), 19–20; John M. Lea to Governor Brownlow, July 26, 1868, Reel 1, Box 2, Folder 8, Governor Brownlow Papers; Wills, *Battle from the Start,* 348–49; White, Ash, and Moore, *Messages* 5:617–19.

15. Tennessee General Assembly, *Senate Journal,* 35th General Assembly, extra sess. (1868), 65, 90–91, 116–23; Tennessee General Assembly, *House Journal,* 35th General Assembly, extra sess. (1868), 17, 28, 68–72, 148. The three Conservatives members, all in the House, were William H. Johnson (Hardeman County), Isaac J. Roach (Carroll, Gibson, Henry, and Madison Counties), and W. P. H. Turner (Lawrence County). McBride and Robison, *Biographical Directory* 1:620–21, 2:468–69, 928–29.

16. Tennessee General Assembly, *House Journal,* 35th General Assembly, extra sess. (1868), 68–71; Tennessee General Assembly, *Public Acts of Tennessee,* 35th General Assembly, extra sess. (1868), Resolution Nos. 21 and 23.

17. Hamer, *Tennessee* 2:641; *The American Annual Cyclopedia and Register of Important Events* (New York, 1868), 722–23; Queener, "Decade of East

Tennessee Republicanism," 63; Arnell, "Southern Unionist," 341; R. R. Butler to Governor Brownlow, Aug. 11, 1868, Patton Papers; Tennessee General Assembly, *House Journal,* 35th General Assembly, extra sess. (1868), 135.

18. Tennessee General Assembly, *House Journal,* 35th General Assembly, extra sess. (1868), 145–48, 153–60; *Nashville Daily Press and Times,* Aug. 26, 1868; *Nashville Republican Banner,* Aug. 28–29, 1868.

19. Graf, Haskins, and Bergeron, *Papers of Andrew Johnson* 14:553–55; *Nashville Republican Banner,* Aug. 28–29, 1868; *Nashville Daily Press and Times,* Aug. 17, 1868; Arnell, "Southern Unionist," 339–40; Wills, *Battle from the Start,* 349–52; Stanley F. Horn, *Invisible Empire: The Story of the Ku Klux Klan, 1866–1871* (Boston: Houghton Mifflin, 1939), 411–13.

20. *Nashville Daily Press and Times,* Aug. 29, 31, Sept. 1, 3, 1868; Tennessee General Assembly, *Senate Journal,* 35th General Assembly, extra sess. (1868), 116; Tennessee General Assembly, *House Journal,* 35th General Assembly, extra sess. (1868), 172–75; Tennessee General Assembly, *Public Acts of Tennessee,* 35th General Assembly, extra sess. 1868, Resolution No. 23.

21. Samuel M. Arnell to Governor Brownlow, Sept. 1, 1868, Patton Papers; Tennessee General Assembly, *Senate Journal,* 35th General Assembly, extra sess. 1868, 131–68; Tennessee General Assembly, *House Journal,* 35th General Assembly, extra sess. (1868), 185–223.

22. Tennessee General Assembly, *Senate Journal,* 35th General Assembly, extra sess. 1868, 184–87; Tennessee General Assembly, *House Journal,* 35th General Assembly, extra sess. (1868), 252–55; Tennessee General Assembly, *Public Acts of Tennessee,* 35th General Assembly, extra sess. (1868), chap. 2. A legal definition of "infamy" is provided in *Tennessee Code Annotated* (Charlottesville, VA 1997), 7A:300–304.

23. Tennessee General Assembly, *Senate Journal,* 35th General Assembly, extra sess. 1868, 195–203; Tennessee General Assembly, *House Journal,* 35th General Assembly, extra sess. (1868), 258–59; Tennessee General Assembly, *Public Acts of Tennessee,* 35th General Assembly, extra sess. (1868), chap. 3; *Nashville Republican Banner,* Sept. 11, 1868.

24. Tennessee General Assembly, *House Journal,* 35th General Assembly, extra sess. (1868), 153–54; Tennessee General Assembly, *Senate Journal,* extra sess. (1868), 186–87, 198; Samuel M. Arnell to Governor Brownlow, Sept. 1, 1868, Patton Papers. Thomas Alexander mentions the Radical division over the force bills, but he provides no detailed analysis of either the debates or the roll-call vote. *Political Reconstruction,* 201.

25. *Nashville Daily Press and Times,* Sept. 17, 1868.

26. Graf, Haskins, and Bergeron, *Papers of Andrew Johnson* 15:37–38, 44–51, 69; *Nashville Daily Press and Times,* Sept. 17, 1868; Simpson, *Let Us Have Peace,* 250.

27. Congress, *House Executive Documents, Report of the Secretary of War* (1868), xxx–xxxi; Sefton, *United States Army and Reconstruction,* 262; Porter Diary, Oct. 3, 5, 7, 9, 1868.

28. Trelease, *White Terror,* 45–46, 175; Hamer, *Tennessee* 2:642–43; Owens, "Union League of America," 201; Porter Diary, Oct. 3, 1868. Following the election in 1867, the Tennessee General Assembly decided to hold the state's congressional races in even-numbered years in conjunction with national elections. Bergeron, Ash, and Keith, *Tennesseans and Their History,* 174.

29. Sefton, *United States Army and Reconstruction,* 224; Phillips, "History of the Freedmen's Bureau," 314, 318; House, *Sheafe v. Tillman,* 61, 248; Congress, *House Executive Documents, Report of the Secretary of War* (1868), 152–55; Alexander, *Political Reconstruction,* 194–95; Coulter, *Brownlow,* 366; Trelease, *White Terror,* 175–76; *Nashville Daily Press and Times,* Nov. 10–13, 1868; *Autobiography of Oliver Otis Howard* 2:381.

30. Hopkins and Lyons, *Tennessee Votes,* 48–49; Alexander, *Political Reconstruction,* 193; Trelease, *White Terror,* 177.

31. House, *Sheafe v. Tillman,* 145–49, 237–38; Hopkins and Lyons, *Tennessee Votes,* 49; Trelease, *White Terror,* 176; *Nashville Daily Press and Times,* Nov. 13, 1868.

32. *Nashville Daily Press and Times,* Nov. 7, 10, 12, 1868; Frederick M. Culp and Mrs. Robert E. Ross, *Gibson County Past and Present: The First General History of One of West Tennessee's Pivotal Counties* (Trenton, Tenn.: Gibson County Historical Commission, 1961), 43; Hopkins and Lyons, *Tennessee Votes,* 49.

33. House, *Sheafe v. Tillman,* 193–95; Coulter, *Brownlow,* 66–67. William B. Stokes, who easily won his third district with the aid of the militia in 1867, won again in 1868, but with twenty-one hundred fewer votes. Darrah, "Political Career of W. B. Stokes," 282.

34. White, Ash, and Moore, *Messages* 5:624–25, 627–28, 633.

CHAPTER 8

1. White, Ash, and Moore, *Messages* 5:652–53.
2. *Nashville Daily Press and Times,* Nov. 13, 1868, Jan. 10, 12, 14, 15, 18, 19, 27, 1869; *Knoxville Whig,* Jan. 20, Feb. 3, 1869; Trelease, *White Terror,* 177–78; Horn, *Invisible Empire,* 80.
3. Trelease, *White Terror,* 149–74; Richard N. Current, *Those Terrible Carpetbaggers: A Reinterpretation* (New York: Oxford Univ. Press, 1988), 137–42; Thomas A. DeBlack, "A Harnessed Revolution: Reconstruction in Arkansas," in *Arkansas: A Narrative History,* by Jeannie M Whayne, Thomas A. DeBlack, George Sabo III, and Morris S. Arnold (Fayetteville: Univ. of Arkansas Press, 2002), 219–27.
4. Tennessee General Assembly, *Senate Journal,* 35th General Assembly, adjourned sess. (1869), 72, 82, 101, 109, 135, 171; Tennessee General Assembly, *House Journal,* 35th General Assembly, adjourned sess. (1869), 168, 177, 236–41; *Nashville Daily Press and Times,* Jan. 15, 16, 1869; Tennessee General Assembly, *Public Acts of Tennessee,* 35th General Assembly, 2nd sess. (1869), chap. 13; *Nashville Republican Banner,* Jan. 17, 1869; *Nashville Union and American,* Jan. 19, 23, 24, 1869. In 1868, the anti-Radical *Union and Dispatch* was renamed the *Union and American.*
5. *Nashville Republican Banner,* Jan. 17, 1869; White, Ash, and Moore, *Messages* 5:650.
6. Patton, *Unionism and Reconstruction,* 198–99; Alexander, *Political Reconstruction,* 188; *Knoxville Whig,* Oct. 7, 1868; Daniel T. Boynton to John N. Ellis, J. W. Bowman, Joseph Moore, and D. F. Smith, Jan. 18, 1869, Reel 2, Box 3, Folder 1, Brownlow Papers; *Nashville Republican Banner,* Jan. 22, 28, Feb. 5, 1869; Census of Tennessee, 1870 (Robertson County), 74; Muster Roll for Company C, 1st Regiment, Tennessee State Guard, Reel 8, Vol. 12; State Guard Officer Roster (1869), Reel 13, Vol. 85, both in TAGO. During the Civil War, Winters served in the First Michigan Engineers. Hewett, *Roster of Union Soldiers* 17:450.
7. General Order No. 1, Jan. 25, 1869, Reel 9, Vol. 27; Special Order No. 2, Jan. 26, 1869, Reel 9, Vol. 33, both in TAGO; Census of Tennessee, 1870 (Washington County), 232; Reel 1, CSR Index.
8. *Nashville Daily Press and Times,* Jan. 22, 25, 1869; *Nashville Republican Banner,* Jan. 20, 21, 22, 1869.
9. Tipton County Petition to Governor Brownlow, Jan. 26, 1869, Reel 1, Box 2, Folder 4, Brownlow Papers; *Nashville Daily Press and Times,* Jan. 26, 1869; *Nashville Republican Banner,* Jan. 24, 26, 28, 29, 31,

Feb. 4, 6, 1869; *Nashville Union and American,* Jan. 30, 31, Feb. 6, 1869; *Fayetteville Observer,* Feb. 4, 28, 1869.

10. *Nashville Union and American,* Jan. 31, 1869; *Nashville Republican Banner,* Jan. 28, 1869; *Nashville Daily Press and Times,* Jan. 26, 1869; *Memphis Appeal,* Jan. 25, 1869.

11. *Nashville Republican Banner,* Jan. 24, 31, Feb. 4, 1869; House, *Sheafe v. Tillman,* 252–53; *Fayetteville Observer,* Feb. 4, 1869; Susan Lawrence Davis, *Authentic History: Ku Klux Klan, 1865–1877* (New York: American Library Service, 1924), 125–28; Trelease, *White Terror,* 179–80; Wills, *Battle from the Start,* 350, 357–59.

12. General Order No. 2, Feb. 12, 1869, Reel 9, Vol. 27, TAGO; *Nashville Republican Banner,* Jan. 31, 1869.

13. State Guard Officer Roster (1869), Reel 13, Vol. 85; Special Order Nos. 3 (Jan. 28, 1869) and 6 (Feb. 2, 1869), Reel 9, Vol. 33, both in TAGO; *Nashville Republican Banner,* Jan. 31, Feb. 14, 1869; *Nashville Union and American,* Feb. 11, 1869; Reels 15, 16, CSR Index; Hewett, *Roster of Union Soldiers* 20:575–76, 590; *Report of the Adjutant General,* 199, 230, 418, 435, 439; Census of Tennessee, 1870 (Meigs County), 395, and (DeKalb County), 128. Blackburn himself might also have offered his services to the 1869 State Guard, but at the time he appears to have been earning a lucrative living as a special bounty hunter for the Brownlow administration. Manson M. Brien to Governor Brownlow, Oct. 18, 1868, Patton Papers.

14. Muster Roll for Company B, 1st Regiment, Tennessee State Guard, Reel 8, Vol. 14; State Guard Officer Roster (1869), Reel 13, Vol. 85, both in TAGO; Census of Tennessee, 1870 (Bradley County), 314, 323; Reel 9, CSR Index; Hewett, *Roster of Union Soldiers* 20:503; *Report of the Adjutant General,* 401; *Nashville Union and American,* Feb. 17, 1869.

15. State Guard Officer Roster (1869), Reel 13, Vol. 85, TAGO; Census of Tennessee, 1870 (Sevier County), 426; Reel 15, CSR Index; Hewett, *Roster of Union Soldiers* 20:572; *Report of the Adjutant General,* 115; *Nashville Union and American,* Apr. 22, 1869.

16. Muster Roll for Company F, 2nd Regiment, Tennessee State Guard, Reel 8, Vol. 15; State Guard Officer Roster (1869), Reel 13, Vol. 85, both in TAGO; Census of Tennessee, 1870 (Greene County), 336; Reels 3, 4, CSR Index; Hewett, *Roster of Union Soldiers* 20:431, 435; *Report of the Adjutant General,* 630; Phillip Shaw Paludan, *Victims: A True Story of the Civil War* (Knoxville: Univ. of Tennessee Press, 1981), 26–27, 84–98.

17. State Guard Officer Roster (1869), Reel, Vol. 85; Morning Report for Company G, 1st Regiment, Apr. 21, 1869, Reel 8, Vol. 17, both in

TAGO; Reels 13, 14, 15, CSR Index; Hewett, *Roster of Union Soldiers* 20:546, 560, 573; *Report of the Adjutant General,* 80, 417, 558, 633.

18. *Knoxville Whig,* Feb. 10, 1869; Robert L. Hall to Capt. L. B. Gamble, Feb. 6, 1869, Reel 2, Box 9, Folder 5; State Guard Officer Roster (1869), Reel 13, Vol. 85; Morning Report for Company I, 1st Regiment, Feb. 18, 1869, Reel 8, Vol. 19; Morning Report for Company E, 1st Regiment, Apr. 21, 1869, Reel 8, Vol. 17, all in TAGO; *Nashville Republican Banner,* Jan. 29, Feb. 16, 1869; Reels, 3, 6, 10, 16, CSR Index; Hewett, *Roster of Union Soldiers* 20:423, 464, 471, 505, 582; *Report of the Adjutant General,* 33, 288, 314; Census of Tennessee, 1870 (Sevier County), 413; General Order No. 3, Feb. 22, 1869, Reel 9, Vol. 27, TAGO.

19. Muster Roll for Company D, 1st Regiment, Tennessee State Guard, Reel 8, Vol. 13; State Guard Officer Roster (1869), Reel 13, Vol. 85, both in TAGO; Census of Tennessee, 1870 (Union County), 241, 245, 282; D. T. Boynton to Daniel F. Smith, Jan. 18, 1869, Reel 2, Box 3, Folder 1, Governor Brownlow Papers; *OR,* ser. 2, 1:863, 870, 881; Jacob Sharp to Governor Brownlow, Apr. 27, 1867, Reel 1, Box 2, Folder 2, Governor Brownlow Papers; Reels 2, 14, CSR Index; Hewett, *Roster of Union Soldiers* 20:414, 554, 559; *Report of the Adjutant General,* 23.

20. State Guard Officer Roster (1869), Reel 13, Vol. 85, TAGO; *Nashville Union and American,* Feb. 18, 1869; Reel 5, CSR Index; Hewett, *Roster of Union Soldiers* 20:453; *Report of the Adjutant General,* 488; Census of Tennessee, 1870 (Jefferson County), 303, and (Davidson County), 3–293; *Knoxville Whig,* Apr. 24, 1867; Graf, Haskins, and Bergeron, *Papers of Andrew Johnson* 15:399–400.

21. Morning Report for Company A, 1st Regiment, June 25, 1869, Reel 8, Vol. 17; State Guard Officer Roster, Reel 13, Vol. 85, both in TAGO; Inez Burns, *History of Blount County, Tennessee: From War Trail to Landing Strip, 1795–1955* (Nashville: Benson, 1957), 319; Reel 3, CSR Index; Hewett, *Roster of Union Soldiers* 16:337, 20:431; *Report of the Adjutant General,* 357; *Goodspeed's History of Tennessee, Containing Historical and Biographical Sketches of Thirty East Tennessee Counties* (Nashville, 1972), 1089; S. A. Cowan to Ben Cunningham, Mar. 2, 1867, Reel 1, Box 2, Folder 1, Governor Brownlow Papers; Census of Tennessee, 1870 (Blount County), 127, 161; Benjamin H. Severance, "Loyalty's Political Vanguard: The Union League of Maryville, Tennessee, 1867–1869," *Journal of East Tennessee History* 71 (1999): 25–46. On April 27, 1865, the steamboat *Sultana,* carrying liberated Union prisoners of war, exploded on the Mississippi River, killing hundreds on board. See James M. McPherson, *Battle Cry of Freedom: The Civil War Era* (New York: Oxford Univ. Press, 1988), 853.

22. *Nashville Daily Press and Times,* Feb. 16, 1869; State Guard Officer Roster (1869), Reel 13, Vol. 85, TAGO; McBride and Robison, *Biographical Directory* 2:375–76; Census of Tennessee, 1870 (Sevier County), 353, 378; Reels 2, 6, CSR Index; Hewett, *Roster of Union Soldiers* 20:406, 466, 468; *Report of the Adjutant General,* 602, 667.

23. *Nashville Union and American,* Feb. 12, 1869; State Guard Officer Roster, Reel 13, Vol. 85, TAGO; Census of Tennessee, 1870 (Carter County), 60, 73; Reels 7, 13, 16, CSR Index; Hewett, *Roster of Union Soldiers* 20:473, 549, 585; *Report of the Adjutant General,* 515, 558, 624; *OR,* ser. 1, 39 (1): 489–92; Samuel W. Scott and Samuel P. Angel, *History of the Thirteenth Regiment, Tennessee Volunteer Cavalry, U.S.A.* (Philadelphia: P. W. Ziegler, 1903), 167–70, 451; Temple, *East Tennessee and the Civil War,* 572.

24. *Knoxville Whig,* Feb. 10, 1869; *Nashville Daily Press and Times,* Jan. 27, 1869; *Nashville Union and American,* Feb. 11, 1869; Morning Reports for Companies F and K, 1st Regiment, Apr. 21, 1869, Reel 8, Vol. 17; State Guard Officer Roster (1869), Reel 13, Vol. 85, both in TAGO; Reels 12, 13, 16, CSR Index; Hewett, *Roster of Union Soldiers* 20:539, 544, 588; *Report of the Adjutant General,* 33, 38, 280; *OR,* ser. 1, 45 (1): 428–29. Captain Gurney apparently recruited men from McMinn, as well as Roane and Anderson counties, angering the officers of Roach's command. J. S. Riggs to General Cooper, Feb. 3, 1869, Reel 2, Box 9, Folder 5, both in TAGO.

25. *Nashville Republican Banner,* Feb. 20, 1869; State Guard Officer Roster (1869), Reel 13, Vol. 85; J. Murray to Capt. L. B. Gamble, Feb. 18, 1869, Reel 2, Box 9, Folder 5, both in TAGO. A man named McWhiney informed State Guard headquarters that he had organized a full company from McMinn County, but General Cooper never granted him a commission. McWhiney to General Cooper, Feb. 3, 1869, Reel 2, Box 9, Folder 5, TAGO.

26. Special Order Nos. 7, 8, and 10, Feb. 5, 6, 10, 1869, Reel 9, Vol. 33, TAGO; *Nashville Union and American,* Feb. 4, 16, 1869; General Order No. 3, Feb. 17, 1869, Reel 9, Vol. 27, TAGO. The incidents that prompted Cooper to lock down the militia encampment included a militiaman's refusal to pay for breakfast at a black-owned restaurant and the killing of a Federal soldier by a militiaman during a brawl. *Nashville Republican Banner,* Feb. 7, 11, 12, 1869.

27. Special Order Nos. 17 and 22, Feb. 20, 25, 1869, Reel 9, Vol. 33, TAGO; *Nashville Daily Press and Times,* Feb. 18, 1869.

28. General Order Nos. 4, 6, and 7, Feb. 23, Mar. 1, 2, 1869, Reel 9, Vol. 27; Major Bayless to Lieutenant Colonel Gamble, Mar. 15, 1869, Reel 9, Vol. 28, both in TAGO; *Nashville Republican Banner,* Feb. 4, 1869, Major Bayless to General Cooper, Mar. 13, 1869, Reel 2, Box 10, Folder 4, TAGO.

29. Tennessee General Assembly, *Senate Journal,* 35th General Assembly, adjourned sess. (1869), 226, 258; Tennessee General Assembly, *House Journal,* 35th General Assembly, adjourned sess. (1869), 371–72; *Nashville Union and American,* Feb. 9, 20, 1869; Graf, Haskins, and Bergeron, *Papers of Andrew Johnson* 15:421, 436.

30. *Knoxville Whig,* Feb. 20, 1869; *The American Annual Cyclopedia and Register of Important Events* (New York, 1869), 662; Trelease, *White Terror,* 470; *Nashville Union and American,* Feb. 23, 1869; *Nashville Republican Banner,* Feb. 21, 23, 1869.

31. Alexander, *Political Reconstruction,* 196–97; Trelease, *White Terror,* 178; *Nashville Republican Banner,* Feb. 4, 1869; Tennessee General Assembly, *House Journal,* 35th General Assembly, adjourned sess. (1869), 470. Stanley Horn offers a lively account of Barmore's ill-fated exploits in *Invisible Empire,* 108–12.

32. General Order No. 4, Feb. 23, 1869, Reel 9, Vol. 27; Post Order Nos. 1–2, Feb. 25, 26, 1869, Reel 9, Vol. 28, both in TAGO; *Nashville Republican Banner,* Feb. 24, 1869; Porter Diary, Feb. 28, 1869.

33. House, *Sheafe v. Tillman,* 242–43; *Nashville Daily Press and Times,* Apr. 1, 1869; Trelease, *White Terror,* 182; Horn, *Invisible Empire,* 81; *Nashville Republican Banner,* Feb. 25, 1869.

34. *Nashville Union and American,* Feb. 27, 1869; T. H. Reeves to James Thompson, Feb. 28, 1869, Reel 18, BRFAL.

35. Hamer, *Tennessee* 2:645–46; White, Ash, and Moore, *Messages* 6:3–5; *Nashville Union and American,* Feb. 23, Mar. 4, 1869; General Order No. 5, Feb. 27, 1869, Reel 9, Vol. 27, TAGO; *Nashville Republican Banner,* Feb. 28, 1869; Post Order No. 4, Mar. 1, 1869, Reel 9, Vol. 28, TAGO. Curiously, Senter made no specific mention of the militia deployment in his inaugural address.

36. Tennessee General Assembly, *Senate Journal,* 35th General Assembly, adjourned sess. (1869), 317; A. Cox to Governor Senter, Feb. 25, 1869, Box 1, Folder 2; Giles County Petition to Governor Senter, Feb. 26, 1869, Box 1, Folder 6; Lawrence County Petition to Governor Senter, Feb. 26, 1869, Box 1, Folder 3, all in DeWitt C. Senter, Papers of the Governors, Tennessee State Library and Archives, Nashville (hereafter cited as Governor Senter Papers); *Nashville Republican Banner,* Mar. 6,

1869; *Nashville Union and American,* Apr. 28, 1869. William J. Smith, chairman of the Senate military committee, appears to have been absent when the resolution to disband the militia was reintroduced.

37. *Nashville Republican Banner,* Feb. 27, Mar. 6, 9, 1869; *Knoxville Whig,* Mar. 24, 1869.

38. General Order No. 7, Mar. 1, 1869, Reel 9, Vol. 27; Special Order Nos. 29–30, Mar. 5, 1869, Reel 9, Vol. 33, both in TAGO; *Nashville Union and American,* Mar. 7, 1869; *Nashville Republican Banner,* Mar. 4, 11, 1869; Captain French to Captain Yates, Mar. 5, 1869, Reel 9, Vol. 32; C. Beaty to Governor Senter, Mar. 24, 1869, Reel 2, Box 11, Folder 4, both in TAGO; Robert L. Eldridge and Mary Eldridge, *Bicentennial Echoes of the History of Overton County, Tennessee* (Livingston, Tenn.: Enterprise Printing, 1976), 67; *Nashville Daily Press and Times,* Mar. 16, 1869. In addition to hunting down the Klan, militiamen may have also helped the U.S. Army destroy some illicit distilleries in Overton County. See *Nashville Press and Times,* Mar. 31, 1869.

39. J. Womack to Governor Senter, late Mar. 1869, Box 1, Folder 6, Governor Senter Papers; Special Order No. 52, Mar. 24, 1869, Reel 9, Vol. 33, TAGO.

40. *Nashville Daily Press and Times,* Mar. 24, 25, Apr. 9, 1869; *Nashville Republican Banner,* Mar. 25, 1869. On March 20, General Cooper ordered Sheriff Beaty to disband his unit and return to Fentress County. Special Order No. 51, Reel 9, Vol. 33, TAGO.

41. General Order No. 6, Mar. 2, 1869, Reel 9, Vol. 27; Special Order Nos. 23 (Feb. 28, 1869) and 26 (Mar. 2, 1869), Reel 9, Vol. 33, both in TAGO; *Memphis Appeal,* Mar. 1, 1869; W. H. Stilwell to John Eaton, Jan. 28, 1869, Box 1, Folder 9, John Eaton Papers, Special Collections, Univ. of Tennessee, Knoxville (hereafter cited as Eaton Papers); J. C. Reaves to G. Underwood, Feb. 27, 1869, Reel 2, Box 11, Folder 4, TAGO.

42. *Nashville Daily Press and Times,* Mar. 19, 20, 1869; *Nashville Union and American,* Mar. 16, 1869; *Nashville Republican Banner,* Mar. 23, 1869.

43. *Nashville Daily Press and Times,* Mar. 23, 26, 30, 1869; *Nashville Republican Banner,* Mar. 27, 1869; *Nashville Union and American,* Mar. 23, 1869. The *Memphis Avalanche* (as reported in the *Daily Press and Times,* Mar. 26, 1869) falsely stated that the townspeople of Woodville killed fifteen militiamen during Clingan's occupation.

44. *Nashville Daily Press and Times,* Mar. 29, 30, Apr. 1, 1869; *Nashville Republican Banner,* Mar. 27, 1869.

45. *Nashville Republican Banner,* Apr. 7, 13, 15, 30, 1869; *Nashville Daily Press and Times,* Apr. 14, 1869; Culp and Ross, *Gibson County,* 43. Culp and Ross incorrectly state that Richardson was executed by hanging.

46. *Nashville Republican Banner,* Apr. 27, 30, May 4, 1869; Culp and Ross, *Gibson County,* 43. Contending that the criticism of Clingan was overblown, a number of residents from the Humboldt military district commended the conduct and behavior of the major and his officers. M. G. Senter to Governor Senter, Apr. 28, 1869, Box 1, Folder 6, Governor Senter Papers; Haywood Petition to Governor Senter, May 4, 1869, Reel 2, Box 11, Folder 4, TAGO.
47. *Nashville Union and American,* Mar. 2, 3, 1869; *Nashville Republican Banner,* Mar. 2, 3, 1869; Porter Diary, Mar. 3, 1869.
48. *Nashville Union and American,* Mar. 4, 9, 1869; Giles County Petitions to Governor Senter, Mar. 6, 7, 8, 1869, Box 3, Folders 2, 6, Governor Senter Papers; *Nashville Republican Banner,* Mar. 9, 11, 1869.
49. Post Order No. 3, Feb. 26, 1869, Reel 9, Vol. 28, TAGO; *Pulaski Citizen,* Mar. 19, 26, Apr. 23, 1869; *Nashville Union and American,* Mar. 19, 21, 1869; Court Martial Proceedings, 1st Regiment, Tennessee State Guard, Mar. 1, 3, 4, 19, 20, 27, 1869, Reel 9, Vol. 28, TAGO; *Nashville Republican Banner,* Mar. 19, 1869. Capt. James P. Edmondson investigated a robbery allegedly perpetrated by some of his men, but he found that local whites in "soldier's garb" committed the crime. Pulaski residents appear to have accepted Edmondson's findings. See *Republican Banner,* Mar. 20, 1869.
50. *Nashville Republican Banner,* Mar. 20, 1869; *Pulaski Citizen,* Mar. 26, 1869; *Columbia Herald,* Mar. 12, 1869; *Nashville Union and American,* Apr. 3, 1869.
51. *Nashville Daily Press and Times,* Mar. 17, 20, 23, 24, Apr. 13, 1869; *Nashville Republican Banner,* Mar. 20, 25, Apr. 1, June 1, 1869; *Nashville Union and American,* Mar. 20, Apr. 10, 1869; *Pulaski Citizen,* Mar. 26, Apr. 2, June 4, 1869; Hugh D. Barker to Tennessee Adjutant General, Apr. 9, 1869, Reel 10, Vol. 46; State Guard Officer Roster (1869), Reel 13, Vol. 84; Medical Supply Inventory Sheets, Reel 13, Vol. 83; Sanitation Directive, Apr. 27, 1869, Reel 9, Vol. 28, all in TAGO. Sickness in 1867 appears to have been a minor problem for the State Guard, probably because the units then were deployed in smaller, more mobile detachments as opposed to the larger, permanent encampments of 1869.
52. *Nashville Daily Press and Times,* Apr. 3, May 5, 1869; *Nashville Union and American,* Mar. 10, 27, 1869. The observations presented here corroborate the general findings of historian Allen Trelease. In a chapter aptly titled "Abortive Martial Law," Trelease describes the militia campaign of 1869 as an anticlimax. See Trelease, *White Terror,* 175, 182.
53. General Order No. 9, Mar. 26, 1869, Reel 9, Vol. 27; Special Order Nos. 55, 57, 58, and 68, Mar. 26, 29, Apr. 12, 1869, Reel 9, Vol. 33,

TAGO; *Nashville Daily Press and Times,* Mar. 31, Apr. 3, 6, 1869; *Nashville Republican Banner,* Apr. 1, 3, 7, 9, 1869; Regimental Order No. 7, Apr. 11, 1869, Reel 9, Vol. 28, TAGO.

54. Special Order Nos. 70, 74, and 75, Apr. 13, 16, 17, 1869, Reel 9, Vol. 28; General Order Nos. 11–13, Apr. 24, 30, 1869, Reel 9, Vol. 27, both in TAGO; *Nashville Republican Banner,* Apr. 15, 1869.

55. *Nashville Republican Banner,* Apr. 13, 1869; *Nashville Daily Press and Times,* Apr. 14, 1869; *Nashville Union and American,* Apr. 13, 1869. Somewhat overshadowed by Hathaway's misdemeanor was an embarrassing incident involving Lt. D. F. Smith of the militia. "Under the influence of John Barleycorn," Smith reportedly roamed the streets of Nashville on the night of April 14, randomly firing pistol shots into the air or at passersby. He was arrested and fined fifty-five dollars. *Daily Press and Times,* Apr. 16, 1869.

56. *Nashville Daily Press and Times,* Apr. 23, 26, 1869; *Nashville Republican Banner,* Apr. 25, 1869; *Pulaski Citizen,* Apr. 23, 30, 1869.

57. *Columbia Herald,* Mar. 12, 1869; *Nashville Republican Banner,* Apr. 9, 16, 1869; *Nashville Daily Press and Times,* Apr. 12, 1869; Giles County Petition to Governor Senter, Apr. 12, 1869, Box 1, Folder 2, Governor Senter Papers.

58. *Nashville Daily Press and Times,* May 6, 1869; A. Cullom to I. D. Louis, June 1, 1869, Box 3, Folder 2, Governor Senter Papers.

59. *Pulaski Citizen,* May 7, 14, 1869.

60. Major Clingan to Governor Senter, May 15, 1869, Box 1, Folder 2, Governor Senter Papers; *Nashville Union and American,* Apr. 25, 1869; *Nashville Daily Press and Times,* Apr. 26, 1869; W. H. Stilwell to John Eaton, Apr. 26, May 10, 1869, Box 2, Folders 1, 2, Eaton Papers; Haywood County Petition to Governor Senter, May 4, 1869, Reel 2, Box 11, Folder 4, TAGO.

61. *Pulaski Citizen,* May 7, 1869; Major Clingan to Governor Senter, May 15, 1869, Box 1, Folder 2, Governor Senter Papers; W. H. Stilwell to John Eaton, May 17, 1869, Box 2, Folder 2, Eaton Papers.

62. O. K. Reeves to Governor Senter, Apr. 29, 1869, Box 1, Folder 5; J. B. to Governor Senter, May 18, 1869, Box 1, Folder 2; Major Clingan to Governor Senter, May 15, 1869, Box 1, Folder 2, all in Governor Senter Papers.

63. General Order Nos. 14–17 and 22–23, May 6–9, 14, 1869, Reel 9, Vol. 27; Special Order Nos. 97, 101, and 104, May 7, 9, 17, 1869, Reel 9, Vol. 33; General Order Nos. 1 and 2, May 17, 18, 1869, Reel 8, Vol. 26, all in TAGO; *Nashville Daily Press and Times,* Apr. 24, May 5, 6, 12, 1869. On his return to East Tennessee, Martin L. Helton, a for-

mer militia sergeant, discovered that Hawkins County was being terrorized by a band of Rebels. In addition to harassing blacks and discharged
militiamen, these Rebels beat a Unionist preacher and drove him out of
the county. Helton requested permission from the governor to form a
special company of State Guard to punish the Rebel vigilantes, but he
never received a commission. See Martin L. Helton to Governor Senter,
June 5, 1869, Box 1, Folder 3, Governor Senter Papers.

64. Major Bayless to Governor Senter, May 14, 1869, Box 1, Folder 2,
Governor Senter Papers; *Nashville Daily Press and Times,* Apr. 22, 24,
1869; G. W. Blackburn to Governor Senter, Apr. 23, June 29, 1869, Box
1, Folder 2, Governor Senter Papers; *Nashville Republican Banner,* May
4, 5, 1869; Tennessee General Assembly, *Senate Journal,* 36th General
Assembly, 1st sess. (1869), Appendix, Comptroller's Report, 76–77.

65. *Nashville Union and American,* Jan. 23, Mar. 24, Apr. 7, 8, 1869;
Memphis Appeal, Jan. 19, 26, 1869; *Nashville Republican Banner,* Jan. 30,
Feb. 20, 28, Mar. 24, May 1, 1869; *Nashville Daily Press and Times,*
Apr. 13, 1869; Executive Order, June 11, 1868, Reel 1, Box 1, Folder 1,
Governor Brownlow Papers; *E. D. Wright v. Claiborne Beaty,* May 17,
1869, Houk Papers. In 1874, Louisiana Republicans also tried in vain to
make the citizens of violence-ridden regions pay for law enforcement.
See Joe Gray Taylor, *Louisiana Reconstructed, 1863–1877* (Baton Rouge:
Louisiana State Univ. Press, 1974), 259.

66. White, Ash, and Moore, *Messages* 6:8–16; Hamer, *Tennessee* 2:646–49.
Cooper was present at the convention and considered it a farce. Urging
the delegates to "drink less bad whiskey," the militia general left in disgust after the first day. White, Ash, and Moore, *Messages* 6:11.

67. White, Ash, and Moore, *Messages* 5:553; Coulter, *Brownlow,* 332;
Nashville Union and American, Mar. 2, 10, Apr. 6, 1869; *Nashville Daily
Press and Times,* Mar. 11, 1869; *Knoxville Whig,* Mar. 17, 1869; Cooper,
Survivor of Two Wars, 18; *Pulaski Citizen,* June 4, 1869. During the
1869 deployment, General Cooper received $1,360 for his four months
of service. State Guard Officer Payroll, Reel 13, Vol. 84, TAGO.

68. White, Ash, and Moore, *Messages* 5:595–97; Hamer, *Tennessee* 2:647;
Captain Hammer to Governor Senter, May 22, 1869, Box 8, Folder 10,
Governor Senter Papers.

69. Peter H. Argersinger, "The Conservative as Radical: A Reconstruction
Dilemma," *Tennessee Historical Quarterly* 34 (1975), 183–85; *Nashville
Republican Banner,* May 29, 30, June 4, 1869; W. A. Peffer to Governor
Senter, May 31, 1869, Box 1, Folder 5, Governor Senter Papers;
Clarksville Weekly, June 5, 1869; *Nashville Union and American,* May 29,
1869.

70. Special Order No. 112, May 28, 1869, Reel 9, Vol. 33, TAGO; W. A. Peffer to Governor Senter, May 31, 1869, Box 1, Folder 5, Governor Senter Papers; *Clarksville Weekly,* June 5, 1869; W. S. Cheatham to Governor Senter, June 6, 1869, Box 1, Folder 2, Governor Senter Papers.

71. Alexander, *Political Reconstruction,* 214–18; Bergeron, Ash, and Keith, *Tennesseans and Their History,* 177–78; White, Ash, and Moore, *Messages* 6:25–26; Frank Hyberger to selected Commissioners of Registration, May–July 1869, Reel 2, Box 3, Folder 1, Governor Brownlow Papers; General Order Nos. 18 and 19, June 18, 21, 1869, Reel 9, Vol. 27, TAGO; Giles County Petitions to Governor Senter, June 16, 17, 1869, Box 1, Folders 2, 3, Governor Senter Papers.

72. Major Bayless to Captain Edmondson, June 23, 1869 and Regimental Order Nos. 2–5, June 24, 29, July 6, 14, 1869, Reel 9, Vol. 28, TAGO; Court of Inquiry, Captain Hammer presiding, July 7, 1869, Box 3, Folder 2, Governor Senter Papers.

73. Court of Inquiry; Captain Edmondson to Frank Hyberger, July 7, 1869, Box 3, Folder 2, Governor Senter Papers; *Nashville Daily Press and Times,* July 15, 1869; General Order Nos. 22 and 23, July 10, 12, 1869, Reel 9, Vol. 27, TAGO.

74. *Nashville Daily Press and Times,* July 13, Aug. 19, 1869; *Jonesboro Union Flag,* July 16, 1869; H. Pomeroy to John Eaton, June 9, 1869, Box 5, Folder 2, Eaton Papers; *Knoxville Whig,* June 2, 9, 1869; McBride, "Blacks and the Race Issue," 314–15; Hamer, *Tennessee* 2:651–52; *Nashville Union and American,* Aug. 18, 1869; Anonymous to Governor Senter, Aug. 19, 1869, Box 3, Folder 2, Governor Senter Papers; Singletary, *Negro Militia and Reconstruction,* 50–65; Taylor, *Louisiana Reconstructed,* 249, 254. W. H. Stilwell of Gibson County contended that Senter's withdrawal of the militia coupled with his tacit approval of ex-Confederate registration guaranteed Stokes's defeat in West Tennessee. "No colored man will now be permitted to vote for Gen. Stokes," he noted just before the election, adding that the challenger was "certainly the choice of almost all." W. H. Stilwell to John Eaton, July 20, 1869, Box 5, Folder 2, Eaton Papers.

75. S. Webb to Frank Hyberger, Aug. 28, 1869, Box 3, Folder 2; Thompson McKinley to Governor Senter, Sept. 1, 1869, Box 1, Folder 6; Maj. Gen. Oliver O. Howard to Governor Senter, Sept. 13, 1869, Box 1, Folder 3; Lewis M. Williams to Governor Senter, Sept. 14, 1869, Box 1, Folder 6, all in Senter Papers; Frank Hyberger to Thompson McKinley, Sept. 1, 1869, Houk Papers.

76. Tennessee General Assembly, *Public Acts of Tennessee,* 36th General Assembly, 1st sess. (1869), chaps. 112, 116; White, Ash, and Moore, *Messages* 6:75–77; Queener, "Decade of East Tennessee Republicanism," 72; Trelease, *White Terror,* 278–79; F. Wayne Binning, "The Tennessee Republicans in Decline, 1869–1876," *Tennessee Historical Quarterly* 39 (1980): 478–79; Sefton, *United States Army and Reconstruction,* 262.

77. Hamer, *Tennessee* 2:653–57; Hale, *History of DeKalb County,* 195, 248; Bergeron, Ash, and Keith, *Tennesseans and Their History,* 178–79; Porter Diary, Aug. 5, 1869. The militia clauses of the 1870 Tennessee Constitution are Art. I, Sec. 25 and Art. III, Sec. 5.

CONCLUSION

1. *Jonesboro Union Flag,* Feb. 18, 1870; W. H. Stilwell to Senator Brownlow, Apr. 18, 1870, Box 1, Folder 13, Brownlow Papers. Ex-Confederate political terrorism in Middle and West Tennessee continued until at least 1874. Trelease, *White Terror,* 279–80; William Gillette, *Retreat from Reconstruction, 1869–1879* (Baton Rouge: Louisiana State Univ. Press, 1979), 29, 37, 230.

2. Trelease, *White Terror,* 216; McBride and Robison, *Biographical Directory* 2:168; Robert K. Cannon, *Volunteers for Union and Liberty: History of the 5th Tennessee Infantry, USA, 1861–1865* (Knoxville, Tenn.: Bohemian Brigade, 1995), 119; Lovett, *African-American History of Nashville,* 209; *Survivor of Two Wars,* 5–6, 14–19. In the late 1870s, Cooper was on the losing side of yet another intraparty power struggle, this one involving rival Republican factions in East Tennessee. As a result, Cooper lost his position as internal revenue collector. Gordon B. McKinney, *Southern Mountain Republicans, 1865–1900: Politics and the Appalachian Community* (Chapel Hill: Univ. of North Carolina Press, 1978), 85, 234.

3. General W. P. Carlin to General O. O. Howard, Oct. 9, 1867, Reel 16, BRFAL.

4. Charles J. Rector, "D. P. Upham, Woodruff County Carpetbagger," *Arkansas Historical Quarterly* 59 (2000): 59; Otto H. Olsen, ed., *Reconstruction and Redemption in the South* (Baton Rouge: Louisiana State Univ. Press, 1980), 181.

5. Olsen, *Reconstruction and Redemption,* 181–84; Foner, *Reconstruction,* 440–41; Trelease, *White Terror,* 208–25.

6. Tennessee General Assembly, *Senate Journal,* 35th General Assembly, 1st sess. (1868), Comptroller's Report, 100–102; *Senate Journal,* 36th General Assembly, 1st sess. (1869), Comptroller's Report, 73, 77; Singletary, *Negro Militia and Reconstruction,* 148–50. Historian Ira P. Jones claims, without documentation, that the total cost of the State Guard was actually in excess of $668,000. See Jones, "Reconstruction in Tennessee," 213.

7. Graham and Gurr, *Violence in America,* 472–78, 639.

8. Baenziger, "Texas State Police," 474–77; Foner, *Reconstruction,* 440; Trelease, *White Terror,* 147–48. The high volume of arrests in Texas requires qualification, for it includes all lawbreakers, not just Klansmen, whereas the Tennessee State Guard generally targeted only the Klan and similar Rebel vigilante groups.

9. This hypothetical cost analysis assumes that companies remain at full strength, including horses, and that the men incur no "stoppages" in pay. Yearly expenses for five companies (wages, subsistence, uniforms, and horse maintenance only) come to $145,060. Monthly logistical support for five companies comes to $6,301, a sum derived from an average of quartermaster figures for May and October 1867, months during which no more than six companies were on active duty. For one year, logistical support comes to $75,612. Finally, rail transportation for five companies comes to $6,837, a sum that is one-fourth the total spent on twenty-one companies in 1867. Overall, the yearly cost of a five-company State Guard comes to $233,810.

10. After the state election in 1867, Tennessee senator Joseph S. Fowler wrote Governor Brownlow an intriguing letter in which he stated, "I think some years will elapse before the genuine rebel will be fit to vote. My impression is it will be in the second generation." Like some other Radicals, Fowler later softened his views as evidenced by his 1868 vote to acquit President Johnson during the congressional impeachment proceedings. See Fowler to Governor Brownlow, Aug. 30, 1867, Box 1, Folder 10, Brownlow Papers.

Bibliography

Primary Sources

Manuscript Collections

Arnell, Samuel Mays. Papers. MS 823. Special Collections, Univ. of Tennessee, Knoxville.

Brownlow, William G. Papers. MS 1940. Special Collections, Univ. of Tennessee, Knoxville.

Brownlow, William G. Papers of the Governors. GP 21. Tennessee State Library and Archives, Nashville.

Colyar, Arthur S. Papers. Southern Historical Collection, Univ. of North Carolina, Chapel Hill.

Eaton, John. Papers. Special Collections, Univ. of Tennessee, Knoxville.

Houk, Leonidas Caesar. Letters. Calvin M. McClung Historical Collection, East Tennessee History Center, Knoxville.

Patton, E. E. Papers. Calvin M. McClung Historical Collection, East Tennessee History Center, Knoxville.

Porter, Nimrod. Diary. MSS 1094. Nimrod Porter Papers. Southern Historical Collection, Univ. of North Carolina, Chapel Hill.

Senter, DeWitt C. Papers of the Governors. Tennessee State Library and Archives, Nashville.

Smith, William Jay. "Autobiographical Sketch (1823–1913)." MS 909. Special Collections, Univ. of Tennessee, Knoxville.

Government Documents

Tennessee Adjutant General's Office. Papers. RG 21. Tennessee State Library and Archives, Nashville.

———. *Report of the Adjutant General of the State of Tennessee on the Military Forces of the State, from 1861–1866.* Nashville, 1866.

Tennessee General Assembly. *House Journal.* Nashville, 1865–70.

———. *Public Acts of Tennessee.* 34th, 35th, and 36th General Assemblies. Nashville, 1865–70.

———. *Senate Journal.* Nashville, 1865–70.

Index to the Compiled Service Records of Volunteer Union Soldiers Who Served in Organizations from the State of Tennessee. National Archives and Records Service. Washington, D.C., 1962.

Southern Claims Commission. Tennessee Case Files. Tennessee State Library and Archives, Nashville.

Tennessee Blue Book, 1999–2000, Tennessee Secretary of State, Nashville, 2000.

Tennessee Code Annotated. Charlottesville, VA, 1997.

U.S. Bureau of the Census. *Eighth Census of the United States.* 1860. Schedules of Population for Tennessee.

———. *Ninth Census of the United States.* 1870. Schedules of Population for Tennessee.

U.S. Bureau of Refugees, Freedmen, and Abandoned Lands, 1865–72. Records of the Assistant Commissioner for the State of Tennessee. RG 105, National Archives.

U.S. Congress, both houses. *Ku Klux Conspiracy: Report of the Joint Select Committee to Inquire into the Condition of Affairs in the Late Insurrectionary States.* 13 vols. Washington, D.C.: GPO, 1872.

U.S. Congress. House. *House Executive Documents, Report of the Secretary of War.* 40th Cong., 2nd sess., 1867. Serial 1324.

———. House. *House Executive Documents, Report of the Secretary of War.* 40th Cong., 3rd sess., 1868. Serial 1367.

———. House. *Sheafe v. Tillman.* 41st Cong. 2nd sess., H. Misc. Doc. 53. Serial 1433.

Newspapers

Athens Republican

Bristol News

Clarksville Weekly Chronicle

Cleveland Banner

Columbia Herald

Fayetteville Observer

Harper's Weekly

Jonesboro Union Flag

Knoxville Whig

McMinnville Enterprise and New Era

Memphis Daily Appeal

Nashville Daily Press and Times

Nashville Republican Banner

Nashville Union and American

Nashville Union and Dispatch

Paris Weekly Intelligencer

Pulaski Citizen

Books

The American Annual Cyclopedia and Register of Important Events. New York, 1865–69.

Graf, LeRoy P., Ralph W. Haskins, and Paul H. Bergeron, eds. *The Papers of Andrew Johnson.* 16 vols. Knoxville: Univ. of Tennessee Press, 1967–2000.

Hewett, Janet B., ed. *The Roster of Union Soldiers, 1861–1865.* 21 vols. Wilmington, Del.: Broadfeet, 1997–2000.

Hopkins, Anne H., and William Lyons. *Tennessee Votes: 1799–1976.* Knoxville: Univ. of Tennessee Press, 1978.

Howard, Oliver Otis. *Autobiography of Oliver Otis Howard, Major General United States Army.* 2 vols. New York: Baker & Taylor, 1908.

Inman, Myra. *A Diary of the Civil War in East Tennessee.* Edited by William R. Snell. Macon, Ga.: Mercer Univ. Press, 2000.

Miller, Charles A., ed. *The Official and Political Manual of the State of Tennessee.* 1890. Reprint, Spartanburg, S.C.: Reprint Company, 1974.

Pitts, John A. *Personal and Professional Reminiscences of an Old Lawyer.* Kingsport, Tenn.: Southern Publishers, 1930.

Powell, William H. *List of Officers of the Army of the United States from 1779 to 1900.* Detroit: Gale Research, 1967.

Simon, John Y., ed. *The Papers of Ulysses S. Grant.* 24 vols. to date. Carbondale: Southern Illinois Univ. Press, 1967–.

A Survivor of Two Wars: Biographical Sketch of General Joseph A. Cooper. Knoxville, J. H. Bean and Co., 1895.

U.S. Department of War. *The War of the Rebellion: A Compilation of the Official Records of the Union and Confederate Armies.* 70 vols in 128 parts. Washington, D.C.: GPO, 1880–1901.

Welles, Gideon. *Diary of Gideon Welles, Secretary of the Navy under Lincoln and Johnson.* John T. Morse, jr. ed. 3 vols. Boston: Houghton Mifflin, 1911.

White, Robert H., Stephen V. Ash, and Wayne C. Moore, eds. *Messages of the Governors of Tennessee.* 11 vols. to date. Nashville: Tennessee Historical Commission, 1952–.

Secondary Sources

Books

Alexander, Thomas B. *Political Reconstruction in Tennessee.* Nashville: Vanderbilt Univ. Press, 1950.

———. *Thomas A. R. Nelson of East Tennessee.* Nashville: Tennessee Historical Commission, 1956.

Ash, Stephen V. *Middle Tennessee Society Transformed, 1860–1870: War and Peace in the Upper South.* Baton Rouge: Louisiana State Univ. Press, 1988.

Baggett, James Alex. *The Scalawags: Southern Dissenters in the Civil War and Reconstruction.* Baton Rouge: Louisiana State Univ. Press, 2003.

Benedict, Michael Les. *The Fruits of Victory: Alternatives in Restoring the Union, 1865–1877.* Philadelphia: Lippincott, 1975.

Bergeron, Paul H., Stephen V. Ash, and Jeanette Keith. *Tennesseans and Their History.* Knoxville: Univ. of Tennessee Press, 1999.

Burns, Inez. *History of Blount County, Tennessee: From War Trail to Landing Strip, 1795–1955.* Nashville: Benson, 1957.

Cannon, Robert K. *Volunteers for Union and Liberty: History of the 5th Tennessee Infantry, USA, 1861–1865.* Knoxville, Tenn.: Bohemian Brigade, 1995.

Coulter, E. Merton. *William G. Brownlow, Fighting Parson of the Southern Highlands.* Chapel Hill: Univ. of North Carolina Press, 1937.

Culp, Frederick M., and Mrs. Robert E. Ross. *Gibson County Past and Present: The First General History of One of West Tennessee's Pivotal Counties.* Trenton, Tenn.: Gibson County Historical Commission, 1961.

Current, Richard N. *Those Terrible Carpetbaggers: A Reinterpretation.* New York: Oxford Univ. Press, 1988.

Curry, Richard, ed. *Radicalism, Racism, and Party Realignment: The Border States During Reconstruction.* Baltimore: Johns Hopkins Press, 1969.

Davis, Susan Lawrence. *Authentic History: Ku Klux Klan, 1865–1877.* New York: American Library Service, 1924.

Davis, William C. *Rebels and Yankees: The Fighting Men of the Civil War.* New York: Gallery Books, 1989.

Deaderick, Lucile, ed. *Heart of the Valley: A History of Knoxville, Tennessee.* Knoxville: East Tennessee Historical Society, 1976.

Durham, Walter T. *Rebellion Revisited: A History of Sumner County, Tennessee from 1861 to 1870.* Gallatin, Tenn.: Sumner County Museum Association, 1982.

Eldridge, Robert L., and Mary Eldridge. *Bicentennial Echoes of the History of Overton County, Tennessee.* Livingston, Tenn.: Enterprise Printing, 1976.

Fisher, Noel C. *War at Every Door: Partisan Politics and Guerrilla Violence in East Tennessee, 1860–1869.* Chapel Hill: Univ. of North Carolina Press, 1997.

Foner, Eric. *Reconstruction: America's Unfinished Revolution, 1863–1877.* New York: Harper & Row, 1988.

Franklin, John Hope. *Reconstruction After the Civil War.* Chicago: Univ. of Chicago Press, 1961.

Gillette, William. *Retreat from Reconstruction, 1869–1879.* Baton Rouge: Louisiana State Univ. Press, 1979.

Glatthaar, Joseph T. *Forged in Battle: The Civil War Alliance of Black Soldiers and White Officers.* New York: Free Press, 1990.

Goodspeed Histories of Cannon, Coffee, DeKalb, Warren and White Counties. 1887. Reprint, McMinnville, Tenn.: Ben Lomand Press, 1972.

Goodspeed's History of Tennessee, Containing Historical and Biographical Sketches of Thirty East Tennessee Counties. 1887. Reprint, Nashville: Charles and Randy Elder Booksellers, 1972.

Graham, Hugh Davis, and Ted Robert Gurr, eds. *Violence in America: Historical and Comparative Perspectives.* 2 vols. Washington, D.C.: GPO, 1969.

Hale, Will T. *History of DeKalb County, Tennessee.* 1915. Reprint, McMinnville, Tenn.: Ben Lomand Press, 1969.

Hamer, Philip M. *Tennessee: A History, 1673–1932.* 4 vols. New York: American Historical Society, 1933.

Hoffer, Eric. *The True Believer: Thoughts on the Nature of Mass Movements.* New York: Harper & Row, 1951.

Horn, Stanley F. *Invisible Empire: The Story of the Ku Klux Klan, 1866–1871.* Boston: Houghton Mifflin, 1939.

Humphrey, Steve. *That D—d Brownlow . . .* Boone, N.C.: Appalachian Consortium Press, 1978.

Lovett, Bobby L. *The African-American History of Nashville Tennessee, 1780–1930.* Fayetteville: Univ. of Arkansas Press, 1999.

Maslowski, Peter. *Treason Must Be Made Odious: Military Occupation and Wartime Reconstruction in Nashville, 1862–1865.* Millwood, N.Y.: KTO Press, 1978.

McBride, Robert M., and Dan M. Robison. *Biographical Directory of the Tennessee General Assembly.* 6 vols. Nashville: Tennessee Historical Commission, 1975–.

McKinney, Gordon B. *Southern Mountain Republicans, 1865–1900: Politics and the Appalachian Community.* Chapel Hill: Univ. of North Carolina Press, 1978.

McPherson, James M. *Battle Cry of Freedom: The Civil War Era.* New York: Oxford Univ. Press, 1988.

———. *What They Fought For, 1861–1865.* Baton Rouge: Louisiana State Univ. Press, 1994.

Miller, Francis T., ed. *The Photographic History of the Civil War.* 10 vols. New York: Thomas Yoseloff, 1957.

Olsen, Otto H., ed. *Reconstruction and Redemption in the South.* Baton Rouge: Louisiana State Univ. Press, 1980.

Paludan, Phillip Shaw. *Victims: A True Story of the Civil War.* Knoxville: Univ. of Tennessee Press, 1981.

Patton, James Welch. *Unionism and Reconstruction in Tennessee, 1860–1869.* Chapel Hill: Univ. of North Carolina Press, 1934.

Perman, Michael. *Reunion Without Compromise: The South and Reconstruction, 1865–1868.* Cambridge: Cambridge Univ. Press, 1973.

Rable, George C. *But There Was No Peace: The Role of Violence in the Politics of Reconstruction.* Athens: Univ. of Georgia Press, 1984.

Scott, Mingo. *The Negro in Tennessee Politics and Governmental Affairs, 1865–1965: "The Hundred Years Study."* Nashville: Rich Print, 1965.

Scott, Samuel W., and Samuel P. Angel. *History of the Thirteenth Regiment, Tennessee Volunteer Cavalry, U.S.A.* Philadelphia: P. W. Ziegler, 1903.

Seals, Monroe. *History of White County, Tennessee.* 1935. Reprint, Spartanburg, S.C.: Reprint Company, 1974.

Sefton, James E. *The United States Army and Reconstruction, 1865–1877.* Baton Rouge: Louisiana State Univ. Press, 1967.

Simpson, Brooks D. *Let Us Have Peace: Ulysses S. Grant and the Politics of War and Reconstruction, 1861–1868.* Chapel Hill: Univ. of North Carolina Press, 1991.

Singletary, Otis A. *Negro Militia and Reconstruction.* New York: McGraw-Hill, 1957.

Taylor, Alrutheus A. *The Negro in Tennessee, 1865–1880.* Washington, D.C.: Associated Publishers, 1941.

Taylor, Joe Gray. *Louisiana Reconstructed, 1863–1877.* Baton Rouge: Louisiana State Univ. Press, 1974,

Temple, Oliver P. *East Tennessee and the Civil War.* Cincinnati: R. Clarke, 1899.

———. *Notable Men of Tennessee, 1833–1875: Their Times and Their Contemporaries.* New York: Cosmopolitan, 1912.

Trelease, Allen W. *White Terror: The Ku Klux Klan Conspiracy and Southern Reconstruction.* Baton Rouge: Louisiana State Univ. Press, 1971.

Watauga Association of Genealogists. *History of Washington County, Tennessee.* Jonesboro, Tenn.: Walsworth Press, 1988.

Webb, Thomas G. *DeKalb County.* Memphis: Memphis State Univ. Press, 1986.

Williams, Emma Inman. *Historic Madison: The Story of Jackson and Madison County Tennessee, from Prehistoric Moundbuilders to 1917.* Jackson, Tenn.: Madison County Historical Society, 1946.

Wills, Brian Steel. *A Battle from the Start: The Life of Nathan Bedford Forrest.* New York: HarperCollins, 1992.

Wilson, Joseph T. *The Black Phalanx.* 1890. Reprint, New York: Arno Press, 1968.

Articles and Book Chapters

Argersinger, Peter H. "The Conservative as Radical: A Reconstruction Dilemma." *Tennessee Historical Quarterly* 34 (1975): 168–87.

Ash, Stephen V. "Postwar Recovery: Montgomery County, 1865–70." *Tennessee Historical Quarterly* 36 (1977): 208–21.

Baenziger, Ann Patton. "The Texas State Police During Reconstruction: A Reexamination." *Southwestern Historical Quarterly* 72 (1969): 470–91.

Binning, F. Wayne. "The Tennessee Republicans in Decline, 1869–1876." *Tennessee Historical Quarterly* 39 (1980): 471–84.

Conklin, Forrest. "Wiping Out 'Andy' Johnson's Moccasin Tracks: The Canvass of Northern States by Southern Radicals, 1866." *Tennessee Historical Quarterly* 52 (1993): 122–33.

Crofts, Daniel W. "Reconstruction in Tennessee: An Assessment for Thaddeus Stevens." West Tennessee Historical Society *Papers* 43 (1989): 13–27.

DeBlack, Thomas A. "A Harnessed Revolution: Reconstruction in Arkansas." In *Arkansas: A Narrative History,* by Jeannie M Whayne, Thomas A. DeBlack, George Sabo III, and Morris S. Arnold, 205–39. Fayetteville: Univ. of Arkansas Press, 2002.

DeLozier, Mary Jean. "The Civil War and Its Aftermath in Putnam County." *Tennessee Historical Quarterly* 38 (1979): 436–61.

Feistman, Eugene G. "Radical Disfranchisement and the Restoration of Tennessee, 1865–1866." *Tennessee Historical Quarterly* 12 (1953): 135–51.

Fisher, Noel C. "Definitions of Loyalty: Unionist Histories of the Civil War in East Tennessee." *Journal of East Tennessee History* 67 (1995): 58–88.

Fraser, Walter J., Jr. "Lucien Bonaparte Eaton: Politics and the Memphis *Post,* 1867–1869." West Tennessee Historical Society *Papers* 20 (1966): 20–45.

Guild, George B. "Reconstruction Times in Sumner County." *American Historical Magazine* 8 (1903): 355–68.

Jones, Ira P. "Reconstruction in Tennessee." In *Why the Solid South? Or Reconstruction and Its Results,* ed. Hilary A. Herbert, 169–215. Baltimore: R. H. Woodward, 1890.

Kelly, James C. "William Gannaway Brownlow." *Tennessee Historical Quarterly* 43 (1984): 25–43, 155–72.

Kornell, Gary L. "Reconstruction in Nashville, 1867–1869." *Tennessee Historical Quarterly* 30 (1971): 277–87.

Lovett, Bobby L. "Memphis Riots: White Reactions to Blacks in Memphis, May 1865–July 1866." *Tennessee Historical Quarterly* 38 (1979): 9–33.

———. "The Negro's Civil War in Tennessee, 1861–1865." *Journal of Negro History* 61 (1976): 36–49.

Lufkin, Charles L. "A Forgotten Controversy: The Assassination of Senator Almon Case of Tennessee." West Tennessee Historical Society *Papers* 39 (1985): 37–50.

Madden, David. "Unionist Resistance to Confederate Occupation: The Bridge Burners of East Tennessee." East Tennessee Historical Society *Publications* 52–53 (1980–81): 22–39.

Maness, Lonnie E. "Emerson Etheridge and the Union." *Tennessee Historical Quarterly* 48 (1989): 97–110.

———. "Henry Emerson Etheridge and the Gubernatorial Election of 1867: A Study in Futility." West Tennessee Historical Society *Papers* 47 (1993): 37–49.

McBride, Robert M. "Northern, Military, Corrupt, and Transitory: Augustus E. Alden, Nashville's Carpetbagger Mayor." *Tennessee Historical Quarterly* 37 (1978): 63–67.

McNeilly, James H. "Reconstruction in Tennessee." *Confederate Veteran Magazine* 28 (1920): 340–42.

Perman, Michael. "Counter Reconstruction: The Role of Violence in Southern Redemption." In *The Facts of Reconstruction: Essays in Honor of John Hope Franklin,* ed. Eric Anderson and Alfred A. Moss Jr., 121–40. Baton Rouge: Louisiana State Univ. Press, 1991.

Queener, Verton M. "A Decade of East Tennessee Republicanism, 1867–1876." East Tennessee Historical Society *Publications* 14 (1942): 59–85.

———. "The Origins of the Republican Party in East Tennessee." East Tennessee Historical Society *Publications* 13 (1941): 66–90.

Rector, Charles J. "D. P. Upham, Woodruff County Carpetbagger." *Arkansas Historical Quarterly* 59 (2000): 59–75.

Severance, Benjamin H. "Loyalty's Political Vanguard: The Union League of Maryville, Tennessee, 1867–1869." *Journal of East Tennessee History* 71 (1999): 25–46.

Sharp, J. A. "The Downfall of the Radicals in Tennessee." East Tennessee Historical Society *Publications* 5 (1933): 105–24.

Zebley, Kathleen R. "Samuel Mayes Arnell and Reconstruction in Tennessee." *Tennessee Historical Quarterly* 53 (1994): 246–59.

Theses and Dissertations

Darrah, Marsha Young. "Political Career of Col. William B. Stokes of Tennessee." Master's thesis, Tennessee Technological Univ., 1968.

Hill, Arthur Cyrus. "The History of the Black People of Franklin County, Tennessee." Master's thesis, Univ. of Minnesota, 1982.

McBride, William Gillespie. "Blacks and the Race Issue in Tennessee Politics, 1865–1876." Ph.D. diss., Vanderbilt Univ., 1989.

McGehee, Charles Stuart. "Wake of the Flood: A Southern City in the Civil War, Chattanooga, 1838–1873." Ph.D. diss., Univ. of Virginia, 1985.

Owens, Susie Lee. "The Union League of America: Political Activities in Tennessee, the Carolinas, and Virginia, 1865–1870." Ph.D. diss., New York Univ., 1947.

Phillips, Paul D. "A History of the Freedmen's Bureau in Tennessee." Ph.D. diss., Vanderbilt Univ., 1964.

Rose, Stanley F. "Nashville and its Leadership Elite." Master's thesis, Univ. of Virginia, 1965.

Ulrich, William J. "The Northern Military Mind in Regard to Reconstruction, 1865–1872: The Attitudes of Ten Leading Union Generals." Ph.D. diss., Ohio State Univ., 1959.

Index

Clapp, A. M., 263n68; operations in Hawkins County, 115, 140, 153–54; operations in Sullivan County, 115; raises a militia company, 45, 52

Clapp, James S., 45

Clark, Joseph B., 265n21

Clarksville Weekly, 224

Clausewitz, Karl von, xii

Clayton, Powell, 194, 196–97, 206, 213, 219, 230–32

Cliffe, D. M., 99, 101

Clift, W. J., 89, 91

Clingan, Alexander A., 39

Clingan, Judge K., 55, 64–65, 76, 82, 156, 171, 205, 226, 229–30, 263n7, 282n21; operations in Gibson County, 147, 212–13, 217, 219–20, 299n46; operations in Haywood County, 73–75, 83, 110, 212–13, 219, 298n43; operations in Madison County, 75, 109–11, 137–38, 141, 146, 170, 219; raises a militia company, 39–40, 198, 258n32

Cocke County, 41

Coffee County, 34, 193

Coltart, John, 163

Colyar, Arthur S., 68, 183, 197

Connecticut, 29

Connelly, William M., xiii

Conservative (anti-Radical) party, 59, 63, 138, 221–23, 227; defined, xii–xiii; Gaut circular, 86–87, 89, 93, 95, 97, 103, 110, 119, 122, 142; Nashville Convention (1867), 61, 87; political conspiracy, 7–8, 166, 230; gubernatorial campaign (1867), 62, 65, 73, 76, 78–81, 87, 89, 91–92, 95, 97, 110, 115–16, 118, 122, 133, 136, 271n35, 273n51, 279n31; presidential election campaign (1868), 183, 188, 190. *See also* Etheridge, H. Emerson

Convention of Union Loyalists (1866), 11

Cooper, Edmund, 92, 95, 116, 129

Cooper, John, 196

Cooper, Joseph A., 82, 90, 105, 110, 113, 148, 150, 152, 172, 208–10, 229, 263n69, 268n1, 279n32; assumes command of the State Guard, 56–58,

83, 195–96, 202, 205; coordinates with the U.S. Army, 102, 106, 124, 129, 163, 271n35, 272n37, 296n25; deploys militia units, 59, 75, 77, 85, 89, 91–92, 96–102, 106–7, 109, 111, 114–16, 119, 121, 125, 129–31, 143–47, 149, 151, 153, 161–62, 164, 206, 210–11, 216, 233, 270n25, 272n45; disbands militia units, 149, 155, 160, 216–17, 298n40; enforces discipline, 107–8, 118, 156, 166–67, 170, 203; political activity, 57–58, 95, 222, 286n50, 301n66, 303n2; public statements, 121–22, 154–55, 196–97, 203, 214, 282n21; relinquishes command of the State Guard, 168, 220, 222–23; salary, 156, 301n67

Cordell, John M., 206

County Guards, 15, 177–78, 195, 211, 221, 289n7

Cowan, Samuel A., 201

Cox, Henry A., 199

Cox, Samuel T., 225

Crane, William, 265n22

Cravens, William F., 33, 71, 89, 125, 158–59, 198

Cromwell, Oliver, xv, 222

Cromwell, Patrick S., 196

Cutshaw, Henry M., 199

Davenport, Daniel E., 66–67, 93

Davidson County, 160, 226; Klan activity, 193; militia activity, 116, 126, 129, 131–32, 141; militia recruitment, 51–52, 195

Davis, Edmund, 233

Davis, Jefferson, 40, 96

Davis, Russ B., 26

Davis, W. B., 90–91

Day (Rebel), 77

DeKalb County, 226; militia activity, 70–72, 82, 125, 147, 152–53, 158; militia recruitment, 31, 33, 198; Klan activity, 153; Union League in, 126

Democratic party, xiii, 188, 224, 226–29, 233. *See also* Conservative party

Dickerson, James M., 27

Doughty, James A., 18, 20
Dowdy, Perry O., 91
Dowdy, Rufus, 194
Duncan, Thomas, 101, 106, 123, 129, 167, 272n37, 290n10; deploys U.S. troops, 99–100, 124, 141, 151, 162, 276n5
Duncan, William, 178
Durham, John S., 52, 129–30
Dyer County, 178; Klan activity, 190, 206, 227; militia activities, 76, 106, 108–9, 135, 148, 158; Union League in, 108

East, Edward H., 17
Edmondson, James P., 203, 220, 225, 299n49; operations in Montgomery County, 224; raises a militia company, 200–201
Edwards, R. M., 39
elections in Tennessee: Congressional election (1865), 6; county elections, 6, 8, 10, 15, 50, 178–79; gubernatorial election (1867), 11, 23, 25, 38, 52, 54, 63–64, 76–77, 83, 87, 97, 101, 105–6, 111, 119, 121, 123–146, 157, 189–190, 230, 233, 292n28; gubernatorial election (1869), 220, 222, 224, 226–27, 302n74; gubernatorial election (1870), 228; judicial election (1869), 223–24; Nashville election (1867), 145, 160–66, 168, 230, 233; presidential election (1868), 176–78, 185, 187–91, 195
Elliott, W. Y., 146
Ellis, John N., 42, 81, 95, 139, 155, 270n23
England, James A., 42, 95–96, 126
Enoch, John, 26
Etheridge, H. Emerson, 69, 95, 116; arrested for sedition, 7, 249n10; Conservative candidate for governor, 38, 51, 61–63, 73, 76, 79–81, 99–100, 103, 115, 118, 125–40, 142, 267n50, 271n35, 279n31
Evans, James, 159
Evans, James R., 58, 65, 118, 155, 282n24; operations in Claiborne County, 79–81; operations in

Grainger County, 79–83, 95; operations in Humphreys County, 95, 126; raises a militia company, 41–42

Farnum, G. W., 34–35
Farquharson, Robert, 105, 134
Farris, Frank, 1, 37
Fayette County, 176, 188, 220
Fayetteville Observer, 24, 63, 66, 118, 150, 152
Featherston, H. D., 106, 127
February, Joseph A., 47, 105, 134
Federal garrison. *See* U.S. Army
Fentress County, 178, 193, 221, 298n40
Ferguson, Champ, 31, 33
Fleming, Eli G., 91, 125–26
Flemming, Philip J., 52, 131, 162
Fletcher, Andrew J., 75, 82, 107, 125, 133
Foote, F. W., 166
Forrest, Nathan B., 88, 177, 181, 183–84, 197–98, 208, 222, 271n34, 273n51
Fort Pillow Massacre (1864), 100, 271n34, 273n51
Fowler, Joseph S., 304n10
Franchise Acts: of 1865, 5, 9, 20; of 1866, 6–8, 10, 17, 20, 62, 64; of 1867, 24–25, 62, 64, 86–87, 97, 126, 142, 161–63, 165, 190–91, 223, 284n36. *See also* Tennessee General Assembly: franchise legislation; Conservative party: Gaut circular
Franklin County, 47, 74, 83, 149; Klan activity, 190, 206, militia activity, 65–70, 73, 82, 92–95, 127–28, 141, 168–69, 158; militia recruitment, 33–34
Freedmen's Bureau, 51, 65, 76, 176–78, 190, 208, 230, 282n21
Freeman, Howard, 130
French, James R., 200
French, Jefferson C., 200, 217, 219–20
Frierson, Joshua B., 210
Fry, Charles, 75
Fulgham (Rebel), 150
Fuller, William G., 37, 135, 158, 167, 170, 178

Galbraith, Robert, 26
Gamble, Larken G., 58, 107, 196, 205, 217, 225; operations in Giles County, 208, 210, 214–15
Garner, William A., 218
Gaut circular. *See* Conservative (anti-Radical) party: Gaut circular
Gaut, Jesse, 39
Gaut, John C., 63, 86–87, 181, 183
Gettysburg, battle of (1863), 41
Gibson County, 36, 73, 124, 302n74; Klan activity, 188, 190, 193, 206, 212, 219; militia activity, 76, 106–8, 114, 136–37, 141, 144, 146–49, 157, 169, 212–13, 216–17, 219–21, 223, 225, 279n32, 299n46; militia recruitment, 37
Giles County: Klan activity, 9, 87–88, 129, 150–51, 169, 174, 176–77, 188, 190, 193, 206, 208, 215, 218; militia activity, 30, 92–93, 129–30, 168–69, 208, 210, 214–18, 220, 224, 299n49; Union League in, 151, 176
Gillem, Alvan C., 17, 46
Gleaves, Alexander, 52, 131
Goodwin, W. H., 103
Grace, Joseph A., 45
Grainger County: militia activity, 79–83; militia recruitment, 42, 45
Grant, Jackson, 199
Grant, Ulysses S., 124, 162–63, 188–89, 227, 285n41
Green, Galen E., 171
Greene County: militia recruitment, 43–44, 49, 198–99
Greeneville Convention (1861), 3, 45, 56, 201
Greer, Nathan H., 201
Grisham, George E., 48, 55, 58, 65, 82–83, 102, 113, 118, 171, 199, 279n29; operations in Lincoln County, 103, 105, 133–35, 149; operations in Sullivan County, 49, 77–80, 98; political activity, 46–47, 168, 226, 229, 267n50; raises a militia company, 46–47, 49, 52
Grundy County, 9
Grundy, Thomas, 152

Gurney, E. H., 201, 296n24
Guthrie, James B., 111, 127, 169

Hacker, Newton, 183, 185
Hackworth, Morgan C., 199
Hall, Edwin R., 41, 54, 270n25; operations in Cheatham County, 96–97; operations in Henry County, 111, 127, 149; operations in Madison County, 169, 171–72
Hall, Robert L., 58, 102; operations in Davidson County, 103, 167; operations in Obion County, 169; operations in Rutherford County, 116, 126, 128, 143, 146; raises a militia company, 40, 80, 199
Hall, W. K., 13
Hamilton County, 39
Hamilton, George, 113; operations in McNairy County, 111–12, 139, 149; raises a militia company, 38, 45, 52
Hamilton, Thomas A. 187
Hammer, Jonathan M., 201
Hammer, Samuel M., 201, 217, 220, 223
Hardeman County, 142
Hardin County, 38
Hardin, James, 112
Harper, Ellis, 10, 50, 99, 132, 189
Harris, Andrew J., 201
Harris, E. B., 96–97
Harris, Isham G., 3, 19
Harris, Shadrick T., 55, 127, 200; operations in Henry County, 111, 115; raises a militia company, 40–41, 96
Harris, T. D., 132
Harrison, Horace, 164
Harrison, Thomas P., 130
Hartmus, Thomas H., 159–60, 171
Hatchet, S., 136
Hathaway, William L., 33, 54, 72, 91, 165, 205, 217–18, 222, 226, 300n55; operations in DeKalb County, 71, 152–53; operations in Overton County, 210–11; operations in Putnam County, 211; raises a militia company, 198

Hawkins County, 301n63; militia activity, 115, 140, 153; militia recruitment, 44–45; Rogersville riot, 115, 119, 140; Union League in, 115
Haynes, John, 200, 217
Haywood County: Klan activity, 206, 219; militia activity, 73–75, 83, 109–10, 212–13, 219, 221; Union League in, 74
Hazen, M. V. B., 101
Heath, Samuel, 67–68
Helton, Martin L., 300–301n63
Hendrickson, Jacob, 201
Henry County, 63, 220; militia activity, 111, 115, 126–27, 149, 169
Hickman County, 151
Hicks, William L., 198, 212–13, 217, 219–20, 225
Holden, William, 231
Holden, William B., 128
Holt, Jordan C., 34–35, 67–70
Holt, William C., 38, 109; operations in Gibson County, 136–37, 141, 148, 169–70, 279n32; raises a militia company, 37, 263n69
Holtsinger, John P., 63, 116
Hood, James R., 13
Hood, John B., 15, 56
Hooks, Tom, 37
Hough, Alfred, 80
Houk, Leonidas C., 23, 47, 62, 79, 221
Houston, Michael, 52, 116, 131, 162
Hughes, John, 94–95
Humphreys County, 38, 95–96, 126, 176
Hunt, Samuel, 27, 34, 69–70, 99, 100, 108, 132, 159, 165, 168, 268n1
Hurst, Fielding, 13
Hurst, Levi, 112
Hurt, W. J., 160
Hyberger, Frank, 220, 224, 227

Indiana, 30
Ireland, 195

Jack, Francis M., 171
Jackson County, 206, 210

Jarmon, Wilson, 225
Jefferson County, 40–41, 45, 96, 200
Johnson, Andrew, 13, 26, 49, 56, 174, 185, 200, 268n4, 304n10; Conservative appeals to, 8, 17, 25, 42, 47, 57, 63, 68, 78, 80, 85–86, 116, 122, 162–63, 181, 183; decrees of 1866, 232; Federal garrison in Tennessee, 10, 15, 46, 70, 184, 187, 194, 285n41; "Swing around the Circle," 11
Johnson County, 45
Johnson, William H., 290n15
Jones, Martin, 94, 121
Jonesboro Union Flag, 46–47, 49
Judd, George E., 190

Kansas, 229
Keith, George W., 157
Kelley, George W., 39
Kelley, James, 75
Kentucky, 10, 43, 211, 223
Kersey, Pomp, 33
Kinman, Moses H., 37, 170
Kirk, Francis M., 44, 93, 158–59
Kirk, George W., 49, 54–55, 113, 158, 205, 217, 226, 283n31; operations in Franklin County, 70, 93–95, 127–28, 141; operations in Madison County, 147–48; operations in North Carolina, 229, 231–32; raises a militia company, 43–44, 81, 93, 198–99
Kirk, John L., 102, 119; operations in Gibson County, 147–48; operations in Madison County, 159–60; operations in Montgomery County, 105–6, 127; raises a militia company, 49, 52, 81, 106, 272n45
Kirkpatrick, James, 134
Knox County, 40, 45, 139, 199, 223
Knoxville, 15, 40–41, 57, 83; militia movements in, 80, 115, 144; Sons of Temperance, 107; Unionist Convention (1861), 3
Knoxville Whig, 5, 58, 81, 87, 162; defends the State Guard, 82, 141; discusses militia legislation, 19, 179

Koger, James F. 176
Ku Klux Klan, xi, xiv, xvi–xvii, 142,
    181–87, 190–91, 196, 198, 203, 205,
    209, 226, 228, 231–34, 248n11,
    250n14, 287n51, 290n10, 298n38;
    formation of, 9, 87–88, 175; member-
    ship in, 177; in Arkansas, 194,
    230–32; in Middle Tennessee, 129,
    150–51, 153, 169, 174, 176–80,
    188–89, 193–95, 197, 206, 208,
    210–11, 214–16, 218–19, 226, 230; in
    North Carolina, 229, 231–32; in
    Texas, 233, 304n8; in West
    Tennessee, 176–77, 188, 193, 197,
    206, 212–13, 219–20, 226, 229–30.
    See also vigilantism; violence

Lauderdale County: militia activity,
    108–9, 114, 139, 141, 149, 212
Law, Joseph, 113
Lawrence County: Klan activity, 194,
    206, 210; militia activity, 92–93, 208
Lawrence, Joseph S., 49
Lea, John M., 181–82
Leib, Edwin H., 10, 98, 133, 141, 178,
    189, 290n10
Lellyett, John, 18
Lewis, Samuel, 112
Lincoln, Abraham, 5, 46, 94
Lincoln County, 150; Klan activity, 177,
    188–90, 197, 206, 218; militia activ-
    ity, 92–93, 103, 105, 133–35, 149,
    169; militia recruitment, 34; Union
    League in, 103, 150
Lincoln County News, 134
Lindsley, A. V. S., 184
Louisiana, xv, 227, 232, 301n65
Love, Isaac, 134
Low, Powell H., 198, 212–13, 225
Loyal Leagues. *See* Union Leagues
Loyalty oaths, 6, 16, 26, 35, 87, 90, 165
Lyle, Berry, 185

Madison County, 154, 178, 190; Klan
    activity, 197, 206; militia activity, 75,

109–11, 137–38, 141–42, 144, 146–48,
    153, 158–60, 169–72, 212, 219–21
Maleer, Burnell, 134, 149
Mankin, John J., 35, 70, 150, 156,
    168–69, 177; operations in Giles
    County, 92–93, 129, 151
Manson, Joseph O., 199, 217–20, 225
Marshall County, 30; elections in, 9–10;
    Klan activity, 176, 178–79, 188–89,
    206, 210, 218; militia activity, 70,
    92–93, 128, 168, 208; militia recruit-
    ment, 34, 269n16; Union League in,
    128
Martin, Stephen, 97
Massachusetts, 195
Matthews, Stephen J., 172
Maury County, 9, 215, 272n37, 276n5;
    Klan activity, 176–77, 180, 188, 190,
    194, 197, 206, 210, 218; militia activ-
    ities, 101, 124, 130–31, 141, 208;
    Union League in, 176
Maynard, Horace, 8, 58, 62, 65, 81, 126,
    182
McClanahan, William C., 127
McCord, Frank, 208
McCornice, William, 139
McCoy, James, 109
McCutchen, J. T., 159
McEwen, J. B., 154
McKenzie, J. M., 218
McKinney, Page, 49
McKinley, Thompson: operations in
    Sumner County, 98–99, 132–33;
    raises a militia company, 50–51, 162,
    261n53; state legislator, 133, 168,
    227, 288n58
McLaughlin, Henry, 146
McLaughlin, Nelson, 47, 49, 77, 103–4,
    135
McMinn County, 39, 45, 201, 296n24
McMinnville Enterprise, 90
McNair, Jesse, 179, 186
McNairy County: militia activity, 111–12,
    121, 139, 149; militia recruitment, 38;
    Union League in, 112
McWhiney, 296n25
Medlin, Robert, 110, 137, 154

Tealey, Frank, 217

Tennessee: Civil War in, 3, 5, 19, 27, 29, 31–34, 39–41, 44, 56, 72, 100, 109, 200–1, 283n27; Constitutional Convention (1870), 228; readmission to the Union, xiv, 8, 10, 25, 123, 143; secession, 1, 3, 65, 77, 79, 92, 95–96, 109, 111–13, 116. *See also* elections in Tennessee.

Tennessee General Assembly, 27, 46, 50, 58, 61, 89, 94, 128, 133, 140, 142, 154, 160, 168, 181, 188, 191, 193–94, 226, 233, 286n50, 292n28; anti-Klan legislation, 182, 185–86, 227; condemns violence, 1, 3, 177–78, 206; franchise legislation, 3, 5–7, 13, 39; militia legislation, 3, 11–13, 15, 17–21, 39, 73, 172–73, 175, 179–80, 182–87, 194–95, 205, 210, 227; petitions Federal government, 25, 29, 184–85, 187; ratifies the Fourteenth Amendment, 8, 39; repeals militia acts, 174, 227; Sedition Act (1865), 7, 89; Sheriff Acts (1865), 15, 177–80, 221

Tennessee State Guard: anti-Radical criticism, 24–25, 30, 34, 36, 42–43, 47, 50–51, 61, 63–66, 68–69, 73–74, 78, 80–82, 85–86, 90, 94, 97–102, 106–7, 113–14, 116, 118, 124, 128, 132, 134, 136, 139, 147, 149, 154, 156, 159–61, 165, 172, 181, 196, 205, 210, 212–14, 221, 226; black militiamen, 17–18, 25, 31, 36, 38, 45–47, 49–52, 54–55, 62, 78–79, 85, 97–103, 105–6, 112, 116, 119, 124, 127, 129–33, 141–43, 145, 147, 152, 154, 157, 159–60, 162, 170, 178, 187, 196, 203, 226, 230, 261n53, 285n39; bodyguard duties, 72, 80, 91, 115, 126; camp life, 29, 63–64, 74–75, 217, 225; carpetbaggers in, 41, 50–51, 195; casualties in, 43, 90–91, 94, 99, 112, 121, 152, 212, 214, 261n57; commission seekers, 26–27, 30–31, 46, 146, 152, 200–201, 269n16, 296n25, 301n63; desertion in, 43, 74, 76–77, 110, 157, 170–71, 214–15, 218; disbandment of, 144–47, 149, 152, 155,

157, 160, 168, 172, 174–75, 177, 180, 190, 205, 210, 213, 216–18, 220, 222, 224–26, 233, 282n21, 298n40; disciplinary actions in, 70, 77, 90, 94–95, 107–8, 156–57, 167–68, 200, 203, 215, 217, 225; evaluation of, xvi–xviii, 55, 59, 82–83, 118, 140–43, 166, 175, 188–90, 222–23, 226, 229–31, 233–34; federal investigations into, 69–70, 80, 83, 151; financial expenditures, 30, 87, 113, 115, 155–57, 168, 172–73, 183, 205, 220–21, 234, 304n6; logistical support, 27–29, 58–59, 75, 81, 96, 102, 109, 111, 113, 149, 171, 196, 205, 263n68, 265n22, 267n49, 287n51; medical conditions in, 58, 75, 136, 156, 211, 215–16, 269n11, 283n31, 299n51; mission of, 64–65, 82, 87, 91, 105, 154, 210; mobilization in East Tennessee, 31, 37–49, 52, 59, 81, 198–202, 296n24; mobilization in Middle Tennessee, 31, 33–36, 49–52, 55, 59, 71, 195, 198; mobilization in West Tennessee, 36–38, 52, 55, 59, 202; Nashville election (1867), 160–66; operations in East Tennessee, 77–81, 113, 115–16, 139–40, 153–54; operations in Middle Tennessee, 65–73, 89–106, 111, 116, 125–35, 146, 149–53, 168–69, 208–11, 214–15, 218–19, 224; operations in West Tennessee, 73–77, 96, 106–114, 127, 135–39, 146–49, 158–60, 169–72, 211–14, 219–20, 223; ordnance, 28–30, 34, 37, 42, 115, 148, 173, 205, 211; scholarly opinion of, xiv–xvi, 54, 81, 195, 230, 258n32, 261n53, 299n52; shooting incidents, 68, 106, 112, 151, 155, 159, 171–72, 211–12, 214; socioeconomic profile, 33, 54–55, 203; "special command," 157–58, 233; transportation, 28, 111, 113–15, 173, 210; troop strength, 31, 52, 55, 59, 85, 116, 121, 125, 155, 163, 198, 217. *See also* militia acts; U.S. Army

Tennessee Supreme Court, 24, 161, 174, 210, 223–24, 284n36

Terry, Pleasant, 261n57

Texas, 233, 304n8

Thomas, George H., 16, 33, 56; describes anti-Radical lawlessness, 9, 70; Federal garrison in Tennessee, 8, 10, 15, 17, 25, 46, 123–24, 162–64, 179–80, 188–89, 276n4, 285n41, 290n10; Radical sympathies, 15, 25, 122, 163

Thomas, Horace H., 27–29, 88, 115, 173

Thornburgh, D. G., 182

Thornburgh, J. W., 216

Thurman, Elijah, 178, 289n7

Tillet, P. A., 195

Tipton County, 142

Tipton, Caswell T., 199

Tompkins (anti-Radical), 98

Toncray, Alexander R. P., 199

Totten, W. W., 81, 267n49

Trezevant (anti-Radical), 149

Trimble, John, 13

Tucker (Private), 34

Turner, James J., 132–33

Turner, John B., 198

Turner, Nelson, 50

Turner, W. P. H., 206, 290n15

Underwood, C., 26

Union County, 200

Union Leagues, 24, 46, 62, 87–88, 181, 191, 268n8; in East Tennessee, 47, 115, 201; in Middle Tennessee, 50–52, 65, 88, 96–97, 103, 126, 128, 150–52, 176; in West Tennessee, 74, 76, 108, 112

U.S. Army (Federal garrison), xiv, 5, 7, 12, 91, 106, 125, 129, 143, 180, 184, 187, 195, 208, 233, 250n14, 272n37, 290n10; black troops in, 46, 50–51, 271n34; operations in Tennessee, 8–10, 15, 75, 98–100, 124, 131, 133, 141–42, 151–52, 159, 162–64, 166, 169, 173, 179, 188–91, 193–94, 197, 215, 271n35, 276n5, 280n42, 285n41, 286n45, 298n38; relation-

ship to the State Guard, xv, 25, 76, 100–102, 122–24, 166–67, 225, 296n26; troop strength in Tennessee, 10, 15, 122, 163, 188, 228

Van Buren County, 35, 91–92

Vanetta, McAdoo D., 198

Viars, S. Bob, 113–14

vigilantism (ex-Confederate), xvii, 144–45, 231–32; Civic Guards, 87, 142; in East Tennessee, 42, 47, 80–81, 153, 300–301n63; in Middle Tennessee, 9–10, 24, 33–35, 87, 90–91, 93, 96, 105–6, 121, 127, 129, 131–34, 149–50, 152–53, 189–90, 219, 224; in West Tennessee, 1,3, 37, 77, 87, 107–8, 110, 112, 114, 121, 135–38, 142, 146, 148, 158, 169, 171, 178, 220. *See also* Ku Klux Klan; violence

violence, 8, 11, 67, 72, 90–91, 93, 95, 97, 112, 131, 148, 153, 174, 176, 185, 189, 220, 282n21, 296n26; Brownsville riot, 73; Case assassination, 1, 3, 6, 17, 36, 62, 76, 160, 177; Franklin riot, 88–89, 99–101, 124, 152; Memphis race riot (1866), 7, 15, 29, 46, 124; Rogersville riot, 115, 119, 140. *See also* Ku Klux Klan; vigilantism

voter analysis, 140–42, 189–90

voter registration, 64–65, 86, 91, 118, 125, 141, 188, 224; in East Tennessee, 81; in Middle Tennessee, 64–67, 71, 89, 92–93, 95–96, 99, 101, 105, 116, 189; in West Tennessee, 76, 108–12, 114, 127, 169, 220, 302n74

Vowel, Martin, 108, 177

Walker, Anderson H., 64, 135–36

Warren County: militia activity, 71, 89–92, 125, 153; militia recruitment, 35

Warren, Thomas J., 95

Washington County, 134–35; militia recruitment, 44, 46–47, 49, 199; Union League in, 47

Washington, D.C., 185
Watson, Isaac H., 40
Watson, Newell, 157
Wayne County, 178, 289n7
Weakley County, 37–38, 64; Klan activity, 212, 227; militia activity, 76, 106–8, 135–37; militia recruitment, 37; Union League in, 76
Weaver, George, 51
Welch, William, 95
West, Noah N., 199
West Tennessee College, 159
Wheeler, Joseph, 31–32
Whipple, M. C., 128
Whipple, William D., 69–70
White County: militia activity, 71–72, 90, 92, 125; militia recruitment, 35–36
White, W. O., 27
Wilcox, Christopher C., 201–2
Wiley, Robert, 92, 176, 269n16
Williams, Elihu S., 183
Williams, J. L., 115
Williams, John, 80
Williams, Joseph, 51, 62, 88

Williams, Wiley, 156
Williamson County: Franklin riot, 88–89, 99–101, 124, 152; Klan activity, 176–77; militia activity, 99–102, 124, 129–31, 141; militia recruitment, 51–52; Union League in, 52, 88, 101, 176
Willis, C. D., 155
Wilson County, 24, 153; militia activity, 71–73, 103, 135, 216
Wilson, Robert P. 166
Wilson, Thomas T., 201
Winters, Edwin E.: operations in Giles County, 214–15, 217–18; raises a militia company, 195–96
Wisener, William H., 187, 194
Wood (Radical), 93
Woodard, J. K., 58
Woodsides, Levi N., 198, 217
Wright, William, 132
Wyatt, William, 177

Yates, Henry C., 199

Tennessee's Radical Army was designed and typeset on a Macintosh computer system using QuarkXPress software. The body text is set in 11/13.5 Adobe Caslon and display type is set in Hingham. This book was designed by Barbara Karwhite and manufactured by Thomson-Shore, Inc.